The Foreign Film Renaissance on American Screens,
1946–1973

WISCONSIN FILM STUDIES

Patrick McGilligan
Series Editor

The Foreign Film Renaissance on

American Screens, 1946–1973

Tino Balio

The University of Wisconsin Press

Publication of this volume has been made possible, in part,
through support from
the ANONYMOUS FUND OF THE COLLEGE OF LETTERS AND SCIENCE
at the University of Wisconsin–Madison.

The University of Wisconsin Press
1930 Monroe Street, 3rd Floor
Madison, Wisconsin 53711-2059
uwpress.wisc.edu

3 Henrietta Street
London WCE 8LU, England
eurospanbookstore.com

1   3   5   4   2

Printed in the United States of America

Library of Congress Cataloging-in-Publication Data
Balio, Tino.
The foreign film renaissance on American screens, 1946–1973 / Tino Balio.
p.   cm. — (Wisconsin film studies)
Includes bibliographical references and index.
ISBN 978-0-299-24794-2 (pbk.: alk. paper)
ISBN 978-0-299-24793-5 (e-book)
1. Foreign films — United States.
2. Foreign films — United States — Reviews.
I. Title.   II. Series: Wisconsin film studies.
PN1995.9.F67B35   2010
791.43´75 — dc22
2010011533

Contents

Illustrations

Acknowledgments

I am grateful to the Academy of Motion Picture Arts and Sciences for award-ing me an inaugural Academy Film Scholar Grant in 2001 to write this book. It was a project I had in mind for years, and the academy's recognition spurred me on. The Graduate School of the University of Wisconsin–Madison also provided me research support for this project for which I am grateful.

I have been fortunate to work with many excellent graduate students in the Department of Communication Arts who took my seminars and joined me in my research. I am indebted to Richard Avol, Teresa Becker, Lisa Dombrowski, Ken Eakin, Kevin Heffernan, Scott Higgins, Heidi Kenaga, Yiota Mini, Chris-topher Sieving, Greg M. Smith, Raphael Vela, and Kelly A. Wolff.

I have presented several of my research findings at the Annual Business and Economics Scholars Workshop Summit of the DeSantis Center for Motion Picture Industry Studies (Florida Atlantic University). My gratitude to Bruce Mallen, the founding director of the center, and to the other invited participants.

My colleague David Bordwell read portions of the manuscript and was a source of ongoing support. Sarah Street and Richard Jewell read the completed manuscript and offered many valuable suggestions. Daniel Talbot, an icon of the art film scene in New York, also graciously agreed to review the completed manuscript. Henry Krawitz copyedited it. They have my special thanks.

The Wisconsin Center for Film and Theater Research provided the illustra-tions for this book. My thanks to Michele Hilmes, Maxine Fleckner Ducey and Dorinda Hartmann.

The Foreign Film Renaissance on American Screens,
1946–1973

Introduction

Roberto Rossellini's *Open City* (*Roma, città aperta*), a low-budget picture about the underground resistance during the Nazi occupation of Rome, opened at the World Theatre in New York on February 25, 1946, and proved a total surprise. Before the war Italian films had never compared favorably with French, German, or British imports and had played mostly in ethnic theaters in immigrant neighborhoods. *Open City*, the first film to come out of Italy after the war, ran for twenty-one months at the World and broke the previous New York City records set by *The Birth of a Nation* and *Gone With the Wind*—an unprecedented achievement for a foreign film. *Open City* went on to win the Grand Prix at Cannes in 1946 and was named Best Foreign Language Film of the year by the New York Film Critics Circle. After going into general release, *Open City* reputedly grossed $5 million at the box office and set another record in the United States for a foreign film.[1]

Rossellini started work on his picture "shortly after American GIs pushed the Germans out," reported *Variety*. He shot it under difficult conditions in the streets of the city, inside actual buildings, and in a makeshift studio. Raw film stock was hard to come by, but Rossellini received "strictly unofficial aid" from U.S. Army Signal Corps technicians to complete his film.[2] Rossellini chose Anna Magnani and Aldo Fabrizi, both seasoned professionals, to play the leads. To fill out the cast he recruited amateurs, and for extras he used the citizens of Rome.

The heroes in *Open City* are the "little people," who struggle for liberation. There's Manfredi, a Communist resistance leader on the run from the Gestapo; Francesco, a friend who operates an underground print shop; Pina, Francesco's pregnant wife-to-be, a widow with a young son who risks her life by hiding the resistance leader in her apartment; and Don Pietro, a simple Catholic priest who "carries money bound in scholarly-looking volumes" and "smuggles ammunition under his priest's robes" across the lines to aid the cause. Pina was played by Magnani and Don Pietro by Fabrizi. The heroes all fall victim to the Germans. Pina is shot down in the street on her wedding day as she rushes after Francesco, who was caught in a sweep of her tenement and is being hauled off to prison. Manfredi is betrayed by his mistress after a falling out and is arrested by the Gestapo along with Don Pietro. At Gestapo headquarters Manfredi is flayed with a blowtorch and dies without informing on his comrades. Don Pietro, who was forced to witness the ordeal, also defies the Nazis and is placed before the firing squad. Awaiting his execution, he blesses the parish children huddled outside the prison fence, who are whistling a resistance tune to give him comfort. Don Pietro's last words are, "It is not difficult to die well; it is difficult to live well."

U.S. critics had never before seen a war film quite like this. Bosley Crowther in the *New York Times* was overwhelmed by its "candid, overpowering realism." *Open City*, he said, had the "wind-blown look" of a "straight documentary" that "was inspired by artists whose own emotions had been deeply and recently stirred." "The feeling that flows most strongly through the film," he added, "is one of supreme admiration for the people who fight for freedom's cause."[3] *Newsweek* described it as "the screen's most eloquent indictment of Nazism by a people who first aided them, then became virtual slaves of the Germans."[4] James Agee in the *Nation* doubted that "institutional Christianity and leftism," as represented by the priest and the Communists, ever coexisted as easily as they do in the film. Nonetheless, he admired the film's immediacy: "Everything in it had been recently lived through; much of it is straight reenactment on or near the actual spot; its whole spirit is still, scarcely cooled at all, the exalted spirit of the actual experience."[5]

Agee wrote off the German characters as "standard villains" but described the acting of most of the Romans—and "especially of a magnificent woman named Anna Magnani"—as "near perfect."[6] *Variety* also singled out Miss Magnani's performance: "She is certainly not a heroine in the Hollywood conception, as she is not only homely, but even quite slovenly and rather ordinary."[7] John McCarten in the *New Yorker* particularly liked Fabrizi's performance as the priest: "Aldo Fabrizi, a famous stage comedian, is superb in all kinds of disparate scenes. At one point, he is slyly humorous as he arranges a statue of a nude woman in an antique shop so that it will not confront the image of St. Rocco; at another, he is solemnly impressive as, for the benefit of a Gestapo searching party, he reads the prayers for the dying over an old man whom he has had to

Aldo Fabrizi as Don Pietro in Roberto Rossellini's *Open City* (1946)

knock out with a frying pan to make him lie quietly beside the weapons that are hidden under his blankets; and at yet another, he is profoundly courageous as he refuses to reveal to the chief of the Roman Gestapo the identity of his fellow-conspirators."[8]

Rossellini's film was a public relations triumph for Italy and whetted America's appetite for Italian neorealist and foreign films in general after the war. Fast-forwarding to 1963, a small but influential art film market now existed in the United States, a legacy of *Open City*. The number of art houses had grown from just a handful in 1946 to around 450, and a vibrant film culture had come into being. Foreign films and their directors were the subjects of reviews and feature stories in the *New York Times*, mass-market magazines, highbrow periodicals, and the trade press. They were also promoted by museums, film festivals, and colleges and universities. Responding to film's new status as "an authentic art form," Lincoln Center for the Performing Arts launched the New York Film Festival in September 1963. To mark the event, *Time* magazine ran a cover story entitled "A Religion of Film," which stated: "By its taste and high excitement, by the quality of its films and the intelligence of its sellout crowds, it may well mark for Americans a redefinition of what movies are and who it is that sees them. For in the decade since Hollywood came unstuck and television became the reigning medium of mass entertainment, the movies have suddenly and powerfully emerged as a new and brilliant international art, indeed as perhaps the central and characteristic art of the age." The article continued: "At the heart of the new movement is a hardy little band of inspired pioneers—Japan's Akira Kurosawa; Sweden's Ingmar Bergman; France's Alain Resnais and François Truffaut; Italy's Federico Fellini, Michelangelo Antonioni, and Luchino Visconti; England's Tony Richardson; Poland's Andrzej Wajda and Roman Polanski; Argentina's Leopold Torre Nilsson; India's Satyajit Ray." It noted that the audience that flocked to their films was young, mostly under thirty. "It is a vehement audience; it applauds what it likes and hisses what it doesn't. It is an expert audience; the new generation of moviegoers believes that an educated man must be cinemate [*sic*] as well as literate. And it is a mass audience; financially, the new cinema is a going concern."[9]

The art film market, which introduced the "hardy little band of inspired pioneers" to American filmgoers, had antecedents as far back as the 1920s, but it was essentially a postwar phenomenon that flourished until 1966. As originally understood by the trade, the art film market was a subindustry devoted to the acquisition, distribution, and exhibition of critically acclaimed foreign- and English-language films produced abroad without Hollywood's involvement. No hard-and-fast definition existed for art films; they encompassed a range of styles, genres, and modes of production. These films were typically made with the support of government subsidies and with international distribution in mind. About the only generalization one could make about the style of these films is that they departed more or less from Hollywood narrative norms.

This history of the art film market begins with the release of Rossellini's *Open City* in 1946 and concludes with the release of Bernardo Bertolucci's *Last Tango in Paris* in 1973. The focus is on New York City, the gateway and launching pad for the market. The importance of this choice has been described by Edward Kingsley, a prominent art film distributor, as follows: "Every picture from abroad is reborn in New York. Each picture starts from scratch when it gets here. The promotion and advertising must be planned for the American market. If it doesn't get off to a good start in New York, it doesn't have a chance anyplace."[10] To be considered a hit, a foreign film had to get a good review from Bosley Crowther in the *New York Times* and run a minimum of eight weeks in a first-class Manhattan art house; anything less would damage if not kill its chances for wider distribution. The Greater New York run could generate as much as half of the total revenue for a film—sometimes more.

To explain the workings of the market, I have singled out the following basics of art film distribution: (1) market structure (2) import trends (3) marketing (4) critical reception (5) censorship (6) audience, and (7) box office. Stated another way, I have identified the key foreign film distributors, their relative size, and methods of operation. In addition, I have identified the film imports that attracted the greatest attention in the press and drove the market. Lastly, I have described the audiences for these pictures and the marketing strategies distributors used to reach them. Since the art film market functioned as a subindustry, I have discussed its operations in relation to mainstream Hollywood. (N.B.: The date in parentheses following a film title indicates the year the film was released in the United States, not the year it was produced. The film title itself is the American release version. Wherever a foreign film is first discussed and not just mentioned, I have inserted its original release title within parentheses.)

This history is divided into three parts. The first describes the emergence of the market immediately after the war brought about by two import trends— Italian neorealism and the British film renaissance. The first chapter sets the stage by describing the import trends of the 1930s and the failed efforts of European producers to gain entree into mainstream U.S. exhibition. Looked at from their perspective, the art film market functioned as a ghetto for foreign films. Italian neorealism flourished until 1951. Like *Open City*, such later arrivals as Rossellini's *Paisan* (1948) and Vittorio De Sica's *The Bicycle Thief* (1949), were admired for "their mixture of realism and fine, voluble acting, their classic pathos and fleshy humor, their background of poverty and the picturesque, and, above all, their new technique, which turns them into documentaries of postwar history, of neighborhoods, or of human hearts and pocketbooks," as Janet Flanner put it in the *New Yorker*.[11] Rossellini and De Sica worked on the fringe of the Italian film industry as independents, and their films kick-started the art film market after the war. In so doing, they also provided Italian producers with the means to break into mainstream U.S. theaters. By discovering ways to exploit elements of the trend, by the early 1950s the Italian film industry ranked "second only to Hollywood as the major supplier of films to the U.S. and the world."[12]

Pictures that signaled the British film renaissance, like David Lean's *Brief Encounter* (1946) and Laurence Olivier's *Hamlet* (1948), appealed to discriminating filmgoers who appreciated tasteful fare with a literary bent. They were produced by J. Arthur Rank, the British motion picture mogul who launched an aggressive campaign after the war to force the Hollywood majors to open their theaters to British films. His effort failed, but certain lines of his films—Michael Balcon's Ealing comedies, for example—helped convince reluctant exhibitors to convert to art films rather than close their doors during the postwar recession. The growth in the number of art houses during the early 1950s created a truly viable art film market with relatively healthy distribution and exhibition arms.

The second part of this study covers the heyday of foreign films, from the early 1950s to 1966. Initially the market was driven by numerous independent distributors headquartered in New York who scoured international film festivals and European production centers to bid on prizewinners and discover new talent. To play it safe, distributors bid on films on the basis of what was popular the year before, or they might go after cutting-edge pictures to try and start a new trend. In either case, they faced the daunting task of making their wares appeal to U.S. audiences. Foreign films were almost always released with subtitles — fans would have it no other way. However, for marketing purposes distributors sometimes retitled their films and edited them to make them more palatable to American tastes. One thing was certain: distributors had little money for promotion and advertising; art films were released unheralded, with the result that few imports grossed over $200,000 at the box office.

Foreign film distributors had to contend with the Production Code Administration (PCA), the Legion of Decency (a Catholic group), and state and municipal censorship boards, each of which presented a separate censorship hurdle. Distributors seldom bothered with the PCA, which would likely have demanded cuts to get a seal; besides, foreign films played in art houses and independent theaters where a code seal did not matter. As a result, foreign films enjoyed one advantage over Hollywood in the United States: sex appeal. From the start, foreign film distributors understood that sex sold films and freely borrowed techniques from the exploitation market to "sex up" film titles and advertising to lure customers. The added revenue saved many a film.

The import trends discussed in this part are arranged chronologically, according to when they generated the greatest interest in the market. Although there is considerable overlap in time with this arrangement, by concentrating on trends rather than a cross section of the market year by year, one can more easily track the rise and fall of trends, general critical reception, and dynamics of film distribution. The accompanying table lists the top foreign films of the period.

French films reentered the United States immediately after the war. Most were made during the occupation in the style of the Tradition of Quality, the dominant French import trend of the 1950s. Based on French literary classics, the films were admired for their craftsmanship and intelligence, as well as for their sophisticated handling of sex. Interspersed among such pictures were a series of films produced by veteran French directors of the 1930s, plus a few modernist works by Jacques Tati and Robert Bresson. Tati's new brand of

Variety's All-Time Foreign Language Films to 1973

Title (distributor and U.S. release date)	Box Office*
I Am Curious (Yellow) (Grove Press, 1969)	$20.2
La Dolce Vita (Astor, 1961)	19.5
Z (Cinema V, 1969)	15.8
A Man and a Woman (Allied Artists, 1966)	14.3
8½ (Embassy, 1963)	10.4
Elvira Madigan (Cinema V, 1967)	10.1
Yesterday, Today and Tomorrow (Embassy, 1964)	9.3
Marriage Italian Style (Embassy, 1964)	9.1
Dear John (Sigma III, 1964)	8.8
Belle de Jour (Allied Artists, 1968)	8.0
Two Women (Embassy, 1961)	7.2
The Garden of the Finzi-Continis (Cinema V, 1971)	6.0
King of Hearts (Lopert, 1967)	5.7

Source: *Variety*, February 21–27, 2000, 16.

* Domestic box office gross in millions of dollars.

comedy as exemplified in *Mr. Hulot's Holiday* (1954) was a bright spot, but Bresson's minimalist style in *Diary of a Country Priest* (1954) found little favor. As a group French films were respected, but they met with little enthusiasm until the arrival of a series of popular thrillers, beginning with Henri-Georges Clouzot's *The Wages of Fear* (1955) and the appearance two years later of Brigitte Bardot in Roger Vadim's *And God Created Woman* (1957), which set a new box-office record for foreign films. The picture was released by Kingsley-International, a subsidiary of Columbia Pictures, and marked the beginning of Hollywood's entry into art film distribution in a significant way. The market was soon flooded with Bardot's films, both old and new. Since Bardot virtually personified the youth of the 1950s and was especially popular with college students, her films set the stage for the reception of the French New Wave.

Japan entered the market in 1951 with the release of Akira Kurosawa's *Rashomon*. Like *Open City*, it was a total surprise. Japan's film industry lay in ruins after the war and its relations with the West had yet to be normalized. To secure a foothold for Japanese films in the United States, Masaichi Nagata, the head of Daiei Studios and *Rashomon*'s producer, attempted to capitalize on the film's reception by devising an export strategy based on stories of old Japan told in a humanistic style. In other words, he hoped that *Rashomon* would do for Japanese films what *Open City* had done for the Italian film industry. Nagata's experiment initially succeeded, but when Daiei introduced films with a more contemporary feel, interest in Japanese films faded.

Toho, Daiei's competitor, had a go at the American market by introducing samurai action films, most notably Kurosawa's *The Magnificent Seven*, which was picked up by Columbia Pictures in 1956 and mishandled as a "Japanese Western." The experience convinced Toho to open showcase theaters for Japanese cinema in Los Angeles, San Francisco, and New York City and to take over the distribution of its pictures—all to no avail. Cultural differences may have prevented Japanese films from attracting a significant following in the United States. In Kurosawa's case, poor distribution also played a role; Kurosawa had many distributors, and no effective marketing strategy was devised to attract more American filmgoers.

Such was not the case with Ingmar Bergman. The handling of his films demonstrated what good distribution could do for an auteur on the cutting edge. Bergman rose to prominence in the late 1950s, when art films were being equated with sexploitation films thanks, in part, to the Brigitte Bardot craze. Bergman began to be taken seriously in 1956, with the release of *Smiles of a Summer Night*. By 1959 he had become a one-man production trend with a cult following. His pictures were being compared to the works of James Joyce, Marcel Proust, and Jean-Paul Sartre. Bergman's films were distributed by Bryant Haliday and Cy Harvey of Janus Films, who devised a successful campaign to craft an image of Bergman as auteur and to carefully control the timing of each release. By 1960 Bergman had made the cover of *Time* magazine and was the subject of numerous feature stories that examined his themes, working methods, and personal life. The national press coverage was unprecedented and conditioned the critical reception of his films. Equally important, Janus released the films in an orderly fashion to prevent a glut on the market and to milk every last dollar out of the box office. No other auteur received such treatment. Bergman's reputation peaked when *The Virgin Spring* (1960) and *Through a Glass Darkly* (1961) each won Oscars for Best Foreign Language Film.

The French New Wave arrived in 1959 after winning top honors at Cannes. The first entries were Louis Malle's *The Lovers*, François Truffaut's *The 400 Blows*, Claude Chabrol's *The Cousins*, and Marcel Camus's *Black Orpheus*. A diverse lot, they were released within weeks of each other in late 1959 and temporarily overshadowed Bergman. The directors were unknowns. They typically started out as movie critics at the influential *Cahiers du Cinéma* and had railed against the Tradition of Quality directors. Beyond that they shared only two things, according to reviewers: youthful exuberance and love of cinema. Their films were based on what they knew best, "the anarchic, spasmodic, lawless, and rebellious lives of certain modern young French."[13] Like the Italian neo-realists, these budding auteurs worked with small budgets and shot their films on location with portable, flexible equipment in whatever style inspired them. Their actors were also young and mostly unknown. By breaking the rules of storytelling and adopting new modes of production, the French New Wave pushed the boundaries of what was acceptable as art house fare. As Hollis Alpert has stated, "These movies seem more than anything else an outburst of energy and protest against the stupefying and banal that have glutted theatres for so long and will continue to do so."[14]

Later arrivals included Alain Resnais's *Hiroshima Mon Amour* (1960) and *Last Year at Marienbad* (1962); Jean-Luc Godard's *Breathless* (1961); and Truffaut's *Jules and Jim* (1962). Godard emerged as the most experimental member of the group. Like Bergman, he attracted a cult following. However, after *Breathless* reviewers were either unable or unwilling to keep up with his rapidly evolving style. He was deemed totally uncommercial. By 1962 the French New Wave had run its course, although some of its leaders endured thanks to production deals from the Hollywood majors.

The British New Cinema was also identified with youth, in this case young directors who railed against the British welfare state, complacency in the arts, and the entrenched power of the upper middle class. The first entries, Jack Clayton's *Room at the Top* and Tony Richardson's *Look Back in Anger*, hit the market around the same time as the French New Wave, but the movement didn't really get going until 1961, with the release of Karel Reisz's *Saturday Night and Sunday Morning* starring Albert Finney. British directors borrowed stylistic devices and production practices from the French New Wave, but their narratives were hardly ambiguous or obscure. For source material they adapted the novels and plays of a new generation of writers dubbed the "Angry Young Men" by the media. The settings were the bleak industrial Midlands, which required a new breed of actor—the likes of Albert Finney, Alan Bates, Tom Courtenay, and Rita Tushingham. American film reviewers had little sympathy for the angry young protagonists in these films. Reviewers may have been insensitive to the debilitating effects of British socialism on the lower classes, or perhaps they considered the movement old hat, not much different from the social protest plays of Clifford Odets from the 1930s or more recent Hollywood films like *The Wild One* and *Rebel Without a Cause*. The only thing preventing the British New Cinema from going directly into mainstream exhibition was the Production Code, which was at odds with the blunt dialogue and illicit sex in some of the films.

The second Italian renaissance grabbed the limelight in 1961 with the arrival of Michelangelo Antonioni's *L'Avventura*, Federico Fellini's *La Dolce Vita*, and Luchino Visconti's *Rocco and His Brothers*. Unlike the French and British "new wavers," the Italians were middle-aged men getting their second wind, so to speak. All three were moralists in the tradition of Italian neorealism: Antonioni and Fellini took the pulse of the upper classes, while Visconti chose to focus on the lower class. Only Fellini had an established reputation in the United States. It was built on the reception of *La Strada*, which was awarded a top prize by the New York Film Critics Circle and received the inaugural Academy Award for Best Foreign Language Film of 1956.

Antonioni emerged as the most controversial filmmaker of the group. *L'Avventura* was greeted by incomprehension and hostility, but after the release of *The Night* (1962) and *Eclipse* (1962)—which completed Antonioni's trilogy exploring the "spiritual aridity" and "moral coldness" of Italy's postwar generation—he was regarded as one of the finest stylists in the history of cinema. However, the so-called obscure style of Antonioni's films, with their unresolved endings and deliberate pacing, mostly attracted cineastes.

Fellini emerged as the most flamboyant filmmaker. *La Dolce Vita*'s scandalous portrait of Roman café society generated an enormous amount of publicity and became the film to see. Hollis Alpert, speaking for most critics, hailed *La Dolce Vita* as "the most fascinating three hours of cinema turned out in recent years, a culmination of the Italian realistic approach, the most brilliant of all movies that have attempted to portray the modern temper."[15] *La Dolce Vita* was released as a road show and set a new box-office record. It ranked number one on *Variety*'s All-Time Foreign Language Films, holding that position until 1969. Fellini followed up *La Dolce Vita* with *8½* (1963). Fellini's portrait of a middle-aged artist in crisis elevated him higher in the pantheon of auteurs. It was also a big commercial success, ending up number five on *Variety*'s list.

Visconti was the most maligned filmmaker. The fault largely rested with his distributors. *Rocco and His Brothers* (1961), Visconti's portrait of an immigrant family trying to make a better life for itself in industrial Milan, contained a shocking "rape scene in the mud" and an "intensely violent murder." Astor Pictures, the distributor, had high hopes for it but felt obliged to trim thirty minutes for the New York launch and another thirty for the general in order to make it more marketable. The exercise finally reduced the film to "a formless series of violent climaxes. It was a commercial failure."[16] Visconti's next film, *The Leopard* (1963), suffered a similar fate at the hands of its distributor, 20th Century-Fox.

Thanks mainly to Joseph Levine, the second Italian renaissance was the most commercially successful import trend of the 1960s. A look at *Variety*'s All-Time Foreign Language Films shows why. Prior to releasing *8½*, Levine had linked up with Italian producer Carlo Ponti to market a series of pictures starring Sophia Loren, Ponti's wife. The films were directed by Vittorio De Sica, who had been reduced to directing other people's pet projects after the failure of his *Umberto D.* The Levine-Ponti collaborations began in 1961 with *Two Women* and continued until 1964 with *Yesterday, Today and Tomorrow* and *Marriage Italian Style*, which paired Miss Loren with Marcello Mastroianni. Although the films were released with subtitles, they contained conventional plots and a star who had earlier become an international sensation in Hollywood pictures. As a result, the Loren vehicles had the side effect of diluting the meaning of the terms "art film," "foreign film," and "art film market." They also raised the expectations of art house managers, who wanted to play it safe.

This part concludes with a survey of imports from outside the epicenter, which is to say outside the production centers of Western Europe. The main players include Luis Buñuel, Satyajit Ray, and Akira Kurosawa, auteurs whose films left an enduring legacy in the U.S. art film market despite poor distribution. As a group they found the going rough. Ray's films probably would never have made it to an art house without the perseverance of Edward Harrison, his sole distributor. Beginning with the Apu trilogy, Ray soon attracted a cult following. However, despite all the fine reviews and awards, his films generated little business. By 1960 Kurosawa was being compared favorably to Ingmar Bergman, yet no distributor came forward to give him the Janus treatment. Although Toho opened a Manhattan showcase for Japanese cinema and briefly took over the distribution of Kurosawa's pictures, the efforts yielded little in the way of results. Of all the auteurs from outside the epicenter, Luis Buñuel fared the best. During the 1960s he became a one-man import trend and a darling of the New York Film Festival.

Secondary players included filmmakers from Soviet Russia and Poland. A series of Russian films was introduced to the market beginning in 1960, the result of a U.S.-Soviet film exchange arranged by the State Department during a thaw in the cold war. Hollywood companies dutifully stepped forward to take on the films, but after observing the box office returns, they opted out of the exchange in 1963 and consigned the Soviet films to the art house market. Subsequently independent distributors dealt directly with the Russians to acquire films. The biggest deal was Walter Reade's acquisition of Sergei Bondarchuk's epic *War and Peace*, the most expensive film ever made up to that time. In 1968 Reade released a dubbed version of the film specifically to bypass the art house circuit. A series of postwar Polish films was introduced to New Yorkers in 1960 by the Museum of Modern Art (MoMA). Two of the films, Andrzej Wajda's

Kanal and *Ashes and Diamonds*, found commercial distribution and served as the harbingers of a surge of creative filmmaking from Eastern Europe that soon attracted international attention.

The third part traces the impact of Hollywood on the art film market. The majors entered the art film market beginning in 1957 and enjoyed a huge advantage over independent distributors by bidding aggressively on imports and attracting promising auteurs with production deals. The cost of doing business now beyond their reach, independent distributors simply closed up shop or went into other lines of work. By 1964 the art film market had become a two-tiered affair. The top tier comprised the Hollywood majors and two prominent indies, Walter Reade's Continental Distributing and Donald Rugoff's Cinema V. This group handled the cream of the crop and pretty much occupied the first-run art houses on Manhattan's so-called Gold Coast East Side. The bottom tier consisted of a handful of newcomers who relied on the New York Film Festival to promote their films. It found outlets for them either at the Fifth Avenue Cinema near Greenwich Village or at the New Yorker Theater on the Upper West Side of Manhattan.

The founding of the New York Film Festival in 1963 thus acquired special significance. At a time when art house managers were looking for safe bets from the top-tier companies, the festival served a cultural purpose by presenting the latest developments in international filmmaking, many of which would probably never have been shown publicly in New York. The festival also served an unintended purpose as a pre-release showcase for films that had previously been acquired by lower-tier distributors. Only a small percentage of the festival presentations were predestined for commercial release, and only a few succeeded at the box office.

Having abolished the Production Code in 1966, the majors could now produce almost anything as long as it was not obscene. The late 1960s witnessed a transition in American moviegoing from a mass family entertainment to a minority art form supported mostly by young people. Hollywood's investment in countercultural films, such as Arthur Penn's *Bonnie and Clyde* (1967) and Dennis Hopper's *Easy Rider* (1969), attracted young people to the box office in record numbers and ushered in a period of unprecedented frankness in Hollywood filmmaking. Looking back at these events, *Variety* stated: "No longer does the elitist end of the American audience look solely to foreign films as the source of intellectual stimulation in the 'wasteland' of U.S. commercial 'trash.' Domestic product, even from the major companies, has passed cinematic puberty in record time, offering films with themes and treatment so adult as to knock the bottom out of what once was an art house market."[17]

Another look at *Variety*'s All-Time Foreign Language Films might suggest that foreign films did quite well in the immediate post-Code period, when six imports made it to the list: Philippe de Broca's *King of Hearts* and Bo Widerberg's *Elvira Madigan* in 1967, Luis Buñuel's *Belle de Jour* in 1968, Costa-Gavras's *Z* and Vilgot Sjöman's *I Am Curious (Yellow)* in 1969, and Vittorio De Sica's *The Garden of the Finzi-Continis* in 1971. Such films, however, were anomalies. By 1967 foreign films had lost their cachet, and critically acclaimed pictures like Alain Resnais's *La Guerre Est Finie* (1967), Ingmar Bergman's *Persona* (1967), Claude Chabrol's *La Femme Infidèle* (1969), Milos Forman's *The Fireman's Ball* (1968), and Elio Petri's *Investigation of a Citizen Above Suspicion* (1970) barely got off the ground. One reason, according to Saul Tureli of Janus Films, was that "American filmgoers [could] see brilliant, sophisticated movies of their own."[18]

By 1970 the majors had abandoned the art film market, as had many of the remaining independents. In 1973 Bernardo Bertolucci's *Last Tango in Paris*, a United Artists release, was thought to signal a new beginning for art films by serving as a model for an adult art cinema, but the majors had by now lost interest in X-rated films as well. Although art houses had been switching to sexploitation films to stay in business, it made no sense to the majors to produce such films, which excluded young people under seventeen. Besides, *Last Tango* was a Marlon Brando spectacle, which would have been tough to replicate.

By 1973 the art film market had reverted to a niche business operated by numerous independent distributors catering to a small but dedicated cadre of mature adults. Every year one or two imports attracted attention and played in New York, Los Angeles, San Francisco, Boston, and a few other cities. Beginning in 1979, the growth of two ancillary markets for feature films—pay television and home video, with their voracious appetites for programming of all types, including foreign films—lured the majors back into art film distribution. The return of the majors started the cycle anew, but the "heroic age of moviegoing," to use Phillip Lopate's phrase, had long since passed.

The critical reception recounted in this history derives exclusively from contemporary sources. Art house operators might first learn about a new foreign film by reading *Variety*, which regularly covered Cannes, Venice, and other international film festivals. Addressed to the trade, *Variety*'s reviews assessed a picture's commercial chances and often contained a recommendation or two about how it should be marketed, in addition to providing a plot summary. In the end, however, it was the New York City launch that established a foreign film's reputation and determined its fate in the market. Unlike regular moviegoers, art house patrons paid little attention to paid advertising and mostly relied on reviews and word of mouth to make their choices. I have therefore cited reviews and articles from a cross section of influential publications of the time that routinely reviewed foreign films and generated the first media response to new releases. They include: a national newspaper, the *New York Times*; a free alternative New York City weekly, the *Village Voice*; weekly news magazines, such as *Time* and *Newsweek*; and specialized magazines, such as the *Saturday Review*, *New Yorker*, *Nation*, *New Republic*, and *Esquire*. These were the publications art house patrons typically read to keep current. *Time* and *Newsweek* had circulations in the millions. Among the specialized magazines, the *New Yorker* had the largest weekly circulation, reaching 450,000 by 1960, followed by the *Saturday Review* with 260,000, and the *New Republic* and the *Nation* with around 30,000 each. *Esquire*, a monthly, had a paid circulation of 750,000 around this time. The principal cast of reviewers include: Bosley Crowther and Vincent Canby (*New York Times*); Andrew Sarris (*Village Voice*); Arthur Knight and Hollis Alpert (*Saturday Review*); Pauline Kael (*New Yorker*); Stanley Kauffmann (*New Republic*); and Dwight Macdonald (*Esquire*). They were all professional journalists who wrote under deadline pressure and whose tastes were presumably aligned with those of their readership. Nevertheless, only Bosley Crowther had major power at the box office.

The *New York Times* was in a class by itself. As I previously noted, a new release had to play a minimum of eight weeks in a first-run art house in New York and receive a positive review from Bosley Crowther to be considered a hit and attract the interest of art house managers. For this reason Crowther plays a major role in this history. A Princeton University graduate, Crowther joined the paper in 1928 as a cub reporter. Serving as the paper's chief film critic from 1940 to 1967, Crowther could "make or break most 'art' films in New York," according to Andrew Sarris, and could "dictate to distributors what films they may or may not import."[19] *Variety* stated that a positive review from Crowther could set "the tone for the rest of the country, both in terms of exhibitor and critics' reaction."[20] No one seriously challenged these assessments. Crowther oversaw a department of six writers and wrote half of the four hundred movie reviews published each year, in addition to contributing longer pieces for the Sunday edition. The readers of the *New York Times* were well educated, affluent, and politically liberal—the exact demographic of the emerging art house audience. In 1944 Crowther was elected chairman of the New York Film Critics Circle, an organization comprising the film editors of New York's daily newspapers, and presided over its annual awards ceremony during his years in office.

Crowther was an ardent booster of foreign films after the war, as well as a champion of freedom of the screen. Yet he was a man of conservative tastes in films, preferring those with social themes—particularly Italian neorealism—to most others. Crowther's power had its downside, of course. Modernist films did poorly by him. For example, Crowther damned such art house classics as Antonioni's *L'Avventura*, Bergman's *Wild Strawberries*, Kurosawa's *Throne of Blood*, Godard's *Contempt*, and Bresson's *Diary of a Country Priest*. In part to counteract Crowther's influence, in 1966 Hollis Alpert of the *Saturday Review*, Andrew Sarris of the *Village Voice*, Richard Schickel of *Life*, and several other reviewers formed the National Society of Film Critics, which instituted its own set of awards.

Crowther stepped down as chief critic of the *New York Times* in 1967. He was done in by Arthur Penn's *Bonnie and Clyde*, which he reviewed—negatively—three times for its "blending of farce with brutal killings." Crowther was clearly out of sync with the new film culture and was replaced by the twenty-nine-year-old Renata Adler, a Bryn Mawr graduate who had never been a regular reviewer. Her appointment was viewed as part of the staid newspaper's "new generation rejuvenation" pattern. Adler lasted a brief fourteen months and was replaced by Vincent Canby, a Dartmouth graduate who had joined the newspaper in 1967 as a member of the theater and film criticism staff after previously serving as a reviewer and reporter for *Variety*. Canby served as the newspaper's chief film critic until 1993.

Though lacking the box office clout of the *New York Times*, the weekly news magazines *Time* and *Newsweek* helped prepare the groundwork for a national art film market. According to Ernest Callenbach's 1951 survey of U.S. film journalism, these magazines appealed "to the 'leaders' of American society—the college graduate, business-executive class. Backed by the prestige of huge circulations and presented in concise form, the film sections of these weeklies are influential in conditioning audience expectations and responses on a national scale." The reviews appeared without bylines and, like newspaper reviews, contained plot summaries, comments on performances, and brief evaluations. The tone of these reviews, noted Callenbach, was "terse and slightly self-conscious."[21]

The postwar film renaissance obviously upped the ante on traditional journalistic criticism. Foreign films could be radically different from conventional Hollywood fare in terms of style, narrative structure, and mode of production. They required more than a "I liked it or didn't like it" judgment to satisfy interested readers. What constituted the correct standards of film criticism led to heated arguments in the press and in cult film magazines. By 1968 film critics had become celebrities; they had their own television segments and their reviews were collected and published in book form to demonstrate definitions of "true" film criticism.

Among the first reviewers in specialized periodicals to promote the film renaissance were Arthur Knight and Hollis Alpert. They were members of an impressive stable of critics publisher Norman Cousins had assembled during the 1940s to revitalize the *Saturday Review*, which was originally known as the *Saturday Review of Literature*. A City College of New York graduate, Knight had worked as a film curator at MoMA before joining the *Saturday Review* in 1949. After serving in the army as a combat historian, Alpert worked simultaneously as an assistant fiction editor for the *New Yorker* and as a freelance film critic for the *Saturday Review*, eventually joining the latter full time in 1956. In addition to filing balanced and appreciative reviews, Knight and Alpert interviewed auteurs to explain the ways of filmmaking to their readers and wrote carefully researched background stories to introduce the latest import trend. For their efforts they received the Screen Directors Guild Critics Award for 1957. That same year Knight published a pioneering text, *The Liveliest Art: A Panoramic History of the Movies*, which became required reading for the new generation of cineastes. In 1960 he joined the faculty of the University of Southern California and became a founder of academic film studies. Knight and Alpert coauthored an authoritative series on motion picture censorship, "The History of Sex in the Cinema," which ran in *Playboy* from 1965 to 1973. Foreign films and stars played a major role in their history.

Stanley Kauffmann and Dwight Macdonald, two highbrow critics in the cast, wrote in the humanist/literary tradition. Kauffmann studied drama at New York University and worked in book publishing before joining the *New Republic* in 1958. He was among the first to ponder in print the role of the film critic in the postwar scene. In his review of James Agee's edited volume of film criticism, *Agee on Film*, Kauffmann appraised Agee's stature as follows: "The best critic is one who illuminates whole provinces of an art that you could not see before, who helps to refine the general public's taste (which is never good enough—they haven't time, they're busy studying something else or doing their jobs) and who serves as a sounding board for serious artists. . . . But fundamentally you take a critic's hand and let him lead you further, perhaps higher, only if you are initially convinced of a substantial area of mutual sympathy and interest."[22] Agee served as the film critic for the *Nation* from 1942 to 1948 and wrote anonymous reviews for *Time* during the same period. *Agee on Film* was published in 1958, three years after his death at the age of forty-six and the year his posthumous novel, *A Death in the Family*, won the Pulitzer Prize in fiction.

Kauffmann aspired to this ideal. He was regarded as a "committed, serious, literate, and objective" critic who was adept at interpreting intellectually complex films and who had a thorough appreciation of film acting.[23] Without declaring his criteria for judging a film, Kauffmann was willing to go against the critical consensus. He praised Antonioni but was underwhelmed by films that achieved fame because of their "difficulty," or because they claimed to be "advanced" or "pioneering," such as *Last Year at Marienbad, 8½, A Woman Is a Woman*, and *Wild Strawberries*. Kauffmann observed that Agee's greatest asset as a critic was passion: "He takes films seriously . . . cares greatly about them, what they are doing and where they are going."[24] Kauffmann, however, was generally considered too impersonal and too dignified to convey a sense of enthusiasm even if he liked a film. His initial stint at the *New Republic* lasted eight years, until 1965, when he served briefly as the drama critic for the *New York Times*. He returned to the magazine in 1967, where he has remained to the present. His first collection of reviews, *A World on Film*, was published in 1966. Writing in the *New York Times Book Review*, Laurence Goldstein said that after reading Kauffmann on Antonioni's *L'Avventura* and *La Notte*, he knew more about himself, adding, "That, possibly, is the great strength of Mr. Kauffmann's criticism. He is concerned with film not only as an esthetic but as a moral force. His sense of values is dynamic. . . . His perspective encompasses the development of the modern film in a world where new visions often anticipate new values. There is little more one can ask of a critic."[25]

Dwight Macdonald was the film critic at *Esquire* from 1960 to 1966. Educated at Phillips Exeter Academy and Yale University, Macdonald started out as an associate editor at Henry R. Luce's *Fortune* magazine (1929–36) before going into radical politics as an editor of the socialist literary journal *Partisan Review* (1938–43), as the editor and publisher of the pacifist magazine *Politics* (1944–49), and as a staff writer for the *New Yorker* (beginning in 1951). It was during his stint at *Esquire* that Macdonald wrote *Against the American Grain* (1962), which contained a withering critique of American mainstream culture in the essay "Mass Cult & Mid Cult." As a film critic, Macdonald subordinated his sociological interests and placed aesthetic concerns foremost. "Being a congenital critic, I know what I like and why. But I can't explain the *why* except in terms of the specific work under consideration, on which I'm copious enough. The general theory, the larger view, the gestalt—these have always eluded me." Macdonald felt that "the reasons a critic gives for his judgments are more important than the judgments themselves; one may agree with his taste and find his writing unprofitable; also vice versa." Having said that, Macdonald offered up his criteria for a good motion picture: "Did it change the way you looked at things?" "Did you find more, or less, in it the second, third, etc., time?"[26] Macdonald, like Kauffmann, was hard to please; the few foreign film he liked included *L'Avventura, 8½, The 400 Blows, Jules and Jim*, and *Hiroshima Mon Amour*. Writing for a monthly limited Macdonald's coverage of new releases and sometimes prevented his reviews from appearing in a timely manner. Nevertheless he was generally admired for the "breadth of his vision," for the "leanness and sprightliness in his writing," and for his "sense of humor." So said John Simon in his review of Macdonald's collection of film reviews spanning four decades, *Dwight Macdonald on Movies*, which was published in 1969.[27]

Andrew Sarris and Pauline Kael, the two remaining names in the cast, represented a new generation of film critics. As Emanuel Levy put it, they belonged to a "small group of intellectuals who have shaped American culture, entering the lives of cinephiles as representatives of a new way of life, one dominated by the movies." Sarris, of course, was responsible for introducing the auteur theory to the United States. He attended Columbia University and drifted into film reviewing in 1955 as a contributing editor to *Film Culture*, a new cult magazine devoted to American underground cinema founded by Jonas and Adolfas Mekas. In 1960 he started writing for the *Village Voice*, rising from "obscurity to notoriety" in 1963 following the publication of a two-part article in *Film Culture*. According to Levy, "In the first, 'Notes on the Auteur Theory,' Sarris Americanized Truffaut's 'la politique des auteurs,' suggesting the director as the author of a film and visual style as the key to assessing a director's standing as auteur. In the second piece, Sarris evaluated 106 American and 7 foreign directors, placing them in categories that ranged from 'the Pantheon' to 'Oddities and One Shots.'"[28]

It was generally agreed that the auteur theory certainly applied to the great European filmmakers, but Sarris's attempt to elevate the status of Hollywood directors working within the studio system was greeted as heresy—or worse—by the cultural establishment. The first to attack him was Pauline Kael, who quashed Sarris's argument in a notorious piece entitled "Circles and Squares," which appeared soon after in *Film Quarterly*.[29] Kael, who attended the University of Calfornia at Berkeley, started out in the 1950s managing a pair of art film houses in Berkeley and reporting on movies for Pacifica radio. By 1960 she was freelancing, with reviews and articles appearing in cult film magazines and other specialized journals. *Film Quarterly* published Sarris's rebuttal to the "Circles and Squares" piece, but it hardly quelled the controversy.[30] Dwight Macdonald, Arthur Knight, John Simon, and others joined the attack, yet the theory retained an elemental force, and by the time Sarris's influential book *The American Cinema: Directors and Directions* was published in 1968, auteurism was taken for granted.

The impact of auteurism on film criticism was profound. As Levy summarized it, "Sarris altered irreversibly the way movies were seen, revealing dimensions that traditional literary-based criticism had ignored. By treating movies as movies, not as poor relations or extensions of books and plays, Sarris introduced a new method of criticism. Auteurism raised the issue of whether a film should be judged as an individual work unto itself or with reference to the director's other films, both those that preceded and those that followed that work."[31] Sarris's collected reviews, *Confession of a Cultist*, was published in 1970. Writing in the *New York Times Book Review*, Stuart Byron stated that "no American has written better criticism than Andrew Sarris, and in the past two or three years it has become clear that none has had a more profound influence on those who came after him to a serious contemplation of the movies."[32]

Kael's impact of film criticism was equally profound. She came to national prominence in 1965, when her first book of collected reviews, *I Lost It at the Movies*, sold more than 150,000 copies in paperback in its first year. After moving to New York City, Kael found reviewing jobs at *McCall's* and *New Republic* before landing at the *New Yorker* in January 1968. That spring *Kiss Kiss Bang Bang*, her second collection of reviews, was published. Until her arrival at the magazine, *New Yorker* reviews were written mostly by men of letters who had "well-bred and supercilious disdain for most films."[33] For Kael movies were not a peripheral affair: "Good critics see movies as part of the experience of their time, they help us understand what the new work they championed meant to them, they help us understand what the work they found objectionable represented in the culture. The good critic is also a crusader who helps to bring an audience to this good new work."[34]

Kael was at the height of her power while writing for the *New Yorker*. Unlike John McCarten's and Brendan Gill's film reviews for the magazine, which filled two or three columns of type at most, Kael's went on for pages—she was "a literary maximalist." Writing in a slangy, conversational style, she made movie reviewing "highly personal events, bringing all her experience to bear on them and channeling everything she knows into them, including a feeling for politics and literature and all the arts, high and low," remarked Levy. "Kael's response to a movie was often more interesting than the movies itself. She introduced a new trend of criticism, one that placed the critic, rather than the movie, at the center of the review."[35]

Kael adhered to no theory or aesthetic of cinema. Like Macdonald, she was "slightly cranky and thoroughly combative," refusing to join any school. Unlike Sarris, Kael seldom had "anything to say about the visual nature of the medium, or the pictorial quality of a specific film," said Edward Murray. She focused mainly "on the what; what characters stand for; what the film is 'saying'; what it means to her . . . and what it means to others—an interest that frequently carries her into sociological criticism, just as her own feelings often carried her into impressionistic criticism (or noncriticism)."[36]

This survey has only touched upon the issues surrounding the debate to establish correct standards for film criticism. Fuller accounts can be found in the essays by Emanuel Levy collected in his *Citizen Sarris, American Film Critic* and in Raymond J. Haberski Jr.'s *It's Only a Movie! Films and Critics in American Culture*. The attacks and counterattacks certainly enlivened the film culture of the 1960s and made for interesting reading in the *New York Times*, where some of the battles were waged. Wilfrid Sheed has observed, "To your average vague layman, the Wars of the Movie Critics must look like a cross between a 13th-century theological squabble and a fixed wrestling match."[37] To the participants, however, reputations were at stake. Ironically, the elevation of film as an art form and the growing prestige of movie critics that resulted from all the media coverage occurred just when the art film market went into decline. The real winners were the new generation of American directors—Arthur Penn, Stanley Kubrick, and Mike Nichols—who stole the hearts of young cinephiles.

Part One

Emergence

Antecedents

A vibrant art film culture existed in the United States as early as the 1920s, an outgrowth of the Little Cinema Movement, a loose network of small theaters presenting the latest avant-garde and critically acclaimed films from Europe. The Little Cinema Movement was inspired by the Little Theater Movement, a similar network of noncommercial theaters presenting the new drama and stagecraft of Europe, and by the cine clubs of Europe showing avant-garde films. The little cinemas catered to the upper-class elite and to the intelligentsia, people who considered foreign films more artful and sophisticated than standard Hollywood fare.[1]

The Little Cinema Movement took off in 1926 when Symon Gould, the director of the International Film Arts Guild, acquired the Cameo Theater, a legitimate house located on 42nd Street, near Broadway, in Manhattan and transformed it into a repertory theater presenting a series of weeklong programs to a subscription audience. During the first season, the guild showed a mix of films from Germany, France, and the United States, among them Ernst Lubitsch's *Passion*, starring Pola Negri, Fernand Léger's *Ballet mécanique*, and Charlie Chaplin's *The Pilgrim*. Also in 1926 Michael Mindlin, a former Broadway producer, transformed the Fifth Avenue Playhouse into a repertory theater, leading off with the German expressionist classic *The Cabinet of Dr. Caligari*. Mindlin went on to operate a string of art houses in the Greater New York area, as well as other cities, and created a film distribution arm to supply them. The movement received the support of prominent organizations that promoted the "Better Films" idea, in particular the National Board of Review of Films, the former New York City censorship body, which published thoughtful commentaries and reviews about the imports in its magazine. Other journals, such as *Close up* and *Theatre Arts Magazine*, also lent their support.

By the end of the decade little cinemas could also be found in New Haven, Baltimore, Washington, D.C., Rochester, Cleveland, Akron, Chicago, Los Angeles, Berkeley, and San Francisco. Unlike the ornate movie palaces that were being built in most downtown areas, the little cinemas provided an intimate viewing experience and cultivated an aura of "modernity and chicness" by serving coffee and cigarettes in the lounge, exhibiting paintings and sculpture, and distributing programs like the ones in legitimate theaters.[2] It was a short-lived movement, however, a casualty of talkies. As bastions of the silent film, the little cinemas ran out of quality films during the conversion and the first talkies were unsuitable as replacements. The Depression also took its toll.

After the conversion to sound, the number of foreign imports actually increased, but they played almost exclusively in ethnic theaters in immigrant neighborhoods. New York, with over thirty ethnic theaters, showed films in French, German, Italian, Russian, Polish, Greek, Hungarian, Chinese, Spanish, and Yiddish, to name but a few. Producers in the largest overseas markets—France and Germany in particular—would have preferred otherwise. Hollywood had dominated the world film market since the 1920s. To limit Hollywood's incursion, foreign governments instituted import quotas and other protective measures to support their local film industries. However, few of their films returned their investments at home. In order to survive, foreign producers needed to export and wanted reciprocity in the lucrative American market. The majors would have none of it. During the silent era, the majors regularly distributed foreign films and exhibited them in their theaters; it was a simple and inexpensive matter to translate the intertitles of foreign films into English to make them intelligible to American audiences. After the advent of sound, the situation changed. Foreign films had to be dubbed into English—an expensive proposition—to tap the U.S. market. As the principal innovators of sound, the majors had gotten a head start by investing millions to construct sound stages, wire their theaters, and experiment with the new medium. Hollywood easily retained it dominance overseas. In the rush to compete, European producers had to scramble to make the conversion. The first foreign films to reach the United States were often criticized for their poor sound quality and for being "out of touch" with standard production practices.

During the 1930s the majors preferred to handle their own pictures exclusively on their home turf. Moviegoing had become a national pastime, serviced by seventeen thousand theaters in cities, towns, and villages throughout the country. The Big Five—Loew's Inc. (Metro-Goldwyn-Mayer), Warner Bros.,

Paramount, 20th Century-Fox, and RKO—produced and distributed practically all the quality pictures that reached the screen and owned nearly all the important first-run theaters. Together with the Little Three—Columbia, Universal, and United Artists—they filled the playing time of just about every theater of consequence and captured the lion's share of the box-office revenue. To reach mainstream exhibition, a foreign film had to outperform Hollywood's best and somehow worm its way into the key theater chains—which were mostly controlled by the Big Five and were well supplied with product as a result of reciprocal booking arrangements among the majors. To secure a play date in a deluxe house, a foreign film not only had to be good but a smash hit.

The acclaimed foreign imports on the *New York Times*'s annual "Top Ten" were selected by the newspaper's chief film critics. During the 1930s, the latter included Mordaunt Hall (1930–34), Andre Sennwald (1934–36) and Frank S. Nugent (1936–40). Beginning in 1937, foreign films were also honored by the newly organized New York Film Critics Circle, which comprised the film editors of New York's daily newspapers. (Foreign films did not receive Academy Award recognition until after the war.) At the start of the 1930s, New York had four art theaters: the downtown Fifth Avenue Playhouse and the 55th Street Playhouse, Little Carnegie Playhouse, and the Plaza, all of which were located north of the Broadway theater district. The number briefly rose to six when the John Golden, a legitimate theater on West 58th Street, and the World, a midtown movie house, converted to art films, but by 1940 the number had fallen to three.[3] These theaters—plus a few others in Boston, Chicago, and elsewhere— kept the flame alive.

German Films

German films were the most popular imports during the early 1930s. In New York they played on Broadway and in German-speaking neighborhoods, often in theaters owned by the majors.[4] Three German companies—UFA, Tobis, and Capitol, all with offices in New York—distributed nearly seventy pictures a year as a group.

Géza von Bolváry's *Two Hearts in Waltz Time*, Leontine Sagan's *Mädchen in Uniform*, and Fritz Lang's *M* were the most impressive. A breed apart from *Caligari*, *The Golem*, *The Last Laugh*, and other German expressionist silents that played the Little Cinema circuit, *Two Hearts in Waltz Time* (*Zwei Herzen im Dreivierteltakt*) was a filmed German operetta about a composer who is cured of writer's block when he meets a pretty young blonde. Here is how Mordaunt Hall described the movie's reception on opening day: "The Fifty-fifth Street

Playhouse was packed with Germans yesterday afternoon, as sunny an October day as it was, and the presumption is that many in the gathering had heard from the fatherland of this film. They laughed and enjoyed the music and the tuneful melodies as they evidently almost forgot that the singing came from the mere shadows of the performers."[5] The film ran for more than a year at the theater and was seen by an estimated 250,000 people. Hailed by critics as "the first outstanding music and dialogue film to reach this country from abroad," it was repeatedly revived in New York and in many other American cities.

Mädchen in Uniform opened on September 20, 1932, at the Criterion after taking Berlin, Paris, and London by storm. It reached the United States via John Krimsky and Gifford Cochran, both newcomers to the business, who happened to see it in Paris and flew to Berlin the same afternoon to secure the U.S. rights to the film. Adapted from Christa Winsloe's play *Gestern und Heute*, it was "a simple human account" of a young woman's attachment to a sympathetic teacher in an authoritarian Prussian boarding school for girls. Hertha Thiele played Manuela, the young woman, and Dorothea Wieck played Fräulein von Bernburg, the teacher. Carl Froelich, the distinguished German director, produced it as a collective enterprise, employing most of the original cast of the Berlin stage production.

Mädchen was originally denied an exhibition license by the New York Board of Censors because Manuela's "unnatural affection" for her teacher "too intimately explored female adolescence." However, the board reversed itself when the presenters argued that the film should be interpreted as a comment on the rising spirit of militarism in Weimar Germany.[6]

Variety had a dim view of the film's chances: "Here's still another in the series of European importations that fall into that curious division of pictures that are artistically meritorious and abroad mean something at the box office but in the United States will mean very little from a cash standpoint. New York's picture critics threw their literary bonnet high in the air upon seeing this film, one of them even going so far as to call it the 'year's ten best pictures rolled into one.' All that may help in New York for the first week or so of the film's run, but after that, and outside of New York, the film will have to stand on its own. And as entertainment, it hasn't a leg to stand on."[7]

Nevertheless, *Mädchen* played in more than a thousand independent theaters and was revived at the Criterion in 1934 with a synchronized English soundtrack. That it never played in an affiliated theater was the direct result of Hollywood's new Production Code. When Krimsky submitted the film to the Production Code Administration (PCA) for a seal, Joseph I. Breen, the head man, replied that "in our judgment the picture is a violation of the production

Peter Lorre in Fritz Lang's *M* (1933)

code and unacceptable for public exhibition in theatres before mixed audiences."[8]

Fritz Lang's *M*, a chilling portrait of a serial child killer played by Peter Lorre, was produced in 1931 but was banned in Germany for being overtly anti-Nazi. Paramount Pictures, which had opened its doors to émigrés from the German film industry, acquired the distribution rights to the picture and released it at the Mayfair in early April 1933, a few months after the Nazi takeover. Hall described Peter Lorre's Murderer as "a repellent spectacle, a pudgy-faced, pop-eyed individual who slouches along the pavements and has a Jekyll-and-Hyde nature. Little girls are his victims. The instant he lays eyes on a child homeward bound from school, he tempts her by buying her a toy balloon or a ball. This thought is quite sufficient to make even the clever direction and performances in the film more horrible than anything else that has so far come to the screen."[9] *M* was originally released with subtitles, but two weeks into the run it was replaced by a dubbed version. Hall explained that the subtitles left too much out and that the patrons of the Mayfair "wanted to understand all that was being said by the characters." In the end, it was the dubbed version that was used for the general release.[10]

Demand for German films plummeted after Hitler came to power in January 1933. New York's Europa Theatre, which catered mainly to German Jews, stopped showing German imports almost immediately. German-language theaters elsewhere followed suit. After the Nazis nationalized the film industry, the Reich offered pictures to American exhibitors at no cost up front and requested just a percentage of the take, but only a few German-language theaters accepted the offer.[11]

French Films

Bosley Crowther described the 1930s as the golden age of French cinema. "Americans were led to discover the unique qualities of these finer French films—their intelligence and comprehension and honest realism which was quite distinct from the average juvenility out of Hollywood's glamour mills. Technical perfection was often lacking in these films," he said, "but they had something much more desirable which brought the customers in." In reality, the customers for French films were few and comprised "those who spoke the language through the circumstance of birth, rearing or higher education and, to a lesser extent, those who felt vague stirrings of discontent with Hollywood." In short, "They combined to form an audience of insignificant size."[12]

René Clair amused francophiles during the Depression with such films as *Sous les toits de Paris* (1930), *Le Million* (1931), and *À nous la liberté* (1932). Clair was described by Frank Nugent as a master of satire, "a fellow of impudent wit and bubbling humor" who seemingly "carried the entire French motion-picture industry on his shoulders."[13] The French films that later struck the public's fancy included Jacques Feyder's *Carnival in Flanders* (1936), Anatole Litvak's *Mayerling* (1937), Jean Renoir's *Grand Illusion* (1938), and Marcel Pagnol's *Harvest* (1939) and *The Baker's Wife* (1940)—all winners of the New York Film Critics Circle award for Best Foreign Film. They were also the biggest box-office draws: *Mayerling* grossed $240,000, *Grand Illusion* $100,000, *Harvest* $65,000, *Carnival* $50,000, and *Baker's Wife* over $80,000 during its first eleven weeks at the World. Herman Weinberg, the man who wrote the subtitles for the films, claimed this was "an all-time record for the French film in America."[14]

The exhibitor mainly responsible for cultivating an audience for French films was Jean H. Lenauer, manager of the Filmarte. In 1936 Lenauer took over the John Golden Theatre and converted the eight-hundred-seat house into a showcase for quality foreign films. Lenauer opened each new season with a distinguished French film; Feyder's *Carnival of Flanders* opened the 1936 season, with *Mayerling* and *Grand Illusion* opening the next two seasons. *Carnival in Flanders* (*La Kermesse héroïque*), Feyder's ribald satire, told how the women of a village in Belgium pacified the invading Spanish army in 1616 with "Gallic" hospitality while their men cowered and hid. The most expensive picture ever produced in France up to that time, *Carnival* was admired for Lazare Meerson's rich settings and costumes, which were based on the paintings of Dutch masters, as well as for its urbane comedy and its acting. "On a performance basis," said Nugent, "Alerme's mock heroic portrait of the Burgomaster is superb, Louis Jouvet's sardonic characterization of the friar a model of comic implication, Mlle [Françoise] Rosay's lively sketch of the Burgomaster's wife thoroughly delightful and Jean Murat's gallant Spanish grandee suavely perfect."[15]

Mayerling had much going for it. It starred the great romantic lead Charles Boyer and the exquisite Danielle Darrieux in a tragic love story based on the mysterious deaths of Crown Prince Rudolph, heir apparent to the Hapsburg throne, and his notorious mistress, the seventeen-year-old Marie Vetsera, which occurred at an Austrian hunting lodge at Mayerling in January 1889. The scandal shook the Austro-Hungarian Empire to its foundations. "Was it suicide or was it murder that accounted for their demise? And why?" Maxwell Anderson's take on the mystery in the Theatre Guild production of *Masque of Kings* was still a fresh memory in New York. Anderson's play suggested "that political intrigue drove the lovers to the final frustration of suicide." Litvak's version suggested that "it was nothing but beautiful, passionate love, finally forbidden by the Emperor, that caused the inseparable couple to make their ends."[16] Frank Nugent described *Mayerling* as "one of the most moving dramas the screen ever has unfolded." "Through the matchless performances of Charles Boyer as Rudolph and the unbelievably beautiful Danielle Darrieux as Vetsera," he said, "we are carried breathlessly along an emotional millrace, exalted and made abject as the dramatist directed. It is impossible to remain aloof, to regard the romance

Danielle Darrieux and Charles Boyer in Anatole Litvak's *Mayerling* (1937)

dispassionately. There is no resisting the fire that players, writer and director have struck from the screen."[17] *Variety* thought the film's title would be meaningless to average Americans and that the picture should have been dubbed into English to attract a wider audience. (Boyer would not permit it based on "artistic scruples.")[18] *Mayerling* ran for three months at the Filmarte and was booked into commercial chains to gain national exposure.

    Grand Illusion appeared when Europe was again a tinder box. Banned in Germany and Italy, it was unusual for being "a war film without a war scene, without horror, hysteria or heroics."[19] Boasting a distinguished cast headed by Jean Gabin, Pierre Fresnay, Eric von Strohheim, and Marcel Dalio, *Grand Illusion* depicted the efforts of captured French officers to escape from a German prisoner of war camp in World War I. According to Nugent, Renoir was less concerned with "the success or failure of this enterprise" than he was with character relationships: "Renoir cynically places a decadent aristocrat, a German career officer, in command of the camp; he places his French counterpart among the prisoners. Theirs is an affinity bred of mutual self-contempt, of the realization of being part of an outgrown era. The other prisoners are less heroic, but more human. They are officers, of course, but officers of a republic, not an aristocracy. One is Maréchal, ex-machinist; another is Rosenthal, a wealthy Jew. Von Rauffenstein, the German commandant, held them both in contempt. The elegant Captain de Boeldieu respected them as soldiers, admired them as men, faintly regretted he could not endure them as fellow beings.[20] Renoir's title alluded to the reference to World War I as "The War to End All Wars." *Variety* said, "There are only two references to the title but both are pertinent. Once when a French soldier exclaims 'what an illusion,' when a comrade says that the war will be over before they have time to escape from military prison, and again when he describes the end of all wars as an illusion."[21] Von Stroheim's performance, perhaps the finest of his career, helped the film earn an Academy Award nomination for Best Picture—a first for a foreign film.

Marcel Pagnol's *Harvest* (*Regain*), based on a novel by the contemporary Provençal author Jean Giono, told a story "of two lonely people who find each other amid a world of accident and sordid contacts and who cause dead fields to flourish anew by the miracle of their happiness." It was originally banned by the New York Board of Censors on the ground that "because its peasant lovers were not married, the picture tended to corrupt morals." After critical and editorial protest, the board's governing body, the Board of Regents, overruled the decision.[22] Nugent considered it one of the finest films of the year, "a film of utter serenity and great goodness, so reverently played and so compassionately directed that it is far less an entertainment work than it is a testament to the dignity of man and to his consonance with the spinning of the spheres." "Pagnol's cameras have delved the soil of Provence as understandingly as Giono's pages, winning for the film an atmospheric as well as thematic authenticity. The scenes of the sowing, the harvest, the gift of bread, the wife's brave and exultant announcement of her pregnancy (in such welcome contrast to the sickeningly coy manner of most screen ladies in the circumstance) are poetically cinematic."[23] *Harvest* enjoyed a long run at the World Theatre.

The Baker's Wife (*La Femme du boulanger*) was also derived from a Giono novel and starred Raimu, the renowned French comedian whom Nugent described as "the great God Pan . . . with an equatorial waistline, a buttony mustache, a foolscap of knitted wool and the true clown's genius for pathos." It told the story of a baker who stops working when his wife runs off with a shepherd on the marquis's best horse. The villagers, prizing his bread, "bring his wife back, and the marquis gets his horse, and the baker bakes again, with five extra loaves for the poor. The wife? Oh, she's forgiven. We've said this is a French picture." Nugent pointed to *The Baker's Wife* as "proof that the French have not lost the gift of laughter and the ability to communicate it to others."[24]

Russian Films

Russian films had been playing regularly in the United States since 1926, the year Sergei Eisenstein's *Battleship Potemkin* and the Soviet montage movement made their marks. During the 1930s, the period of socialist realism, Russian films found homes at the Cameo Theater, which had an average weekly attendance of fifteen thousand, the Eighth Street Playhouse, and the Acme, as well as ethnic theaters in Russian-speaking neighborhoods around the city.[25] Amkino, the distribution company the Soviets set up in the 1920s to distribute Russian films in the United States, remained the sole distributor. As Thomas Pryor recalled, "The Soviet's realistic approach to contemporary subjects acquired new significance in this country with the reawakening of the mass social consciousness after the stock market crash of 1929. [During the 1930s] it was practically impossible to mention a Soviet film within earshot of the intelligentsia without being drawn into a lengthy argument about the superior artistic craftsmanship of the Soviet technicians and the sociological content of the subject-matter. The lounges of the little art cinemas, which specialize in Soviet productions, were crowded with earnest young groups of young and old, rich and poor—all intently discussing and dissecting, according to their individual philosophies, the drama which had just been unfolded on the screen."[26]

Nikolai Ekk's *The Road to Life* (*Putyovka v zhizn*), the first successful Russian talkie to reach the United States, depicted the plight of Moscow street children orphaned during the Bolshevik Revolution. The film is "frankly propaganda," said *Time*. "It exhibits, with great self-satisfaction, Soviet methods of dealing with the problem of the wolfish ragamuffins. . . . Corralled by the police, the wild boys are set to work in a juvenile Commune, superintended by a tactful and vigorous social worker (Nikolai Batalov). From time to time they are obstreperous but gradually they become addicted to honesty and industry."[27] Ekk's appealing portrait of the "wild children of Russia" convinced RKO to book the film in its theater chain—"the only Soviet film to claim that distinction"—and inspired Warner Bros. to produce an American version, William Wellman's *Wild Boys of the Road* (1933), a social problem film about middle-class teenagers who hit the road as hobos rather than remaining a burden to their families when their fathers lose their jobs. Like *The Road to Life*, *Wild Boys* had an upbeat ending. The kids' plight is resolved when they are brought before a kindly judge, who looks very much like FDR, and are told, "There's a new day coming."[28]

Interest in Soviet films peaked in 1936 with the release of Sergei and Georgy Vasiliev's *Chapayev* (1935) and Efim Dzigan's *We Are from Kronstadt* (1936), two propaganda films that celebrated the individual heroism of the Soviet military during the Russian civil war. *Chapayev* had special appeal, winning a top award from the National Board of Review, among other honors. Immensely popular in Russia, *Chapayev* told the story of an illiterate Red Army general who leads a troop of peasants against the Whites before falling in battle. "Though it includes few of the salaamings that make most such 'documentary' films impenetrably dull to non-Communist audiences," said *Time*, "it makes the Robert Clive of the Russian Revolution appear more heroic and more human than the central figure in Hollywood's current excursion into the realm of British imperialism. Good shot: Chapayev (Boris Bobochkin) using a crock of potatoes and a package of cigarets to show Furmanov where a commander should stand when his soldiers are in action."[29]

Demand for Soviet films declined after 1936 and came to a halt in 1939, after the Germans and the Soviets signed a nonaggression pact. The market for French films in the United States collapsed as well after Germany invaded France. Cut off from their main sources of supply, art houses and ethnic theaters had to make do somehow or go out of business. By 1940 only three art houses were still operating in New York City: the 55th Street Playhouse, the Little Carnegie, and the World. According to Herman Weinberg, by war's end the number of art houses in the United States had dwindled to eighteen.[30]

British Films

British films fared better than foreign films, albeit not as well as the British had hoped. Because the United States and Great Britain shared a common language, the British film industry convinced itself that its films could find an audience in the American mainstream market if given a chance. The British clung to this belief against all odds for over thirty years.

During the 1930s the principal distributor of British pictures in the United States was United Artists and its main supplier was Alexander Korda, a Hungarian-born producer and director who had settled in England. Exclusively a distributor of high-class independent productions, United Artists linked up with Korda thanks to the Cinematograph Films Act of 1927. The legislation required British distributors—including American companies operating in Great Britain—to distribute a certain percentage of British-made pictures and insisted that British exhibitors devote a portion of their playing time to showing them. A form of protectionism designed by Parliament to safeguard the British film industry, the act had the unintended effect of stimulating the production of so-called quota quickies, films produced on the cheap that distributors and exhibitors could use to adhere to the letter of the law. Needless the say, the latter gave British films a bad name. Since the reputation of United Artists rested on quality pictures, distributing quota quickies in Great Britain could damage the company's name—and certainly such films were of no value to the company in the United States.

Korda came to the company's attention after making a better-than-average quota picture for Paramount called *Service for Ladies*, starring Leslie Howard. To test Korda's potential as a producer of class-A pictures, United Artists signed him to a two-picture contract. Korda's first effort, *The Private Life of Henry VIII*, was directed by Korda himself and starred Charles Laughton in a tongue-in-cheek and somewhat risqué chronicle of the much-married sixteenth-century British monarch. It premiered at Radio City Music Hall on October 12, 1933, and was a big hit. *Variety* called it "the finest picture which has come out of England to date."[31] To support this claim *Variety* noted that Korda's direction completely eliminated any broad British accent by members of the cast: "This amounts to the focal point of Korda's astuteness and is invaluable to the picture's gross possibilities in the States." It also noted that Korda "slipped in another surprise by placing before the king not one but many dainty dishes; for instance, Merle Oberon and Binnie Barnes." (Henry's other wives were played by Wendy Barrie, Elsa Lanchester, and Everley Gregg.) Of course it was Charles Laughton's performance that made the picture. Mordaunt Hall remarked, "Mr. Laughton not only reveals his genius as an actor, but also shows himself to be a past master in the art of make-up. In this offering he sometimes looks as if he had stepped from the frame of Holbein's painting of Henry. He appears to have the massive shoulders and true bearded physiognomy of the marrying ruler. Mr. Laughton may be guilty of caricaturing the role, but occasionally truths shine in the midst of the hilarity."[32] Korda's film grossed a respectable $500,000 in the United States and Charles Laughton won an Academy Award in the title role, the first Oscar awarded to a British-made film.

Korda's second effort, *Catherine the Great*, directed by Paul Czinner, premiered at the Astor on February 14, 1934, and succeeded Rouben Mamoulian's *Queen Christina*, starring Greta Garbo. Catherine was played by the Austrian actress Elizabeth Bergner in her first English-speaking role; Douglas Fairbanks Jr. co-starred as the insane czar Peter III. Mordaunt Hall called the picture "a further illustration of the marked progress made in British film production. . . . If anything, this current offering is even more elaborately staged than its illustrious predecessor and therefore it can boast of being the most lavish screen offering to emerge from England's studios." He particularly liked Miss Bergner's astute portrayal of the empress, the Czarina of All the Russias.[33] *Variety* called it "another ace from England and out of the same deck, Korda. Its success before a better class audience is assured."[34]

Charles Laughton and Binnie Barnes in Alexander Korda's *The Private Life of Henry VIII* (1933)

The first two entries earned Korda a long-term contract with United Artists and a partnership in the company in 1935. Korda was heralded at home as the man who single-handedly put the British film industry back on its feet. Building on this track record, Korda took his London Films production company public in 1934 and convinced the mighty Prudential Assurance to finance the construction of Denham Studios, located just outside London, one of the most up-to-date and best-equipped studios in Europe.

Korda went on to deliver two more costume biopics, both of which he personally directed: *The Private Life of Don Juan* (1934) and *Rembrandt* (1936); a pair of H. G. Wells's fantasies: William Cameron Menzies's *Things to Come* (1936) and Lothar Mendes's *The Man Who Could Work Miracles* (1937); a series of three imperial pictures directed by his brother, Zoltán Korda: *Sanders of the River* (1935), *Drums* (1938), and *The Four Feathers* (1939); and the René Clair comedy *The Ghost Goes West* (1936). As a group they were considered prestige pictures, a term used by the trade to designate production values and promotion treatment. A prestige picture was typically a big-budget special of any genre based on a presold property and injected with plenty of star power, glamorous and elegant trappings, and elaborate special effects. Some examples that came out of Hollywood include MGM's *Queen Christina*, Fox's *Stanley and Livingstone*, RKO's *Little Women*, Warner Bros.' *The Life of Emile Zola* and *The Adventures of Robin Hood*, Paramount's *Cleopatra*, Samuel Goldwyn's *Wuthering Heights*, and David O. Selznick's *Gone With the Wind*.

The Kordas' pictures clearly fit into this category. His leading players— Charles Laughton, Leslie Howard, Robert Donat, Merle Oberon, and Elsa Lanchester—were popular with American audiences and had dual careers in England and Hollywood. Moreover, his budgets compared favorably to Hollywood's. For example, *Things to Come*, a science fiction film about the devastating effects of a disastrous world war, cost $1 million and was the most expensive picture produced in England up to that time. To make these films palatable for exhibitors, United Artists downplayed their "Englishness" by pro- moting Alexander Korda as an international producer who had worked in Paris and Hollywood as well as in London. In its advertising the company placed Korda's name above the title and consigned the production company name, London Films, to small print at the bottom.[35]

Korda made a valiant effort to gain a foothold for British films in the American market. However, only one of his pictures for United Artists after the first pair could be considered a financial and critical success, namely, René Clair's *The Ghost Goes West*, a satire about an American chain store mogul who buys a haunted castle from a Scottish nobleman (Robert Donat) and orders it shipped stone by stone "to a palm-bordered oasis in Florida." This was Clair's first picture in English and his first bid for "mass approval." Frank Nugent's ver- dict was decisive. *Ghost* was "a sparkling jest—a brilliant satire and as perfect a romantic comedy as one has any right to expect this year."[36] Korda lost control of his company in 1938 when his creditors seized Denham Studios and merged it with the interests of a rising motion picture mogul named J. Arthur Rank.

During the war British propaganda films such as Michael Powell's *The Lion Has Wings* (1940), Noel Coward and David Lean's *In Which We Serve* (1942), and Michael Powell and Emeric Pressberger's *One of Our Aircraft Is Missing* (1942) fared well at the box better, no doubt because of "the temporary feeling of emotional unity which the war had created between Americans and English- men."[37] After the war, however, things returned to normal.

Postwar Conditions

By the time *Open City* arrived in New York in February 1946, the fighting had been over for nearly a year. Immediately following the Axis defeat, Hollywood set out to recapture lost markets by unloading its huge backlog of unreleased pictures produced during the war. Hollywood met little resistance; over six hundred American films were exported to Italy alone in 1946. Similar numbers were shipped to France, West Germany, and Japan. The protective barriers countries had erected during the 1920s and 1930s had disappeared and national film industries were left in shambles. Rome's principal studio complex, Cinecittà, had been bombed by the Allies and was being used as a displaced person's camp at war's end. Film production had continued in France during the occupation, but top personnel had fled into exile or joined the resistance, and film stock was scarce. After Germany's defeat, the country was divided into east and west. In East Germany the Soviets took over the old UFA studios outside Berlin and created a state film monopoly that conformed to socialist realism. In West Germany British and American authorities dismantled all the organizations for producing films and instituted a policy of denazification. The policy restricted the size of the new producing companies and removed all restrictions on film imports. West Germany was soon flooded with American films to the point where its film industry went into a decline that lasted twenty-five years. Only the British film industry survived the war intact. During the war, Great Britain accounted for nearly 50 percent of Hollywood's overseas earnings. Its industry remained under the control of Rank, who had succeeded in creating a vertically integrated film empire, with himself at the top.

Europe reacted to Hollywood's postwar expansion by imposing currency restrictions and import quotas to curtail the flow of imports and by providing production subsidies to local filmmakers, as they had done earlier. In order to survive, Europe's film producers again demanded reciprocity in the American market. Italy and France were content to use the art film market to gain a toehold, but only Italy discovered a way out of the "art house ghetto." Rank, who had the biggest claim on the American market after the war, was denied immediate access. Viewed against this backdrop, the postwar art film market was created, in part, out of the dashed hopes of European producers.

2

Italian Neorealism

Assessing the impact of *Open City* on the postwar art film market in 1948, Thomas Pryor noted, "Distributors, who in prewar days wouldn't go around the corner to see an Italian picture, much less undertake to sell one, now are frantically scrambling to get their hands on anything coming out of Italy. Whereas French pictures used to be most in demand, today it is Italian films, of which, incidentally, there seemingly is a never-ending flow."[1] Neorealism as a distribution trend flourished in the United States until 1951. The most honored imports included: Roberto Rossellini's *Open City*, *Paisan*, and *The Miracle*; Luigi Zampa's *To Live in Peace*; and Vittorio De Sica's *Shoe Shine*, *The Bicycle Thief*, and *Miracle in Milan*. These films were named Best Foreign Language Film by the New York Film Critics Circle six years in a row, from 1946 to 1951. In addition, *Shoe Shine* and *The Bicycle Thief* won honorary Oscars in 1948 and 1950, respectively. Moreover, *The Miracle* was the centerpiece of an historic censorship decision handed down by the U.S. Supreme Court in 1952.

The enduring reputation of Italian neorealism was nicely summed up by Robert Hawkins in a 1952 piece for the *New York Times Magazine*, in which he noted that after the war Italy had "little or no money for movies, and practically no movie industry. . . . For lack of proper writers, [directors] worked without a script. For lack of satisfactory actors, they used the man on the street. The natural histrionic flair of the Italian people replaced experienced talent. They saw, created, shaped, improvised." Rossellini and De Sica made films "which bit sharply into life, which tackled its problems, films with undictated, true endings, pessimistic films as a reaction to the forced optimism under fascism, but pessimistic also in the pessimistic world which surrounds them. *Open City*, *Paisan*, and

Shoe Shine were cruelly real, and they shocked moviegoers the world over. 'New Realism' had come into its own."[2]

Although Hawkins captured the spirit of the trend that kick-started the U.S. art film market after the war, he exaggerated somewhat. From the start these directors worked with scripts prepared by experienced writers and used professional actors. Rossellini collaborated with screenwriter Sergio Amidei for most of his postwar features and De Sica teamed up with Cesare Zavattini, a writer and political theorist. Both writers were important figures in the development of the movement. Rossellini cast Aldo Fabrizi and Anna Magnani for his leads in *Open City*. Fabrizi was a popular music hall comedian and Magnani was a pro, with nearly twenty years of experience in the movies. Rossellini continued to cast seasoned professionals, the most famous being Ingrid Bergman in *Stromboli*.

Two men were mainly responsible for introducing Italian neorealism to American filmgoers, namely, Joseph Burstyn and Bosley Crowther. Burstyn, in partnership with Arthur Mayer or on his own, distributed the best of the lot, including *Open City*, *Paisan*, *The Bicycle Thief*, *The Miracle*, and *Miracle in Milan*. A Polish Jewish immigrant who arrived in the United States in 1921, Burstyn started out as a press agent for the Yiddish theater in New York before going into foreign film distribution with Mayer in 1936. Known as "the merchant of menace," Mayer managed the Rialto Theatre, an exploitation house near Times Square that ministered to the "masculine escapist urge."[3] The partnership, called Mayer-Burstyn, lasted until 1949, after which Burstyn continued in the business on his own, although both remained close friends.

Being a foreign film distributor is "the most heartbreaking business in the world," Burstyn contended. "There is no demand for foreign pictures like there is for Hollywood films. . . . Distributors like me must go out and create a market for each picture, and that is a challenge that is both heartbreaking and fascinating." Realizing it would take time to cultivate an audience for foreign films, Burstyn used venerable exploitation techniques to attract attention. Take the case of *Open City*. A print of the film had come to Mayer-Burstyn by way of Rodney E. Geiger, an American GI who got to know Rossellini during the filming and purchased the U.S. rights for $20,000.[4] Returning home with a print of the film in his duffel bag, Geiger, who had no experience in distribution, turned it over to the company for handling.

Although the New York Board of Censors passed the film "with but insignificant scissorings," according to *Variety*, Mayer-Burstyn decided to bypass the Production Code Administration (PCA) to avoid having to make further cuts. The same article continued: "Its got plenty to make [Hollywood censors] blanch if and when it is shown them. Principal sympathetic femme character speaks openly of her pregnancy, although she's not wed, and the traitoress who leads to the capture and death of the partisans betrays them for a combination of cocaine and the love of a lesbo German spy. That's just a sample of the angles for the PCA to mull, while the handling of the priest will no doubt make the Legion of Decency gulp hard, although the film has been okayed by the Vatican."[5] Unlike the Vatican, the Legion of Decency found much to fault in the film and gave it a condemned rating. Lacking the Production Code seal and the C rating meant that *Open City* would not be booked by the major theater chains.

The Mayer-Burstyn partnership made the best of circumstances. First, it released *Roma, città aperta*, the original title of the film, as *Open City*. The original referred to Rome's protected status during the war as a historical city. Burstyn's title suggests something quite different—a wide-open city where anything goes. In line with this title change, Mayer-Burstyn promoted the film as "Sexier than Hollywood ever dared to be!" and ran ads with fake publicity stills, one showing "two young ladies deeply engrossed in a rapt embrace" and another of "a man being flogged," both of which were "designed to tap the sadist trade," according to Mayer.[6] As *Variety* explained, two types of audiences existed for foreign films: the "fairly discriminating filmgoers," who were taken with the "raw, unvarnished approach to sex" in the films, and the "transients, the misfits . . . and the loose-jawed brethren," who normally get their thrills vicariously from exploitation films."[7] At first *Open City* played in art houses and independent theaters. Mayer-Burstyn later toned down the torture scenes and removed an offending shot of a toddler on a potty to secure a coveted code seal and entrée to mainstream theaters.

Even more significant, Burstyn single-handedly defended the cause of foreign films by combating motion picture censorship in all its forms. Burstyn defied the PCA by releasing *The Bicycle Thief* to mainstream theaters without a seal following the initial art house run. He is best remembered for waging a landmark censorship battle involving Rossellini's *The Miracle* all the way to the U.S. Supreme Court. Deciding the case on May 26, 1952, the Court read the movies into the First Amendment, which marked the beginning of the end of motion picture censorship as an institution in this country. Motion picture censorship as an institution had existed since 1915, when the Supreme Court decided the *Mutual* case, in which the movies were defined as a "business, pure and simple . . . not to be regarded as part of the press of the country or as organs of public opinion." The case legitimated the system of prior restraint and led to the creation of numerous state and local censorship boards around the country. When the Court agreed to hear the *Miracle* case, the outcome was by no means assured. In fact, the unanimous verdict handed down by the Court was a complete surprise.[8] Burstyn understood the publicity value of fighting a censorship battle. Yet he also knew he was taking a calculated risk, given the expense of litigation and the uncertain impact of the decision on the box office.

Joseph Burstyn died in 1953, aged fifty-three, while en route to Europe on a shopping expedition. In his laudatory obituary Bosley Crowther described Burstyn as "a top importer of foreign-language films and an indomitable champion of the screen's freedom in the famous case of *The Miracle*." Although Burstyn's "fight was largely overlooked by important people in the motion picture business," said Crowther, his death "seems to have drawn the silent tribute of poetic justice from a beneficent fate." The week before two courts had overruled governmental censorship actions by citing the *Miracle* case as a precedent.[9]

Crowther had supported Burstyn's cause from the very beginning. The chief film critic of the *New York Times* was "an early, ardent booster of foreign films." As Arthur Mayer recalled, "When a handful of pioneers—Joseph Burstyn, Ilya Lopert, Irvin Shapiro and I—first began to import foreign-language films, Crowther was the newspaper critic who encouraged us and urged the public to appreciate pictures strikingly different in content and technique from American productions."[10] Crowther clearly preferred movies with strong social themes. His tastes in films were in line with many of the pundits from the 1920s on who had criticized Hollywood for ignoring its alleged responsibility to enlighten as well as to entertain. His favorite prewar Hollywood films were *Citizen Kane*, *Grapes of Wrath* and *Gone With the Wind*. His postwar favorites included *The Lost Weekend*, *Crossfire*, and *Gentleman's Agreement*.

As an advocate for more mature and socially meaningful films, Crowther was an outspoken critic of all forms of film censorship. When *The Miracle*'s exhibition license was revoked, Crowther covered Burtyn's counterattack from court to court, all the while decrying Hollywood's acquiescence to state censorship and religious pressure groups. Crowther answered Cardinal Spellman's diatribe against the film with an article in the *Atlantic Monthly*, which suggested that the vehemence of the Catholic campaign directed against *The Miracle* was part of a larger strategy to extend the Church's control over the content of foreign films in addition to those produced by Hollywood.[11]

When the Supreme Court ruled in favor of Burstyn, Crowther observed, "The greatest, most heartening thing about the *Miracle* case decision to the progressive elements in Hollywood is that it comes at a time when reavowal of democratic principles is most urgently in demand. It is significant to these elements that the *Miracle* case was fought by an independent importer of foreign pictures, Joseph Burstyn, without the support of the organized American film industry, and that its outcome reasserts that freedom of thought and expression which other elements in the industry seem ready to resign in the face of dubious pressure and dark, depressing fears. The Supreme Court has reminded the film-makers that they live in a society of free men."[12]

A savvy, small-time distributor and an emboldened film critic—albeit one with the backing of a powerful national newspaper—generated a level of respect and recognition for foreign films that they had never previously enjoyed. Italian neorealism marked an auspicious beginning for the postwar art film market.

The Masterpieces

After *Open City*, New Yorkers had to wait eighteen months to see their next neorealist hit, Vittorio De Sica's *Shoe Shine*. De Sica, like Rossellini, worked on the fringe of the Italian film industry as an independent producer and had to raise his own financing. This status made the two of them receptive to offers from American entrepreneurs who wanted to exploit the trend. *Shoe Shine* was produced by Paolo W. Tamburella, a thirty-eight-year-old Columbia University graduate who put up financing for the film and may have suggested the idea for the story as well.[13] De Sica, like Rossellini, was also unknown in the United States. In Italy De Sica was an established stage actor, film producer, director, and a top leading man in the movies. His first directorial efforts were only moderately successful. His star began to rise when he teamed up with Zavattini. Together they collaborated on many Italian neorealist masterpieces, beginning with *The Children Are Watching Us* (*I Bambini ci guardano*), made in 1942.[14] The film was released in New York in 1947 by Superfilm Italia under the title *Il Piccolo Martire* (*The Little Martyr*) and played for three weeks at the Cinema Verdi, an Italian ethnic theater, but went unobserved by the press, including the *New York Times*.

Shoe Shine (*Sciuscià*), the second De Sica-Zavattini collaboration, was released in this country by Lopert Pictures and opened at the Avenue Playhouse on August 26, 1947. Lopert Pictures, headed by Ilya Lopert, was another pioneering film importer that introduced many fine Italian and French films after the war. The company would go on to play a major role in the art film market in the 1960s after it was acquired by United Artists to serve as its foreign film subsidiary.

A social problem film unlike anything served up by Hollywood, *Shoe Shine* depicted "the plight of Italy's homeless, hungry children in the days immediately after the downfall of fascism." "De Sica got the inspiration for this film from the hordes of sickly, undernourished and ill-clothed street urchins who followed American troops into Naples, Rome and other cities with their shoe-shine boxes, badgering the GIs with their cries of 'Shoosa Joe,'" said Thomas Pryor. "Some of these pathetic youngsters become pawns of unscrupulous black marketeers and, like Giuseppe and Pasquale [in the film], were tossed into jail to languish and lose whatever vestige of goodness remained in them while inefficient police authorities half-heartedly sought the real criminals." De Sica cast Rinaldo Smordoni as Giuseppe and Franco Interlenghi as Pasquale. They had never before "faced a movie camera, much less acted," said Pryor. Their performances were "so genuine one never for a moment thinks of them as actors, and, indeed, they are not, for theirs are naturalistic performances devoid of any histrionic techniques." "*Shoe Shine* is not an entertainment; rather, it is a brilliantly-executed social document."[15]

Time was equally laudatory: "*Shoe Shine* may strengthen a suspicion that the best movies in the world are being made, just now, in Italy. U.S. audiences have seen only one other important Italian picture, *Open City. Shoe Shine*, in some respects, is even better. . . . *Shoe Shine* was intended as a furious and moving indictment of a postwar society, and of the world, in which such things could happen. It is all that, and more. It makes the oversimplified diagnosis and prescription of most social tracts look like so much complacent blueprint. It is filled, in every scene, with an awareness of the pitiful complexity of the causes of even simple evil. The jailers, bureaucrats, magistrates, lawyers and priests who are cogs in the machinery of destruction are savagely caricatured, but each one of them is presented with compassion and understanding, as well as rage."[16]

The sense of hopelessness in the film led Philip T. Hartung of *Commonweal* to comment, "In spite of the fact that *Shoe Shine* will probably break your heart, I must advise you to see this extraordinary Italian film. It was made on a small budget in Rome, but like so many simple, foreign pictures, it puts most of our expensive Hollywood productions to shame—because it has above all else a quality of sincerity. As its tragic story moves to an inevitable conclusion you are stirred beyond words by the power of its vivid sequences. . . . The acting throughout this movie is so real that in many cases it does not seem like acting at all, but more like the events in a documentary actually taking place before our eyes. . . . This film is not only powerful as a tract on the evils of juvenile prisons, but it is equally powerful for its picture of post-war Europe; and it merits the attention of everyone who wants further argument against the horrors of war and especially the attention of adults who think of boys not as good or bad but as boys who will soon assume the dignity of men."[17]

Crowther was so taken with the film that he used it to take Hollywood to task. In his weekly column he stated that Hollywood films fell short of *Shoe Shine* in significant ways, arguing that movies need not always "divert the thoughts and the feelings of people with the blandest theatrical make-believe," and pointing to *Shoe Shine*, "which is one of the least diverting and yet one of the most engrossing films that we have seen. For here, in this one little drama, is evidenced all that need be said for the movies' particular capacity to searchlight the world in which men live. And if this isn't valid movie business, you can have every share of our Hollywood stock." Moreover, movies need not always aspire to have slick production values. *Shoe Shine* "is not a well-made picture in the Hollywood sense of the word. The photography, continuity and even some of the performances are crude. A suede-coated Hollywood director would probably sniff in contempt at it. . . . But the crudities of its construction, whether come by of necessity or design, are distinctly expressive virtues. Indeed, they mark it as truly 'well-made.' . . . No expense or contriving could achieve such convincing effect."[18]

Having said that, Crowther also took the movie public to task for not adequately supporting films like *Shoe Shine*. After telling a story about a "rather well-fed lady" who disliked the film because it did not "add to her happiness," he compared people like her to the French, who made the film "a huge success," and who, "one might imagine, would most desperately hunger for 'escape.'" "Could it be," wondered Crowther, that "the French have less illusion about a leisurely and comfortable life yearning for preservation? Could it be that they are leery of escape?"[19]

Luigi Zampa's *To Live in Peace* (*Vivere in pace*) was released by Times Film Corporation shortly after *Shoe Shine* and replaced *Open City* at the World Theatre on November 24, 1947. *To Live in Peace* was produced by Carlo Ponti for Lux Films, which was rapidly becoming the largest film studio in Italy. Lux started its expansion program by exploiting Aldo Fabrizi and Anna Magnani in vehicles that played off their original roles in *Open City*. *To Live in Peace* was made for Fabrizi.[20] Times Film was headed by Jean Goldwurm, the owner of the World Theatre. Like Burstyn, he was a staunch defender of movies and later fought two successful censorship battles to finish what Burstyn had started. Zampa had trained at Rome's famed cinema school, Centro Sperimentale, and had made "white telephone" romantic comedies during the war. Thereafter he became a leading exponent of neorealism.

To Live in Peace is set during the German occupation, but unlike *Open City* it takes place in a remote Italian village and is a comedy-drama. As the title suggests, its theme is the brotherhood of man. In Crowther's words, the film tells the story of "the reactions of some Italian villagers to their moral responsibilities when they suddenly find in their midst a wounded American Negro soldier (John Kitzmiller) and an American journalist (Gar Moore), both of whom have escaped from their Nazi captors and are lost behind the lines. And particularly it is the story of one stout and self-respecting villager [Fabrizi] who is sick of political dogmatism and who rallies the other villagers to the moral test."[21]

John McCarten, who so admired Aldo Fabrizi's performance in *Open City*, commented that "Signor Fabrizi dominates the proceedings. . . . He can play anything from low comedy to tragedy without a flicker of uncertainty." He singled out one scene that best illustrates the film's theme: "Among the scenes that struck me as particularly funny is the one portraying the antics of the American Negro and a Nazi soldier, who meet when they are both far gone in wine, and immediately forget about the war and tear an Italian town apart in excess of camaraderie."[22]

Kitzmiller, a former captain in the U.S. Army Corps of Engineers attached to the port city of Leghorn, made his screen debut in this film. He remained in Italy after the war and went on to act in nearly fifty European films. Moore, a stage actor, had served with the American occupation forces in Italy, and had earlier made his screen debut in Rossellini's *Paisan*, which had yet to be released in this country.

Rossellini's *Paisan* (*Paisà*) was produced by the same Rodney Geiger who had returned from Italy with a print of *Open City*. Encouraged by its success, Geiger urged Rossellini to make another film about the resistance and agreed to co-finance the film with Italian backers. Geiger even supplied Rossellini with raw film stock and four American actors for the cast: Gar Moore, Dale Edmonds, Dots M. Johnson, and Harriet White. In readying *Paisan* for release, the Mayer-Burstyn company added an "n" to *Paisà*, the original title, to clarify its meaning. American audiences were unlikely to know that "paisà" meant the same as "paisan," a familiar term of affection similar to "buddy." Becoming more inventive, the company hired Stuart Legg and Raymond Spottiswoode, two prominent British documentary filmmakers, to edit the film down from 115 to 90 minutes and to insert maps and narration to connect the six segments of the film, thereby enabling the audience visually to trace the American army's progress up the boot of Italy from Sicily to the Po River in the north. For the ads the company used a still from a nonexistent scene showing, in Mayer's words, "a young lady disrobing herself with an attentive male visitor reclining by her side on what was obviously not a nuptial couch."[23] Such advertising led Richard Griffith, curator of the MoMA Film Library, to speculate that neorealism's success in the United States might have been due less to their quality than to the

The black American MP Joe (Dots Johnson) and the Italian street urchin Pasquale (Alfonsino Pasca) in Roberto Rossellini's *Paisan* (1948)

"frankly pornographic advertising used to promote them here."[24] Al Hine was less disturbed by the practice: "It may be deplorable that this is so, but it can't be denied that sex bait pulled more people to see *Open City* than if the picture had been presented deadpan as a stark but moving, almost documentary story of Italians under the German yoke. Ditto most of the advertising and publicity for *Paisan*."[25]

Paisan is an Italian resistance film of sorts. As Crowther put it, where *Open City* "was an overpowering drama about the wartime 'underground' movement in Rome—a drama which flashed the first real insight into the feelings and characteristics of the people involved—*Paisan* builds up a comprehension of the whole nature of the war in Italy and of its impact upon American soldiers, Italian civilians and, especially, Partisans."[26] *Variety*, which had first crack at the film when it opened in Italy, commented, "Roberto Rossellini has again turned out a film that must rank near the great foreign pictures of all time." The trade paper was especially impressed with the way Rossellini overcame the problems of location shooting "to give rugged honesty and realism" to the picture.

"Rossellini's cold, gray photography most of all catches what ex-G.I.s who've seen Italy or France or China or Korea, after the enemy occupation, will particularly appreciate—a sense among the people of an urgency for living, a constant subsurface excitement, a whole speedup of existence as they feverishly try to get themselves back to a norm that the destruction of war has decreed can never be."[27]

Paisan opened at the World on March 29, 1948. Crowther regarded it "as one of the strongest antiwar films ever made."[28] Robert Hatch of the *New Republic* agreed: "By itself, *Open City* might have been a superlatively lucky accident; *Open City* and *Paisan* together are conclusive proof that Roberto Rossellini is among the greatest living practitioners of the motion picture." *Paisan* "is a reconstruction, by episodes, of the American Army's progress from Sicily, through Naples, Rome, Florence and the Gothic Line, to the swamplands of the Po River," said Hatch. "It is not an account of war, however, but of people at war; and particularly of the special circumstances that arise when soldiers and civilians find themselves cooperating at war. It presupposes the question 'How did the Americans and the Italians get along together?' and answers it in several ways and at several different levels. The composite answer is that they got along very well—increasingly well as they gained in understanding and trust. That, if you want, is the ulterior message of the film."[29]

Paisan was a significant box office success, taking in more than $1 million.[30] Although the presence of Americans and American GIs conversing in English helped overcome the language barrier, it led *Time* to comment, "Although there seems to be an honest attempt to show Americans complete with their faults, the emulative tone of the picture is painfully sycophantic towards the United States; so much of it is recorded in English that one wonders whether it was made for home [Italian] consumption at all."[31]

The Bicycle Thief (*Ladri di biciclette*), the third De Sica-Zavattini collaboration, premiered on December 12, 1949, at the World and ostensibly dealt with postwar unemployment. De Sica based his film on the Luigi Bartolini novel, which tells the simple story of Antonio Ricci, a humble bill poster, whose bicycle (which is required for his work) is stolen before his eyes on the first day of his new job. The incident sends Ricci and his young son Bruno on an odyssey throughout the city in search of the thief.

Burstyn released the film as *The Bicycle Thief* instead of "Bicycle Thieves," the literal translation of the original Italian title. The original is true to the plot—there is more than one thief in the picture—and suggests that Italy's postwar unemployment had the potential of turning desperate people into lawbreakers. However, the original title lacked punch, so Burstyn probably changed it to arouse curiosity and to make it conform to Hollywood narrative norms, which dictated a single protagonist. To compensate for the film's lack of "any erotic embellishments," Burstyn-Mayer devised an ad campaign that contained "a highly imaginative sketch" of a young man riding off right on a bicycle, his hat flying in the air and a woman's bare legs dangling languorously from the handlebars.[32]

The critics admired almost everything about the film. Crowther was impressed with the message: "De Sica is concerned here with something which is not confined to Rome nor solely originated by post-war disorder and distress. He is pondering the piteous paradoxes of poverty, no matter where, and the wretched compulsions of sheer self-interest in man's desperate struggle to survive. And while [De Sica] has limited his vista to a vivid cross-section of Roman life, he actually is holding a mirror up to millions of civilized men."[33]

John Mason Brown of the *Saturday Review* admired the humor: "This humor is not of that obvious, palliative kind known as comic relief. It is as human, as quiet and real as are those sufferings which are the picture's uncompromising concern." Brown gave two examples — "A church service disturbed by the father's whispered but insistent questioning of an evil old man, a confederate of the real thief," and Bruno's angry refusal to walk on the same side of the street with his father — which demonstrated "De Sica's refusal to overplay the sentimentalities of a story which in other hands could easily have been sentimentalized."[34]

Cue magazine liked the documentary look and compared it to the lyric "city symphonies" of the 1920s: "Viewed simply as a piece of motion picture making, *The Bicycle Thief* is a superbly assembled progression of poetically contrived, magnificently photographed and exceptionally well-acted dramatic sequences. It is a realistic tour through contemporary Roman society — ranging from richly humorous to acidulously satiric — as it follows the confused and frustrated workingman and his worried little boy. Their search takes them past the venerable palaces, arches and memorial staircases that are monuments to the ancient glories of Rome, through broad, landscaped boulevards and narrow, dirty alleys, through crowded black markets and sports arenas, into ornate churches rearing their marbled magnificence amid squalid streets, into bordellos, soup kitchens, police stations, union halls and poverty-stricken tenements."[35]

The total effect rested in no small measure on the nonprofessional actors. Here is how Brown described them: "They have no tricks to unlearn, these actors of his. They have only their lives to remember. . . . De Sica must have looked far, and could not have done better, in selecting his principals. Lamberto Maggiorani is a gaunt, harried man; modest and determined as the

Enzo Staiola and Lamberto Maggiorani in Vittorio De Sica's *The Bicycle Thief* (1949)

father. . . . Enzo Staiola, as his little son, is equally impressive, indeed unforgettable. He is a child uncursed by any of the regrettable qualities of the average child actor. He is older, tragically older, than his years. His childhood is shown as having none of the natural childish diversions."[36]

Thinking that *The Bicycle Thief* had crossover potential, Burtyn submitted it to the PCA for approval in 1950. It wanted two cuts: a brief shot of Bruno about to urinate against a wall and a scene where the father and the boy chase the old man through a bordello. Burstyn appealed the decision to the Motion Picture Association of America (MPAA) executive board—to no avail. The press was quick to take Burstyn's side in the controversy. Crowther led off with a piece for the *New York Times* entitled "The Unkindest Cut," which stated that the decision "illustrates the sort of resistance to liberalization or change that widely and perilously presses the whole industry today." *Life* asserted that the MPAA "made a fool of itself" in the ruling: "This act of censorship effectively prevents all major U.S. movie houses from showing a film that has been generally regarded as one of the finest ever made. . . . [T]he film's appeal is to the mind, not the glands."[37] Burstyn defied the PCA and put his film on the market without a seal. Surprisingly, he obtained major circuit bookings and "came to be regarded in the field as a conquering hero because he dared to flaunt Hollywood's Production Code authority."[38] Burstyn's decision paid off, with *The Bicycle Thief* grosseing $1 million at the box office.

Burstyn did not anticipate a problem with Rossellini's *The Miracle* (*Il Miracolo*). It passed the New York censors twice, first in its original version and then subtitled as part of the trilogy *Ways of Love* accompanied by Jean Renoir's *A Day in the Country* and Marcel Pagnol's *Jofroi*. Burstyn acquired the three shorts when he found no feature film to his liking for the 1950–51 season. Lasting around forty-five minutes each, the films had little commercial value individually, but if released as a trilogy, he reasoned, they might draw as well as *Quartet* and *Trio*, two popular British omnibus films then in release. Burstyn came up with the title after concluding that each film revealed a different aspect of love. To link the stories he decided to introduce each film with a shot of a dictionary showing the various definitions of the word.

Ways of Love opened at the Paris Theatre on December 12, 1950, and received a rave review from Bosley Crowther: "[J]udged by the highest standards, on either its parts or the whole, [*Ways of Love*] emerges as fully the most rewarding foreign-language entertainment of the year."[39] Twelve days into the run, *Ways of Love* was withdrawn on orders of Edward T. McCaffrey, New York City's Commissioner of Licenses, who notified the theater manager that he personally found *The Miracle* "a blasphemous affront to a great many of our fellow citizens" and "threatened to revoke the theater's operating license unless the film was dropped."[40] McCaffrey also notified Burstyn that he would revoke the license of any other theater under his jurisdiction that showed the film. Meanwhile, the Legion of Decency classified the entire trilogy as "Class-C or Condemned," with the explanation that *Ways of Love* "presented a sacrilegious and blasphemous mockery of Christian and religious truth."[41] Burstyn had invested heavily in the picture and these actions threatened to destroy his business.

Crowther anticipated the picture would cause a stir: "For *The Miracle* tells a violent story of an idiot woman [Anna Magnani] in a raw Italian town who, in a transport of religious emotion, is seduced by a stranger whom she thinks is her special saint. Found pregnant and revealed as a transgressor, this poor, mad woman is ridiculed for harboring the crazy notion that she has conceived immaculately. And thus, cast out by her cruel neighbors, she suffers her time in solitude until she is ready to be delivered of a baby when she crawls alone and bears her child in an empty church."[42]

Burstyn secured a temporary injunction from the New York State Supreme Court to lift the ban. On Sunday, January 7, 1951, a letter from Francis Cardinal

Federico Fellini and Anna Magnani in Roberto Rossellini's *The Miracle* (1950)

Spellman was read at all masses in St. Patrick's Cathedral calling on every Roman Catholic in the United States to boycott any theater showing this film. *The Miracle*, it said, is a "despicable affront to every Christian" and "a vicious insult to Italian womanhood" that threatens to "demoralize Americans, so that the minions of Moscow might enslave this land of liberty."[43] That afternoon, Catholic War Veterans began picketing the Paris Theatre, carrying signs proclaiming: "This Picture Is an Insult to Every Decent Woman and Her Mother," "This Picture Is Blasphemous," and "Please Stay Out of This Theater." Although the theater received bomb threats and was harassed by the fire department, the cardinal's edict did not have the desired effect. In fact, the picketing, harassment, and ensuing court battle—which was reported on the front pages of most New York newspapers—generated an enormous amount of "free ballyhoo" and attracted an estimated 100,000 patrons during the following two months.[44]

In February 1951, the New York censorship authorities reconsidered its original decision and revoked the film's license on the grounds that it was "sacrilegious." Burstyn withdrew the film from the Paris Theatre and proceeded to fight the case all the way to the U.S. Supreme Court. On May 26, 1952, the Court handed down a landmark decision that extended to the movies the constitutional protections long enjoyed by newspapers, books, magazines, and other organs of communication.

The Miracle returned to the Paris in June 1952 to good business. There was no picketing. *Newsweek* noted that after the Supreme Court's decision, dozens of theaters were eager to show the film. The article also mentioned supportive quotes from such liberal Hollywood producers as Sam Goldwyn, Stanley Kramer, and Dore Schary, whose voices had been silent throughout the struggle.[45]

The interesting thing about the return engagement was the ad campaign, which again illustrated Burstyn's "cool, calculating commercial mind."[46] Burstyn's original ads merely displayed the title of the film, with little graphic embellishment. Having presumably exhausted the audience for the dignified approach, Burstyn switched to the exploitation mode for the return engagement. The new ads naturally mentioned the Supreme Court decision and the New York Film Critics Circle award. Yet they also contained a triangular-shaped drawing that showed a man and woman lying on the grass kissing; below them, another woman was lying on her back with her arms outstretched; above them, peeping from behind a gnarled tree, was an aged farmer; with his horse-drawn cart in the background. The caption read: "This illustration derived from the film 'Ways of Love' suggested by 'Persephone' by Thomas Hart Benton." "Persephone" was a notorious nude Benton had painted in 1939 that led to his dismissal from a teaching position at the Kansas City Arts Institute. The nude, resembling a 1930s pin-up, had hung for a while at the Diamond Horseshoe, Billy Rose's refurbished Manhattan cabaret. Nowhere in the trilogy were there any traces of licentiousness suggested by the drawing.[47] The court battle had generated an enormous amount of free publicity, to be sure, but Burstyn knew the art film audience, and it was still small.

De Sica's *Miracle in Milan* (*Miracolo a Milano*), the winner of the Grand Prix at Cannes, opened at the World on December 17, 1951. De Sica described it as a "fable suspended half-way between whimsey and reality—a fable that is intended more for grown-ups than for children, but still nothing but a fable," adding "I have taken a holiday from my usual style, but I think that the picture nevertheless expresses the artistic credo and the moral convictions from which I have never deviated—'Love thy neighbor as thyself.'"[48] Based on Zavattini's novel *Totò, il buono*, it told the story of Toto (Francesco Golisano), an orphan who inspires an army of homeless beggars to build a model village in their shantytown outside Milan. When the beggars discover oil on the land, the owners move to evict them. With the help of "a miraculous dove," Toto repels a private police force, fulfills all the beggars' desires, and ultimately "takes his whole colony to the great plaza before the Milan cathedral, and there launches it off to heaven on a flight of broomsticks."[49] *Miracle in Milan* is today considered a precursor to "rosy realism," a production trend that emphasized "the sunnier side of Italian life."[50]

Crowther advised the public not to read too much into the film, "except that man is essentially good but the various corruptions which society has worked upon his nature make life tough. However, De Sica's reflections of people are so witty and warm, his interests are so fundamental and he has directed his pick-up cast so well that he presents us with a catchy entertainment, nonetheless."[51] *Time* agreed: "*Miracle in Milan* is the freshest movie in years. . . . De Sica this time accents the positive ideal of human brotherhood in a warm, exhilarating, richly comic picture. . . . [I]ts deft use of music, its passages of bitter-sweet humor, stylized playfulness and social satire . . . recalls the best of Charlie Chaplin and René Clair. But it is also an original work of art, touched in its finest moments with the elusive magic of poetry."[52] Manny Farber demurred, calling the film a "sententious documentary fable [that] walked away with most of the best foreign-film awards [and] will doubtless delight every filmgoer who seriously believes he loves his fellow men."[53] Although *Miracle in Milan* ran for twelve weeks at the Little Carnegie, interest in Italian neorealism was tapering off. American art house patrons were showing more interest in such films as *Rashomon* and *The Lavender Hill Mob.*

De Sica followed up *Miracle in Milan* with *Umberto D*, the final neorealist masterpiece to come out of postwar Italy. Produced in 1952, it was attacked by Giulio Andreotti, state under-secretary in charge of regulating the Italian film industry, because it imparted a "pessimistic vision" of life. The attack put an end to neorealism as a production trend. *Umberto D* was a box-office failure in Italy, but that did not explain why it had to wait nearly four years before being picked up for distribution in the United States. Crowther offered one possible explanation by pointing to the picture's theme of neglect and isolation of the elderly, which "is supposed to be a subject that just won't 'sell.'" "If such is the case—as tradesmen argue—then it is truly a tragic commentary upon the taste and moral strength of humankind, even those who plausibly reason that they go to the theatre to be 'entertained.' And if such is the public disposition toward the current *Umberto D*, then a lot of people will miss an experience such as seldom is afforded by the screen."[54]

Umberto D opened at the Guild on November 7, 1955. De Sica cast nonactor Carlo Battisti, a professor of philology at the University of Florence, in the title

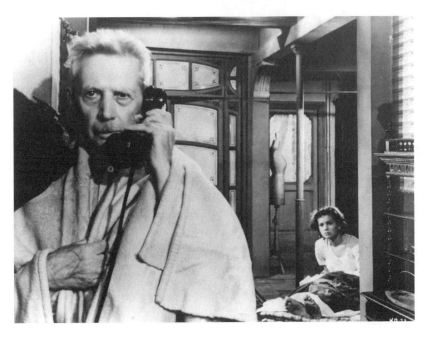

Carlo Battisti in Vittorio De Sica's *Umberto D* (1955)

role. Battisti was "a perfect reflector of the character of his lonely old man," Crowther said. "Never have we seen shame and torment so clearly revealed on a man's face as when this old gentleman endeavors, unsuccessfully, to beg—or such absolute desolation as when he makes his decision to die. Signor De Sica has used him like a wonderfully mellow violin."[55] The New York Film Critics Circle named *Umberto D* Best Foreign Language Film of 1955.

Umberto D was released two years after Burstyn's death by Joseph Burstyn Inc.; it was only fitting for his company to take on the distribution of this fine film. Burstyn had begun to despair of the art film market when *Miracle in Milan* did only so-so business. *Variety* reported that he was ready "to confine himself to importing only such product as offers the possibility of being advertised and exploited for its sex content."[56] With none of the latter to exploit, *Umberto D* did little business yet managed to keep alive the spirit of the art film trend.

Italian neorealism provided a welcome relief from the "harmless entertainment" produced by Hollywood. The films provided no easy solutions to social and economic problems. As *Time* put it, they recognized "the complexity of the causes of even simple evil." The films were made on a shoestring and appeared crude by Hollywood standards, but the "crudities" of their construction achieved a "convincing effect." And the acting was more realistic: "In many cases it does not seem like acting at all, but more like the events in a documentary actually taking place before our eyes."[57] As a group, they captured the highest awards and enjoyed a level of prestige seldom if ever experienced by foreign films in the United States. By performing well at the box office, they transformed the art film market into a viable business enterprise.

However, back at home neorealism was a commercial disaster. Because these films dealt with the miseries of war and postwar unemployment, Italians understandably preferred "Miss Hayworth, or Tyrone Power, dubbed . . . over any bicycle thief," reported Janet Flanner.[58] Hollywood films flooded the market as early as 1944, preventing Italian filmmakers from obtaining screen time in their own land. To support its film industry, the Italian government curbed the number Hollywood imports and instituted a series of protective measures to make Rome the "Hollywood of Europe." Italian producers needed to export in order to survive and used the trappings of neorealism to gain access to the American market. Their goal was not to reach foreign film aficionados in art houses but rather the average Joe in regular theaters, where the real money was.

New Directions for Italian Film

Two neorealist films offered a way out of the "art house ghetto"—Rossellini's *Stromboli* and Giuseppe De Santis's *Bitter Rice (Riso Amaro)*, both released in 1950. The new direction for Italian films was set the day Ingrid Bergman told Rossellini that she greatly admired *Open City* and *Paisan* and would very much like to make a film with him. Rossellini's reputation in the United States had declined after *Paisan. Germany Year Zero*, which completed Rossellini's war trilogy in 1948, was picked up for distribution by Superfilm in 1950 and was largely ignored. Ingrid Bergman was at the peak of her popularity when she wrote to Rossellini. His response was to fly to Hollywood and offer her the lead in his new film *Stromboli*. To help raise the money for the project, Bergman introduced Rossellini to Howard Hughes, the new owner of RKO. Hughes was willing to listen. Of all the U.S. majors, RKO was in the worst financial shape after the war and was seeking ways to bolster its roster. On the strength of Bergman's name, Hughes put up the financing. The deal required Rossellini to shoot two versions: an English version for the American and British markets and an Italian version for Italy and other foreign markets. With financing assured, Rossellini set up production on the island of Stromboli, off the coast of Sicily.

Press reports from Sicily intimating that Rossellini and Bergman—both of whom were married—were having an affair ignited a scandal. When it became known that Bergman was expecting Rossellini's child, "church groups, women's clubs, legislators and local censors in more than a dozen states" became outraged and wanted the picture banned even before its release.[59] Jane Cianfarra, the *New York Times* correspondent in Rome, described the film as follows: "A typical Rossellini neo-realist work. However, while in previous films the Italian director portrayed the despair and life in all its crudeness and ugliness, in this picture he is mainly concerned with a profound religious struggle to which he gives a simple dramatic solution. The problem he develops and explains is the transformation of a woman who, as so many today, lives only a materialist existence into a woman who comes to realize that there are spiritual values in the world. This realization is brought about by motherhood, which is therefore one of the principal elements of the drama."[60]

Cianfarra also reported that RKO planned to release an edited version of the film that contained a voice-over to clarify the ambiguous ending. RKO defended its decision by saying that "certain scenes in the picture" would likely remind viewers "of recent highly publicized rumors concerning the Swedish actress and the Italian director." In particular, the company felt that Karin's lines in the film, "referring to her incipient motherhood and coming after the newspaper reports which have depicted Miss Bergman as being in that condition in real life, might make Karin look somewhat ridiculous in the film, and cause audiences to find the coincidence rather amusing."[61] Rossellini publicly disowned the film before it was released.

To protect its investment, RKO capitalized on the Bergman-Rossellini scandal by ballyhooing the movie "as a kind of lurid peepshow" for a full week prior to the February 1950 opening. The ads proclaimed: "Raging Island, Raging Passions." Fearing the effect of any early negative reviews, RKO canceled all press screenings. Finally, RKO opened *Stromboli* wide—in some thirteen theaters in the Greater New York area and in more than four hundred theaters nationwide—to earn as much money as possible before the critics had their say.

Here is how Crowther opened his review: "It comes as a startling anticlimax to discover that this widely heralded film is incredibly feeble, inarticulate, uninspiring and painfully banal." It went downhill from there: "Let's be quite blunt about it. The story is a commonplace affair, completely undistinguished by inventiveness or eloquence in details."[62] The magazine critics agreed. *Time* said, "For Actress Bergman, *Stromboli* is a triumph of sorts. It gives her the 'different' role she has longed for, with a shabby $30 wardrobe and a full range of seamy emotions, and she gives it the full measure of her considerable talent and beauty. But she is surrounded by such mediocrity that her performance seems pathetically wasted. Would-be moralists who are trying to punish her and Director

Rossellini for their private transgressions by banning *Stromboli* might serve their own ends better by having the picture shown as widely as possible."[63]

RKO had cut nearly forty minutes from the film and had given it a new ending to dispel any ambiguity. *Time* described the latter as follows: "Overcome by black fumes at the rim of the volcano, [Karin] spends the night on a lava bed and awakens (without a smudge on her face) to a morning scene of serene grandeur. Then, with no dramatic preparation but her awed look and a line of dialogue ('What mystery! What beauty!), an offscreen narrator baldly announces that she has found the religious strength to return to her husband."[64] Crowther naively believed that Hughes should have held up the release of the film "at least until the sensation of the romance had died down. Now the detractors of the movies as a medium which plays to cheap, low tastes have something about which to holler. And a lot of customers are going to feel themselves bilked."[65]

Stromboli severely damaged Bergman's and Rossellini's careers. The two went on to make five more films together, and all were rejected by the public. Nonetheless, the original collaboration marked the start of "runaway production" to Italy. The number of American actors who worked in Italy during the 1950s skyrocketed as Hollywood producers set up production in Rome to take advantage of the country's natural beauty, cheap labor, and government incentives.

Bitter Rice caused a sensation of another sort. Produced by Dino De Laurentiis for Lux Films, it was released in Italy in 1949 and earned more money in three months than *Open City* had earned in three years. It broke box-office records in Paris and London as well. Its biggest success, however, was in the United States, and there was no doubt that De Laurentiis had an eye on the American market when he produced the film. *Bitter Rice* starred Silvana Mangano, the former Miss Rome of 1946. The film was ostensibly an exposé of the shocking working conditions in the Po Valley rice fields, where itinerant women laborers, known as *mondine*, had to stand knee-deep in bogs to harvest and plant the rice crop and were forced to live in dormitories under wretched conditions. As one reviewer commented, "These women are not allowed to talk while they work—so they sing instead."[66] All this served as a backdrop for an elemental melodrama involving Mangano, who takes up with a gangster (Vittorio Gassman) and, to quote from *Variety*, "helps him steal the rice crop, but ends up by killing him out of remorse, before committing suicide."[67]

Robert Hatch called the film a "routine sex-and-slaughter yarn that could have been filmed as well on any studio lot."[68] John McCarten claimed that *Bitter Rice* "pushes mayhem to the edge of absurdity."[69] Clearly the main attraction of the film was Silvana Mangano. As Al Hine put it, "For every viewer

Silvana Mangano in Giuseppe De Santis's *Bitter Rice* (1950)

who carried away a shred of indignation over conditions in the rice fields, several thousand carried away only the image of Miss Mangano sloshing in extra-short, extra-tight shorts and a well-filled sweater. Miss Mangano let her sex hit the movie audience without any of the popular barriers or trimmings— kittenishness, fancy dress, careful *maquilage* [*sic*]—long considered essential by Hollywood and most other film capitals. And the panic was on."[70] Bosley Crowther considered Mangano "nothing short of a sensation on the international film scene. Full-bodied and gracefully muscular, with a rich voice and a handsome, pliant face." He went on to describe her as "Anna Magnani minus fifteen years, Ingrid Bergman with a Latin disposition and Rita Hayworth plus twenty-five pounds!"[71]

Bitter Rice was distributed by Lux's U.S. distribution arm and opened at the World on September 18, 1950. After playing in U.S. art houses for almost a year in a subtitled version, Lux rereleased it in a dubbed version and sold it directly to national theater chains, bypassing local independent exhibitors. *Bitter Rice* became "the most popular foreign-made film ever shown in America," claimed *Newsweek*, which named Miss Mangano "Italy's prize export."[72]

After *Bitter Rice*, Americans were introduced to other prize Italian exports, among them Gina Lollobrigida, Rossana Podestà, Sophia Loren, and Eleanora Possi-Drago. Like Silvana Mangano, these starlets were featured on the covers of national magazines and, in the cases of Lollobrigida and Loren, were given Hollywood contracts. As a group they represented a new type of glamour, said *Life*, a "mixture of sex and naturalism, which is the trademark of the postwar Italian film."[73] The Italian exports were typically tailored for the regular U.S. market and were released by Lux and IFE in a dubbed version with risqué titles. The favored venues were drive-ins.

Such a state of affairs led Arthur Knight to lament: "After *Umberto D*, the Italian film had degenerated into a sleazy succession of exploitation pictures featuring well-endowed damsels in situations that permitted them to display as much of their endowment as the producers thought they could get away with. There was still lip service to realism, if realism could be defined simply in terms of natural backgrounds and the seamiest side of life—drugs, perversion, adultery, and prostitution. But the high ideals of the neo-realist movement, using the film to create a greater understanding among people in the building of a better world—these had all but disappeared."[74]

British Film Renaissance

A small but dedicated audience for British films existed in the United States at war's end, cultivated in part by the Alexander Korda prestige pictures of the 1930s. Bosley Crowther insisted that British film aficionados "are not the sort who go to the movies with untrained or juvenile minds." On the contrary, "they have had some considerable advantages in the cultivation of their tastes. They know a good thing when they see it and react favorably to sense and style."[1] This was precisely the audience Hollywood generally ignored. British films experienced a renaissance after the war, and the patron who backed it was J. Arthur Rank. The Rank films that stimulated the emerging art film market included: David Lean's *Brief Encounter* (1946) and *Great Expectations* (1947); Laurence Olivier's *Henry V* (1946) and *Hamlet* (1948); Carol Reed's *Odd Man Out* (1947); Michael Powell and Emeric Pressburger's *I Know Where I'm Going* (1947) and *The Red Shoes* (1948); the Sydney Box production of *Quartet* (1949); and Anthony Asquith's *The Winslow Boy* (1950).

Unlike the Italians, who found inspiration for their films in recent history and economic conditions of their country, British filmmakers turned to Shakespeare, Charles Dickens, and contemporary authors such as Graham Greene, Rumer Godden, Noël Coward, and Terence Rattigan for source material. Their films followed conventional narrative lines and were often crafted by director-writer teams such as David Lean and playwright Noël Coward (*Brief Encounter*), Carol Reed and novelist Graham Greene (*Fallen Idol* and *The Third Man*), and Anthony Asquith and playwright Terence Rattigan (*The Winslow Boy*).

The defining characteristic of the trend was "theatrical class," which Crowther defined as "a literate quality, an honest restraint in visual treatment and excellent acting."[2] The actors in these films were drawn from London's West End theater, and a distinguished lot they were: Laurence Olivier, Trevor Howard, James Mason, Margaret Leighton, Wendy Hiller, Cedric Hardwicke, and Ralph Richardson, to name just a few. "The British produce good actors. That's a recognized fact," said Crowther, "just as the Irish produce good politicians and the French produce good wines. Perhaps it's because British actors usually get more experience on the legitimate stage. Perhaps they have a tradition of the theatre that our people do not have. Perhaps on the whole, in British pictures there is a greater tendency toward restraint. Anyhow, good British acting is hard to beat."[3]

If the Italian imports were distinguished by their location shooting and their documentary visual style, the British imports were products of a studio tradition organized around skilled craftsmen. Many of the films contained distinctive elements that set them apart. For example, Robert Hatch said of *Great Expectations*: "This new film is made with great care and taste — almost lovingly. The English do period movies better than we do. There is a slick, expensive perfection about Hollywood costume plays that asks to be looked at and that reduces the performers, however competent, to a kind of puppetry. In the English movies the locale, the sets, and particularly the costumes, even after the research departments are through with them, seem so real, so commonplace even, that you are not conscious of extras passing before canvas-and-lath sets in getups hired for the day."[4]

J. Arthur Rank had no abiding interest in supplying prestige films for the American art film market; like his Italian counterparts, he wanted access to the mainstream.[5] The dominant figure in the British film industry, Rank owned more than half of the studio facilities in the country and financed a full roster of around twenty-five films a year through affiliated production companies. In the realm of exhibition, Rank owned two of the three big theater circuits. In the realm of distribution, his General Film Distributors regulated the flow of pictures to the two circuits. Rank also had extensive motion picture holdings in the Commonwealth. The British market was not large enough to support indigenous production, and Rank had to export to survive. To get playing time in the United States, he had to convince the majors to make room for his pictures in theaters they owned and to allow his pictures to compete against those the majors produced. Alexander Korda attempted to do just that during the 1930s and failed. Rank had much more clout. On a goodwill tour of the United States during the summer of 1945, Rank told studio bosses that if they wanted access to his theaters in Great Britain, they had better reciprocate here. The majors would not budge. For one thing, the motion picture business was booming during the war and future prospects looked even better. For another, American exhibitors generally disliked British pictures, claiming that audiences had problems with the British accent, the longhair themes, and unfamiliar actors. As *Variety* put it, "Pix from abroad . . . are still a very long way from achieving parity of interest with the home-grown product. Imports made box office inroads only in such areas as New York, Los Angeles, San Francisco, and Boston, which had cosmopolitan populations. The midwest and south continue to be as much citadels of isolationism in their picture tastes as in their politics."[6] Only an unusual and highly exploitable foreign film could break down this resistance.

Rank secured a foothold in the United States in 1937, when he purchased an interest in Universal Pictures and used the company as a distribution outlet for his films. During the war he arranged with United Artists to release a series of prestige pictures that included David Lean's *Blithe Spirit* (1945), Gabriel Pascal's *Caesar and Cleopatra* (1946), and Laurence Olivier's *Henry V* (1946). After the war, he continued to rely on Universal-International, as it was now called, but the company lacked the capacity to handle the entire line. Rank therefore needed an additional outlet for his pictures, which he found by forming a partnership with Robert Young, an American railroad tycoon who was branching out into movies. The partnership resulted in the formation in September 1946 of a production-distribution company called Eagle-Lion Films. Rank and Young reached a reciprocal agreement whereby Eagle-Lion would distribute a portion of Rank's pictures in the United States and Rank would handle Eagle-Lion's pictures in Europe. Rank's attempt to crack the mainstream U.S. theatrical market ultimately failed, leading to the collapse of his motion picture empire in 1949. However, a by-product of this effort benefited the art film market. To understand how this happened, it is necessary to divide Rank's films into two groups based on budget size.

The Art Films

The smaller films like *Brief Encounter* and *I Know Where I'm Going* mainly appealed to a mature audience and were pitched accordingly. Universal released these films through a new distribution subsidiary called Prestige Pictures and placed them in art houses. *Brief Encounter*, the first such release, opened at the Little Carnegie on August 25, 1946. It was based on Noël Coward's one-act play *Still Life* and starred Celia Johnson and Trevor Howard. Set just before the war, *Brief Encounter* told "the barest wisp of a story" about a middle-class housewife and a married doctor who meet by chance in a railway station and fall in love." The love affair "is of the simplest," said Crowther, "just a couple of

Celia Johnson and Trevor Howard in Noël Coward's *Brief Encounter* (1946)

harmless rendezvous in which the two have luncheon together, go to the movies, and take a modest country drive. But it is in the story's simplicity—and in the simplicity with which it is told—that its honest credibility and emotional integrity reside."[7] The romance was made all the more poignant by being related in flashback by the woman (as she listens to Rachmaninoff's Piano Concerto No. 2), so that the audience knows from the start the outcome of the ill-starred affair. The New York Film Critics Circle voted Celia Johnston Best Actress of 1946. *Time* said, "Miss Johnson seems to be exactly what the plot calls for: thirtyish, of middling looks and income, the mother of two children. She has an imperfect hairdo, a few undisguised wrinkles, often gets caught in unflattering camera angles, appears more than once in the same old none-too-chic hat. When they are making a movie about average people, the British apparently do not know how to turn their heroines—and thus their plots—into something more gorgeous than life."[8]

I Know Where I'm Going opened at the Sutton, a 561-seat house on East 57th Street, on August 19, 1947. It starred Wendy Hiller and Roger Livesey. A romantic drama shot largely on location in the Hebrides, it told the story of a headstrong girl who is determined to marry a rich industrialist many years her senior. Prevented by the weather from crossing to the island of Kiloran to see her husband-to-be, she takes refuge with some locals on the island of Mull, where she meets and falls in love with a young naval officer, the penniless laird of Kiloran. Pryor called it "one of the most satisfying screen romances of many a season. *I Know Where I'm Going* is boy-meets-girl, but developed in an adult, literate style—a sort of romantic suspense drama which is as beautifully performed as it is beautifully written and directed."[9] *Time* said, "The love story develops, deftly and gently, not between the customary movie paper dolls, but between two sympathetic, strongly individualized human beings, beautifully embodied by Miss Hiller and Mr. Livesey. It is no mere ripening towards a clinch. Before she is capable of love, the heroine has come of age by learning how much better a woman she is than she had ever realized. . . . The film is an achievement in civilized comedy; even in its grave and noble moments it preserves a graceful, tender gaiety."[10]

I Know Where I'm Going played at the Sutton for almost a year. As Richard Griffith reported, "Its audience was not confined to the Manhattan intelligentsia; it drew patrons from the remotest sections of Queens and the Bronx, and even from towns in New Jersey and Connecticut. And those who saw it not only told their friends but went back a second time themselves."[11] The Sutton had previously played second-run films, but as a result of *I Know Where I'm Going* it became a first-run house as well as a "mecca for discriminating audiences" that enjoyed British films. Universal's handling of Rank's specialized pictures demonstrated that if hard-to-publicize films were placed in intimate-sized houses with moderate overhead, they could slowly attract a discerning audience and run up a decent gross.

The Road Shows

The big-budget pictures obviously presented a different kind of challenge, namely, how to recoup their heavy investments in the face of stiff resistance from mainstream audiences. United Artists's handling of Laurence Olivier's *Henry V* provided the template.[12] Produced in 1944 at a cost of $2 million, *Henry V* was an enormous hit in England, yet its fate in the United States was by no means assured. Olivier produced, cowrote, and directed *Henry V* and was its star. Regarded by many as the greatest actor on the British stage and a movie star of international stature, Olivier was best known to American moviegoers for his roles in William Wyler's *Wuthering Heights* (1939) and Alfred Hitchcock's *Rebecca* (1940). The British Ministry of Education persuaded Olivier to make

Henry V in an effort to lift public morale on the eve of the Allied invasion of Normandy. Olivier condensed the play to make it more accessible without sacrificing the essence of the piece. The film begins on the bare stage of the Globe Theatre and presents the play as an Elizabethan audience might have seen it. Slowly the story expands beyond the confines of the stage until, on the eve of the Battle of Agincourt, the action is totally cinematic. As United Artists may have viewed it, *Henry V* was Shakespeare and had Olivier in the lead. Moreover, it was in Technicolor and contained an epic battle sequence accompanied by a brilliant William Walton score. This was the plus side. On the minus side, it was a British picture about that country's history, with actors speaking verse—elements that were sure to scare off the average moviegoer.

United Artists decided to market the film as a road show. A venerable method of film distribution, a road show release presented a picture as if it were a stage play. In practice this meant booking the film in legitimate theaters and showing it twice a day on a reserved-seat basis, with the tickets sold in advance and at higher admission prices. *Henry V* was preceded by a a six-minute overture by William Walton and ran for two and a quarter hours—roughly the same length as most plays. By mimicking the trappings of the legitimate theater, complete with intermissions and free programs, and dropping the popcorn sales, this approach attempted to instill an aura of sophistication to the presentation and attract a higher class of clientele. Targeting this audience, United Artists hooked up with the Theatre Guild. Dedicated to producing and touring meritorious plays for a subscription audience across the country, the Theatre Guild sent mailings to its subscribers recommending the film and allowed United Artists to use the Theatre Guild name on promotional material in return for a small percentage of the film's rentals.

The *Henry V* road show began on April 3, 1946, at the Esquire Theatre in Boston, the doyen of American movie theaters specializing in British films. James Agee described the event as follows: "At last there had been brought to the screen, with such sweetness, vigor, insight and beauty that it seemed to have been written yesterday, a play by the greatest dramatic poet who ever lived. It had never been done before."[13] The New York premiere took place on June 17, 1946, at the City Center, located on West 55th Street, under the auspices of the Theatre Guild. Olivier and his wife, Vivien Leigh, were in attendance and attracted a capacity crowd. Crowther gave it a rave review, enumerating all the ingredients that made it "a box-office attraction in any town in the United States."[14] After running eleven weeks at City Center, *Henry V* was booked into the John Golden, a legitimate house on West 45th Street, near Broadway, where it played another thirty-five weeks before going into general release in the area.[15] The New York Film Critics Circle named Olivier Best Actor of 1946 and the Academy presented him with an honorary award "for his outstanding achievement as actor, producer and director in bringing *Henry V* to the screen."

United Artists decided to market the film as a road show in twenty more cities across the country. Although metropolitan areas generated the most money, United Artists was able to garner healthy returns from moderate-size cities by hiring a cadre of special field representatives. The latter usually arrived in town a week before an engagement to discuss the film at local high schools, libraries, churches, radio stations, record stores, and Rotary Clubs. They were also charged with generating tie-ins, such as theater parties, book displays, charity events, and sound-track album sales. United Artists' technique succeeded. This slow and deliberate method of release, which lasted from 1946 to the end of 1950, generated a distribution gross of nearly $2 million—a success by any standard. What it succeeded in doing was to turn a film whose appeal might be quite limited into one whose appeal was broad. Stated another way, United Artists sold the American public an art film.

"Hank Cinq" (as it was known in the trade) laid the groundwork for handling Rank's other prestige productions—Olivier's *Hamlet* and Michael Powell and Emeric Pressburger's *The Red Shoes*, which were distributed by Universal and Eagle-Lion, respectively. *Hamlet* was produced at a cost of $2 million by Filippo Del Guidice's Two Cities Films. Playing opposite Olivier were Eileen Herlie as the queen, Basil Sydney as the king, and Jean Simmons as Ophelia. Olivier and Alan Dent, his Shakespeare consultant, eliminated characters, scenes, and soliloquies from the play to create a film with a playing time of two and a half hours. (An uncut version would have lasted four hours.) According to *Newsweek*, Olivier settled on the theme "the tragedy of a man who couldn't make up his mind" and was determined "to make the play clear in every line and every word—even to those who know nothing of Shakespeare." As Dent said, "One has to choose between making the meaning perfectly clear, here and elsewhere, to 20,000,000 cinemagoers and causing 2,000 Shakespearean experts to wince."[16] Unlike *Henry V*, *Hamlet* was shot in black and white because Olivier saw the court at Elsinore "as an engraving rather than a painting." The sets were designed as abstractions to emphasize the timelessness of the theme. Olivier had his hair bleached platinum-blond so the audience would not think "there's Olivier as Hamlet." For Hamlet's asides and soliloquies he used subjective sound.[17]

Hamlet had its American premiere on August 18, 1948, at the Astor Theatre in Boston. It opened in New York on September 29, 1948, at the Park Avenue under the auspices of the Theatre Guild. Crowther raved, "Laurence Olivier

Laurence Olivier's *Hamlet* (1948)

gives absolute proof that these classics are magnificently suited to the screen. . . . Just as Olivier's ingenious and spectacular *Henry V* set out new visual limits for Shakespeare's historical plays, his *Hamlet* envisions new vistas in the great tragedies of the Bard."[18] He went on to predict that Olivier's *Hamlet* "will be one of the great popular pictures of our times."[19] *Hamlet* played for over sixty weeks at the Park Avenue and grossed more than $700,000.[20] *Hamlet* won four Oscars, including Best Picture—the first for a British film—and Best Actor.

For the road show Universal copied many the promotional techniques United Artists had used for *Henry V*. In fact, the company hired an ex-employee and road show expert to develop the *Hamlet* campaign. The target audience, he said, comprised "'discriminating' theatre-goers; school and college students; a large female following and, to some extent, the regular cinema-goer who appreciated it as 'entertainment.'"[21] Placing the picture in general release after the road show, Universal downplayed the high culture elements of the film and promoted it as "the greatest ghost story of them all" in its ads, accompanied by the caption, "Shrouded in mist, clad in rusty armor, a horrifying spectre stalks the great stone battlements of the ancient castle. Its one command is . . . kill . . . kill . . . KILL!"[22] *Hamlet* became a crossover hit, grossing over $3 million at the box office—a record sum for British films.

For *The Red Shoes* it was Eagle-Lion's turn to use the road show technique. Written, produced, and directed by Michael Powell and Emeric Pressburger, *The Red Shoes* premiered at the Bijou, a shuttered legitimate Broadway house, on October 22, 1948. The Theatre Guild sponsored the presentation. Starring Moira Shearer, an eighteen-year-old ballerina from the Sadler's Wells dance company, *The Red Shoes* was a conventional backstage melodrama about a young dancer in a famous ballet troupe who defies the great impresario's dictum that marriage and a career are incompatible and consequently suffers tragic results. Shot in Technicolor on location in London, Paris, and Monte Carlo, *The Red Shoes* contained a score performed by the Royal Philharmonic Orchestra under the direction of Sir Thomas Beecham. The main attraction was a fifteen-minute sequence in the middle of the film entitled "The Ballet of the Red Shoes," based on the Hans Christian Andersen fable about a young girl who becomes possessed by a pair of magical red slippers and dances herself to death. The story of the ballet paralleled the story of the film itself and was performed by Shearer. Brilliantly choreographed and edited and containing not a single spoken line, the sequence garnered most of the critical attention. Pre-release publicity in *Life*, which ran a two-page photo spread of the ballet, noted that it was "the first ballet written expressly for the motion pictures and performed without the limitations of the stage"[23]

Variety was dubious about the film's prospects: "Although good ballet is assured box office in London and possibly other big cities, its popularity in smaller town and country districts is dubious. And in America, too, it will probably only attract a limited audience. . . . It will disappoint the ballet fans, who won't be satisfied with a 15-minute show, and there isn't enough in the story for the general public to hold interest for two and a quarter hours."[24] A surprise hit, *The Red Shoes* played for more than a year at the Bijou and was booked into two hundred theaters across the country. Because Powell and Pressburger insisted that an accomplished ballerina play the principal role, *The Red Shoes* attracted more than just school girls and balletomanes; like *Hamlet*, it reached people who infrequently or rarely—if at all—attended the movies.[25] In Los Angeles alone more than 100,000 saw the film at the Fine Arts Theater. In Philadelphia the film outperformed any other picture in the city during its forty-week run at the Trans-Lux. A quality picture like this helped to account for the increase in the number of sure seaters in the United States from 226 to 270 in just one year, according to *Time*.[26] *The Red Shoes* grossed over $1 million in rentals from the road show and another $863,000 in rentals from the general release as of 1950. By 1954 its total box office gross came to $5 million—a new record for British films.

Despite the impressive results of the road show campaigns, Rank posted a loss of more than $9 million by 1949. Rank had been releasing a full roster of pictures each year through Universal and Eagle-Lion. Most were unsuitable for American audiences and were shunned by exhibitors. Rank's financial straits were exacerbated by British politics. In an effort to shore up the British economy, on August 7, 1947, the Labour government instituted a 75 percent import tax on American films. In retaliation, the American majors boycotted the country for over a year. But the majors suffered little since they already had a substantial backlog of pictures in the country lined up for release. As a compromise, the Labour government dropped the tax in March 1948 and permitted Hollywood to withdraw a portion of its earnings from the country over a period of two years; the remaining amount was frozen. By instituting this form of protectionism, the Labour government hoped that American distributors would invest their frozen funds in British productions. Later that year, Parliament passed a new Quota Act that more than doubled the number of British pictures local exhibitors were required to present. Rank increased production to meet the demand, but Britain did not have enough movie-making talent to support Rank's expansion, which resulted in a dreary parade of box office flops. In March 1949 Rank fired 1,800 production workers, sold off several of his studios, and cut back drastically on production.

The Ealing Comedies

Although much diminished, Rank continued to satisfy loyal Anglophiles by supporting a series of little comedies from Ealing Studios, each of which, said Arthur Knight, had "an unmistakable stamp of intelligence, freshness, and creativity about it."[27] A tiny studio outside London headed by Sir Michael Balcon, Ealing invented a new type of comedy that played off of British reserve and normalcy. As *Time* observed, each film rests on a fantastical yet possible situation: "a small section of postwar London is discovered to be foreign soil" (*Passport to Pimlico*, 1949); "a whisky famine makes criminals of a whole island" (*Tight Little Island*, 1949); "a likable young man kills off six of his relatives" (*Kind Hearts and Coronets*, 1950); and "a mild-mannered clerk pulls off a bank robbery" (*Lavender Hill Mob*, 1951).[28] Shot on location whenever possible to save money, the films made no concession to popular American tastes and were designed to recoup their production costs in the British market. In the United States they were distributed by Universal and Eagle-Lion.

Passport to Pimlico, directed by Henry Cornelius and written by T.E.B. Clarke, featured a cast of veteran British character actors headed by Stanley Holloway. The zany situation in this film played off the privations the British endured as a result of postwar rationing. After the citizens of Pimlico discover that the district belongs not to Britain but to the French duchy of Burgundy, according to *Newsweek* they "tear up their ration cards, repeal the curfew laws, and proceed to live handsomely under an impromptu government headed by a storekeeper (Stanley Holloway), a bank manager (Raymond Huntley), and several other civic-minded Burgundians." The *Newsweek* article went on to state that "director Henry Cornelius doesn't seem to have omitted much that could be satirized to good advantage: the black market and the currency muddle, the closed borders and the subway trains halted for Burgundy's customs inspection, the siege, the airlift, and the Bundles for Burgundy."[29]

Tight Little Island, directed by Alexander Mackendrick, starred Basil Radford and Joan Greenwood. It was adapted by Compton Mackenzie from his novel *Whiskey Galore!*, which was inspired by on an actual incident in 1941. *Time* described it as follows: "To the rugged inhabitants of the mythical Hebridean island of Todday, off the Scottish coast, the middle of the war brought a calamity 'wor-r-rse than Hitler-r's bombs': there was no more whisky. Then a U.S.-bound vessel carrying 50,000 cases of Scotch ran aground off Todday's craggy harbor. All that stood between the parched islanders and a joyously illegal salvage job was the bumbling Englishman (Basil Radford) who, as the island's Home Guard captain, felt constrained to enforce the letter of the law."[30] Bosley Crowther remarked, "Never, we're sure, has Scotch whiskey been more temptingly advertised than it is in this beguiling little picture."[31]

Kind Hearts and Coronets made Alec Guinness an international star and a top box office draw. Directed by Robert Hamer, who cowrote the screenplay with John Dighton, the film also starred Dennis Price, Valerie Hobson, and Joan Greenwood. The satire in this film was of a darker sort. It follows the progress of Louis Mazzini (Dennis Price), a disowned relative of an aristocratic family (the Ascoynes), as he struggles to obtain the title of duke by murdering those in line to inherit it before him. "Imagine yourself young, proud and ninth in line to inherit a dukedom," said *Life*. "What's more natural than to slaughter the intervening eight persons? Such is the opinion of a personable and cold-blooded young man in a new English comedy, *Kind Hearts and Coronets*. Moving with deadly, deadpan wit, he presides over the demise of eight members of the D'Ascoyne family, all of whom are acted, in a remarkable burst of versatility, by a single actor, Alec Guinness."[32]

Crowther marveled at Guinness's versatility: "In this delicious little satire on Edwardian manners and morals, Mr. Guinness, we believe, sets a record by playing eight supporting roles. That's right. . . . He plays first an insufferable dandy, then the latter's dyspeptic old man, then a dull dilettante, a vicar, an admiral, a general, and a suffragette. Finally he gets off a rare bit as the crusty and doomed incumbent duke. In each of these capsule characterizations Mr. Guinness destroys with merciless strokes one of the standard symbolizations of the British upper class. The charming thing is that he does it with humor, integrity and wit. No wasted motions. No splashy takeoffs. Just shrewd, deft, decisive mimicry."[33]

The Lavender Hill Mob was chosen to open the new Fine Arts Theatre, located on 58th Street between Park and Lexington Avenues, on October 15, 1951. Starring Alec Guinness and Stanley Holloway, it was directed by Charles Crichton and written by T.E.B. Clarke. Like *Kind Hearts and Coronets*, it involved criminal activity. Alec Guinness plays Henry Holland, a mild-mannered bank clerk who masterminds the theft of a million pounds (sterling) of gold bullion from the Bank of England and smuggles it out of the country in the form of souvenir replicas of the Eiffel Tower. By now Ealing had become synonymous with "dexterous rib-ticklers," "irrepressible English satires," "jolly trifles," and the like. *Theatre Arts* had this to say about Guinness: "To the role of the little Mr. Holland, the white-collar drudge who nurses a secret dream of glory, Guinness brings that deceptively casual competence gained only by years of training and stage experience and the love for his metier so often lacking in the work of our own, better-publicized stars."[34]

Stanley Holloway and Alec Guinness in Charles Crichton's *The Lavender Hill Mob* (1951)

The last of the Ealing comedies, Alexander Mackendrick's *The Lady Killers*, was released in 1956, five years after *The Lavender Hill Mob*. By then Balcon had sold his studio to the BBC; Eagle-Lion had long gone out of business; and Universal had concluded its distribution agreement with Rank. *The Lady Killers* was released by Continental Distributing and opened on February 20, 1956, at the Sutton, which had become the home for British imports. Guinness etched another memorable comic character, playing the ringleader of a group of gang-sters who use a sweet old lady as an unwitting dupe in a daring caper to steal sixty thousand pounds from an armored car. As *Time* described him, "Guinness oozes all the manic charm of Jack the Ripper. False upper teeth give him the fleeting smile of a criminal mastermind: his askew eyes gleam with demented intelligence; his secondhand clothes and yards-long scarf bespeak the professor of the streets." But as good as he was, *Time* said, "he is topped by the chirrupy stylishness of Katie Johnson as a frail lath of a lady with a heart of oak."[35]

Rank's pictures did more than cultivate an audience for art films; they also assuaged the concerns of prospective art house managers. As will be discussed in the following chapter, the majors cut back on production beginning in 1948 in response to an industry-wide recession. Faced with a product shortage, inde-pendent exhibitors in certain situations had the option of converting to foreign films rather than closing down. For those exhibitors who were reluctant to rely exclusively on subtitled films, British pictures, which did not have to be read to be enjoyed, had special appeal. *Variety* tracked this development as early as 1951, noting that the excellent quality of British and other English-language films had accounted for "such recent additions to the art film field as the Trans-Lux houses at 52nd and 60th streets and the Sutton," among other houses.[36]

Part Two

Import Trends

4

Market Dynamics

Art House Growth

Although Italian neorealism and the British film renaissance laid the foundation of the postwar art film market, it was the growth of art house exhibition in the 1950s that led to the expansion of this market. In 1946 art houses were rarities outside New York; whereas by 1960 the number had risen to around 450.[1] By comparison, there were approximately eleven thousand four-wall theaters and six thousand drive-ins operating in the United States

The art house expansion did not reflect a sudden affection for foreign fare on the part of American exhibitors but rather harsh economic realities. Beginning in 1947, Hollywood entered a decade-long recession. Movie attendance dropped by half, four thousand theaters went out of business, and profits plummeted. Although the increasing popularity of television was the major cause, the move to the suburbs after the war, the baby boom, and a shift in consumer spending to durable goods also affected attendance. Instead of enjoying sustained prosperity after the war, Hollywood retrenched. The majors ceased producing B pictures, shorts, cartoons, and newsreels, and instead concentrated on making fewer and more expensive A pictures. The studio system that had supported the industry since the 1920s went by the boards as companies disposed of their back lots, film libraries, and other assets, and dropped producers, directors, and stars from their payrolls. This state of affairs was a boon to the art film business. Subsequent-run houses (the "nabes"), which showed double bills that changed two or three times a week, found themselves scrambling for product after the cutback. Those that could switched to foreign films to avoid closing.

The Greater New York area had the largest concentration of art houses in the country (150), which generated nearly 60 percent of the total art film business. Numerous art houses existed in the Boston–Washington, D.C.–Philadelphia corridor. Farther west, they were clustered in major metropolitan hubs like Chicago, Los Angeles, and San Francisco–Berkeley. Elsewhere they could be found in college and university towns. In 1953 Arthur Mayer lamented, "Until we have art theaters in the Fargos as well as in New York and Pittsburgh, the movement will never be built on a solid national foundation."[2]

A few regional chains existed: Louis Sher's Art Theatre Guild, which comprised over twenty theaters stretching from Cleveland to Denver; Louis Leithold's six-theater chain in Arizona, which included the Portofino in Scottsdale, billed as "the smallest art theater in the country" with ninety-two seats; and Ted Mann's circuit of four theaters in Minneapolis, which *Newsweek* claimed did very well selling Bergman to the "svenskas."[3] Sher's Art Theater Guild was the biggest success story outside New York. He built his chain by buying up declining neighborhood houses. They were invariably located in the suburbs and had plenty of parking. In taking over a theater, Sher would reduce the size of the auditorium and install such amenities as air conditioning, subdued lighting, and new seats and carpeting. Playing foreign films almost exclusively, the goal of these theaters was to "present pictures for an adult audience that appreciates adult themes presented in an adult manner."[4] In line with this policy, Sher did not admit anyone under seventeen to his theaters, which reduced the noise level and placated the local censors, who wanted to protect the morals of youth. The Art Theater Guild also refrained from using unseemly ballyhoo to promote its films; its advertising was always low-key and in good taste even for erotic films.

Neighborhood houses had the advantage of being relatively intimate in size compared to the cavernous downtown movie palaces. Yet most were old and needed refurbishing, and only a few could offer the upscale amenities found in Sher's theaters or in some of the newer art houses. Still, enterprising theater managers could create the proper art house ambience by converting their lobbies into art galleries, installing racks for film books and magazines in lounges, and refitting concession stands to offer freshly brewed coffee, fine teas, and Swiss chocolates. Art houses naturally charged higher admission prices and typically showed single features to emphasize the importance of the main attraction and to erase any memory of their past as neighborhood houses. The exhibition policy of these houses varied considerably. Some occasionally showed foreign films, while others presented a mix of documentaries, classic Hollywood films, and award-winning imports.[5]

Art houses were sometimes labeled "TV-proof." According to *Variety*, "Appellation arises from the conviction that the specialized houses get a discriminating-type audience that won't be wooed by the tele. These patrons are choosey about what they go to see, even in the specialized theaters, but they'll travel far out of their way to view a film they think they'll like. They are not the casual cinemagoers who easily fall for substitute entertainment just because it is easier and cheaper to use."[6]

To build a loyal clientele, exhibitors set out guest books to solicit opinions and comments from patrons and sent out mailings to regular customers announcing upcoming programs and events. Max Laemmle, who operated the Los Feliz in Los Angeles, stated that "our mailing list is our most important means of publicity. . . . The list is in excess of 10,000. We do our own mailing. We usually get out a mailing for several programs at a time. About four times a year." He reported that customers often waited anxiously for their programs, and that if they didn't get them they might call or write to complain.[7]

According to *Variety*, the untapped audience for art films was large. Labeled the "Lost Audience," it comprised "mature, adult, sophisticated people who read good books and magazines, who attend lectures and concerts, who are politically and socially aware and alert. These people have been literally driven out of the motion picture theater by the industry's insistence on aiming most of its product at the lowest level."[8] *Variety*'s take on the art house audience was pretty much in line with academic studies published in the 1950s. For example, Geoffrey Wagner found that the "lost audience" was overwhelmingly over thirty, with an average age of thirty-five, and not necessarily addicted to television. Kenneth P. Adler's survey of two South Side Chicago theaters—an art house and a movie palace—found that "eggheads"—his term for fans of art films—were better educated and engaged in more prestigious occupations than those who preferred conventional fare: "College students, and persons in professional, technical, and managerial work, made up the bulk of the art-film public, while the conventional Hollywood movies had greater appeal for white-collar, blue-collar, and service workers." Adler also noted that art film fans kept current by reading the out-of-town *New York Times* rather than the *Chicago Tribune* or the *Chicago American* and "sophisticated news-feature magazines such as the *New Yorker*, *Harper's*, [the] *Atlantic*, and the *Reporter*."[9]

Unlike regular moviegoers, art house patrons relied mostly on reviews and word of mouth rather than paid advertising to make their choices. Unlike most Hollywood films, art films did not produce the immediate box office rush at the beginning of a run, nor did they have the same "drop-off" in attendance after the second and third weeks; in other words, art films, had staying power.

As Lillian Gerard, then managing director of the Paris Theatre in New York explained: "The facts prove . . . that the specialized theatre with smaller seating capacity and lower overhead and advertising costs, can attract a steady patronage, week after week. . . . During this time the film of merit acquires, through word of mouth recommendation, a solid reputation that draws a growing audience in the subsequent neighborhood showings. . . . The accolades of the press will pack a small theatre, while the more discerning audience, attracted by critics' acclaim, and better acquainted with the nature of the film, is undoubtedly more appreciative. This audience may be in the minority, but its influence eventually permeates the majority of filmgoers, who come either out of curiosity or because a hit inevitably attracts." As proof of her claims, Gerard noted that the French film *Symphonie Pastorale* had been seen by 100,000 people by the end of its ninth week at the new Paris Theatre and would continue to play there for many weeks to come.[10] It will be recalled that *Open City* played for twenty-one consecutive months at the World.

Manhattan, with seventeen first-run art houses during the 1950s, was the gateway to the art film market. The theaters included the Paris, the Baronet, the Beekman, the Plaza, the Sutton, and two Trans-Lux houses on the Upper East Side; the Normandie, the Little Carnegie, and the Fine Arts on the 57th Street corridor and the 55th Street Playhouse nearby; the World in midtown; the Fifth Avenue Cinema in Greenwich Village; and the Murray Hill on East 34th Street. The Sutton, Normandie, and Fine Arts theaters were former subsequent-run houses that converted to first-run art houses after the war. The Trans-Lux houses were former newsreel theaters. Two important theater chains—the Walter Reade Organization and Rugoff Theaters—owned most of these houses; the former operated the Baronet, the De Mille, and the 34th Street East, while the latter ran the Sutton, Beekman, Gramercy, and Murray Hill.

To ensure a first-run booking in the competitive New York market, foreign film companies sometimes operated their own theaters. Pathé Cinema, the pioneer French company, opened the Paris in 1948 as a showplace for French films. Located on the ground floor of a new sixteen-story office building located on 58th Street just west of Fifth Avenue, the Paris was described as the "first motion-picture house in Manhattan to be built from the ground up since the war." Designed by the architectural firm of Warner-Leeds, the Paris contained a curved auditorium with a seating capacity of 571, a compact lobby with "a clear view of the Pulitzer Memorial Fountain in the plaza," and "a wooden-banistered open-well stairway bordered by plants" that led to a lounge below, which contained glass showcases exhibiting artworks and "a kitchen for the serving of coffee and tea."[11] The Rank Organization leased the Sutton Theatre on East 57th Street after its failed attempt to break into the mainstream exhibition market. The Toho Company, the largest film producer in Japan, opened the Toho Cinema, located on West 45th Street, just off Times Square, in 1963.

The Distributors

The art film market of the 1950s was run almost exclusively by independent distributors operating out of New York. The importing fraternity comprised sixty companies and constituted "an extremely individualistic lot," according to *Variety*. "Perhaps in no other branch of the film business are there so many strange juxtapositions of high art and low commerce. Thus the same guy who may gamble his shirt to acquire and promote an avant garde pic about Uruguayan social conditions may also with another subsidiary, be distributing a nudie pic entitled *Falling Fig Leaves*. Another distrib may be fighting the Legion of Decency tooth and nail one minute, anent a Legion condemnation of an exploration of love, French-style, and the next minute courting Catholic cooperation for the promotion of a film biography of a noted saint. The derby hat operators are still functioning, but only on the fringes of the business. Not seen in New York for some time is the distrib who, to spruce up a couple of innocuous Swedish imports, shot some nudie footage on a New Jersey beach which he spliced, indiscriminately into both an urban drama and a rural slapstick farce."[12]

Foreign film distributors were linked together in a trade association called the Independent Film Importers & Distributors of America (IFIDA). It was formed in March 1953, with Joseph Burstyn at the helm, to fight a move by the Italian government to subsidize the new Italian Film Export Corporation (IFE) by using blocked funds of the American majors. IFE was formed in 1952 ostensibly to promote Italian films but soon branched out into distribution by bypassing independent distributors and dealing directly with theaters, especially drive-ins. In a suit it brought before the Federal Trade Commission IFIDA claimed that the move represented unfair competition. As a result of the action, IFE continued to distribute Italian films minus the subsidy. Among its various activities, IFIDA presented annual awards honoring foreign film achievements, including the Joseph Burstyn Award for best foreign language film; supported the censorship battles waged by its members; and attempted to convince the Academy to revise its rules governing the best foreign film Oscar.

The first distributors on the scene—Joseph Burstyn, Edward Kingsley, Irvin Shapiro, and Ilya Lopert—got their start in the 1930s. Lopert started out dubbing films into Spanish for Paramount Pictures in Paris. Settling in the United States in 1936, he went into foreign film distribution and made a name for himself by handling Anatole Litvak's *Mayerling* and other French films. During the war, he worked for MGM International, distributing the company's foreign films in the United States. In 1946 he formed Lopert Pictures and went into independent production while continuing to import and distribute such films as Roberto Rossellini's *Shoe Shine* (1947), Alexander Korda's *Richard III* (1954), and Federico Fellini's *Cabiria* (1957). As a producer, he scored a hit with David Lean's *Summertime* (1955), a romantic drama set in Venice and starring Katharine Hepburn and Rossano Brazzi. Lopert also managed various art houses in Washington, D.C., and New York. In 1958 his company was acquired by United Artists to serve as its art film subsidiary, under the name Lopert Films. Lopert went on to release such art house hits as Jules Dassin's *Never on Sunday* (1960) and Tony Richardson's *Tom Jones* (1963).

Edward Kingsley began as a publicist for Paramount in 1933. After serving in the infantry during the war, he went to work for Joseph Burstyn and Arthur Mayer. In partnership with Arthur Mayer beginning in 1949, he distributed such art house classics as Luis Buñuel's *Los Olividados* (1950), Jacques Tati's *Jour de fête* (1952), and Max Ophül's *Le Plaisir* (1954). Branching out on his own, he formed Kingsley-International Pictures, which in 1956 became the art film subsidiary of Columbia Pictures. Kingsley-International is best known for introducing Brigitte Bardot's *And God Created Woman* (1957) to American audiences and starting a Bardot craze. On his own, Kingsley went on to release Andrzej Wajda's *Kanal* (1957), Marc Allegret's *Lady Chatterley's Lover* (1959), Grigori Chukhrai's *Ballad of a Soldier* (1960), and Luis Buñuel's *Viridiana* (1962). He died in 1962 at the age of forty-seven.[13]

The newcomers included Harrison Pictures, Janus Films, and Continental Distributing. Harrison Pictures, the smallest company in this group, was founded by Edward Harrison, a former press agent who handled U.S. publicity for Akira Kurosawa's *Rashomon* (1951), the film that focused world attention on Japanese cinema. Harrison at first specialized in Japanese films, releasing Kenji Mizoguchi's *Ugetsu* (1954) and *Street of Shame* (1956), Teinosuke Kinugasa's *Gate of Hell* (1954), later releasing the films of Satyajit Ray beginning with the "Apu Trilogy."

Janus Films was founded by Bryant Haliday and Cy Harvey in 1956. Haliday operated the 55th Street Playhouse in Manhattan, while Harvey ran the Brattle Theater in Cambridge. The company made a name for itself by devising an innovative distribution campaign for the films of Ingmar Bergman, including *The Seventh Seal* (1958), *Wild Strawberries* (1959), and *The Virgin Spring* (1960). The campaign paid off handsomely at the box office and garnered many awards, including two Oscars for Best Foreign Language Film.

Continental Distributing, a subsidiary of the Walter Reade Organization, functioned as an exhibitors' cooperative by putting up financing for new films in return for exclusive first-run exhibition rights and a share of the profits. Continental released over 150 films, including nearly all the important recent British imports as well as René Clément's *Gervaise* (1956), Robert Bresson's *A Man Escaped* (1957), Jacques Tati's *Mon Oncle* (1958), Akira Kurosawa's *High and Low* (1963), Pietro Germi's *Seduced and Abandoned* (1964), István Szabó's *Father* (1966), Pasolini's *The Gospel According to St. Matthew* (1966), and Joseph Strick's *Ulysses* (1967), among other art house classics.

To acquire films, a distributor had only two choices. He could either purchase the U.S. distribution rights to completed pictures by shopping around European production centers and attending international film festivals or put up production financing to secure the distribution rights to new films. Film festivals offered distributors the most efficient way to acquire product. Going to Cannes or Venice, a distributor could view "a preselected group of major international films in a concentrated period of time [to] get some sense of the probable critical and public reaction."[14] Films from France, Italy, and England were the most coveted. However, going the festival route left the acquisition process to chance. It could sometimes lead to bidding wars where for every winner many returned home empty-handed.

Given the precariousness of the art film market, distributors were only willing to spend between $15,000 and $20,000 to acquire a new film. Foreign producers initially acquiesced to these terms, but as the market heated up, the asking price for the U.S. rights escalated. In 1960 Joseph E. Levine paid $300,000 for the U.S. rights to Vittorio De Sica's *Two Women*. In 1961 Astor Pictures astonished the trade by paying $350,000 apiece for Luchino Visconti's *Rocco and His Brothers* and Roger Vadim's *Les Liaisons Dangereuses* and a whopping $625,000 for Fellini's *La Dolce Vita*.[15] Continental opted out of competitive bidding and acquired its films by putting up production financing in return for distribution rights. Hollywood companies also preferred this option when they entered the art film business.

International Film Festivals

"Scarcely a foreign film reaches these shores without having won some kind of award somewhere," said Arthur Knight.[16] The most prestigious showcases for international cinema during the 1950s were the Venice International Film Festival and the Cannes International Film Festival. Both received government support and were highly competitive. Foreign film producers vied to have their films presented at these festivals since winning a prize at either virtually guaranteed international distribution. Venice, the oldest film festival in the world, was established in 1932 with Mussolini's support. After the war, the annual two-week festival was held in early September on the Lido of Venice. In addition to presenting ten films in formal competition, each submitted by the participating film-producing countries, the festival also showed nearly twice that many films out of competition. Venice's top prize—the Golden Lion of Saint Mark—was named after the city's patron saint and was awarded by an international jury of professionals. Other prizes were given to directors, actors, scriptwriters, and cinematographers. Venice served as a showcase for Italian neorealism after the war, but the festival transcended national boundaries by bestowing its top honors to Czechoslovakia's *Siréna* (Karel Stekly, 1947), Japan's *Rashomon* (Akira Kurosawa, 1951), France's *Jeux interdits* (René Clément, 1952), Denmark's *Ordet* (Carl Dreyer, 1955), and India's *Aparajito* (Satyajit Ray, 1957), among others.

Cannes, the most famous film festival in the world, was founded in 1939 as an alternative to the politicized Venice festival. After the war, Cannes started off slowly and did not become an annual event until 1951. Originally held at the Palais du Festival in September in direct competition with Venice, the festival was moved to early May in 1951 and soon became the premier showcase for international cinema. As Todd McCarthy later described it, "Virtually throughout its history, Cannes has been the place, more than any other, where talents are discovered, reputations are made and deals are done, where someone can arrive a nobody and depart a star . . . where the true internationalization of film [takes] place."[17]

Films in competition were submitted by the participating nations themselves. To be eligible for submission, an entry could not have been shown outside its country of origin prior to the festival. According to McCarthy, "This process resulted in choices that were made often for political, propaganda, and inscrutable reasons."[18] Films out of competition were selected by the festival staff and were equal in number to those in competition. Because Cannes positioned itself earlier in the year than Venice, it had the pick of the new releases. The amount of media coverage garnered by the festival was enormous; by 1960 the festival was attracting eight hundred newspapermen and thousands of film representatives from around the world.

The Cannes award for best picture, originally called the Grand Prix, was changed to Palme d'Or (Golden Palm) in 1955. Until then more than one "Grand Prix" could be awarded each year. Like Venice, prizes were also given to directors and actors. Jury picks at Cannes were sometimes odd and whimsical, yet the festival nevertheless made many important discoveries, including the French New Wave.

What set Cannes apart from Venice and other film festivals was the creation in 1959 of the Marché du Film, or International Film Market. An informal film market had always existed in cinemas around the city, but the Marché du Film provided producers and distributors with a permanent location to conduct their business.[19]

The number of film festivals proliferated during the 1950s. "Soon every resort town with an adequate auditorium, hotel facilities and (preferably) a beach where starlets could cavort for the benefit of photographers was vying for the privilege of staging a festival of its own," said Knight.[20] The new ones included Edinburgh, Locarno, and Berlin. Not every festival gave out prizes, but the proliferation of such honors led A. H. Weiler of the *New York Times* to wonder if "the festivals and medals [had] become so numerous, the publicity-mongering and wheeling and dealing [had] become so flamboyant as to leave the moviegoing public confused or, at best, apathetic?"[21]

Preparing the Release Print

In purchasing the rights to a film, a distributor typically acquired a negative and a positive print. The next step was to get the film through U.S. Customs and the New York Board of Censors, which was officially known as the Motion Picture Division of New York State Board of Regents. After passing through customs and receiving an exhibition license from the New York censors, the distributor could then prepare the release prints, trailers, and press kit. Foreign films were released in their original language with English subtitles. The rare crossover hit—a subtitled film that generated big box office during its opening run—would then be released subtitled for the art house circuit and in a dubbed version for commercial theaters and/or drive-ins. Certain films with plenty of sex interest (e.g., the Bardot films) might open in New York day-and-date in two versions, subtitled for a classy first-run art house and dubbed for a Times Square grind house.

Subtitling supposedly retained the flavor of the original film and was a major draw for the "lost audience." Retaining the flavor of an import challenged the ingenuity of the translator. Herman G. Weinberg, who did the subtitles for Rossellini's *Open City* and Vittorio De Sica's *Shoe Shine*, stated that his goal was to treat the original "with a genuine appreciation of its atmosphere, spirit, and intent." A properly subtitled film, he said, should retain "the full subtlety and meaning" of the spoken dialogue. A translator obviously had to find English equivalents for the colloquialisms and humor of the original. To do the job right, a translator also had to deal with a technical handicap. As Weinberg explained, "He must try to retain as much of the original flavor and meaning of the spoken dialogue as possible in far fewer words than are given the actors in their lines. Since dialogue is spoken on the screen faster than it is possible to read a translation of it, the actors' speeches must be highly condensed in the titles, withal retaining the essence of what was said."[22] More often than not, in Crowther's opinion, the translations were just barely adequate and difficult to read. Arthur Knight hoped a "way could be found to move the subtitles off the picture and into a blank area all their own."[23]

For marketing purposes, simply translating the film title into English might not work. The U.S. market was "title conscious," according to Edward Kingsley, and since foreign stars often lacked name recognition, distributors could attract attention only through "a snappy name switch."[24] As a result, distributors sometimes gave their films more racy titles. Rossellini's *Roma, città aperta* was released as *Open City*, but other examples abound. Luis Buñuel's *Los Olividados* was released as *The Young and the Damned*, Max Ophüls's *Le Plaisir* as *House of Pleasure*, and Ingmar Bergman's *Summaren Med Monika* as *Monika, the Story of a Bad Girl*. Even English imports needed help. The title of the British comedy *Laxdale Hall* meant nothing to most Americans and was changed to something with a more familiar ring, *Scotch on the Rocks*. Similarly, the title of the British crime thriller *Brighton Rock* was changed to *Young Scarface*.

To make foreign films acceptable to U.S. audiences, distributors sometimes engaged in the controversial practice of editing. More often than not, editing meant "cutting out" scenes and shots to get past the New York censors. As Eugene Archer put it, "New York's foreign film audiences, long accustomed to visions of a continental starlet seductively beginning to unbutton her blouse, followed abruptly by a fully clad breakfast scene, have had ample cause for reflection on the . . . meaning of the term [cut out]."[25] Less frequently, the practice meant altering the original to make it more marketable. Joseph Burstyn, it will be recalled, added explanatory material to unify the separate stories of *Paisan*.

So-called slow films, such as Visconti's *The Leopard* and *Rocco and His Brothers*, were sometimes shortened, leading foreign filmmakers to complain that their works were being "butchered, violated, and destroyed" by U.S. distributors. But distributors "have their ready reply," said Crowther. "They say that foreigners have the inclination to make their pictures 'too long' and that trimming and sometimes rearrangement are often essential to satisfy the American taste."[26] Such concerns abated somewhat when Hollywood successfully released three- and four-hour spectacles during the 1960s. Longer foreign films like Rossellini's *General della Rovere* and Fellini's *La Dolce Vita* "proved that the public would rather see a film as its director made it," according to Cy Harvey of Janus Films.[27]

The lure of the larger theatrical market was always there, and dubbing remained an option for foreign film distributors. Regular theaters refused to play subtitled films. Although subtitles appealed to the "lost audience," they could repel most moviegoers, "who simply won't go to a film they have to read, rather than watch and listen to," said Crowther.[28] To dub a picture cost anywhere from $10,000 to $20,000, and was a significant added marketing expense. Done right, a dubbed film was "indistinguishable from an original version," said *Variety*, which elaborated on the process involved: "This naturally calls for very special casting so that the English voice blends perfectly with the face and characteristics of the actor of the original version. . . . Also the writing of the American script is extremely difficult and can be compared to translating poetry: The same idea needs to be expressed in character with the role, and words have to be found which have almost identical lip movements. The directing of the actors is even more difficult, as the director of a dub has to guide his actors to express the emotions in exactly the same way as the original cast, and in lip sync."[29] Few dubbed films attained this level of craftsmanship.

To dub or not to dub was exhaustively debated in the pages of the *New York Times*. Bosley Crowther was originally against it. "A dubbed English dialogue soundtrack vastly changes a foreign language film. In the first place, it taints the natural flavor of the locale in which the film is set and of which the original native language is an important communicator." When the actors in *Rififi* spoke French, "the film seemed to bring us in contact with the true Parisian criminal element, which had a peculiar raciness and quality of corruption all its own. But when a synthetic flow of hard-boiled American gangster dialogue came from their French lips, they seemed no more than average Hollywood hoodlums, very badly misplaced geographically."[30] Dubbing also changes the persona of the performers, and "this could not be more clearly illustrated than in the case of Mlle. Bardot, who loses all of her tangy French flavor when endowed with an American chippy's voice."[31]

Crowther later came out in favor of dubbing when it became apparent that subtitles created an impenetrable barrier to the commercial market. In 1960 he argued that "much of the original meaning of a film is lost through inadequate titles, in addition to which a large number of foreign pix are shot silent and dubbed later anyway."[32] Crowther's article struck a nerve and unleashed a deluge of mostly angry letters from readers. The dubbing controversy abated temporarily when Fellini's *La Dolce Vita* hit the market in 1961. Released in a subtitled version by Astor Pictures, the film became a crossover hit and played in theaters that had never before shown a subtitled film. "As a result, subtitles became somewhat more acceptable in the market-at-large," said *Variety*.[33] Yet the controversy refused to go away. During the 1960s international coproductions dominated the market, complicating the very definition of a foreign film with an original language.

The New York City Launch

New York City's position as the gateway to the U.S. art film market was described by Edward Kingsley as follows: "Every picture from abroad is reborn in New York. Each picture starts from scratch when it gets here. The promotion and advertising must be planned for the American market. If it doesn't get off to a good start in New York, it doesn't have a chance anyplace. You might as well burn the film. The foreign film market follows the pattern of the legitimate stage. There are only hits and flops. Only occasionally will the public support a picture which the critics turn down."[34] To be considered a success by the trade, a film had to receive a favorable review from Bosley Crowther and to run a minimum of eight weeks in New York; anything less would kill its chances for wider distribution. The New York run could generate as much as half—and sometimes more—of the total revenue for a film.

New foreign films opened in the city's first-run art houses—in what the industry called exclusive engagements. Distributors fought hard to secure an appropriate theater for their premieres. As *Newsweek* noted, art houses had "almost mystical reputations." The World was associated with Italian neorealism, the Paris with French films, the Sutton with British imports, the Beekman with Ingmar Bergman's films, and so forth.[35]

Distributors sold, that is, rented their films to exhibitors on a percentage basis. Standard practice called for a 90-10 split of the box-office take, with 90 percent going to the distributor and 10 percent to the exhibitor. The distributor needed the lion's share to offset his greater financial risk in bringing the film to market. However, the terms were not as one-sided as they might at first appear. Under this arrangement, the distributor paid all the advertising costs. After the latter were deducted from the box-office take, the exhibitor deducted the "house nut"—the weekly overhead expenses—before dividing the receipts. Clearly, it was a buyer's market; the theater owner came out ahead no matter what.[36]

Whereas Hollywood films went to the market backed by lavish advertising campaigns; this was not the case with imports. As Robert J. Landry stated in *Variety*, "there's nothing wrong with British, Italian, French, and even Swedish product which couldn't be cured by money. Money meaning adequate capital for the promotion of the imports. Mostly foreign pictures go to the U.S. wickets on gumshoes. Americans don't know the stars, don't know the titles, are confused as between 'titling' and 'dubbing.'"[37] Importers could only afford to spend between $8,000 and $10,000 on a New York launch, most of which went toward paid advertising. The daily newspapers reached the entire metropolitan market and their advertising rates were priced accordingly. Since the average art house had a capacity of four hundred and drew "only an infinitesimal number of people exposed to the various media," much of the money distributors spent to open a new film was wasted.[38] Fortunately, art house patrons relied less on advertising and more on reviews and word of mouth to make their choices.

By the 1960s the traditional launch had become "senseless and archaic," according to Dan Talbot, the legendary manager of the New Yorker Theater. "It involves a series of pre-opening screenings for critics, tastemakers and trade people. Overnight, an aggressive publicity machine goes into competition with other aggressive publicity machineries, whose aims are to get a still from the movie in the papers on opening day, or to extract some advance quote from an 'influential,' or even the foolish attempt to 'prime' critics to write favorably. In this auction market atmosphere very few films receive good reviews. The day after reviews appear, they are raked over for good quotes. Then, in proportion to the Machinery's pocketbook and ego, all those noisy advertisements you see every day fight each other for audience attention. Out of this confusion, the ultimate metamorphosis takes place: movie-goers become passive, subject to easy manipulation."[39]

A national distribution system for foreign films did not exist. After a successful New York run, a distributor might place his film in a few art market hubs, such as Boston and San Francisco, to build up publicity. He would then get on the phone or send letters to theater owners around the country to sell his film. Following the initial run, the distributor contracted with sub-distributors to wring whatever additional revenue they could from the market. Films in sub-run were sold to art houses for flat fees. Leading distributors like Janus Films and Continental had branch offices in the larger cities to do their selling. Regardless of such arrangements, the take was small. Cyrus Harvey, president of Janus Films, estimated that most foreign films "whether made in English or released with subtitles are normally limited to bookings of 150 to 200 theaters in the United States, of which 50 to 60 are in New York."[40] A top Hollywood film, by comparison, received 10,000 bookings—and sometimes more.

Oscar Recognition

Did winning an Oscar help? The Academy of Motion Picture Arts and Sciences first recognized foreign films in a separate category in 1947 when it awarded an honorary Academy Award to Vittorio De Sica's *Shoe Shine*. Honorary awards were handed out at the discretion of the Board of Governors until 1956, when the Academy instituted a competitive Oscar for Best Foreign Language Film. Nothing in the rules prevented British films from being considered for the Best Picture Oscar; which occurred when Olivier's *Hamlet* won the top honor in 1949.

Under the new rules, Academy members voted for the foreign film contenders by secret ballot from a slate of five nominees submitted by an Academy selection committee. Bosley Crowther outlined the process as follows: "The rule is that the academy invites each country to submit one film each year, and from these films its screening committee selects five candidates. These may or may not be pictures that already had been released in the United States. Then these five candidates are screened for members of the academy in Hollywood. A member is free to vote for the best foreign-language picture whether he has seen all the candidates or not."[41]

In 1960 IFIDA asked the Academy to change the rules to allow all foreign films released in the United States in the previous calendar year to be eligible for consideration. Speaking for IFIDA, Richard Brandt, president of Trans-Lux Entertainment, said, "Under the current system the best foreign films have little chance even for consideration for awards. The winning picture is neither the best film made abroad during the year, nor the best film seen by American audiences."[42] For example, in 1960 the Italians nominated Gillo Pontecorvo's *Kapò* over *La Dolce Vita*, *L'Avventura*, and *Rocco and His Brothers*. As of December 1961, *Kapò* had yet to be acquired for American distribution. The Academy rejected the proposed rule change on the grounds that it was "motivated by financial self-interest."[43] Winning the Oscar for Best Foreign Language Film did not significantly improve its commercial value. The first film to receive such an award was Federico Fellini's *La Strada* in 1956. At Academy Award time, it had been playing for over thirty weeks at the Trans-Lux and was still going strong. After winning the award, *La Strada* was re-released in a dubbed version for a commercial run. "In theory it should have been a tremendous grosser," said *Variety*, but it wasn't."[44] Other highly acclaimed winners—such as Jacques Tati's *Mon Oncle*, *Sundays and Cybele*, and *Closely Watched Trains*—experienced similar fates after receiving the award.

By the same token, Ingmar Bergman's *The Virgin Spring* fared extremely well following the awards ceremony, grossing $700,000 at the box office. According to Cy Harvey, most of this derived from the dubbed version and "the many extra bookings [the film received] as a result of its Academy Award."[45] Yet it is also likely that the brutally realistic rape scene in the picture may have been just as big a draw in the mainstream market.

As will be seen, Oscar recognition benefited those films that already contained proven commercial ingredients, such as topical political content (Z), star power (*Yesterday, Today and Tomorrow*), notoriety of the auteur (*8½*), and youth appeal (*A Man and a Woman*). An Oscar win did not necessarily impress art house patrons. Distributors of such films therefore had to decide whether it was worth spending the additional money in an attempt to reach the mainstream.

Censorship Hurdles

Foreign film distributors had to function in a highly regulated market that was subjected to government censorship, industry self-regulation, and pressure-group censorship—a triad of controls that Hollywood had embraced since the 1930s to keep the distribution pipeline open. Postwar government censorship boards existed in seven states and nearly eighty cities and towns throughout the country. They exercised prior censorship, that is, they reviewed new films before their release and had the statutory right to deny exhibition licenses to those they found offensive. According to Michael F. Mayer, executive director and general counsel of IFIDA, "local censors have banned in various communities such distinguished foreign films as the magnificent, award-winning *Room at the Top*, the delightful comedy *Never on Sunday*, the remarkable anti-bomb drama *Hiroshima Mon Amour*, and *The Case of Dr. Laurent*, which shows on the screen the actual birth of a baby."[46] The legal status of these boards was established in 1915 by the *Mutual* case, the first censorship case heard by the United States Supreme Court. The Court ruled unanimously that the "exhibition of moving pictures is business, pure and simple . . . not to be regarded as part of the press of the country or as organs of public opinion."[47] As commercial products, the movies could be treated in much the same way as hazardous materials and prevented from reaching consumers through prior censorship.

In New York City films were licensed by the New York Board of Censors. Obviously, it was important to get a clean bill of health in New York, not only because of its market size but also because "a ban in New York based on Catholic protests threatened to set off censors in other key cities such as Chicago or to frighten away theater owners even in cities without government censorship."[48] Dealing with a ban, a distributor could either cut out the offending parts, fight the decision in court, or face being shut out of an entire market. According to Laura Wittern-Keller and Raymond J. Haberski Jr., prior censorship had been stacked against distributors: "In determining why a license should not be revoked, the distributor had to bear the burden of proof and explain to the state why it should nor rescind a duly issued license. A backward burden of proof."[49] Moreover, the distributor was denied a jury trial.

Industry self-regulation was administered by the Production Code Administration (PCA). Created by the Hollywood majors in 1930 as a branch of the Motion Picture Producers and Distributors of America (MPPDA), the industry's trade association, the PCA was designed to keep the distribution channels open by anticipating the objections of state and municipal censorship boards. The PCA required producers to submit all new films to industry-appointed censors at progressive stages of development to ensure that the content of the films conformed to the tenets of the code. To force compliance with the regulatory process, the majors agreed not to release or exhibit any picture without the code seal.

The *Paramount* antitrust decision of 1948, which forced the Big Five companies to divorce their theater chains, was supposed to have weakened the enforcement mechanism of the code, but the former affiliated theater chains and many independent theaters continued to ban films lacking the PCA seal throughout the 1950s. European film producers regularly complained that the code was a de facto barrier to entry in the American market for foreign films because the PCA was more lenient toward Hollywood films than imports. As *Variety* stated, foreign film distributors mostly ignored the code for two reasons: "First, the vast majority of these pictures go into art situations where no question is ever raised whether or not the Code has approved them. Secondly the circuits, if they want a picture, will play it anyway, seal or no seal. Also, a number of the more provocatively 'sexy' imports couldn't get Code approval anyway and so they don't bother with applying for it."[50]

Taking the form of boycotts, picketing, and police action, pressure-group censorship was directed at the local theater owner. As the *Miracle* case demonstrated, the actions were extralegal—in other words, generally beyond legal remedy—and had the goal of affecting the patronage of the theater. The most powerful pressure groups were Catholic fraternal organizations such as the Catholic War Veterans and the Knights of Columbus. They took their cues from the Legion of Decency. Formed in 1933 by the Catholic Church as a watchdog group monitoring screen morals, it reviewed and classified films according to their moral content and suitability for adults and adolescents. The group wielded considerable clout at the box office because the church asked its members to take an annual pledge "to stay away altogether from places of amusement which show [indecent and immoral films] as a matter of policy." A film that received a "C-Condemned" rating meant that it would certainly be boycotted by Catholics and be denied a booking in any major circuit. In some cities local newspapers refused to accept ads for such films.[51]

The *Miracle* case of 1952 marked the beginning of the end of motion picture censorship as an institution in the United States The Supreme Court's decision did not outlaw state and municipal censorship boards per se, according to Richard Randall, but it did "provide a constitutional basis for challenging their rulings and those of the Federal Bureau of Customs in the case of imported films. Specifically, it held that a film could not be denied exhibition merely because it was found to be 'sacrilegious.'" During the following thirteen years, independent distributors such as Edward L. Kingsley, Jean Goldwurm, Dan Frankel, and Walter Reade Jr. continually attacked the standards and procedures of state and local censor boards by challenging their decisions in court. In addition to "sacrilegious," various other statutory censorial criteria—such as "harmful," "immoral," and "indecent"—were struck down as unconstitutional. "By a process of elimination," said Randall, "these decisions made it clear that obscenity would be the only permissible criterion for governmental prior restraint of movies."[52]

Although the number of state and municipal censorship boards steadily declined during the 1950s, the New York Board of Censors, which served as the gatekeeper to the art film market, persisted to the bitter end. The end came in 1965, when the Supreme Court decided the *Freedman v. Maryland* case by doing away with prior censorship altogether. No longer would foreign films have to be submitted to a state agency to secure a license for public exhibition. No longer would distributors have to bear the burden of proof when contesting a decision. A film could now be banned only if it was deemed obscene by a jury following its release.

Although the Production Code was liberalized several times following the *Miracle* decision, it endured until 1968, when it was replaced by a rating and classification system. Although the Legion of Decency continued to review films—it condemned such classics as Antonioni's *L'Avventura* and *La Notte*, Ingmar Bergman's *The Silence*, Truffaut's *Jules and Jim*, and Leopoldo Torre Nilsson's *The Terrace*—its power within the industry declined. In 1965 it renamed itself the National Catholic Office for Motion Pictures and announced its intention "to support worthy films and a widespread educational campaign to develop a new appreciation of the medium among Catholic laymen."[53] The end of motion picture censorship proved a mixed blessing for the art film market. The newly won freedom meant that foreign films had lost their cachet and could no longer be billed as "sexier than Hollywood ever dared to be."

Television Syndication

The foreign film market extended beyond the art house. Some foreign films went on to television. Until the major TV markets were hooked up by coaxial cable to form national networks, local stations had to fill out their programming schedules pretty much on their own. Foreign films, particularly British imports, were attractive programming options for the afternoon and late evening slots—and occasionally even in prime time. Feature films had higher production values than locally produced live shows and were less expensive to present. By the 1950s *Variety* reported that TV had become "the 'third' step in standard playoff of foreign films, following first the theatrical release of the titled film and the theatrical release of the dubbed version."[54] Some parts of the country preferred dubbed foreign films over British imports because dubbing was done using American voices and could be understood more easily than British accents. According to *Variety*, films with big-name stars like Sophia Loren, Curt Jurgens, Fernandel, and Alec Guinness were in greatest demand and could earn as much as $100,000 or more from TV syndication, whereas most of the films that went into the pipeline fetched only token amounts.[55] Films for TV were handled by television syndicators, such as Flamingo Films and Art Theatre of the Air, which acquired TV rights from producers and distributors and put together packages of fifty films or more for lease to local stations. Demand for such product declined after 1955, when the major Hollywood studios revised their attitude toward the new medium and sold off their pre-1948 film libraries for television syndication.

Nontheatrical Distribution

Some foreign films went on to nontheatrical distribution as well. A lucrative market grew up after the war comprising numerous distributors that specialized in the rental of sixteen-millimeter films to film societies, community groups, clubs, and universities—particularly in towns without art houses. Such films were acquired by lease from foreign film distributors. In 1949 the *New York Times* reported that "somewhere in the neighborhood of 200 film societies have been organized by persons whose interest in the film medium goes beyond the purely entertainment functions of the commercial theatre," and that "practically every college town in the country has a going film society composed of groups numbering from as few as twenty to 500 or more."[56] Many of these film societies were likely serviced by the Museum of Modern Art Film Library, which began distributing selected titles from its holdings to museums, schools, and nonprofit organizations beginning in 1937. MoMA's catalog originally comprised silent narrative and avant-garde films. Under the direction of Iris Barry, the library packaged features, excerpts, and shorts with accompanying study material for use in courses in the history, art, and technique of the motion picture. By the 1950s the number of film societies had grown to over fifteen hundred. They were loosely held together by the American Federation of Film Societies, a nonprofit volunteer organization located in Queens, New York.

The largest and most successful of the lot was Cinema 16, based in New York. Founded in 1947 by Amos Vogel, an Austrian émigré who fled the Nazis in 1939. Cinema 16 was modeled after European ciné-clubs and incorporated as a nonprofit membership organization in order to avoid the usual censorship constraints placed on commercial exhibition.[57] Vogel's original aspirations were modest. He wanted to reach stalwarts willing to support an annual program of avant-garde films, which he intended to presented at the old Provincetown Playhouse in Greenwich Village. Cinema 16 became an instant hit and moved to a more spacious venue in 1950, the sixteen-hundred-seat Central Needle Trades Auditorium at the Fashion Institute of Technology.

During the 1950s Cinema 16 presented a new program every month from fall to spring. The programs ran for about two hours and usually consisted of a mix of four or five short films, which Vogel obtained from film festivals, private collectors, foreign film distributors, scientific film libraries, MoMA, and the filmmakers themselves. Regardless of the source, all films were projected on sixteen millimeter arc equipment at a standard which demonstrated that "16-mm projection can be as satisfactory as 35-mm."[58]

Cinema 16's Special Events series included lectures and interviews with filmmakers and critics, symposia on film-related topics, and premieres of award-winning films. The speakers included both independent and mainstream filmmakers, such as Salvador Dali, Maya Deren, Norman McLaren, Hans Richter, Alfred Hitchcock, Stanley Kramer, Fritz Lang, Jean Renoir, King Vidor, and Robert Wise. Film scholars who spoke at Cinema 16 included, Parker Tyler, Richard Griffith, and Roger Manvell.

Cinema 16's audience, according to *Holiday*, was "a little younger than the crowd at your nearest art theater; it has a good sampling of students, those who are simply interested in all the arts and some who are making a serious study of the motion picture. It's a quiet audience, attentive and appreciative. It doesn't applaud every selection, but when it does clap it claps loud. . . . All in all, a healthy cross section bound together by mutual interest in good moviemaking."[59]

To expand Cinema 16's "sphere of influence across the country," Vogel founded the Cinema 16 Film Library, the first distribution company devoted primarily to contemporary documentary and experimental film. Despite Vogel's pioneering efforts, Cinema 16 was unable to contain the spiraling costs of running the society or to retain its members; fees alone were no longer sufficient to keep the society solvent. After peaking at seven thousand in 1957, membership dropped by almost 50 percent the next year. Although members were sometimes annoyed by Cinema 16's esoteric programming, the main cause for the drop in membership was increased competition from art houses. Cinema 16 audiences wanted to see more foreign features, and Vogel responded accordingly, but the city was already awash in foreign films. Cinema 16 also lost its privileged status as the primary showcase for independent and underground films as art houses, museums, and other film societies added such films to their programs. Now in deep financial trouble, Vogel closed Cinema 16 at the conclusion of the 1962–63 season. Soon thereafter he was appointed codirector of the newly organized New York Film Festival.

During the 1950s the principal distributors of foreign features to the non-theatrical market were Brandon Films, Contemporary Films, and Cinema Guild. Headed by Thomas J. Brandon, Brandon Films possessed the largest collection of films for general sixteen-millimeter release in the United States, among them *Grand Illusion, The Rules of the Game, Open City, The Bicycle Thief, La Strada,* and *Breathless.* The nontheatrical market expanded in the 1960s due in large part to the increased interest in film art on college campuses. The core audience for foreign films now consisted primarily of America's "cinephile" generation—university students born during the late 1930s and 1940s. They were described by *Variety* as "partly sophisticated, partly idealistic, somewhat dreamy about professional careers in some aspect of the film industry. Almost to a man or girl, they are more influenced by Paris and Rome than by Hollywood."[60] These were the students who helped support an estimated three thousand campus film societies by 1968.

To meet the growing demand, in 1961 Janus Films, a leading distributor of theatrical foreign movies, formed a subsidiary, Janus Film Library. Its first releases were sixteen-millimeter prints of Bergman's films. Then, in 1964, Janus curtailed regular theatrical distribution and bolstered its sixteen-millimeter operations. As the *New York Times* reported, Janus "found it more profitable to release specialized foreign films to universities and film societies in 16mm. size than to go to the expense of a commercial New York opening. 'There is not enough potential revenue to justify the expense of bringing in small films,' Mr. Harvey said. He added that he considered it impossible for any distributing company to make a profit on small art films in the present market."[61] Janus provided film societies with advertising and promotion material, including posters, which helped student-showmen to develop audiences for their attractions with a minimum of effort. Other companies that branched out into nontheatrical distribution during the 1960s included Donald Rugoff's Cinema V and Dan Talbot's New Yorker Films. Some had hoped that college film societies would provide an alternative channel of distribution for specialized foreign films, given the fact that art houses had "virtually joined the establishment" and came to rely on offbeat Hollywood films and sexploitation pictures to remain in business.[62] Although film societies held on throughout the 1970s, they were never able to pick up the slack.

This portrait of the art film market remained pretty much unchanged until Hollywood entered the business in a big way in the 1960s. The majors, with their deep pockets, absorbed all the top European auteurs with commercial potential by providing them with full financing. Their presence raised expectations: abroad foreign producers demanded more money for the distribution rights to their films, and at home art theaters wanted to book only sure-fire hits. Changing circumstances created a two-tier market with a much diminished independent foreign film distribution sector at the bottom.

5

French Films of the 1950s

At one time the words 'French film' and 'foreign film' were practically inter-changeable," commented Arthur Knight in 1952. "Since the war, how-ever, English and Italian pictures have increasingly been edging in, often se-curing extended playing time in the most desirable theatres. No exhibitor now books a French picture simply because it is French." The French faced the daunting task of reconstructing and modernizing their studios and theaters after the war. The task was made all the more difficult by the backlog of Holly-wood films that had glutted the market. Although the government came to the aid of the industry in 1948 by negotiating the Franco-American Film Agree-ment, which restricted the number of American imports into the country and broadened subsidy benefits, in Knight's opinion the assistance seemed "de-signed to encourage mediocrity and stereotyped production."[1] The U.S. box office returns for French films supported Knight's contention. As late as 1955, the United States ranked ninth among the export markets for French films, be-hind West Germany, French-speaking Belgium and Luxembourg, as well as other countries.[2]

The principal distributors of French films after the war were old-line French companies such as Pathé Cinema and Siritzky International, who were anxious to release a backlog of films produced since the 1930s. To guarantee outlets for their films, Pathé Cinema and Siritzky operated their own theaters. Siritzky, which owned a chain of sixty theaters in France, took over the Ambas-sador Theatre at 49th Street and Broadway, and Pathé, the pioneering French company, opened the new Paris Theatre on 58th Street just west of Fifth Avenue. The principal American distributors of French films were Lopert

Films, Irvin Shapiro's Films International, Kingsley-International, Distributors Corporation of America (DCA), and United Motion Picture Organization (UMPO).

The Tradition of Quality

French films had gotten off to an auspicious start beginning in 1946 with pictures made during the occupation, such as Marcel Pagnol's *The Well-Digger's Daughter*, a vehicle for the great French character actor Raimu, and Marcel Carné's *Children of Paradise*, a romantic allegory set in the demimonde of nineteenth-century Paris, which starred Arletty and Jean-Louis Barrault. However, the newer imports just didn't measure up, leading Crowther to complain, "And this is the more depressing in view of the notable fact that there has been a strong revival of interest in foreign pictures since the war."[3] The few films that came close to the classics of the "French Screen's Golden Age" were Jean Cocteau's *Beauty and the Beast* (1947), Jean Delannoy's *Symphonie Pastorale* (1948), Maurice Cloche's *Monsieur Vincent* (1948), and Claude Autant-Lara's *Devil in the Flesh* (1949).

Beauty and the Beast (*La Belle et la bête*), based on the fairy tale by Madame Le Prince de Beaumont, starred Josette Day and Jean Marais. Crowther particularly admired the whimsical touches in Cocteau's film — "the long corridor of candelabra, held out from the walls by living arms," "the dreamy, fitful music of Georges Auric," and the "glittering and imaginative" costumes and scenery designed by Christian Bérard." The Beast as rendered by Jean Marais "has the grace of a dancer, the voice of a muffled baritone. Although his grossly feline make-up is reminiscent of some of the monsters of Hollywood (and could drive the little kiddies to hysterics), he wears it exceedingly well. And Beauty, by Josette Day, is truly lovely, youthful and delicate, a convincingly innocent maiden and student to the mysteries of life." What did the film mean? "Freudian or metaphysician," said Crowther, "you can take from it what you will. The concepts are so ingenious that they're probably apt to any rationale."[4] Released by Lopert Films in December 1947, *Beauty and the Beast* became an early art house classic.

Symphonie Pastorale, *Monsieur Vincent*, and *Devil in the Flesh* were examples of films made within the Tradition of Quality, a production trend that typified most French films of the 1950s. The trend emerged during the occupation and avoided any reference to social conditions or politics to prevent interference from the Germans. Directors working within this tradition typically relied on literary classics and built their films around big name stars, utilizing the full

Michele Morgan, Pierre Blanchar, and Line Noro in Jean Delannoy's *Symphonie Pastorale* (1948)

resources of the French studio system. "Collectively they made few innovations in film technique and virtually no revolutionary changes in subject matter," according to film historian Roy Armes. The latter also noted that because these directors relied "on the quality of the script for the success or failure of their films," they worked closely with established screenwriters whom they considered their co-equals in the creative process.[5] The most prominent collaborations were between director René Clément and the screenwriting team of Jean Aurenche and Pierre Bost and between Charles Spaak and screenwriter André Cayatte. Among the memorable French stars who won international fame during this period were Martine Carol, Michèle Morgan, Simone Signoret, Danielle Darrieux, Jean Gabin, Gérard Philipe, Yves Montand, and Fernandel, to name just a few.

Symphonie Pastorale (*La Symphonie pastorale*) opened the new Paris Theatre on September 13, 1948. It arrived in the United States, via Irvin Shapiro's Films International, laden with honors from Cannes—the Grand Prix and Best Actress award for Michèle Morgan. The Aurenche-Bost screenplay was based on the André Gide novella about "a pastor steeped in piety" who takes a blind girl into his home and raises her "into a lovely young woman." In the process, "his charitable feelings toward her are slowly transformed into an overpowering love, the nature of which he does not understand until his son becomes his rival for the girl's affections." Crowther commented, "It is gratifying and encouraging to see at last a new French film which has the depth and maturity of some of the great pre-war pictures from France. And, indeed, it is even more encouraging to have a new theatre open here with emphasis on taste and decorum and dedicated to the decent showing of foreign films."[6] As was previously noted, *Symphonie Pastorale* enjoyed a long run at the Paris that lasted eight months.

Cloche's *Monsieur Vincent*, an award-winning biopic of St. Vincent de Paul, starred Pierre Fresnay. Lopert Pictures released it at the 55th Street Playhouse in late 1948, just after the opening of Victor Fleming's *Joan of Arc*, starring Ingrid Bergman. Comparing the two pictures, John McCarten said, "As an antidote to the Technicolor hash called *Joan of Arc* Hollywood recently dished up, I prescribe *Monsieur Vincent*, a French film that records the long struggle of Vincent de Paul to improve the wretched lot of the poor in seventeenth-century France. Concerned with a saint whose claim to Heaven was based emphatically upon good works, the picture takes a realistic view of its protagonist, and his times. In *Monsieur Vincent*, there are none of the trappings usually associated with movies describing sanctified characters. No doves flutter around the head of the hero, nor does he go bathed in mysterious celestial light to the accompaniment of angelic choruses. Instead, he is shown as he probably was, a man toughened by a life of adventure and beset by constant frustration during his campaign to set up organized charity in France."[7] Fresnay was awarded the Volpi Cup at Venice in 1947 for his performance. *Monsieur Vincent* won an honorary Oscar in 1948 and played for six months at the 55th Street Playhouse.

Devil in the Flesh succeeded *Symphonie Pastorale* at the Paris Theatre on May 9, 1949. It was released by Paul Graetz, the film's producer. The Aurenche-Bost screenplay was based on Raymond Radiguet's autobiographical novel, which became something of a literary sensation when it was published in 1922. *Devil in the Flesh (Le Diable au corps)* starred two of France's up-and-coming talents, Gérard Philipe and Micheline Presle, and used flashbacks to tell the story of a doomed love affair between a seventeen-year-old schoolboy and a young married woman whose husband is fighting at the front during World War I. *Time* said, "Director Claude Autant-Lara has produced an extraordinarily flouroscopic [*sic*] effect of life-in-depth. The lovers' moments of clandestine passion (as frank as any that have recently reached the screen), their childish gaiety, their anguish and fears have an almost unbearable intimacy. Sensitively conceived and superbly acted—notably by Micheline Presle and Gérard Philipe— *Devil* makes most cinema explorations of the human heart appear strictly two-dimensional.”[8] Although the film was condemned by the Legion of Decency because it presented “a sympathetic portrayal of illicit actions” and was pervaded by “a sordid and suggestive atmosphere,” it too enjoyed a long run at the Paris.[9] To mark the eighth month of the run, the Paris republished the full *Time* magazine review in the *New York Times*.

Moving into the 1950s, French imports comprised mostly prestige pictures in the Tradition of Quality. They were interspersed with films produced by veteran French directors of the 1930s, plus a few modernist experiments by Jacques Tati and Robert Bresson. Like before, they played in Manhattan and a few key cities. Jacques Flaud, director of the Centre National du Cinéma (CNC), the coordinating body of the French film industry, complained to *Variety* in 1956 that the loosely knit independent distributors in the United States could not even guarantee a minimum of five hundred bookings, which, in his opinion, “should constitute the minimum circulation for French features” in the United States. Distributors responded by saying, “There literally exists no ‘grass-roots’ market for the French product unless it is dubbed.”[10] The CNC opened the French Film Office in New York in 1956 with the goal of expanding the market for its films, but it was underfunded from the start.[11] Despite all this, French films made a comeback of sorts in 1955.

René Clément’s *Forbidden Games* and André Cayatte’s *Justice Is Done* are two examples of prestige pictures with fine reputations that never really got off the ground during the early 1950s. *Forbidden Games* (*Jeux interdits*), the winner of the Golden Lion at Venice in 1950 and a box office success in Europe, was released by Times Films on December 8, 1952, at the Little Carnegie. According to Crowther, Clément’s adaptation of François Boyer’s novel told the story of “a pitiful orphan of the war—a child who has seen her two parents and her little dog killed on the road while they were fleeing from the oncoming Germans.” She finds “sanctuary in a peasant home and in the wonderfully sympathetic companionship of a slightly older peasant boy,” who “comforts her by killing other animals and burying them, with ceremonials, beside the grave of her dog.” The parts of the children were played by Brigitte Fossey and Georges Poujouly.[12]

Crowther placed the film “in a class with the best French films. . . . It is strong and profound, as was *Grand Illusion*; earthy, as were *Harvest* and *The Baker’s Wife*; sensitive, as was *Ballerina*, and droll, as were the films of René Clair. It is full of a tenderness towards children, an awareness of the vagaries of man and a sense of accepted fatalism—all of which are familiar in French films. What’s more, it is written and directed with mature intelligence and skill, and it is acted by a cast of performers who seem absolutely native to their

Georges Poujouly and Brigitte Fossey in René Clément's *Forbidden Games* (1952)

roles."[13] *Forbidden Games* ran for over three months at the Little Carnegie and was named Best Foreign Language Film by the New York Film Critics Circle. However, following the New York run the film found few takers among exhibitors. It did not play Los Angeles until 1954, when it opened in a small theater in Westwood Village called the Uclan.

Cayatte's *Justice Is Done (Justice est faite)*, which won top honors at Venice in 1950 and Berlin in 1951, was not released until 1953, when it was finally picked up for distribution by Joseph Burstyn. A successful criminal lawyer who turned to filmmaking during the occupation, Cayatte teamed up with screenwriter Charles Spaak to make a film based on a case Cayatte handled in 1930 involving a "a woman on trial for the mercy killing of her common-law husband." Unlike a typical courtroom drama, *Justice Is Done* attempted to explore the meaning of justice by examining the lives and character of the seven jurors as well as the accused. (Burstyn added a brief voiceover prologue in English that explained how the French trial system worked and subtitled the film "The Secret Lives and Loves of a French Jury.") The jury was charged with deciding: "Was it a mercy killing—or murder?" *Newsweek* described the script as "a model of economy and eloquent detail" that "richly suggested" the motivations of all the principals. "They remain thoroughly human—to a degree unpredictable—and the picture is, among other things, a fascinating guessing game until the jury's vote is in. But it is more than that. It includes a sensitive debate on euthanasia and it is, as a whole, an exceptionally subtle study of human judgment."[14] Although *Justice Is Done* was named Best Foreign Language Film by the New York Film Critics Circle, it had only a brief run at the Trans-Lux 60th Street, where it opened on May 2, 1953. *Time* may have put its finger on the reason by insisting that the film "is far too talky."[15]

The films produced by veteran French directors fared no better. Jean Renoir, Julien Duvivier, René Clair, and Max Ophüls—all important figures from the golden age of poetic realism—had returned to France after the war, having found work in Hollywood during the occupation. Some of their films that reached the United States during the 1950s include: Renoir's *The Golden Coach* (1954) and *French Cancan* (1956); Duvivier's *Under the Paris Sky* (1952) and *The Little World of Don Camillo* (1953); Clair's *Beauties of the Night* (1954) and *The Grand Maneuver* 1956); and Ophüls's *La Ronde* (1951), *Le Plaisir* (1954), and *The Earrings of Madame de* (1954). As a group, they received lukewarm reviews, and did little to disprove Arthur Knight's 1952 assessment of French films: "In general the vigor, the creativity, even some of the taste that distinguished the French cinema of the late Thirties seems to have burned itself out."[16]

The Little World of Don Camillo and *La Ronde*, two very different films, received the widest distribution. A French/Italian coproduction, *The Little World of Don Camillo* (*Le Petit Monde de Don Camillo*) was shot in Italy and released in French. Distributed by the Italian Film Export Corporation, it opened at the Bijou, a faded Broadway house, on January 13, 1953. Based on Giovanni Guareschi's best seller, it described a "spirited but friendly rivalry" between the militant parish priest Don Camillo (Fernandel) and his longtime adversary Peppone (Gino Cervi), the Communist mayor of a village in the Po Valley. "Much of the charm of the picture is due to Fernandel," commented Crowther, "who plays the priest with explosive gusto and infinite alteration of moods. His Don Camillo is a horse-faced bumpkin, just this side of a high-class clown, and his grotesqueries are outrageous, but his spirit is plainly generous and warm. Even the private conversations the priest holds with his God in the church are played by Fernandel with credibility and are staged with simplicity and restraint."[17] An international hit, the film spawned a sequel and a "Don Camillo" series starring Fernandel and Cervi.

La Ronde's notoriety arose from the censorship controversy it generated. Based on Arthur Schnitzler's play *Reigen*, *La Ronde* was set in Vienna at the turn of the century and presented ten interlocking love affairs held together by a "worldly-wise" master of ceremonies. According to Arthur Knight and Hollis

Alpert, "Ophüls made the work more a bittersweet romantic comedy than a social satire, with emphasis upon the inconstancy of lovers rather than the milieu that encourages profligacy."[18] Its cast included Anton Walbrook, Simone Signoret, Serge Reggiani, Gérard Philipe, Isa Miranda, and Danielle Darrieux.

After playing successfully in Paris and London, it was brought to the United States in late 1951 by Commercial Pictures, a new distribution venture headed by French producers Robert and Raymond Hakim. *La Ronde* passed through U.S. Customs without incident but was denied a license by the New York Board of Censors on the grounds that it was "immoral" and would "tend to corrupt morals." The distributors appealed the decision while proceeding to open the film in Washington, D.C., and Los Angeles, both censor-free cities. As *Time* reported, "In both U.S. cities, the film drew cheers from the critics—and not a murmur of protest from any guardian of public morals."[19] In Los Angeles *La Ronde* ran for five months at the Beverly Canon Theater, setting a house record. As the case wended its way through the courts, *La Ronde* played in one hundred cities in twenty-four states before the United States Supreme Court struck down the ban in January 1954. The Court held that the New York censors had failed to provide "definite standards on what constituted an 'immoral' picture."[20]

La Ronde finally arrived in New York in March 1954. It opened in two theaters simultaneously—the Bijou and the Little Carnegie. Crowther's review pulled no punches: "After all the censorial tumult over the forbidden French film, *La Ronde* . . . is going to shock a lot of people [when they] discover that this saucy little film is about as nifty and naughty as a lady's slipper filled with champagne. As a matter of fact, the idea of it is so sadly disenchanting and grimly moral that it somewhat defeats the pleasant purpose of its elegant wit and old-world charm. For the frank demonstration of the picture . . . is that love affairs, taken in passing, are ephemeral and disappointing, and that romance—the romance of sly meetings and faint deceptions—is a vain, illusory thing."[21] John McCarten agreed: "Sex is revealed as a carrousel, on which all kinds of people take a short spin. While the characters are varied, their proclivities are not, and before all the affairs are over and done with, you'll probably be longing to get out of the bedroom and into a cold shower."[22] *La Ronde* played for four months in New York.

Modernist Experimenters

Jacques Tati's first feature film, *Jour de fête*, was released in 1952 by Arthur Mayer and Edward Kingsley in an English-language version. Tati played François, a village postman, "who is inspired to heroic speed and daring when he sees an American documentary film describing the mechanized swiftness of the postal service in the United States. And so, mounted on his trusted bicycle, he tries to imitate 'les yanks,' to the utter astonishment and confusion of the placid villagers," said Crowther.[23] *Time* described Tati's François as "a sad-faced, gangling, rural postman who looks like a cross between General Charles de Gaulle and old time silent Comic Charles Chase." *Jour de fête* was "no weightier than a postcard, and its contents are no more momentous," said *Time*. "But in the sprightly pantomiming of Actor Tati (who also directed and coauthored the screenplay), the picture occasionally seems to be arriving by special delivery."[24] *Jour de fête* played at the 55th Street Playhouse for over three months. However, as Crowther later observed, the film's "modest distribution was nothing to what it deserved."[25]

Tati confirmed his reputation as a new brand of comedian in *Mr. Hulot's Holiday* (*Les Vacances de Monsieur Hulot*). Advance word from Genêt (a.k.a. Janet Flanner) in the *New Yorker* said, "The film depicts the vacation horrors of the sturdy, celibate, ridiculous, kindly, over polite young M. Hulot at a French seaside resort, with its screaming brats, its mean pension food, its frightening old ladies, and its disastrous sightseeing excursions, as well as its pretty and disappointed vacation girl to whom he never dares mention his love. And, above all, the film features his irascible private companion—his homemade sports roadster on bicycle wheels, one of the funniest, most unreliable old automobiles seen since Mack Sennett days."[26]

A GDB International release, *Mr. Hulot's Holiday* opened on June 16, 1954, at the Fine Arts. Noting that Tati has often been compared to the great clowns of the silent cinema, Arthur Knight said, "Actually the aptest comparison would be to a particularly well-intentioned bull in the proverbial china shop. M. Tati is utterly unable to turn around without upsetting something or somebody. His slightest gesture creates chaos. When he tries to be helpful, the results are catastrophic. Even walking, on tip-toes, as he generally does, he leave a trail of destruction in his wake. He is the kind of man who is forever at odds with the world—machinery misbehaves, objects are always in the wrong place at the wrong time when he is around, the most docile animals invariably act up wherever he appears. As a result, humans tend to run from him. Not that they dislike him or suspect his motives. It's simply that bitter experience has taught them that propinquity breeds disaster."[27]

Time was impressed with the style of the film: "*Mr. Hulot's Holiday* appears to be a contemporary French attempt to make a silent film in sound . . . . Dialogue is so infrequent that it hardly matters that much of it is in French. The sound track carries little but the punctuation marks—burps, dings, splats, oogahs—for the strictly visual language in which the silly story is told . . . The beauty of

Jacques Tati and Nathalie Pascaud in Tati's *Mr. Hulot's Holiday* (1954)

Mr. Hulot's Holiday is its elegant sparsity."[28] The film went on to become an art house classic and continued to draw large audiences, many of whom could follow it by heart.

My Uncle (*Mon oncle*) confirmed Tati's status as an auteur. In addition to directing, starring in, and coauthoring his films, Tati functioned as his own producer to make his first color film, a satire that juxtaposed Hulot's eccentric, independent way of life with the "super-modern, hygienic, materialistic" world of his brother-in-law.[29] *My Uncle* attracted international attention at Cannes, where it won the Special Jury Prize in 1958. The film was presented by Continental Distributing on November 3, 1958, in two versions, subtitled at the Baronet and dubbed and slightly shortened at the Guild. *Newsweek* hailed Tati as "the first man since Chaplin to create a unique and individual comedy tradition. Tati's success with comic motion stems from two special characteristics. First, his humor has great variety—outright slapstick (his clever direction of fat men bumping into lampposts makes that old stand-by funnier than ever), personal eccentricity (Hulot's jaunty stride is as memorable as Chaplin's duck-footed shuffle), and natural pantomime (the transformations he imposes on a symmetrical fruit tree when one of its branches breaks off are indescribable).

Second, as a film maker Tati seldom uses a mobile camera or a close-up lens. He sets his camera in one position, then fills its range, both foreground and background, with furious activity. It is a difficult technique, both photographically and directorially, but the happy result is like watching a three-ring circus—there is always something for everybody."[30] *My Uncle* went on to win best foreign film awards from the New York Film Critics Circle and the Academy of Motion Picture Arts and Sciences.

Robert Bresson's first films to reach the United States—*Diary of a Country Priest (Journal d'un curé de campagne)* and *A Man Escaped (Un Condemné à mort s'est échappé)*—were characterized by *Variety* as the types of films "art house managers cry for and yet often are afraid to show."[31] Produced in 1951, *Variety* said *Diary* collected "almost as many medals as a field marshal," but it wasn't until 1954 before it was finally acquired for distribution in this country by Brandon Films. Despite the awards, the picture was considered a commercial risk. Bresson was unknown in the United States and his film contained little to exploit. *Variety* described it as "a conscientious rendering of a literary study [by Georges Bernanos] of the spiritual anguish of a shy, young priest. . . . Made with taste and reverence, pic is slow-moving but impressive. Film shows the priest's entries in the journal, underlines it with his soliloquies, and then shows it through images. The priest (Claude Laydu) suffers the hostility and misunderstanding of the townspeople. Suffering from a severe stomach ailment, he subsists on bread and wine. The hostile villagers soon take him for a drunkard. All his attempts to win the confidence of his flock lead to failure, except in the eyes of the curate, who understands his internal suffering."[32]

Diary opened at the newly refurbished Fifth Avenue Cinema, near Greenwich Village, on April 5, 1954. Formerly known as the Fifth Avenue Playhouse—one of the first art houses in America—this 275-seat showcase had been taken over by Pathé Cinema, which also operated the Paris, for the purpose of presenting "in an atmosphere of some elegance, the sort of pictures that are too limited in appeal to last very long in the larger movie houses."[33] The new management agreed to play the film if fifteen minutes were cut "to eliminate scenes which were felt to be superfluous and tended to retard the pace." Brandon agreed with the condition.[34]

Even with the cuts, Crowther found the film hard to understand. He admitted that *Diary* "has ponderous dignity" and was made "with taste and reverence," but he didn't understand what motivated the characters: "What is the deep and dark misgiving that seems to be eating on [the priest] as he takes up his clerical duties in a curiously churlish little town? Why do the children torment him—especially one little girl, whose peculiarly sadistic taunting is never made reasonably clear? And what is this complicated business of a slyly adulterous Count, his neurotic wife and their strange daughter, who seems to have some complex towards the priest? Don't ask us."[35]

Arthur Knight picked up on this and said, "Our cinema habits have long been used to a sort of comic-strip clarity, and it is quite possible that *Diary of a Country Priest* calls for the exercise of faculties more often required by the serious novel. . . . It seems to me that we have here an example of moviemaking on the highest possible level; a notable technique wedded to an austere and searching subject."[36]

A Man Escaped was released by Continental Distributing and opened at the Baronet on August 26, 1957, with little or no notice. *Variety* described it as "an offbeat film that should insure arty house interest. Its break with film convention in detailing the escape of a French resistance fighter from a Gestapo prison is done with relentless use of the mechanics of the getaway without any recourse to familiar suspense tactics. This actually stresses a man's innate need for liberty without any shouting."[37] Crowther warned his readers that "this is not the sort of picture that one should view without knowing what it is. The strain is hard and the reward is limited. But it is a fine reflection of a cruel experience."[38] Bresson would not get the attention he deserved until the New York Film Festival premiered his new works beginning in 1963.

The Comeback

The tide turned for French films beginning in 1955. Prestige films such as René Clément's *Gervaise* (1957), Claude Autant-Lara's *Le Rouge et le Noir* (1958), and Marc Allégret's *Lady Chatterley's Lover* (1959), which were based on novels by Emile Zola, Stendhal, and D.H. Lawrence, respectively, were duly evaluated for their seriousness of purpose, craftsmanship, and faithfulness to their literary sources. *Lady Chatterley's Lover* achieved some added notoriety because of the censorship controversy it engendered. But the biggest successes were of a different sort. The comeback was fueled by a series of thrillers that included Henri-Georges Clouzot's *The Wages of Fear* (1955) and *Diabolique* (1955), Jules Dassin's *Rififi* (1956), and Jean-Paul Le Chanois's *The Case of Dr. Laurent* (1958), and by the arrival of Brigitte Bardot in 1957. All of these films started out as art house hits, but didn't earned real money until they were released to mainstream theaters in dubbed versions.

The thrillers relied upon gimmicks to attract attention and were handled by exhibitor-owned distribution companies. These companies came into existence in the 1950s as exhibitors searched for ways to secure a steady supply of films while Hollywood cut back on production. They seemed to be on the hunt for pictures with sure-fire box-office potential. *Wages* was released by Distributors Corporation of America (DCA), a cooperative representing thirty exhibitors who operated an estimated seven hundred theaters. Founded in 1954 by Fred Schwartz, president of the Century theater circuit in New York, DCA distributed sixty pictures during the 1950s. *Diabolique* and *Rififi* were released by the United Motion Picture Organization, which was founded by Richard Davis, the owner of the Fine Arts Theater in New York and the Ziegfeld in Chicago. The company distributed twenty-four mostly French pictures during the 1950s. *The Case of Dr. Laurent* was released by Trans-Lux Distributing, an arm of the Trans-Lux theater chain owned by Richard Brandt.

The thrills in *The Wages of Fear* (*Le Salaire de la peur*) emanated from the "harrowing odyssey of four derelicts inching two trucks loaded with nitro-glycerine over a tortuous terrain" to a burning oil field in Central America.[39] The derelicts were played by Yves Montand, Charles Vanel, Folco Lulli, and Peter van Eyck. "Whatever else may be said of it," said *Time*, *The Wages of Fear* is "one of the great shockers of all time. The suspense it generates is close to prostrating. Clouzot is not interested in tingling the customer's spine, but rather in giving him the symptoms of a paralytic stroke."[40] *Wages* was produced in 1953 and went on to win the grand prize at Cannes and the Golden Bear at the Berlin Film Festival before it found a distributor for the United States The delay had to do mainly with the so-called vicious and irresponsible anti-American propaganda in the film, which "cast as villains—that is, the only people with any money—the representatives of an American oil company." To get it passed by the New York censors, DCA eliminated the offensive material and cut over forty minutes from the film. "Nevertheless, the picture's essential power was such that, cuts notwithstanding, *The Wages of Fear* became one of the most successful foreign films of the Fifties in this country."[41]

The claim to fame of *Diabolique* (*Les Diaboliques*) was its trick ending. When the film opened at the Fine Arts, newspaper ads stated, "Don't Reveal the Ending!" At the door ticket holders were asked to sign a "contract" swearing them to secrecy and were not allowed to enter the theater after the start of the film in order to "gain the full flavor of the horror." *Life* reported that "most audiences endure the mounting suspense with dumb fascination, giving way only to giggles and hysterics. A few weeks ago a New York lady fainted in the audience, was revived in the lounge, insisted on going right back to witness the devilish climax."[42] *Diabolique* started out in small art houses, then branched out into the "nabes" and the drive-ins, eventually earning an estimated $1 million at the box office, outperforming *Wages*.

Véra Clouzot, Simone Signoret, and Paul Meurisse in Henri-Georges Clouzot's *Diabolique* (1955)

The main attraction of *Rififi* (*Du rififi chez les hommes*), of course, was the thirty-minute safecracking centerpiece of the film, which *Time* described as "one of the most engrossing sequences since the invention of talking pictures. . . . Not a word is spoken once the robbery is under way. Moving into an apartment above the store, they bind and gag the concierge and his wife, roll back the living-room rug and begin cutting through the concrete floor. When the hole is the width of a man's wrist, an umbrella is lowered through it and opened to catch the fragments of plaster as the gap is widened. Once in the store, the alarm is swiftly disconnected, the safe opened with an electric drill, and the loot removed. The entire operation simulates major surgery. there is the same mute reaching for instruments, the same intensity of purpose, the same growing strain as the operation approaches completion."[43] *Rififi* ran for over twenty weeks at the Fine Arts before going wide in a dubbed version.

No one was admitted during the final fifteen minutes of *The Case of Dr. Laurent* (*Le Cas du Docteur Laurent*). The ending represented "the first completely undisguised commercial filming of a woman giving birth to a child."[44] The film premiered at the Trans-Lux 52nd Street on June 25, 1958, setting a new opening-day record at the theater. Jean Gabin starred as the Paris doctor who converts a cloistered village to his method of natural childbirth. Surprisingly, *Dr. Laurent* received a seal from the Production Code Administration (PCA), an endorsement from the American Medical Association, and an exemption from the Legion of Decency. The latter placed *The Case of Dr. Laurent* in a "'separate classification' given to 'certain films which, while not morally offensive, require some analysis and explanation. The announcement by the Roman Catholic reviewing body states that while the film's medical theme of 'natural childbirth' is 'handled with discretion and good taste' and is of educational value for adults and older adolescents, 'the subject matter itself is too sacred, private and personal' for indiscriminate showing."[45]

The ad campaign featured a picture of the young mother and a caption that asked: "Why does this beautiful French girl want to have her baby born in public?" For the national release, Trans-Lux prepared a dubbed version and booked it into 160 showcases around the country. The company also offered a promotional "servicing plan" for each booking and offered a series of sales "seminars" in key cities to promote the film.[46]

The Bardot Craze

A seismic shift in the market for French films occurred on October 21, 1957. On that day Roger Vadim's *And God Created Woman* (*Et Dieu créa la femme*), starring Brigitte Bardot, opened at the Paris Theatre. The film carried the promotional tagline "but the devil gave shape to Bardot!" The house manager expected it to play a fast two weeks; instead, the film ran for almost a year. Produced in CinemaScope and in color by Raoul Lévy for $400,000 and directed by Roger Vadim, Bardot's new husband, *And God Created Woman* gained entry where "foreign films have never seen the light of the screen," said *Variety*.[47] It did this without a seal of approval from the PCA and a "Condemned" rating from the Legion of Decency. Commenting on the impact of the rating, a Columbia Pictures spokesperson said that *And God Created Woman* would have received twice as many bookings with a less restrictive "B" rating from the legion but would have done only half the business. As Juliette Hardy, a sexually liberated eighteen-year-old orphan who is the talk of Saint-Tropez, Bardot scandalized the censors. Nevertheless the film grossed over $4 million *in rentals* in the United States to set a new record for foreign films.[48]

And God Created Woman was distributed by Kingsley-International, a subsidiary of Columbia Pictures. As a member of the Motion Picture Association of America (MPAA), the industry trade association, Columbia was forbidden

Brigitte Bardot in Roger Vadim's *And God Created Woman* (1957)

to distribute any picture that was denied a seal from the PCA or received a C rating by the Legion of Decency. Independent distributors had earlier rejected the picture, presumably because it was too controversial to handle. Undeterred, Columbia took advantage of a loophole in the MPAA's rules by hiring Kingsley-International, a prominent independent foreign film distributor, to handle the picture.

Kingsley's ad campaign used a pen-and-ink drawing of Brigitte Bardot in the nude, seen from behind. Above it a blurb described the film as "a frolic in sensuality." Below it a review quote read, "A study in rounded surfaces to delight anyone who likes to study rounded surfaces."[49] So what was special about the film? According to Kingsley, the campaign "'gave people what they were led to expect. They weren't promised one thing in the ads and given something else on the screen."[50] Bosley Crowther agreed: "This round and voluptuous little French miss is put on spectacular display and is rather brazenly ogled from every allowable point of view. She is looked at in slacks and sweaters, in shorts and Bikini bathing suits. She wears a bed sheet on two or three occasions, and, once, she shows behind a thin screen in the nude. What's more, she moves herself in a fashion that fully accentuates her charms. She is undeniably a creation of superlative craftsmanship."[51]

Bardot's sex appeal certainly attracted crowds, especially college students. For example, *Variety* reported that the film broke attendance records at the University of Texas, Austin, and started a Bardot craze with simultaneous showings of *Woman* and *Mam'zelle Pigalle*, a recent Bardot film, at separate campus theaters. *Variety* quoted one of the theater managers as saying, "'*And God Created Woman* is a sex film. It's called art because it's foreign.'"[52] Arthur Knight and Hollis Alpert suggested another reason for Bardot's appeal: "Brigitte Bardot virtually personified the youth of the Fifties. And in many of her films, the plots were so contrived as to emphasize the ambivalent reactions of an older generation to her unconventional behavior. American audiences professed to be shocked by Bardot, but they were also intrigued by—and perhaps secretly envied—her emancipated attitudes toward love and life. Certainly, by the end of the Fifties her name had become as potent a box-office lure as that of any home bred Hollywood star."[53]

As might be expected, the art film market was soon flooded with Bardot films, both old and new. As Knight and Alpert reported, "Distributors dipped back into the grab bag of previous Bardot pictures, hoping to cash in on the phenomenon. . . . Although the films were far from distinguished, by early 1958 all New York was a Bardot festival: her pictures, duly dubbed and scrubbed, were playing not only in the art houses but in exploitation grind houses and in respectable neighborhood theaters as well."[54]

Having started the Bardot craze, Columbia capitalized on its lead by teaming up with Raoul Lévy to acquire more Bardot pictures for Kingsley-International distribution. "B.B. now stands for Brigitte Bardot, but has practically become synonymous with blockbuster on a world scale as far as pix in which she appears are concerned," said *Variety*.[55] Lévy delivered Roger Vadim's *The Night Heaven Fell* (1959), Claude Autant-Lara's *Love Is My Profession* (1959), Christian-Jaque's *Babette Goes to War* (1959), and Henri-Georges Clouzot's *The Truth* (1960). In terms of style, the films ranged from torrid melodrama to psychological thriller to light comedy.

Commentators had little good to say about the scripts, but they were sure to always comment on the extent of Bardot's dress or undress and on the quality of her acting. Writing in the *New York Times Magazine*, Seymour Peck said, "Bardot audiences know that at regular intervals, arranged with no greater ingenuity than in a burlesque show, the young woman will become as disengaged as possible from her outer garments. She will swim in a bikini, or sun-bathe; she will take a bath and run around in a towel; she will go to sleep—or wake up in the morning." "Even in clothes," Peck added, "Mlle. Bardot is provocative. She walks in a wiggle; when she stands still, her shoulders shake compulsively; and it takes little more than a coin in a jukebox to start her dancing a frantic mambo or cha cha."[56]

Crowther despaired of such behavior. French films "are losing their subtlety and wit," he said. "Cast your mind back, for a moment, on such a long ago jewel as the satiric *Carnival in Flanders* or the more recent *La Ronde, Le Plaisir* and *Fanfan la Tulipe*. They displayed the old Gallic capacity to be romantic and risque, ribald yet not offensive to a person of intelligence and taste. . . . But something's been happening lately, and we have an uneasy fear it reflects a commercial reaction to the movement Brigitte Bardot. Suddenly, it seems, the French pictures on the delicate subject of sex are being deliberately erotic and laced with uncouth suggestiveness."[57] Regardless of the critical commentary, by 1959 Bardot had become the highest-paid actress in France and her pictures continued to do well in the United States—even when *Babette Goes to War* showed "not a single suggestive inch of Bardot's skin."[58]

The arrival of the thrillers and Brigitte Bardot beginning in 1955 finally increased the demand for French films, but as *The Economist* pointed out, much of this increased revenue was generated by films that were "not particularly 'foreign' in their appeal."[59] The Bardot craze, however, had special significance for the market by attracting the college crowd as well as younger patrons. Bardot stood for youthful rebellion and became a harbinger of the French New Wave.

6

Japanese Films of the 1950s

Akira Kurosawa's *Rashomon*, the surprise winner of the Golden Lion at the 1951 Venice Film Festival, was described by *Time* in its cover story as "a cinematic thunderbolt that violently ripped open the dark heart of man to prove that the truth was not in it. In technique the picture was traumatically original; in spirit it was big, strong, male. It was obviously the work of a genius, and that genius was Akira Kurosawa, the earliest herald of the new era in cinema."[1] A dark horse, according to Jane Cianfarra it was "slipped into the festival unheralded" by the festival director to make "the representation as wide as possible." Members of the jury knew nothing about the picture or the director, but they "were sure, they said, that the 'masterful handling of the Pirandello-esque twists of mood and action, its exciting photography and the superb performances of its seven actors, struck a fresher, more novel and poetic note than the Venice festival had seen in years."[2]

Rashomon opened the newly rebuilt Little Carnegie on December 26, 1951. RKO, the distributor, was another surprise.[3] Under the helm of Howard Hughes, RKO had fallen on hard times during the postwar recession and had shuttered its studio. In need of films for its distribution arm, it went on the hunt for independent products. Taking on a subtitled Japanese film was a gamble, but it paid off.

Rashomon, which stars Toshiro Mifune and Machiko Kyo, is set in twelfth-century Japan and presents as flashbacks four contradictory accounts of a rape and murder as related by a bandit, a noblewoman, the ghost of her slain husband, and a woodcutter. Crowther advised his readers to abandon normal expectations of plot development: "[T]he wonderful thing about this picture—the

118

Toshiro Mifune and Machiko Kyo in Akira Kurosawa's *Rashomon* (1951)

thing which sets it up as art—is the manifest skill and intelligence with which it has been made by Director Akira Kurosawa, who moves to the top ranks with this job. Everyone seeing the picture will immediately be struck by the beauty and grace of the photography, by the deft use of forest light and shade to achieve a variety of powerful and delicate pictorial effects. Others, more attentive, will delight in the careful use of music (or absence of music) to accompany the points of view. But only the most observant—and most sensitive—will fully perceive the clever details and devices by which the director reveals his character, and, in this revelation, suggests the dark perversities of man."[4]

In a later piece for the *New York Times*, Tokyo-based Ray Falk described Kurosawa as "Japan's Top Director" and an "artist to the core," a master of the most popular Japanese film genres of his era, the *jidai-geki* (a costume-action film involving medieval samurai) and the *gendai-geki* (a more realistic, often domestic drama rooted in contemporary Japanese life). Falk noted that the Japanese themselves failed to comprehend *Rashomon*'s theme, which asked: "Is there a truth? Can this truth be grasped by man's mind? If there is a truth, will not man's egotism make it difficult to grasp this truth? Up to this point the novelist and scenarist agree. But Mr. Kurosawa went a step further," said Falk. "As a solution to the dilemma he wants us to believe in man's good will, and begs us to have faith in goodness. That is why he added the last scene in which the woodchopper adopts the orphan child, a chapter not in the original book."[5]

Arthur Knight admired the film as a humanist document: "Its greatest novelty is its story which is non-narrational, timeless, and universal. More, it is a story about men and women—about sex—and it results, unless I am very much mistaken, in one of the two or three films ever made for grown-ups, instead of for kiddies six to sixty."[6] *Time* was impressed with Mifune's flamboyant performance as the bandit, "an unforgettable animal figure, grunting, sweating, swatting at flies that constantly light on his half-naked body, exploding in hyena-like laughter of scorn and triumph."[7] Other critics admired *Rashomon*'s exotic qualities and compared the film to Japanese fretwork, an Oriental glass puzzle, Kabuki theater, or simply Japanese aesthetics in general.[8]

RKO's press kit offered exhibitors two ways to promote the film: for art houses the company created a dignified ad containing favorable quotes from reviews and a listing of its major awards; for mainstream houses the company created a series of ads showing Mifune and Kyo wrestling over a knife, with the caption reading: "The Husband Said: 'SHE BETRAYED ME!' The Bandit Said: 'SHE OFFERED HER LOVE!' The Wife Said: 'I WAS ATTACKED!'" Machiko Kyo was clearly the major selling point. The ads for local newspapers featured a drawing of Kyo's face, which was partially hidden behind a veil, under which were the words: "Introducing the beautiful Machiko Kyo." Publicity stills typically showed her in period dress. The accompanying text read: "In three years, Miss Kyo has carved out a remarkable career for herself on the screen. Often described as the Jane Russell of Japan, because of her physical attributes, Miss Kyo has now established herself as Nippon's foremost actress. She is the winner of the 1950 best actress award. She graduated to the movies following ten years in musical revues." For good measure the press kit included the traditional cheesecake photo of Miss Kyo lying on a rocky beach in a bikini.[9]

Masaichi Nagata's Export Strategy

The Japanese film industry lay in ruins following World War II. Efforts to rebuild it were hampered by an annual flood of Hollywood films that catered to the public's need for entertainment. However, when *Rashomon* won the top honor at Venice, economic conditions had improved. When the Allied occupation forces rescinded the restrictions on film production in 1953, Japan's producers set their sights on export markets.[10] The types of films Japanese audiences enjoyed—Oriental musicals, domestic dramas, and "samurai horse operas"—were thought to be unsuitable for export. To discover what the rest of the world might enjoy, Masaichi Nagata, the head of Daiei Studios and *Rashomon*'s producer, embarked on a tour in 1954 to study "the action pictures from the United States, the sophisticated love stories from France, the English comedies, [and] the Italian realistic dramas." Nagata concluded that the West might be receptive to "a series of stories of old Japan told in a 'humanistic' style and 'with a delicacy of composition and refinement of gesture.'"[11]

Nagata had three such pictures ready for release—Kenji Mizoguchi's *Ugetsu*, Teinosuke Kinugasa's *Gate of Hell*, and Koji Shima's *Golden Demon*—all produced in 1953. To distribute them, he worked with Edward Harrison, a former press agent and publicist for *Rashomon*, who had gone into foreign film distribution. Invariably *Rashomon* served as the standard against which these releases would be judged.

Harrison released *Ugetsu* and *Gate of Hell* within three months of each other in the fall of 1954. Both had won major awards at Venice and Cannes, respectively, and both starred Machiko Kyo. To provide an added boost, Harrison arranged for them to be presented under the sponsorship of the Japan Society. Their arrival generated a lot of press. *Life* published a six-page color photo spread of the Daiei films and explained that the Japanese were working "to establish a product identity" for their exports and "to show that *Rashomon* was no beginner's luck."[12]

Ugetsu (*Ugetsu monogatari*) opened at the Plaza on September 7, 1954. Based on a collection of short stories written by Akinari Ueda in 1768, *Ugetsu* told a "weird, violent tale of two poor 16th Century villagers, eaten by ambition and greed, who satisfy their lust only to find tragedy and bitterness. It could easily be taken for a modern parable of wartime Japan," said *Life*.[13] Like *Rashomon*, Crowther found *Ugetsu* "steeped in a cultural climate so misty and rarefied that an awareness of what was happening in the picture was not at all easy to perceive. But the sensuous details are intriguing, the acting is hypnotically formalized—especially that of Machiko Kyo, the ghostly princess—and the whole composition of it is a challenge for the student of films."[14] *Time* also compared it to *Rashomon*, saying, "*Rashomon* was the first to be shown in this country; *Ugetsu* is the second, and in many ways it is a jewel of an intenser ray than *Rashomon*. *Rashomon* was orgiastic, almost Western in its race for the things of the world. *Ugetsu* is contemplative in the midst of violence, wholly Oriental in its lidded introspection. As a result, its beauty and its meaning are more remote from Western audiences, but not too remote." Linking this to the idea of art, the review continues:

Machiko Kyo and Masayuki Mori in Kenji Mizoguchi's *Ugetsu* (1954)

"Even the most violent scenes are dissolved in a meditative mist, like terrors in the mind of a sage. The moviegoer has the sense of living in a classic Japanese watercolor or of walking on a world that is really a giant pearl."[15]

Gate of Hell (*Jigokumon*) opened at the Guild on December 13, 1954. Based on a contemporary play by the late Kan Kikuchi, the film, set in the twelfth century, tells a tragic tale "of unrequited passion and of a wife who sacrifices her life for her husband's honor."[16] Its main attraction was the color cinematography. Arthur Knight reported that "Japanese technicians spent three years in Hollywood mastering the techniques of color; to this they added centuries of accumulated wisdom in the psychology and philosophy of color. As a result, *Gate of Hell* is not only the most handsome picture yet shown on any screen anywhere, but color plays an emotional role as well. . . . Unquestionably, *Gate of Hell* will become an important influence in refining the future use of color on the screen. It is, in the fullest sense, a true work of art."[17]

The other attraction was Miss Kyo. Crowther said, "One could write reams of lush enthusiasm for the porcelain beauty and electrifying grace of Machiko Kyo. . . . For it is she, with her great power of suggestion with a minimum of gesture and a maximum of use of the tiny mouth and eyes, who conveys the

sense of sadness and despair that suffuses this film."[18] *Gate of Hell* ran for eleven
months at the Guild. The New York Film Critics Circle named it Best Foreign
Language Film and the National Board of Review named Miss Kyo Best
Actress. The latter award confirmed Miss Kyo's status as an international star.
Newsweek described her as "the subtly beautiful girl from Osaka . . . the star
whose performances in prizewinning Japanese period films *Rashomon*, *Ugetsu*,
and *Gate of Hell* took the customers in at least 30 countries back some eight or
ten centuries and made them want to stay there."[19]

    Ugetsu and *Gate of Hell* had proven that *Rashomon* was no "beginner's luck."
Arthur Knight said, "At the moment Japan's film studios seem to be doing the
most interesting, most creative job of movie-making in the world. . . . While our
Occidental films have leveled off at a plateau of technical perfection, the films
from Japan are exploring psychological, physiological, and esthetic paths that
are, in their implications, not merely new but revolutionary." For example, said
Knight, Japanese films convey emotions in an extraordinary way: "We do not
'identify' with the characters, nor are the psychological tensions heightened
by editing techniques. They reach us through the mind rather than through the
nerves. But the formalism of camera movement and the almost ritualistic
performances of the actors achieve the ultimate effect. They create a new level
of emotional gratification in the motion-picture theatre."[20]

    Having scored two critical successes with films of old Japan, Harrison
decided to test the waters with a film having a more contemporary feel. Koji
Shima's *Golden Demon* (*Konjiki yasha*) opened at the Guild on January 30, 1956. It
was a type of film the Japanese categorized as "Haha no Mono," which translates as "Things About Mother." It was called that because "the mere mention
of mother brings sentimental tears to Japanese eyes."[21] *Life* had predicted that
Golden Demon "will probably be more acceptable to American audiences than its
more stylized predecessors." Set in Tokyo in the 1890s, "its story, a sort of modern *Romeo and Juliet*, tells of two unhappy lovers forced to separate by one of
their parents' greed for money—the 'golden demon.' But the 'demon' is finally
exorcized and, unlike Shakespeare's pair, these lovers are happily united at the
end."[22] *Golden Demon* starred the twenty-four-year-old Fujiko Yamamoto, a former "Miss Nippon." Crowther called it "an outrageous piece of sentimental
fiction about love and greed in comparatively modern Japan" and predicted
that "its main interest to American audiences will be the prettiness of its décor.
This seems to be the one distinction we can look for in Japanese films. Goodness knows, *Golden Demon* has few others."[23]

    Harrison made one final attempt to broaden interest in Japanese films by
relying once again on Machiko Kyo, the star of Kenji Mizoguchi's last film,

Street of Shame (*Akasen chitai*), which appeared in 1956. Set in modern-day Tokyo, it examines the lives of young prostitutes working in a legal brothel known as the Dreamland. Harrison claimed that Mizoguchi's film helped put an end to legalized prostitution in Japan.[24] Harrison avoided the New York gauntlet by opening the film at the Vagabond Theatre in Los Angeles on February 15, 1957. The timing enabled Harrison to capitalize on Miss Kyo's starring role in MGM's *Teahouse of the August Moon*, which had recently concluded its run in the same city. A Vagabond ad stated, "Machiko Kyo, star of 'Teahouse' and 'Gate of Hell,' plays a born tramp." To increase its allure, the film was restricted to "Adults Only." *Street of Shame* ran for over five weeks at the Vagabond theater.

After playing in San Francisco, *Street of Shame* finally arrived in New York on June 4, 1959. It played at the World Theater on a continuous basis, with no age restrictions. Crowther wrote, "Pretty Machiko Kyo . . . has, to put it bluntly, assumed the role of a prostitute . . . and as such she is about as coarse and vulgar as previously she was delicate and pure."[25] *Time* noted, "In the U.S., where prostitution has seldom been seriously discussed on the screen, audiences will no doubt be stunned by the film's unblinking realism. But they will probably not be startled by the scriptwriter's discovery that every whore has a heart of gold. . . . [F]or the most part, the acting is excellent. Machiko Kyo is particularly good. She slips so naturally into lace undies and Americanized manners that she is hard to recognize as the stilted medieval heroine of *Rashomon* and *Gate of Hell*. If the story seems repetitive and interminable, so indeed must the life of a prostitute."[26] Harrison was smart to open his film out of town.

Toho's Exports

Nagata's export strategy failed. During the 1950s Toho, Japan's largest film company, also had a go at the American market. The first films to reach the United States included two "samurai horse operas"—Hiroshi Inagaki's *Samurai* and Akira Kurosawa's *The Magnificent Seven*—and one monster movie—*Godzilla*. *Samurai* (*Miyamoto Musashi*) reached the United States through the efforts of William Holden, the Hollywood star, who saw the film in production in Tokyo and arranged for Fine Arts Films to distribute it. Starring Toshiro Mifune, it told the story of "a bullnecked, snarling ruffian who dreams of avenging the lost battle by becoming a great samurai."[27] To help American audiences follow the plot, the distributor added an unobtrusive voice-over narration spoken by Holden.

Samurai premiered at the Vagabond Theatre in Los Angeles in November 1955. The placement gave the film exposure in Los Angeles in time for Academy

Award consideration and allowed the distributor to test the waters before deciding on a New York release. The *Los Angeles Times* basically liked the film, stating, "Many of the shortcomings of a film as colorful as *Samurai* . . . can be forgiven simply because it is so colorful and lovely. . . . Certainly Mifune is unbeatable, even against odds that would confound a Hollywood director. His escapes are miraculous and his luck incredible."[28] *Samurai* opened in New York on January 9, 1956. Crowther described it as "an Oriental Western, dressed in sixteenth-century get-ups and costumes, but as violently melodramatic as any horse opera out of Hollywood."[29] John McCarten of the *New Yorker* said, "After *Gate of Hell*, I was hopeful that the Japanese would keep on with the good work. But *Samurai* would seem to indicate that the Hollywood-B virus has infected them."[30]

A more prescient review from *Time* suggested its appeal: "Director Hiroshi Inagaki uses color film with as much facility as if he had invented it, and sometimes, in following one of Toshiro's berserk rages, the camera appears to circle warily as though a closer approach would invite its own destruction. The girl, Kaoru Yachigusa, splendidly suggests the tempered steel that lies beneath the mannered poise of a Japanese maiden, and Toshiro packs his role with all the deadly menace of a human grenade with the pin of reason removed."[31] *Samurai* received an honorary Oscar for best foreign film and spawned a trilogy. Inagaki went on to make *Samurai* II and *Samurai* III with Mifune in 1955 and 1956, respectively, but they were not seen in the United States until Toho released all three sequentially at the 55th Street Playhouse in 1967.

Akira Kurosawa's *The Magnificent Seven* (*Shichinin no samurai*) was released by Columbia Pictures on November 19, 1956. Columbia decided to go into foreign film distribution in a limited way in 1955 and formed a subsidiary to handle subtitled product that would not pose problems for the censors.[32] *The Magnificent Seven*, which won the Silver Lion at the 1954 Venice Film Festival, was among its first acquisitions. *Variety*'s review of the Venice screening probably explains Columbia's attraction to the film: "High adventure and excitement are stamped all over this solid-core film about a group of seven samurai warriors who save a little village from annihilation at the hands of a group of bandits in 15th Century Japan. . . . Director Kurosawa has given this a virile mounting. It is primarily a man's film, with the brief romantic interludes also done with taste. Each character is firmly molded. Toshire Miifue as the bold, harebrained but courageous warrior weaves a colossal portrait. He dominates the picture although he has an extremely strong supporting cast. . . . Style of the film is the most occidental seen in recent Japanese films but locale is still oriental in flavor."[33]

Columbia opened *The Magnificent Seven* at the Guild, the same theater that earlier had screened *Gate of Hell* and *Golden Demon*. *The Magnificent Seven* had a running time of 158 minutes, a bit shy of the 161-minute international version shown at the Venice Film Festival and nearly an hour shorter than the original Japanese release. *Variety*'s review had just about said it all. Crowther agreed, calling *The Magnificent Seven* an "extraordinary film" which matched *Rashomon* "for cinema brilliance, but in another and contrasting genre." That genre, said Crowther, "bears cultural comparison with our own popular western *High Noon*. That is to say, it is a solid, naturalistic, he-man outdoor action film, wherein the qualities of human strength and weakness are discovered in a crisis taut with peril."[34] Robert Hatch, writing in the *Nation*, said that *The Magnificent Seven* "is much more easily accepted by Western audiences than the earlier film, or for that matter any of the major Japanese films that have been shown here." However, he added that defining it as an "Oriental Western" is about as helpful as calling a bullfight a Latin rodeo. . . . This is melodrama, romance, knight errantry—universal material."[35] Writing in the *Saturday Review*, Arthur Knight said, "It is in the wealth of detail, the richness of characterization, and the robust quality of its physical action—as well as in the sheer technical virtuosity with which Kurosawa has managed each sequence—that lies the ceaseless fascination of the film. For he has taken a theme as familiar and standardized to Japanese audiences as our own Westerns are to us and treated it with a freshness, a directness, a sensitivity to texture and tempo and psychological truth that impart new excitement and meaning to the old form."[36]

The Magnificent Seven performed poorly at the box office, however. Michael Roemer, writing in the *Reporter*, recalled: "Late in 1956, a Japanese film entitled *The Magnificent Seven* opened at a small New York theater. . . . The night I saw it, there were eight people in the audience, six of them Japanese. The reviewers, apparently bewildered, called it a 'Japanese Western,' perhaps because there are horses in it. This tag may have killed the picture but evidently drew it to the attention of Yul Brynner, who is currently adapting the story to a Mexican locale."[37]

Many reasons were offered up to explain the slow going for Japanese films in the United States. A. Iwasaki, writing in the *Nation*, blamed the peculiar narrative style of the films: "Remnants of feudalism are found in every phase of Japanese life; the feudal elements in pictures are all an inevitable reflection. This can be seen also in the 'style' of the Japanese film. Its most obvious feature is slowness of tempo, immobility of camera and dull montage. The tempo of a film is naturally defined by the tempo of the society in which it is made, and there can be no doubt that our way of life is slower than that of America and

Europe." Iwasaki added, "But there is another factor in Japan worth consider-
ing, an ancient artistic tradition which does not lay stress on dramatic force.
The Japanese always valued the subtle in art; they hated exactness, definiteness.
Such was and still is the spirit of the old-school Japanese *Tanka, Haikkai* and
other forms of literature. It is still alive in the most modern form of art, the
film."[38] Henry Hart, the editor of *Films in Review*, had a simpler explanation:
"Old Japanese culture is of small interest to non-Japanese, and cultural changes
now in progress throughout Japan are old hat in the West."[39] Crowther blamed
"the extravagant and flamboyant style of acting, derived from Kabuki," evident
in Japanese films. The technique is amusing when one first sees it, but "it can
also be distracting and monotonous."[40] *Variety* pointed to poor distribution, an
affliction that particularly affected Kurosawa's films.

Poor distribution, however, did not affect Toho's *Godzilla (Gojira)*, the first
Japanese film to go into general release. An article by Dave Jamel in *Variety* entitled "Japanese Arties Wow the Critics, but Horror Films Get Coin" stated the
obvious. Ishirô Honda's low-budget picture about a prehistoric monster that
emerges from the sea to devastate Tokyo was acquired by the aspiring mogul
Joseph E. Levine for a mere $12,000. Levine cut it by forty minutes, inserted
new footage of Raymond Burr as an American journalist on the scene in
Tokyo, and opened it in a dubbed version at the Loew's State on April 27, 1956,
backed by a massive publicity campaign. Afterward, Levine booked the film
into more than four thousand theaters and took in a quick $700,000 in rentals,
which topped "all previous Geishaland entries, including such adjective inspir-
ing films as *Rashomon* and *Gate of Hell* at the wickets" and inspired twenty-two
sequels.[41]

"Japanese arties" continued to trickle in, thanks mainly to Thomas J.
Brandon. In an effort to open "a new and eager market for all future Japanese
imports," Brandon sponsored a one-man Japanese film festival at the Little
Carnegie in late 1959. His plan was to show eight films over two months in
order to reveal "a glimpse of Japan as it is today (at least reflected on film)."[42]
His selections included three early Kurosawa films—*The Men Who Tread on the
Tiger's Tail, Drunken Angel,* and *Ikiru*—which Toho produced in 1945, 1948, and
1960, respectively. However, the poor critical and audience response forced him
to cancel the festival midway through.

Kurosawa's *Ikiru*, the most popular in the series, lived on and enjoyed a
three-month extended run at the Little Carnegie. Rick Lyman summarized it
thusly: "Set in contemporary Tokyo, it follows a joyless, dying bureaucrat,
memorably played by Takashi Shimura, who decides to help slum parents build
a playground."[43] Stanley Kauffmann was among its many admirers: "This is a

Takashi Shimura in Akira Kurosawa's *Ikiru* (1960)

film rooted in the most universal of truths, the one that cuts across all cultural barriers, all concepts of love, success, God: the fact of mortality. It confronts the fact with honesty and a touching eagerness. Takashi Shimura . . . is magnificent as Watanabe: an actor who created fiercely the indignity and helplessness and groveling fear of the man newly sentenced, along with the ravening hunger for sensual pleasure, then for spiritual refreshment, then for a crumb of achievement to be his immortality." Kaufmann added, "The only film comparable to this that I can remember is De Sica's *Umberto D*, which too treats the failing of the light, but *Ikiru* is, for me, more *powerful*."[44]

Time called the film "a masterwork of burning social conscience and hard-eyed psychological realism: the step-by-step, lash-by-lash, nail-by-nail examination of the Calvary of a common man." The reviewer added that the film's defects, "along with its Asiatic strangeness and its painful subject, will surely scare away most U.S. moviegoers. Director Kurosawa is in such raging and relentless earnest that he labors almost every point he makes. And the film maintains its intensity at much greater length (2 hr. 20 min.) than the average spectator can be expected to tolerate. Furthermore, Actor Shimura, though at moments transcendently right and revealing, rather too continuously resembles a Japanese Jiggs who has just been beaned by the eternal rolling pin and is about to say tweet-tweet."[45]

The Japanese film industry was the only non-Western venture to make a concerted attempt to break into the mainstream U.S. theatrical market during the 1950s. It was a quixotic effort. Horror films could travel, albeit not those geared primarily for the Japanese home market. In the early 1960s Toho attempted to find a wider audience for its pictures in the art film market by opening showcase theaters for its films in Los Angeles, San Francisco, and New York City and by handling distribution on its own rather than using independent distributors. Unfortunately, this effort failed as well.

7

Ingmar Bergman: The Brand

An Ingmar Bergman craze hit the art film market in late 1959. It arrived two years after the Brigitte Bardot craze—and none too soon. By 1959 more than one commentator had complained that foreign films had reached a new low, having come to mean, in Pauline Kael's words, "Brigitte Bardot in and out of towel and sheet and Italian Amazons in and out of slips and beds."[1] The Bergman craze started in Paris in 1958 and soon spread to London and beyond. Meanwhile, Bergman's films were taking top awards at Cannes, Berlin, London, and other international festivals. In October 1959 as many as five Bergman films were playing simultaneously in New York's best art houses, setting a record for a foreign film director. In early 1960 Bergman made the cover of *Time* magazine—the first foreign filmmaker to do so since Leni Riefenstahl in 1936—and his life and accomplishments were being recorded in the *New York Times*, the *New York Herald Tribune*, *Life*, *Esquire*, the *Saturday Review*, and other publications. The name Ingmar Bergman had become synonymous with auteur. As *Time* put it, "Bergman's work is all Bergman, and few film directors can make a similar claim. He creates his own pictures from the first line of the script to the last snip of the cutting shears, working with concentrated fury. . . . Bergman is unquestionably one of the most forceful and fascinatingly original artists who now confront the U.S. in any medium."[2]

Bergman's swift ascendency in the U.S. art film scene was comparable to that of Vittorio De Sica's and Roberto Rossellini's after the war, although Bergman was a one-man production team who worked outside the usual production centers. As *Variety* observed, Bergman's achievement was buttressed by "a fortuitous combination of American public relations techniques and the unusual

130

imagination displayed in the Bergman films that resulted in bringing world-wide acclaim to the Swedish filmmaker."[3]

Bergman initially attracted attention in the United States because his picture were Swedish, which was synonymous with soft porn in the exploitation market. The first batch was released with such titles as *Torment* (*Het*, 1946), *Frustration* (*Skepp till India land*, 1949), *Illicit Interlude* (*Sommarlek*, 1954), *Monika, the Story of a Bad Girl* (*Sommaren med Monika*, 1956), and *The Naked Night* (*Gycklarnas afton*, 1956). The titles bore little resemblance to the Swedish originals and were conjured up by the distributors. Crowther deplored such tactics. In his review of *Illicit Interlude*, he said, "There is something cheap and unpleasant about the title 'Illicit Interlude' as applied to the handsome Swedish picture. [The film] gives a subtle and sensitive presentation of a strange, youthful love affair, no more meriting the pornographic word 'illicit' than it deserves to be labeled smut."[4] Robert Hatch described the picture as "a flashback tale of first love, a theme that never dates, told in a mannered screen style that dates to the art cameras of UFA in the 1920s." However, he went on to note that Maj-Britt Nilsson, the heroine, "is partial to sleeping in pajama tops and to early morning dips in the nude—habits which may give the picture a welcome notoriety."[5] According to Arthur Knight and Hollis Alpert, the morning dips were likely inserted into the film by Gaston Hakim, the distributor, who hired an American director to shoot the scenes on a private lake in New Jersey.[6]

Monika, the Story of a Bad Girl was handled more egregiously as an exploitation film. Forgoing the New York launch, Jack Thomas, the distributor, opened *Monika* in Los Angeles at the downtown Orpheum and in nine Pacific Drive-ins on February 3, 1956. It played on a double bill with *Mixed Up Women*, a reissue of Kroger Babb's *One Too Many* (1950), which starred Ruth Warwick in "a bleary-eyed story of a female alcoholic whose gin stupors are nothing to her husband's congenital one." The ads for *Monika* featured a head shot of Harriet Andersson, the lead, with headlines announcing "She's Here!" and "Sweden's Answer to Marilyn Monroe!" The ads also contained the notice "Title Song and Musical Score by Les Baxter." Nowhere in the ads did Ingmar Bergman's name appear. The *Los Angeles Times* described *Monika* as another Swedish film centered around "an idyllic summer romance" and noted that "Miss Andersson hardly seems at home in the clean-limbed fjord country through which she passes with varying quantities of clothing." The review also complained about the "incredibly dim" photography and the "strictly juvenile" dubbing job, which used expletives like "Gosh!" "Gee!" and "Nuts!"[7] The following day Morton Lippe, the Orpheum's manager, was arrested by the L.A. vice squad and the film was seized. Not long after that Thomas was tried and found guilty

Gunnar Björnstrand and Ulla Jacobsson in Ingmar Bergman's *Smiles of a Summer Night* (1957)

of selling a lewd and indecent film. He was sentenced to ninety days in a city jail and fined $750.[8] Thomas appealed the decision. While awaiting the outcome, he opened the film in several Minneapolis drive-ins, accompanied by a similar ad campaign.

Bergman was accorded more respect when *Smiles of a Summer Night* (*Sommarnattens leende*) was named Best Comedy of the year at Cannes in 1956. According to *Variety*, the award "laid the cornerstone to his international renown." *Smiles* was released by Rank Film Distributors and opened at the Sutton on December 23, 1957. The cast was headed by Ulla Jacobsson, Eva Dahlbeck, Harriet Andersson, and Gunnar Björnstrand. "It may not be all that funny, but it is sexy enough in a simple, sweaty way," said *Time*, which described the plot as follows: "The interlocking triangles include a prominent Swedish lawyer, his grown son, his young wife, his ex-mistress, the upstairs maid, a Swedish peer and his fun-loving wife. Essentially it is love's old sweet story of how the man chases the woman until she catches him. Everybody ends up at a house party where the moral climate is established by the hostess, who declares that the only time a person needs morals is when he is playing solitaire."[9]

The Janus Buildup

Smiles inspired Bryant Haliday and Cy Harvey of Janus Films to acquire the U.S. distribution rights to Bergman's films. In 1958 a deal was struck with Svensk Films, Bergman's home studio. Janus thereupon devised a successful marketing strategy to create a "Bergman image" and to control the subsequent release of each of his films. "According to vet industryites," said *Variety*, "it was the 'continuity' of Bergman product available, as well as the quality of the films themselves, which was responsible for the general public's awareness and then acceptance of Bergman as a box office figure to be reckoned with."[10] To help create the "Bergman image," Harvey hired the prominent publicity firm of Blowitz & Maskel.

Janus led off with *The Seventh Seal* and *Wild Strawberries*, which were produced in 1957 and had previously established reputations for themselves in Europe. Janus released *The Seventh Seal (Det sjunde inseglet)* at the Paris Theatre on October 13, 1958. *Variety* described Bergman's morality play about a "returning crusader in the 14th century who keeps Death at bay, via a chess game" as "a definite U.S. art house possibility."[11] The memorable cast was headed by Max von Sydow (the Knight), Gunnar Björnstrand (the Squire), and Bengt Ekerot (Death). Crowther was duly impressed: "Swedish director Ingmar Bergman, whose *Smiles of a Summer Night* proved him an unsuspected master of satiric comedy, surprises again in yet another even more neglected vein with his new self-written and self-directed allegorical film." Crowther considered *The Seventh Seal* "a piercing and powerful contemplation of the passage of man upon this earth. Essentially intellectual, yet emotionally stimulating, too, it is as tough— and rewarding—a screen challenge as the moviegoer has had to face this year."[12] Robert Hatch saw in Bergman a new type of committed film artist: "The history of the theatre is full of driven men, but it is more unusual to come upon a movie maker who is really seized by an idea. Therefore Ingmar Bergman's thoughtful, inventive, poetic *The Seventh Seal* can scarcely fail to impress you. Mr. Bergman is haunted by the tragedy of faith and has composed a simple, almost primitive, allegory to elucidate the agony."[13] Jonas Mekas, writing in the *Village Voice*, ranked Bergman as one of the world's "two or three most intelligent film directors." He then went on to praise his insight: "His is a mental adventure. His strength is (as Virginia Woolf would say) to find adventure in the journey itself. Obsessed with the ideas of love, life, death, good and evil, he meditates as he goes, talking in symbols, in parables, and images that often are of breathtaking beauty. There is more cinema in *The Seventh Seal* than in the entire Hollywood production of 1958 (with the exception of Orson Welles' *Touch of Evil*). It is being said that Bergman is bringing Paris intellectuals back to the movies. Eisenstein was the last one to have that honor."[14] Nevertheless *The Seventh Seal* ran for only four weeks at the Paris before making way for the Alec Guinness comedy *The Horse's Mouth.*

Janus opened *Wild Strawberries* (*Smultronstället*) at the Beekman on June 22, 1959. Victor Sjöström, the legendary Swedish director, played Isak Borg, an elderly medical professor who is troubled by a dream of death and recalls incidents in his life as he travels to his former university with his estranged daughter-in-law (Ingrid Thulin) to accept an honorary degree. *Wild Strawberries* confounded Crowther: "If any of you thought you had trouble understanding what Ingmar Bergman was trying to convey in his beautifully poetic and allegorical Swedish film, *The Seventh Seal*, wait until you see his *Wild Strawberries*. . . . This one is so thoroughly mystifying that we wonder whether Mr. Bergman himself knew what he was trying to say." Crowther labeled the film "a surrealist exercise" that failed to clearly convey "the feelings and the psychology of an aging man."[15] Crowther was in the minority. Robert Hatch demurred: Those who alleged that "*Wild Strawberries* is symbolically enigmatic or otherwise obscure," he said, "must be uncommonly serene people, for no one who has ever looked into himself with astonished disgust or rueful acknowledgment of the lateness of the hour can go seriously astray at this picture. . . . *Wild Strawberries* is the testament, I suspect quite directly personal, of a man who thoroughly understands how terrible it is to be a human being, and who is glad to accept the consequences. The screen has never been used with greater art or for more humane ends."[16]

Stanley Kauffmann singled out Sjöström's performance: "Some old actors' faces have an odd childlike purity; it radiates from Sjöström. Of his many moving scenes one moment stands out particularly. In a dream sequence, his parents, as they were when he was a child, are sitting on a rock while Father fishes. They see him, as he was then, and wave to him. We see the old man as he is now, and, with all the sadness of time past and passing, his eyes fill at the sight of them. It is lovely."[17]

Janus opened its next Bergman film, *The Magician* (*Ansiktet*), at the Fifth Avenue Cinema on August 27, 1959. Bergman's tale of a nineteenth-century conjurer and his traveling magic show starred Max von Sydow, Ingrid Thulin, and Gunnar Björnstrand. Rich in atmosphere, characterization, action, and symbolism, *The Magician*, said Crowther, could have "wide popular appeal, for [Bergman] is dealing with magic, spiritual manifestations, spells and 'animal magnetism,' which are more exciting when they are not fully understood. This picture is full of extraordinary thrills that flow and collide on several levels of

Victor Sjöström as Isak Borg in Ingmar Bergman's *Wild Strawberries* (1959)

emotion and intellect. And it swarms with sufficient melodrama of the blood-chilling, flesh creeping sort to tingle the hide of the least brainy addict of outright monster films."[18] It was precisely for these reasons that Janus released the film in a dubbed version for a wider audience and was able to book the film in major circuits around the country.

While *Wild Strawberries* and *The Magician* were still drawing crowds, Janus revived *Smiles of a Summer Night* and *The Seventh Seal* as a double feature at the Art and reissued *Three Strange Loves* (*Törst*), a film Bergman had made in 1949. As of October 1959, five Bergman films were playing simultaneously in the city. *Smiles* and *The Seventh Seal* "were pulling in more customers a week than they did when first released before the Bergman boom took hold," reported Richard Nason in the *New York Times*. The five films brought in "perhaps more than all the other Swedish films shown since the war put together."[19]

Janus's effort generated an enormous amount of press. "The 'metaphysical ambiguities' of [Bergman's] films were dissected and disputed by the kind of people who delight in the *London Times* crossword puzzles, and for the same reasons," said Richard Corliss and Jonathan Hoops.[20] Stories about Bergman's life, working methods, and artistic vision began appearing in major newspapers and magazines. By late 1959, *Variety* reported, "the Bergman cult has grown to such an extent that a report of a screening of *Devil's Eye* in Sweden was cabled and reported in the *New York Times*," adding that "'the Bergman buildup' was accomplished without him ever visiting the U.S."[21]

For those Bergman fans who wanted a deeper understanding of the films, Simon & Schuster published *Four Screenplays of Ingmar Bergman*, with a ten-page introduction by Bergman, to coincide with the New York premiere of *The Virgin Spring*. Translated from the Swedish by Lars Malmström and David Kushner, the screenplays comprised *Wild Strawberries*, *The Magician*, *Smiles of a Summer Night*, and *A Lesson in Love*—Bergman's most successful films.

What emerged from all this press was a composite portrait of Ingmar Bergman, the auteur—or, stated another way, Ingmar Bergman as a brand name.[22] The construction of the image proceeded with a certain logic and was presumably influenced by the background material on Bergman supplied by Janus. In writing about Bergman, the easiest way for writers to differentiate Bergman from the rest of the pack was by nationality. Beginning with *Smiles of a Summer Night*, writers stressed that Ingmar Bergman was "no kin to Swedish actress Ingrid Bergman," not only to separate the director from his notorious compatriot but also to dispel any connection with the scandal surrounding Ingrid Bergman's illicit affair with Roberto Rossellini.[23]

Writers also used nationality to situate Bergman within the traditions of the Swedish film industry. For example, James Baldwin begins his feature for *Esquire* by locating Bergman's studio, Svensk Filmindustri, in Filmstaden, outside Stockholm. He then invokes the names of Victor Sjöström (noting that Americans would know him by the name of Victor Seastrom), Mauritz Stiller, Greta Garbo, and Ingrid Bergman ("she is not related to Ingmar Bergman") before announcing that "Svensk Filmindustri is proud of these alumni, but they are prouder of no one, at the moment, than they are of Ingmar Bergman, whose films have placed the Swedish film industry back on the international map."[24] According to another story, Bergman accomplished this feat because Carl Anders Dymling, Svensk Filmindustri's head man, encouraged the new director "to use the film as a means of self-expression" freed from the demands of the marketplace. Dymling was quoted as saying, "We work for Scandinavia, we must not be dependent on a world market. This gives us freedom. I can't worry what happens to my pictures in foreign countries."[25] An interview with Bergman in the *Saturday Review* ambiguously referred to Svensk as "Bergman's company," suggesting that Bergman produced his own films.[26]

The reality was something else. Svensk, the owner of 107 theaters in Sweden, saw its domestic revenues threatened during the 1950s by the growth of television, dwindling audiences, and high taxes, which meant that Bergman's films did not return their investment in Sweden even though they were made on modest budgets—$160,000 on average.[27] One Svensk employee told James Baldwin that Bergman "wins the prizes and brings us the prestige," but that others could "be counted on to bring in the money."[28]

Having conveyed the notion that Bergman the filmmaker was detached from market forces, writers next examined his working methods. Unlike a Hollywood director, who, according to Arthur Knight, is "handed a completed script (based, often as not, on a hit play or best-selling novel that was bought by a producer and turned into a screenplay by at least two other people)," Bergman starts out by conceiving an idea—"an idea that then is fleshed out with characters, settings, action, and dialogues that have been related to the exigencies of the camera and microphone from the very outset."[29] In other words, he is a creator, not an interpreter. Werner Wiskari, writing in the *New York Times Magazine*, further noted that "the screen credits do not indicate to what extent Bergman controls all phases of his productions. After conceiving the screenplay, Bergman tells the set designer what he wants. He instructs the composer what to compose and even what instruments to compose for. He is to a great degree his own cameraman. He rarely tolerates visitors on the set during filming—even his producer feels it best to stay away—lest his artistic concentration be upset. And finally, he edits the film and supervises the mixing of all sound effects."[30]

Bergman was famous for his use of a stock company, which included Gunnar Björnstrand, Eva Dahlbeck, Max von Sydow, Harriet Andersson, and Bibi Andersson. Here is how a *Time* magazine article described it: "Most of them are prominent players on the Swedish stage; yet year after year they take part in Bergman's pictures, even though it means giving up summer vacations, even though the parts are sometimes small and the pay unexciting. Together, these players form a unit unique in the history of film; a cinema stock company trained by one director and dedicated to his purposes, beyond question the finest collection of cinema actors assembled under one roof."[31] According to *Newsweek*, "As a master of his trade [Bergman] gets unquestioning loyalty from his actors." On the set of *The Devil's Eye*, the "whole atmosphere was one of strictest discipline—no laughing, no time-wasting—and the idle cast members were dead silent, scarcely daring to breathe."[32]

Probing further, writers addressed Bergman's ideas and themes. Wiskari said, "Ingmar Bergman has won international renown by asking searching questions about [man's relation to] God and woman. He has phrased his questions as unusually provocative motion pictures and, in so doing, has generated tremendous excitement in the movie world, here." Bergman refuses to address social problems. "To critics who deplore his sticking to his 'narrow' range, he replies that if dealing with man's relation to God and to woman is narrow, 'then, yes, I am narrow.' . . . To critics who denounced him as adolescent—as not bringing any clear point of view to his pictures, as only asking questions— he replies that he does not presume to have the answers. Who, he asks, can say with final positiveness that there is a God or there isn't?"[33]

Next they examined Bergman the man, his psychological state. Bergman was depicted as a tortured artist totally consumed by his work. *Newsweek* quoted Bergman as saying, "I take my thoughts home with me nightly, though I try to discard them. . . . When I am filming, I feel as if I were suffering from illness."[34] Much was made of Bergman's delicate health. *Time* said, "He has unusually keen hearing and claims that the slightest sound disturbs him. . . . He is equally sensitive to emotional dissonance: 'I cannot work if I have a single enemy on the set.' He nourishes imaginary illnesses but is horrified of real ones; he gets furious if someone with a cold comes near him. He feels 'The Great Fear' whenever he leaves Sweden, and has spent less than six months outside of the country. He sleeps badly and has frequent fantasies of death."[35]

Lastly, it was only natural for writers to look for the cause of his disturbed psychological state. They found it in his early childhood. *Variety* noted that "Bergman was born in 1918, the son of a Lutheran clergyman. It was a strictly religious home, but not a happy one and the chill atmosphere of it has left a deep impression on him. The majority of his films should be seen against this religious background which brought into juxtaposition God and the Devil; good and evil; the decline of spiritualism and the advancement of materialism. In fact, the majority of Bergman's works can be regarded as moralities, the Middle Age plays that personify virtues."[36] Descriptions of his strict upbringing inevitably repeat the anecdote about Bergman's early obsession with a child's magic lantern, suggesting that he was a born filmmaker. For example, *Time* said, "At nine, Ingmar got a magic lantern as a present. ('I can still smell the exquisite odor of hot metal.'), and in it his fantasies came to focus. A year later he got a primitive projector and soon after that a puppet theater. The demon took over."[37]

Reviewing an Ingmar Bergman film eventually became a routine whereby, according to Kelly Wolff, "a critic could plug in a new title and new character names into a standard piece, lament the director's pretensions or praise his seriousness, and chalk it all up to the director's personal demons and the legacy of his tortured nationality."[38]

As a result of the buildup, Bergman's films brought in more than $1 million in film rentals for Janus in 1959, "about 15 or 20 times what we did last year," Cy Harvey reported. Responding to the suggestion that Bergman might not have a long shelf life as a brand name, Harvey linked Bergman to another genius: "Is Picasso a fad?"[39]

To sustain interest in Bergman without glutting the market, Janus withdrew *Wild Strawberries* and *The Magician* from release in the summer of 1960, when demand for the films was still strong, with the intent of reissuing them as a double feature the following year. Meanwhile, Janus released two of Bergman's older films, *A Lesson in Love (En lektion i kärlek)* and *Dreams (Kvinnodröm)*. They were released in Sweden in 1953 and 1955, respectively, and comprised the first two installments of Bergman's comic trilogy, ending with *Smiles*. The three films starred Harriet Andersson, Eva Dahlbeck, and Gunnar Björnstrand. Janus released *A Lesson in Love* on March 14, 1960, at the Murray Hill Theatre, and *Dreams* on May 31, 1960, at the Fifth Avenue Cinema. *Time* described the trilogy as Ingmar Bergman's "front-line report on the war between the sexes. In *Lesson*, the war begins with crockery barrages. In *Smiles*, it ends in a saraband of sophisticated satire that the winners and losers dance together. In *Dreams*, the last of the three released in the U.S., the battle rages in full fury, and Bergman zooms above the field like a happy gadfly, pranging everything in sight."[40]

To build up Bergman in the hinterlands, Janus also announced plans to present a series of Bergman retrospectives in art houses around the country, which would show all of Bergman's American releases in chronological order. "Admirers of Ingmar Bergman who have been confused by the chronology of the distinguished Swedish writer-director's films will soon have the opportunity to set the record straight," the *New York Times* reported.[41]

The value of Bergman as a brand name peaked with the release of *The Virgin Spring (Jungfrukällan)*. Set in fourteenth-century Sweden against "a background of Christianity and heathendom," the film contained a brutally realistic rape scene that shocked audiences. Describing the world premiere in Stockholm on February 8, 1960, the *New York Times* reported that "The first audiences were stunned. Fifteen persons walked out of the film's first showing. . . . A low buzzing swept through the theatre as a realistic scene of the rape and murder of a maiden appeared on the screen. There were gasps as the girl's father brutally executed the two rapists and flung an innocent boy who had been with them against a wall. There was complete silence as the father prayed for forgiveness and upon lifting up his daughter's body found his prayer miraculously answered: a spring welled up from the spot where she had lain. There were tears in many eyes as the first audience left the theatre."[42]

The Virgin Spring opened at the Beekman on November 14, 1960. "Americans saw it with some of the violence of the rape removed; the censors objected to two shots in which the girl's bare legs are pulled by one of the shepherds around the body of the man on top of her."[43] Although Crowther appreciated the simplicity and clarity of the story—"It might be termed a morality play, so direct and uncomplicated is it"—he feared that the scenes of brutality tended "to disturb the senses out of proportion to the dramatic good they do. However much one may welcome an easier clarity in a Bergman theme, there is a point beyond which the sophistication of the artist may be reduced with peril."[44] Stanley Kauffmann was more direct: "The vengeance scene is so long that it verges on the ridiculous. The father and mother enter the murderers' chamber, fasten locks, take bags from one man's arms, slam a knife into a table, yet the sleepers never stir. Then the father wakes them and has to kill them separately. Theatrically and otherwise, it is an irrational scene."[45] Dwight Macdonald faulted the film's logic: "Two commonsensical quibbles: (1) Would a gently bred young girl meeting such hard-looking types in a lonely spot invite them to a picnic and ply them with wine? (2) If God could make a spring gush forth under the body of the murdered girl—it was a very efficient spring right out of Crane Plumbing—why could He not have restored her to life?"[46]

Critics also found fault with the film's heavy symbolism. For example, Crowther explained that "each character may be a representation of some contemporary element in the world. But we rather feel Mr. Bergman has here given us nothing more than a literal, very harsh, very vivid and occasionally touching statement of a moral. When water springs from the earth beneath the dead child, after the father has repented his wrong, the simple—almost naïve—conception is resolved in a miracle. This is a simplification we feel Mr. Bergman is above."[47]

The Virgin Spring went on to win an Oscar for Best Foreign Language Film and the International Critics Prize at Cannes and became the most profitable Bergman film up to that time, bringing in over $500,000 in rentals. Cy Harvey reported that "five percent of this came from the first run in New York, and an additional 5 to 7 percent from second run here. The rest came largely from the dubbed version, which received many extra bookings as a result of its Academy Award."[48]

The Chamber Dramas

After *The Virgin Spring*, Bergman began a new phase of his career. In 1961 he stated that he would now use his film art "to give expression to his personal religious experiences in reaching out for faith."[49] Bergman's decision resulted in the trilogy *Through a Glass Darkly*, *Winter Light*, and *The Silence*. He wrote the screenplays for all three films and employed regulars from his repertory company. Working with Bergman behind the camera was Sven Nykvist, a master of the expressive use of naturalistic light, who had become Bergman's cinematographer of choice. The films were relatively short—lasting around ninety minutes each—and were sometimes referred to as "chamber dramas." Janus released the three films in sequence a year apart, beginning in 1962. The first two opened at the Beekman and the third at the Trans-Lux East and Rialto.

Swedish film critics noted that *Through a Glass Darkly* (*Såsom I en spegel*) marked a turning point in Bergman's art. As reported by Werner Wiskari, "One reviewer says this is the first time the characters in his films seem really to come to life. Another acclaims the natural flow of dialogue that avoids his occasional 'chairborne cadences.' All hail the simple, stark screenplay written for a cast of only four." The cast comprised Harriet Andersson, Gunnar Björnstrand, Max von Sydow, and a newcomer, Lars Passgård. Werner also noted that the critics were especially "awed by the performance of Harriet Andersson as the mentally ill woman who selects delusion as the world in which she wants to live and who finds her God has the face of a spider."[50] Assuming that *Through a Glass Darkly* would be Sweden's nominee in the Oscar competition for best foreign film, Janus held up the New York release until the Academy announced the finalists. When *Through a Glass Darkly* made the short list—along with Bent Christensen's *Harry and the Butler* (Denmark), Keisuke Kinoshita's *Immortal Love* (Japan), Ismael Rodriguez's *The Important Man* (Mexico), and Luis Garcia Berlanga's *Plácido* (Spain)—Janus opened the film at the Beekman on March 13, 1962. The New York reviews were just as positive as the Swedish ones. Brendan Gill described Harriet Andersson's performance as "well-nigh perfect," claiming that "her mad scenes have a terrifying plausibility; she is doomed, and we know she is doomed, but as in real life, we long for her to pull back from the brink in time."[51]

It was obvious to Janus that *Through a Glass Darkly* faced little competition for the award, particularly since the other nominees had yet to be released in the United States. (For unknown reasons *Last Year at Marienbad* and *La Notte*, which were submitted for consideration, did not make the short list.) To help its cause, Janus arranged a special screening of Bergman's film for Academy members in Los Angeles before the balloting and bought over Miss Andersson to introduce it. *Through a Glass Darkly* won the Oscar—the second year in a row for a Bergman film. Immediately following the awards ceremony, Janus opened the film in Los Angeles and naturally hyped the award recognition in New York to extend its run at the Beekman.

Winter Light (Nattvardsgästerna) opened at the Beekman on May 13, 1963. Starring Gunnar Björnstrand, Ingrid Thulin, and Max von Sydow, it depicted a clergyman suffering what Bergman called "the cruelest of torments—the silence of God.'"[52] *Variety* described it as "an extremely moving and fascinating film for the religiously aware and a somewhat boring one for the religiously indifferent."[53] Crowther dutifully considered the serious purpose of Bergman's allegory and concluded that *Winter Light* must inevitably be appraised as a contemplation of the state of Christianity today—or of the efficacy of the clerical function."[54] Dwight Macdonald put his finger on why the film disappointed. "My quarrel is not with the grimness of Mr. Bergman's moral—whether man is 'spiritually empty' or not seems to me about as important, and sensible, a question as what songs sirens sang—but with his failure to express it cinematically. *Winter Light* is exposition rather than drama. We hear the characters, but we don't see them, except in close-ups as they are explaining their problems. Bergman has always had a weakness for philosophizing, but in his best films he has invented visual ways to convey his meaning. Here one gets the feeling he regards art as frivolous decoration that would detract from the message."[55]

With *Winter Light* "Mr. Bergman told associates he was 'through with religious themes.' He turned next to a dramatization of the ugliness of human relations when the only contact is physical."[56] The result was *The Silence (Tystnaden)*, which became one of Svensk's most profitable and controversial films. Werner Wiskari reported from Stockholm that "Ingmar Bergman has shaken the Swedish moviegoing public as never before and the Swedes have reacted by storming the box office." During the first two months of the release, attendance exceeded one million. "This is a phenomenal record in a country that has a population of only 7,500,000," Wiskari said. He characterized *The Silence* as "a nightmarish depiction of a hell on earth in which life is animalistic and meaningless, as humans cannot communicate with each other and there is no sign of God" and described it as follows: "A smoldering voluptuous woman, accompanied by her small son and sick homosexual sister, are seen traveling homeward through a strange country whose citizens mouth an incomprehensible language invented by Bergman. The travelers stop in a city where men shuffle wordlessly through the streets by day and an emaciated horse slowly pulls a wagon. At night a tank rumbles into view in the otherwise empty city. The lesbian sister [Ingrid Thulin], scorned by her earthy sister [Gunnel Lindblom], is shown in a startling scene of self-love. The voluptuous one goes to a theater where she sees a couple in violent embrace in a nearby seat and agitatedly

Ingrid Thulin as Esther, Gunnel Lindblom as Anna, and Birger Malmsten as the Bartender in Ingmar Bergman's *The Silence* (1964)

rushes out to pick up a man for herself. She taunts her sister by letting her watch. The picture ends with the boy and his mother continuing their journey, leaving the sick woman behind to die alone."[57]

Janus opened the film—with "some judicious cuts"—on February 3, 1964, at the Trans-Lux East uptown and at the Rialto in Times Square. In promoting the film, Janus seemed more interested in attracting the crossover audience, hence the choice of the Rialto, the former "old house of horrors" and now a house for striptease movies. After the opening, the *New York Times* ad displayed the headline "Bergman at His Most Powerful!," which was followed by these blurbs: "On incest, self-defilement and nymphomania, this Bergman latest is the most shocking film I have ever seen. I couldn't believe my eyes!" (Wanda Hale, *Daily News*) and "Not for the prudish. It demands maturity and sophistication from the viewer. The glimpses of nudity and sexual activity are inherent to the frankly adult narrative." (Judith Crist, *Herald Tribune*).[58] The Janus trailer for the film contained a voice-over that described the film as "a compelling drama, a fascinating look into the world where people seek to communicate through the rootless gratification of their sexual appetites." Ingrid Thulin's performance revealed the "delicate intimacies of lesbian love." *The Silence* did record business in New York and Los Angeles. It played thirty-five weeks in New York, twelve at the Trans-Lux East and twenty-three at the Rialto and was expected to gross over $1 million at the box office, to equal or exceed the returns for *The Virgin Spring.*[59]

In 1963 Bergman was appointed director of the Royal Dramatic Theater of Stockholm and withdrew temporarily from full-time filmmaking. Janus's handling of Bergman's pictures set a standard of art film distribution that no other auteur enjoyed, including Michelangelo Antonioni, Jean-Luc Godard, and Akira Kurosawa. Although Bergman's genius as an artist secured his admission to the pantheon, Janus expedited the process. *Smiles of a Summer Night* inspired the fledgling company to secure the exclusive U.S. distribution rights to Bergman's films. Although the terms of the deal are not known, Janus took a calculated risk by committing significant resources to promote and distribute the line. Bergman, after all, was a prolific filmmaker and the evolving modernist style of his work would not be an easy sell. Svensk Films also took a calculated risk by entrusting Bergman's future output to the young company, but given the way Bergman's first releases were handled in the United States, Svensk probably had no other option.

Janus's care and feeding of the media resulted in an enormous amount of press coverage that established a consistent image of Bergman the auteur and prepared the way for the positive reception of his films. The careful timing of the releases, the strategic ad campaigns targeting different segments of the audience, and the astute release pattern of Bergman's older films and reissues of his current films wrung maximum revenue from market for the benefit of Janus and Svensk. Moreover, the successful handling of Bergman's works restored the prestige and reputation of the art film business. It was a bravado performance.

The French New Wave

rench New Wave directors skyrocketed in popularity when they swept top honors at the Cannes Film Festival in 1959: Marcel Camus's *Black Orpheus* received the Golden Palm; François Truffaut's *The 400 Blows* won for best direction; and Alain Resnais's *Hiroshima Mon Amour* took the International Federation of Film Critics prize. Bidding on their films heated up as distributors, filmmakers, and audiences around the world welcomed the revolution. As Jonas Mekas put it, "Not since the early postwar years, when Italian neorealist films *Open City* and *Paisan* suddenly revealed to America a completely new school of film making, has any group of film makers attracted as much attention as the so-called Nouvelle Vague."[1] New Yorkers saw their first New Wave films in the fall of 1959, only a few months after the festival, when Louis Malle's *The Lovers*, Truffaut's *The 400 Blows*, Claude Chabrol's *The Cousins*, and Camus's *Black Orpheus* were released in quick succession beginning in October. By year's end the four films were playing concurrently and temporarily eclipsed Ingmar Bergman.

Time hastily described the trend as a "new cult of cinema" espoused by a few young Parisian film critics who contributed to the highbrow film journal *Cahiers du cinéma* and criticized the "factory" method of pumping out films with big stars, big budgets, and little thought. "Les Vagueistes," as the magazine called them, speak of cinema "as of a religion. . . . They hate commercialism. They prefer to make pictures on subjects of their own choice. They would rather use unknown actors." Their films were characterized as "frankly sexy" and their "too clever" camerawork sometimes made it "hard to see the picture for the pictures." *Time* noted that the French "seem to enjoy such youthful excesses, even though many audiences have been disturbed by the curious sense of moral vacuum in many of the pictures. Aside from a general distaste for bourgeois respectability and a slight leaning toward the left, very few of the films express any moral or spiritual convictions whatever." *Time* credited the de Gaulle government with enabling the trend by withholding screen subsidies from the "conservative" French industry and forcing it to try "something new and different." "The public loved it," said *Time*, and "suddenly, the New Wave was rolling, and on the crest of it dozens of ambitious young cinéastes went surfboarding to success."[2]

Journalists later offered up other perspectives on the trend. For example, Maryvonne Butcher in *Commonweal* said that the New Wave directors shared at least two things in common, namely, youth and little money. Their youth gave them "the courage that occasionally verges on recklessness, which gives a wonderful exhilaration to the audience. To see films which have actually been made out of an *excess* of energy rather than pictures laboriously manipulating a paucity of ideas, is like coming to the end of a deadening heat wave." Their lack of money "naturally hampers them in some ways, but in others it has proved of inestimable benefit." For example, "They cannot afford to hire studios and complicated equipment, so they have been forced out on location—in the streets of Paris, the countryside of France, to small properties lent by friends over which they exercise control for short periods, and so on. This has liberated their work to an amazing extent not only from the rigidity and heaviness of the studio set but also from studio conventions and controls, so that they have a fluidity and speed which makes one marvel."[3]

Genêt, who regularly informed *New Yorker* readers about French happenings in her "Letter from Paris" column, reported that the New Wave films "are part of today's intimate fight between the mature and the young on both sides of the Atlantic. What these young directors have shown best is what they know best—the anarchic, spasmodic, lawless, and rebellious lives of certain modern young French, intensely lived within their own cycle. In these films, the shortcut to romance is sex, the stencil for beauty is the nudity of lovers." She added that the minister of justice was "working on a bill for pre-censorship, or censoring the scenario before the film can be made."[4]

The First Entries

The French New Wave flourished as an import trend in the United States from 1959 to 1962. With one exception, the films were introduced by independent distributors such as Daniel Frankel's Zenith International (Malle's *The Lovers*, Truffaut's *The 400 Blows*, Resnais's *Hiroshima Mon Amour*, and Varda's *Cleo from 5 to 7*), Irvin Shapiro's Films Around the World (Chabrol's *The Cousins*, Godard's *Breathless*, Demy's *Lola*, and de Broca's *The Love Game*), and Astor Pictures (Vadim's *Les Liaisons Dangereuses*, Resnais's *Last Year at Marienbad*, and Truffaut's *Shoot the Piano Player*). *Black Orpheus*, the single exception, was released by Lopert Pictures, the new art film subsidiary of United Artists. As we shall see, the majors watched while independents took the risks, and when a new talent with commercial potential appeared, they might dangle a production-financing offer.

Louis Malle was twenty-six when he made *The Lovers* (*Les Amants*), his second film, which won a Special Jury Prize at Venice in 1958. (His first award was as cameraman and codirector of Jacques Cousteau's undersea film *The Silent World*.) *The Lovers* starred Jeanne Moreau as a rich provincial matron who leaves her dull husband and her aimless life after one night of ecstatic lovemaking with a student-guest. "*Les Amants* was the most discussed, and praised, French film at year's end," reported Genêt. Yet she doubted the film could be shown in New York intact. She was referring to a steamy, "passionate love scene in a château park and bedroom" involving Moreau and the young man, which lasted the final twenty minutes.[5]

The Lovers opened at the Paris on October 26, 1959. Zenith International had to cut thirty seconds of lovemaking for the film to clear the New York censors. *Time* described the sequence as follows: "She meets a young archeologist (Jean-Marc Bory), a chance guest in the house. He kisses her. Suddenly, deliriously, they understand that 'this is the real thing'—or so the narrator says. *Les amoureux* then go back to her room, and with the sound track blaring Brahms (a sextet, naturally) and the camera calmly watching almost everything that happens, they make passionate and explicitly French love 1) in her bed, 2) in the bathtub, 3) back in bed again. Whereupon the wife, without a second's hesitation or backward glance, walks out on her husband, her former lover and her small daughter. The couple simply pile into his car and drive off into the dawn. 'But,' the narration concludes in tones of soaring triumph, 'she regretted nothing.'"[6]

Critics were of at least two minds about Malle's handling of sex. *Time* dismissed the film, saying the heroine "will seem to U.S. audiences no more than a roundheeled dunce."[7] Robert Hatch was equally dismissive: "On the evidence of *The Lovers*, M. Malle is about fourteen. He is preoccupied with the sensation of sex at the involuntary level, where satisfaction is the goal and the only relevant comment is clinical; he evades the consequences of sexual alliance, where competing responsibilities come into play and narrative becomes possible. It is very innocent to suppose that the way people make love is dramatically significant, and very youthful to believe that the fact they have done so makes a story."[8]

Hollis Alpert was more appreciative: "Malle has done something rare. He has dealt both boldly and poetically with the story of a love affair. . . . Something of a sexual revolution appears to be going on in the cinema, and Malle may well be one of its prophets. He seems almost frighteningly knowledgeable about the nature of physical passion, and, more important, he has found a way to be expressive in a medium which, for half a century, has been a prisoner of convention when it came to dealing with its favorite subject matter: the varieties of love."[9]

The Lovers broke box-office records around the art house circuit and made Jeanne Moreau an international star. However, censors in many cities either banned the film or demanded further cuts before it was allowed to be shown. Zenith fought one such censorship battle (*Jacobellis v. Ohio*) all the way to the Supreme Court, which in 1964 handed down a landmark decision declaring that the film was not obscene and that "national, not local, 'contemporary community standards' were to be used in determining whether or not a 'work of expression' is to be judged obscene."[10]

François Truffaut, whom Genêt described as "a precocious, authoritative critic," was twenty-seven when he made *The 400 Blows* (*Les Quatre Cents Coups*), his first feature. According to Genêt, Truffaut based it on his own experiences. "In speaking of this film on juvenile delinquency, Trauffaud [*sic*], who is an explosively candid fellow, told the press that he himself had been a delinquent and had been put in a reform school, so he knew that his film represented real life, and he added that he thought it intelligent, and had every reason to expect that it would make money."[11] Truffaut chose the fifteen-year-old Jean-Pierre Léaud as his stand-in to play Antoine Doinel.

The 400 Blows opened at the Fine Arts on November 16, 1959. Bosley Crowther considered the film "a small masterpiece," noting that "not since the 1952 arrival of René Clément's *Forbidden Games*, with which this extraordinary little picture of M. Truffaut most interestingly compares, have we had from France a cinema that so brilliantly and strikingly reveals the explosion of a fresh creative talent in the directorial field." He singled out two aspects for special praise: "The striking distinctions of it are the clarity and honesty with which it presents a moving story of the troubles of a 12-year-old boy." Of Léaud's performance, Crowther said, "Words cannot state simply how fine is Jean-Pierre Léaud in the role of the boy—how implacably dead panned, yet expressive, how apparently relaxed yet tense, how beautifully positive in his movement, like a pint-sized Jean Gabin. Out of this brand new youngster, M. Truffaut has elicited a performance that will live as a delightful, provoking and heartbreaking monument to a boy."[12]

John McCarten also gave it a rave review and said the film will probably be remembered for its final freeze-frame image: "Running with the strength of the demented, he finally comes upon the sea, and there M. Truffaut stops his camera, revealing to us, in one corrosive still-shot, a boy with no place to go. In fact, it could be said that the whole film is corrosive, for it leaves an etching on the mind that deepens with time."[13] The New York Film Critics Circle named *The 400 Blows* the Best Foreign Language Film of 1959.

The 400 Blows earned the reputation as one of the best movies about childhood ever made. Claude Chabrol's *The Cousins* (*Les Cousins*) presented another portrait of youth, Paris's "Beat Generation." Chabrol was twenty-eight when he made *The Cousins*, his second feature, which won Berlin's Golden Bear in 1959. Advance word in the *New York Times* described it as "a story about a young man from the backwoods, conscientious and naive, who is depraved, ruined and, finally, killed by his cousin, a city boy whose life is devoid of meaning and who ruins everything he touches. Gérard Blain and Jean-Claude Brialy brilliantly play the two young cousins."[14]

The Cousins opened at the Beekman on November 23, 1959. Crowther considered the film a "morbid picture of the younger generation in France" and labeled Chabrol "the gloomiest and most despairing of the new creative men. His attitude is ridden with a sense of defeat and ruin. And if his cinema reporting is as reliable as it is clear-eyed, candid and cruel, then others, as well as he, have good reason to be concerned about the youth of France."[15]

Robert Hatch observed: "The student world of Paris has lost its innocence and shattered its health. . . . Their sad clowning is not unlike that of our aboriginal beats. . . . In one striking scene, this elegant young man [the city cousin], half drunk, switches off the lights in his crowded apartment and, wearing an S.S. officer's cap and carrying a lighted candelabrum, stalks among the entwined couples, intoning in German a mawkish plaint of loneliness, disillusion, nostalgia for the lost war and bleating cries for mama. It is a scornful parody; it is also too well done to be entirely unfelt. M. Chabrol evidently finds among his arrogant and ignorant fellows a sympathy with their brothers of a generation earlier across the Rhine. If that Werther-Goebbels obscenity has made any real inroad on French youth, it is as bitter a piece of irony as this most ironic postwar era has produced."[16] *The Cousins* performed the poorest of the first group of New Wave films at the box office, taking in only $52,000 during the first eight weeks at the Beekman.[17]

Camus's *Black Orpheus* (*Orfeu Negro*) performed the best. "Of the three great Cannes triumphs," Marcel Camus's *Black Orpheus* "is the one the French love most and argue about least," reported Genêt.[18] A samba version of the Orpheus

Breno Mello and Marpessa Dawn in Marcel Camus's *Black Orhpeus* (1959)

and Eurydice legend, *Black Orpheus* was shot in color in Rio de Janiero during carnival using untrained black actors. Unlike his New Wave brethren, Camus ("No kin to Novelist Albert Camus," said *Time*) started out as a painter and sculptor before going into film production as an assistant director. He was in his forties when he began work on *Black Orpheus* and was barely able to complete it. According to an article in *Time*, "He slept on the beach to save hotel bills, lived from meal to meal and worked from reel to reel. Down to his last $17, he was rescued by Brazil's President Juscelino Kubitschek, who told the army to get him some electrical equipment." Casting choices were as follows: "For his Orpheus, Camus hired handsome Brazilian futebol player named Breno Mello and for his Eurydice an unknown dancer from Pittsburgh with serenely lovely looks and a name that nobody could possibly forget: Marpessa Dawn."[19]

Black Orpheus was released by Lopert in a Portuguese-language version at the Plaza on December 21, 1959. Hollis Alpert commented that "*Black Orpheus* is perhaps the most fascinating of those we have so far seen here. Without doubt, it is a quite marvelous film experience, blending really gorgeous color, hypnotizing sound and music, the frenetic hi-jinks of the Rio carnival, and the furious display of energy by a largely amateur group of actors."[20] *Time* considered

Black Orpheus "perhaps the most impressive can of film so far cast up on U.S. shores by the New Wave of creation that has swept across the French movie industry. It is an amazing creation."[21] *Black Orpheus* won the Oscar for Best Foreign Language Film. Thereafter Lopert placed it into general release in a dubbed version. The film went on to became the top grossing French import of 1960, bringing in $600,000 in rentals.[22]

The first New Wave films did well both at the box office and with the critics, leading Hollis Alpert to conclude, at the end of 1959, that "France seems to have taken the lead, for this year at least, in the exploring of new film frontiers. . . . In wine terms a very great year. . . . These movies seem, more than anything else, an outburst of energy and protest against the stupefying and banal that have glutted theatres for so long and will continue to do so." He went on to say that the new French directors "have had the luck and the instinctively good sense to choose subjects that have proved commercially feasible. They certainly seem to have widened the areas of what the movie public, certainly in France and in the art houses elsewhere, will accept."[23]

The Later Entries

Interest in the French New Wave continued with the arrival of Alain Resnais's *Hiroshima Mon Amour* and Philippe de Broca's *The Love Game* in 1960; Jean-Luc Godard's *Breathless* and Roger Vadim's *Les Liaisons Dangereuses* in 1961; and Alain Resnais's *Last Year at Marienbad* and Truffaut's *Jules and Jim* in 1962.

In France *Hiroshima Mon Amour* was the most written and talked about European film since the war," reported Genêt. "Every movie critic has had difficulty giving an adequate description of what happens in it, because attempting a verbal translation of its multiple photographic facets would be like trying to summarize the lyric speed and complex structure of some new piece of sensuous poetry."[24] Based on an original story and screenplay by Marguerite Duras, the film, shot in Japan, starred Emmanuelle Riva, a French stage actress in her film debut, and Eiji Okada, an established Japanese star. Although this was Resnais's first feature-length film, unlike other New Wave directors he was "by no means a 'new' director, nor is he, strictly speaking, a member of the French new wave group," commented Hollis Alpert. "He has directed shorts for ten years and won an Academy Award with his *Van Gogh*. Resnais is thirty-seven, and the five years he spent as a film editor would seem to account for the editing technique so strikingly evident in *Hiroshima Mon Amour*."[25]

Hiroshima Mon Amour opened at the Fine Arts on May 16, 1960. *Time* called the film "the acknowledged masterpiece of the New Wave of Gallic

Emmanuelle Riva and Eiji Okada in Alain Resnais's *Hiroshima Mon Amour* (1960)

moviemakers . . . an atomic horror movie, a pacifist tract, a Proustian exercise in recollection, a radioactive *Romeo and Juliet*. As a matter of fact, it is all these things and more—an intense, original and ambitious piece of cinema."[26] Dwight Macdonald concluded, "For the first time since Eisenstein, we have here a cinematic intelligence so quick, so subtle, so original, so at once passionate and sophisticated that he can be compared with Joyce, with Picasso, with Berg and Bartok and Stravinsky."[27]

Resnais's editing style received the most attention. Describing the beginning of the film as "one of the most remarkable opening sequences in film history," Robert Hatch commented: "The film opens with a close-up of two nude bodies entwined. The woman's voice keeps repeating in French, 'I have seen everything in Hiroshima'; and the man's keeps answering in French with a strong accent, 'You have seen nothing in Hiroshima.' Meanwhile, the shots of their intimacy, rendered almost reptilian by extreme close range, are repeatedly broken by details of the most appalling horror taken from the documentary records of the first atomic city."[28]

Summarizing Resnais's technique, *Time* concluded, "[W]hat is most remarkable in the picture is the director's dexterity in combining all these elements and effects. He crosscuts and flashbacks with daring and sureness. He plays words from one sequence against images from another. He dubs sounds from Hiroshima into scenes in France. He chops some episodes off with effective suddenness, and lets others run on like daydreams. And almost everything he does seems brilliantly right. Hiroshima and France, past and present, music and image and language weave together in a seamless mood that is hard to analyze and even harder to resist."[29]

Given America's involvement in the cold war, critics naturally assessed the film as a pacifist statement. Philip T. Hartung, writing in *Commonweal*, said, "I don't believe the film intends to be anti-American; it is anti-war and definitely anti–A-bomb. For my money, *Hiroshima Mon Amour* is the most provocative movie of the year; and however audiences may argue about its moral content and implications, they will agree on its technical brilliance and cinematic stature."[30] *Hiroshima* played for twenty-seven weeks at the Fine Arts and went on to win the New York Film Critics Circle award for Best Foreign Language Film of 1960. Marguerite Duras's screenplay was nominated for an Oscar.

The Love Game (*Les Jeux de l'amour*), the first New Wave comedy to reach the United States, opened on November 8, 1960, at the 68th Street Playhouse. Philippe de Broca had trained as an assistant director under Claude Chabrol and François Truffaut before becoming a director in his own right. A farce about a young couple at odds over the course of their relationship, the film starred Jean-Pierre Cassel and Geneviève Cluny. Here is how Brendan Gill summarized the plot: "The girl wishes the young man to marry her, so she can start having a family; the young man, already a fixture *chez elle*, sees no reason to modify his so convenient arrangements. . . . [H]e fights the inevitable with marvellous gusto, and the consolations of defeat have been sketched so vividly for us that we find ourselves envying him his lifelong Waterloo." He went on to say, "*The Love Game* is a triumph for its director, Philippe de Broca, who stops at nothing in the way of gags and tricks to make us laugh. It is all preposterous, all in fast, freakish fun, and we nearly always do Mr. de Broca's bidding."[31] *Time* concluded that de Broca "now emerges as the biggest comic talent of the new school of Gallic cinema. . . . [I]n Cassel he has found a richly responsive instrument to play on: a comedian who, like Chaplin or Marie Dressler, is more an actor than a performer. And through the character Cassel creates—a ludicrous but lovable mixture of Don Juan and Peter Pan—the moviemaker says something subtle and gently ironic about the character of urban youth in modern France."[32]

The Love Game made de Broca a commercial property, becoming one of the first New Wave directors to be pursued by the majors. He went on to make two more wacky sex comedies starring Cassel, *The Joker* and *The Five Day Lover*, both released in 1961. *The Joker* was released by Lopert Pictures, the art film subsidiary of United Artists, and *The Five Day Lover* by Kingsley-International, the art film subsidiary of Columbia. De Broca consolidated his reputation as the Mack Sennet of the French New Wave after teaming up with Jean-Paul Belmondo in 1962 to make *Cartouche*, a swashbuckler comedy costarring Claudia Cardinale, which led to a multiple-picture contract with United Artists the following year.

Godard's *Breathless* (*A bout de souffle*) opened at the Fine Arts on February 7, 1961. Genêt called it "the chef-d'oeuvre of the new school" and ascribed its drawing power to "the new Paris film star Jean-Paul Belmondo, whose ugly attractiveness is the latest rage—a tiptop young actor who was thrown out of the Conservatoire d'Art Dramatique because he was so remarkably ugly, they said, that he could never appear on their stage with a woman in his arms, since the audience would laugh. He jumped to fame by playing tough parts." Jean Seberg, whom Americans recognized as Otto Preminger's ill-fated discovery in *Saint Joan* (1957) and *Bonjour Tristesse* (1958), was "merely adequate," according to Genêt, "one of the pretty American girls in slacks and sweater whom you now see on the Champs selling the Paris *Herald Tribune* with the name of the paper writ large across their bosoms.[33]

Americans got their first look at Godard a week before the premiere when he visited New York to accept the New York Film Critics Circle award for *Hiroshima Mon Amour* on behalf of Alain Resnais. He was interviewed by Eugene Archer of the *New York Times*, who introduced the thirty-year-old former film critic as "the most representative director of the French 'new wave.'" When asked to describe his working methods, Godard said that while there were three stages to "film authorship"—writing, directing, and editing—"he carefully neglected to supply a complete script to his producer, his technicians or his actors, so that no one could ever be sure of what was going on." Archer went on: "'I'm lazy,' Godard explained. 'As a result, every morning before we went to work I would write the scenes for the day. Some days, we had to stop work at noon when we ran out of script.'" Godard shot his film on location in Marseilles and Paris over four weeks in late summer 1959. Directing the film, Godard "would place his photographer in a wheelchair with his camera on his lap, and then push the wheelchair himself, all the while shouting instructions to the actors at the top of his lungs," reported Archer. When it came time for the editing, Godard was "the only person who could make sense of the assorted footage" and leisurely composed his own montage and sound track, which was post-synchronized. "Despite the radical nature of M. Godard's working behavior," Archer observed, "the young man's conversation conveys a thoroughgoing professionalism." Godard concluded the interview by saying "'In *Breathless* I was out to attract attention. . . . I wanted to end the old tradition in a spectacular way, so I made a gangster film, using all the effects that were supposed to be impossible. It's a film where anything goes.'"[34]

Variety quickly noted the film's resemblance to "such past Yank pix" as *Gun Crazy, They Live by Night,* and *Rebel Without a Cause.*[35] American critics were more interested in Godard's portrait of contemporary youth. Roger Angell, writing in the *New Yorker,* saw Godard's intent as "nothing less than to make comprehensible, and therefore touching and serious, the lives of two disorderly, disconnected, nihilistic young moderns—and to do so, moreover, by seeing and hearing their unlovely world with exactly the same nervous glances and flighty inattentiveness that they themselves must rely on." Angell singled out one scene in particular: "The most important and astonishing passage in *Breathless* is a slow, incredibly protracted bedroom scene between the two lovers that is built out of pauses, non sequiturs, cigarettes, heartbreakingly intimate games, tiny cruelties, revelations, and small talk about death, automobiles, childhood, books, phonograph records, sex, and loneliness. At the end of this, we have not simply 'understood' the murderer and his girl for the self-destructive, attractive,

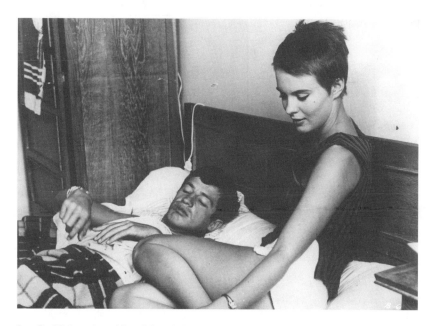

Jean-Paul Belmondo and Jean Seberg in Jean-Luc Godard's *Breathless* (1961)

and frightening narcissists that they are; we have, to a large degree, *become* them, because the scene has been allowed to continue so long that it has taken us into its own time and space." Angell concluded his review as follows: "I cannot conceive of a clearer, more intuitive delineation of the kind of icy animalism that apparently infects so many of our young and terrifies so many of the rest of us."[36]

Time called *Breathless* a "cubistic thriller" and insisted that it "has no plot in the usual sense of the word." The hero "behaves like a personification of Gide's *acte gratuit* ('an action motivated by nothing . . . born of itself'), and his story can be seen as an extemporization on the existentialist tenet that life is just one damn thing after another, and death is the thing after that. But Godard does not pose his philosophical questions very seriously; he seems chiefly concerned with developing an abstract art of cinema, in which time and space are handled as elements in a four dimensional collage." *Time* was particularly impressed with the editing. "More daringly cubistic is the manner in which Godard has assembled his footage. Every minute or so, sometimes every few seconds, he has chopped a few feet out of the film, patched it together without transition. The story can still be followed, but at each cut the film jerks ahead with a syncopated impatience that aptly suggests and stresses the compulsive pace of the hero's doomward drive. More subtly, the trick also distorts, rearranges, relativizes time—much as Picasso manipulated space in *Les Demoiselles d'Avignon*. All meaningful continuity is bewildered; the hero lives, like the animal he is, from second to second to kill. A nasty brute. Godard has sent him to hell in style."[37]

Breathless grossed $200,000 at the box office during its four-month run at the Fine Arts and went on to become Godard's biggest financial success in the United States.[38] Eugene Archer later recalled that "*Breathless* was a classic case of everything working right. Something in the chaos of the structure, the haphazard nature of its dialogue and technique, reflected the tempo of the times. Jean-Paul Belmondo immediately became the Bogart of the sixties and Jean Seberg is still coasting on her success as the uninvolved American expatriate. Outside France, the film's success was more critical than financial, but that was probably even better for Godard. *Breathless* has been extensively discussed and analyzed ever since its appeared. In film societies and revival theaters, it is an established classic."[39]

Les Liaisons Dangereuses, Roger Vadim's fourth feature film, was a modern version of the eighteenth-century classic by Choderlos de Laclos starring Gérard Philipe and Jeanne Moreau. *Variety* called the film "a glossy study of an immoral couple who get their comeuppance. A young diplomat and his wife have found a perfect harmony. He allows her to have all the affairs she wants and she helps him in his conquests. Both seem content until love comes into this completely immoral household to bring on tragedy." The love object was a virtuous young married woman played by Vadim's new wife, Annette Stroyberg Vadim, who becomes a victim of one of the diplomat's "carefully calculated seductions." *Variety* noted that the "picture has plenty of erotica with undressing cunningly suggested via carefully concealed parts of the anatomy. This makes it both exploitable and also able to pass customs nude tests."[40]

Produced in 1959, the film went on to become the greatest box-office success in France since 1954. Nevertheless, the de Gaulle government refused to grant it an export license because it presented contemporary France in an unfavorable light. As Cynthia Grenier reported, "What may have led the officials to their rather unusually severe judgment is the underlying calculated exploitations by young M. Vadim of every possible innuendo through every line of dialogue so as to produce the maximum titillation and licentious undertone. Throughout, the film reflects a kind of cold, clever, rather nasty intelligence at work."[41]

The de Gaulle government did not lift its ban on the film until the middle of 1961, nearly two years after the Paris premiere. It was subsequently snapped up by Astor Pictures as part of a buying spree that included *La Dolce Vita* and *Rocco and His Brothers*. A former Poverty Row distributor headed by Robert M. Savini, Astor originally specialized in rereleasing older films. During the 1950s Astor made it big by going into television distribution. Then, after Savini's death in 1956, it branched out into foreign film distribution under new owners. *La Dolce Vita*, *Rocco and His Brothers*, and *Les Liaisons Dangereuses* were its first foreign film acquisitions.

Astor led off with *La Dolce Vita* by releasing it as a road show at the Henry Miller in April 1961. It was a huge hit. Thinking that it had another hit on its hands, Astor released *Les Liaisons Dangereuses* as a road show at the same theater and at the close of *La Dolce Vita*'s run the following December. The New York censors allowed Vadim's film to be shown after approving a "darkened" print of two "objectionable" nude scenes. The decision came less than five hours before the premiere.[42] Although advance sales looked good, the film ran for only around a month—"an unimpressive and poorly attended run," according to *Variety*.[43] Crowther was equally disapointed by the content: "As much as the international chitchat about this updated eighteenth-century tale of bedroom shenanigans among the haute monde had led us to be prepared for something racy and appropriately informal in the line of Gallic amour, it turns out to be rather solemn, ritualistic and dispassionate display of strictly tactical maneuvers in a bored game of musical beds." Commenting on Annette Vadim's feature film debut, Crowther said, "The mood is neither brightened nor bettered by Annette Vadim in the role of the virtuous young woman. She's a sad one, without beauty, chic or charm—just another little heavy-lipped French girl with a mop of messy hair."[44]

Assessing the impact of the French New Wave on the art film market in its 1963 cover story, *Time* concluded that "the world fame of the new French cinema derives largely from the labors of two men." Resnais is "the supreme theorist and technician, the Schoenberg of the new cinema," while Truffaut is "perhaps the most richly talented," as warm as Resnais is cold. "His films are about real people with real feelings."[45] Both directors solidified their reputations in 1962 with films that are today considered landmarks of the French New Wave, Resnais with *Last Year at Marienbad* and Truffaut with *Shoot the Piano Player* and *Jules and Jim*.

Last Year at Marienbad (*L'Année dernière á Marienbad*) was released by Astor Pictures on March 7, 1962. It played to standing-room-only crowds at the tiny Carnegie Hall Cinema, which showed the film on a continuous basis. Resnais once again collaborated with an avant-garde writer—Alain Robbe-Grillet, "the Prophet of The New Dehumanism that is currently fashionable in French letters," according to *Time*.[46] *Marienbad* had been passed over by Culture Minister André Malraux to represent France at Cannes in 1961 and played outside competition during the festival. French distributors shunned the picture for being "too difficult for the average moviegoer"—that is, until it won the Golden Lion at Venice later that year and was immediately snapped up by "the Paris distributor who handled Ingmar Bergman and Michelangelo Antonioni." According to Cynthia Grenier, *Marienbad* "opened a few weeks later at the small, smart Studio Publicis on the Champs-Elysées and within days broke all attendance records for the house, well outdrawing both Antonioni and Bergman."[47]

To prepare American audiences for the movie, the *New York Times* related the simple plot to its readers shortly before the film opened: "It is set in a huge, ornate, luxurious château in front of which is a large, formal park. The château apparently is a hotel filled with many guests in formal clothes, one of whom is a woman of cameo-like beauty, identified as A. With her is a man, probably, but not positively, her husband, known as M. The triangle is completed with the introduction of a man known as X. X meets A and insists that they had an affair the previous year at Marienbad. She laughingly denies ever having met him before. But he persists and she becomes deeply disturbed. As the picture ends, A flees the château in the company of X."[48] Delphine Seyrig played The Woman, A; Giorgio Albertazzi, The Stranger, X; and Sacha Pitoëff, The Husband, M.

Bosley Crowther warned his readers to "be prepared for an experience such as you've never had from watching a film when you sit down to look at Alain Resnais' *Last Year at Marienbad*, a truly extraordinary French film. . . . It may grip you with a strange enchantment, it may twist your wits into a snarl, it may leave your mind and senses toddling vaguely in the regions in between. But this we can reasonably promise: when you stagger away from it, you will feel you have delighted in (or suffered) a unique and intense experience."[49]

What did the film mean? According to Dwight Macdonald, "Everybody seems to have a different idea of the meaning of *Marienbad*; the hotel is actually a psychiatric sanitarium; the principals are dead; X is a lunatic, he is Life come to free the sleeping beauty from her baroque prison, he is Death come to claim her at last, etc."[50] *Time* cautioned that "customers who expect to be entertained are going to be painfully disappointed. *Marienbad* is not a movie in the publicly accepted sense of the word; it is an enigma, the most monstrously elaborate enigma ever conceived in terms of cinema. As such it is not meant to be seen but to be solved. However, to Resnais' riddle there is not, *hélas*, just one solution; there is an infinite series of solutions and some of them suppose an esthetic, metaphysical, and even mathematical sophistication that few in any audience possess."[51]

Time went on to say that Resnais "has instigated an Einsteinian revolution of cinema. He applies the principle of relativity to the art of film, as Picasso applied it to painting and Schoenberg to music. The result is true cubistic cinema in which reality is 'dismantled,' as Resnais puts it, and reassembled in such a way that it seems to be experienced in every aspect simultaneously—one French critic describes the result as 'total cinema.'" The review concluded sarcastically: "There is one trick that Director Resnais, with all his perspicacity, has failed to bring off; the trick of holding the spectator's attention. Watching this movie is like listening to 93 consecutive minutes of twelve-tone music; the effort exhausts, what is at first hypnotic at last is soporific."[52] Stanley Kauffmann agreed with this assessment, concluding that "the technique becomes the end instead of the means. We find ourselves saying, 'Yes, that is remarkably like the way the conscious and subconscious gambol and struggle with each other,' but of the effect of that gambol and struggle, we feel little."[53]

Truffaut's *Jules and Jim* (*Jules et Jim*) was released by Janus Films and opened at the Guild on April 23, 1962. *Jules and Jim* was Truffaut's third feature film. *Shoot the Piano Player*, his second, failed at the box office in France and was passed over initially by American distributors. According to Richard Neupert, "*Shoot the Piano Player*'s loose, rather convoluted story was accompanied with a quirky, uneven, almost tongue-in-cheek style that left many reviewers

Oskar Werner and Jeanne Moreau in François Truffaut's *Jules and Jim* (1962)

puzzled. . . . Its first run in Paris only sold 70,000 tickets, as opposed to the 260,000 for *The 400 Blows*."[54]

Jules and Jim, which *Time* described as "a near-perfect evocation of Montparnassian *fin de siècle* life, informed with psychological observations of the 60s," showed immediate commercial potential. Based on Henri-Pierre Rouché's semiautobiographical novel about a ménage à trois, *Jules and Jim* starred Jeanne Moreau, Oskar Werner, and Henri Serre. Both the *Time* reviewer and Brendan Gill in the *New Yorker* gave the film rave reviews, which Janus reprinted in their entirety in subsequent ads. Gill's review was the more effusive: "I'm so taken with the beauty and novelty and wit and loving high spirits of François Truffaut's *Jules and Jim* that I scarcely know where to begin."[55] *Time*'s reviewer was more to the point: "*Jules and Jim* . . . is one of the most exciting and likeable films so far produced by the new French school of cinema. . . . The performances are superb. The leading men range with ease from piffle to pathos, and Actress Moreau, who has too long been typed as a gamine Garbo, reveals a pretty capacity to clown. Moreover, the sunny-moony musical score by Georges Delerue is enchanting. The technical effects are formidable. Truffaut employs a hundred subtle tricks of the editor's trade—rapid shifts of image, sudden changes in screen size—to surprise the eye. But in Truffaut's work technique matters less than feeling. His feeling is spontaneous, sincere, generous, naive, natural. It bubbles up like the spring of life itself. A spectator who sits down to this picture feeling old and dry will rise up feeling young and green."[56]

After *Jules and Jim*, the critics became increasingly hostile toward the French New Wave. *Shoot the Piano Player* (*Tirez sur le pianiste*) was released by Astor Pictures on the heels of *Jules and Jim*. The film, which starred Charles Aznavour, was criticized by *Time* for its mixture of styles, being "both a sly, imitative tribute to the Warner Bros. shoot-em-ups of the 30s [and] the existential drama of a man who can no longer respond to life."[57] Crowther's response was even more dismissive: "It looks, from where we are sitting, as though M. Truffaut went haywire in this film. . . . It looks as though he had so many ideas for movie outpouring in his head, so many odd slants on comedy and drama and sheer cliches that he wanted to express, that he couldn't quite control his material. . . . Else why would he switch so abruptly from desperately serious scenes and moods to bits of irrelevant nonsense or blatant caricature?"[58] *Shoot the Piano Player* did not do well in the United States either. It grossed only about one fourth the box office of *The 400 Blows* during the New York first run.

The backlash against the French New Wave increased with the release of Agnès Varda's *Cleo from 5 to 7* (*Cléo de 5 à 7*) in September 1962. Varda's first feature was acquired by Zenith International and came to the United States showered by praise from "some of France's most famous women, from Mme. Simone de Beauvoir to Brigitte Bardot" for its precise detailing "the minute by minute existence of a young woman waiting to learn whether or not she has cancer."[59] Crowther saw the film as "another example of a New Wave picture in which the drama is drowned in a bath of style."[60] Stanley Kauffmann agreed: "The pat shape of the story, its very cleverness, the shallowness of its emotional exploration, the heroine's self-conscious dramatization, make it merely a flashily dressed-up conventional tear jerker, a sob sister of the works of Fannie Hurst. The avant-garde trappings disguise nothing; it is Irving Berlin orchestrated by Stravinsky."[61]

Commenting on Corinne Marchand's performance as Cléo, *Time* said that "the film intends to show . . . 'a profound transformation of the being.' It doesn't. For one thing, Actress Marchand's face is no more capable of transformation than a kewpie doll's. For another, Director Varda suddenly twists the heroine's harm into a happy ending which sentimentally suggests that every shroud has a silver lining."[62] Other reviews were equally harsh. *Cléo* brought in only $22,000 in the five weeks of its first run.[63]

Serge Bourguignon's *Sundays and Cybèle* (*Les Dimanches de Ville d'Avray*), the winner of the 1962 Oscar for Best Foreign Language Film, also felt the backlash. Davis-Royal (Columbia's art film subsidiary) acquired the film even before

it opened in Paris and released it at the Fine Arts on November 12, 1962—
apparently in an effort to capitalize on the recent notoriety of Stanley Kubrick's
Lolita. Based on Bernard Eschassériaux's novel *Les Dimanches de Ville d'Avray*, the
film told a "wondrous story of a magical attachment between a crash-injured
young man who is suffering from amnesia and a lonely little 12-year-old girl."
Crowther considered it a masterpiece, "made by a poet and angled to be a
rhapsodic song of innocence and not a smirking joke," like *Lolita*.[64] Nevertheless, *Sundays and Cybèle* did not perform as expected at the box office. Hollis
Alpert offered the following explanation: "Flotsam from the New Wave has
reached our shores, none of it very stimulating. Serge Bourguignon almost suc-
ceeds for 110 minutes in obscuring a story that could have been told simply and
clearly in a half-hour. A war victim of amnesia creates a fantasy world (and a
very dull one) with a twelve-year-old girl, and is eventually shot down for fear
he will harm the child. Turns out he would have. The unpleasant little tale is
made more so by consciously arty and difficult camera work that comes out
only tricky and empty."[65]

By 1962 the steam had long gone out of the French New Wave as a production trend. Paris became glutted with unreleased pictures as more and more in-
experienced young filmmakers were hopping on the New Wave bandwagon.
Increased opportunities for financing and more channels for production resulted in the inevitable glut of unsuccessful New Wave productions as early as
1961. French producers and distributors subsequently became wary of the New
Wave label, making it extremely difficult for a new director to get his or her first
film into production. Parisian movie tastes were changing as well. The top
money earners in 1961–62 were "broad, rather old-fashioned comedies," the
likes of *La Belle Américaine* and *La Guerre des Boutons* (*The Button War*), noted Cynthia Grenier. "Brigitte Bardot, Jean Gabin, Jean-Paul Belmondo, Jeanne Moreau, Alain Resnais and François Truffaut, with all their glitter and talent, were
not able to bring out the Paris public . . . the way these low-budget films with no
star personalities did."[66] Changing audience tastes and a steady decline in
ticket sales had created a crisis in the industry. Only the authentic film talents of
the New Wave survived, and for some, as we shall see, survival depended on
Hollywood.

The biggest art house hit from France in 1962 was Pierre-Dominique
Gaisseau's *The Sky Above—The Mud Below* (*Le Ciel et la boue*), the Oscar-winning
color documentary, made in 1959, about a French expedition that traversed
Dutch New Guinea from south to north through "largely uncharted jungle,
replete with such obstacles as tricky rivers and head-hunting primitives."[67]
Released by Embassy Pictures with an English voice-over narration, the film

grossed over $1 million in rentals. No New Wave film came close to that figure in the United States until the release of Jacques Demy's *The Umbrellas of Cherbourg (Les Parapluies de Cherbourg)*, the winner of the Golden Palm at Cannes in 1964. An oddball musical with a Michel Legrand score in which all the words are sung, the film starred a twenty-one-year-old Catherine Deneuve in her first major role. *Umbrellas* was released by the Landau Releasing Organization in time for the holidays. Deneuve and Legrand were brought over from Paris to help launch the film. Brendan Gill began his review in the *New Yorker* by saying, "Cain, Herod, Tamerlane, Lady Macbeth—I've been trying in vain to think of someone whose heart would be flinty enough to resist the manifold seductions of *The Umbrellas of Cherbourg*."[68]

Many did. In fact, *Umbrellas* confirmed most critics' low opinion of the New Wave. Crowther said, "A cinematic confection so shiny and sleek and sugar-sweet—so studiously sentimental—it comes suspiciously close to a spoof. . . . Seldom in my recollection has a French moviemaker indulged in such a flow of romantic contrivance and sheer decorative artifice as does Mr. Demy in this picture. . . . Not only has he resurrected the quaint and artificial device of having the dialogue set to music and unrealistically sung, but he uses this operatic method to tell a story that is so banal—so clearly ingenuous and old fashioned that it wouldn't get beyond a reader in Hollywood."[69] Hollis Alpert complained that "people tell me I am supposed to like and appreciate [*Umbrellas*] otherwise I'm a clod lacking in the necessary sensitivity to respond to those marvelous dabs of color . . . the Michel Legrand musical score . . . and the exquisite banality of the plot. Words seem to fail those who like it, because, you see, words can't explain the ineffable charm. . . . I must confess it left me cold, a little bored, and rather annoyed at those who claim it to be an important film."[70] Audiences sided with Brendan Gill. *Umbrellas* ran for nearly six months at the Little Carnegie and then went on to play another ten months in other theaters around town. It also did well outside New York.

The Case of Jean-Luc Godard

Jean-Luc Godard, the most prolific and influential director of the French New Wave, requires individual consideration. By 1964, three years after the release of *Breathless* in the United States, his status as an auteur was secure. Eugene Archer in the *New York Times* said, "Everyone knows about the avant garde in the other arts. In painting, it is Roy Lichtenstein. In drama, it is Ionesco. In fiction, Alain Robbe-Grillet. In music, John Cage. When it comes to movies, the clear leader is a dark-glassed, ascetic featured, wild-haired bundle of temperament named Jean-Luc Godard. Godard fills every avant garde requirement almost too well. His films are eccentric, irritating, rebellious, intellectual, original and totally personal. They are invariably uncommercial. Every film he has made ended in a war with producers, distributors, financiers, stars or the press. . . . He is the center of a widespread cult of film buffs, who consider him the very last word."[71]

Godard made films at a dizzying rate during the 1960s, yet he had difficulty securing satisfactory distribution for his films in the United States. His films arrived in no particular order and were handled by different distributors. As a result, audiences and critics alike were inadequately prepared to appreciate Godard's experimental style. He attempted to solve his distribution problems by linking up with Columbia Pictures in 1963. In the interval between *Breathless* and his first Columbia release, three Godard films reached the United States: *My Life to Live* in 1963 and *A Woman Is a Woman* and *Contempt* in 1964. They were his fourth, third, and sixth productions and were released by Union Films, Pathé Contemporary, and Embassy Pictures, respectively.

The critical reception was overwhelmingly negative. It was not so much that the critics did not recognize Godard's experimental style but rather that they abhorred it. *My Life to Live* (*Vivra sa vie*) opened at the Paris on September 23, 1963. It starred Anna Karina, Godard's new wife, who played Nana, a young Parisian who drifts into a life of prostitution to pay the bills. Noting that the film departed from the "more or less conventional approach" of *Breathless*, Crowther described it as "a simulated documentary film recounting in episodic sections the decline and fall of a pretty shallow girl." Since she "never emerges as much more than an amiable, stupid, helpless thing preyed upon by a standard procurer," the cumulative effect of the film's episodic structure remains "tedious."[72]

Crowther was not alone in his preference for story over style. It seemed that the critics did not want to be confronted with this type of product. Stanley Kauffmann praised *Breathless* as "one of the best films of the new French group" but described *My Life to Live* as "empty and pretentious. Much arty apparatus has been employed in it, but it only emphasizes the absence of content. . . . His picture is only a collection of stylistic devices, without characterization, without credible motivation, without even the pathos of a believable puppet at the mercy of believable, mindless evil."[73] Only *Time* had positive things to say about the film: "*My Life* is a tour de style almost as startling as *Breathless* but more subtly accomplished, more purely felt. It is also a lyric poem in which the camera assiduously adores a beautiful woman. It is finally the tragic allegory of a soul whose pilgrimage to grace goes spiraling ecstatically down the drain."[74]

A Woman Is a Woman (*Une Femme est une femme*) also starred Anna Karina. Produced in 1961, it garnered two top awards at the Berlin Film Festival, a Special Jury Prize for Godard and the Best Actress award for Miss Karina. Nevertheless it languished for three years before it was picked up for distribution by Pathé Contemporary—and the latter had agreed to acquire it only after it was chosen to premiere at the 1964 New York Film Festival on a double bill with Godard's *Band of Outsiders*. The festival's program notes called *A Woman Is a Woman* "Godard's wackiest film" and described the plot in Godard's own words: "A young stripteaser wants a child. Her boyfriend doesn't; he prefers motorcycles. So she asks another young man to oblige. He does." The program notes continued: "Largely improvised, yet shot in Scope and color, the film is pure delight. Partly musical-comedy, mostly just plain comedy, its freshness and excitement cannot fail to charm—as long as you don't expect it to be logical or tidy."[75]

Pathé Contemporary released the film commercially at the Murray Hill in November 1964 and reprinted Eugene Archer's favorable review of the festival presentation in its opening-day ad, which said, "The film has enormous charm, particularly when the characters interrupt the action to imitate actors in a Stanley Donen musical, but it has serious undercurrents. . . . The direction and playing have a youthful exuberance that lend a fresh spontaneity even to the film's excesses."[76]

Time described the film as "an unabashed display of cinematic bravura," adding, "Godard has brought off a flashy little showpiece so full of daring artifice and visual horseplay that it cannot fail to divide viewers into two camps: those who find its excesses unforgivable v. those who find its successes unbeatable."[77] In the former camp, Stanley Kauffmann remarked, "What we have here is a torpid and clumsy picture whose spirit and lightness do not compare with what some other directors have given us while telling a cohesive, well-constructed story. . . . Godard is a magician who makes elaborate uninspired gestures and then pulls out of the hat precisely nothing."[78] In the latter camp, Andrew Sarris commented, "What impresses me most in *Woman* today is not its inventiveness but its intelligence. Too much stress has been placed on Godard's innovations and not enough on his insights. . . . *Woman* is a documentary not merely of Karina but of the sheer otherness of all women. Not since the most tortured days of Sternberg and Dietrich has the female principle been expressed so triumphantly. Far from representing form over content (whatever that means), *Woman* employs all the resources of the cinema to express the exquisite agony of heterosexual love. This is the enchantment of *Women* [*sic*], not the 'inside' jokes."[79]

Brigitte Bardot, Jack Palance, and Georgia Moll in Jean-Luc Godard's *Contempt* (1964)

Critics were at their most obdurate when reviewing *Contempt* (*Le Mépris*). Financed by Carlo Ponti and Joseph E. Levine, the film boasted an international cast comprising Brigitte Bardot, Jack Palance, Michel Piccoli, and Fritz Lang. Godard based his film on the novel by Alberto Moravia and shot it in color and CinemaScope. Godard made the film as he pleased, but, as Sarris explained, "Once *Contempt* was completed, Levine was shocked to discover that he had a million-dollar art film on his hands with no publicity pegs on which to hang his carpetbag. Levine ordered Godard to add some nude scenes, then challenged the New York censors like the great civil libertarian he is, and finally released the film with a publicity campaign worthy of *The Orgy at Lil's Place*. The New York reviewers, ever sensitive to the nuances of press agentry, opened fire on Brigitte Bardot's backside."[80]

Contempt was released by Levine's Embassy Pictures and opened at the Lincoln Art on December 18, 1964, just two days after *The Umbrellas of Cherbourg* opened at the Little Carnegie down the block. After pointing out that *Contempt* "boasts Brigitte Bardot displaying her famous figure in the nude in a number of scenes," Crowther treated the film as a failed domestic melodrama: "It appears he is aiming to tell us why a young French woman grows to hate her loving husband who is making a lot of money as a movie scriptwriter in Italy." Crowther then faulted Godard for failing to "make us understand why the wife in her drama suddenly tells her husband she has contempt for him and decides to leave. Has she lost faith in him? Is she bored? Or is she just fed up with watching him wearing his hat all the time? Evidently, Mr. Godard has attempted to make this film communicate a sense of the alienation of individuals in this complex modern world."[81]

Brendan Gill disliked Godard's improvisatory style: "The screenplay is credited to Mr. Godard, but I doubt whether an actual script could be found; never have I seen a picture that seemed more surely to have been made up as it went along, and while the backgrounds are beguiling . . . what fails to happen in the foreground soon makes one's mind numb with boredom. . . . Miss Bardot has never been so naked or so beautiful in nakedness, but since Mr. Godard has chosen to treat her as an object, alive and lovely but subhuman, the not unimportant matter of her attempting to portray a character doesn't arise."[82] Even *Time* abandoned Godard, calling *Contempt* "doodling disguised as art. . . . In this inflated drama of marital disintegration . . . spontaneity looks more like slackness. *Contempt* subjects Godard's staunchest admirers to a loyalty test that precious few will pass."[83] After a run of about three weeks, Lincoln Art replaced *Contempt* with the new French comedy *Thank Heaven for Small Favors*.

Godard's experience with producers Joseph E. Levine and Carlo Ponti in an international coproduction with a big-name star drove him into the arms of Columbia Pictures. With steady financing and distribution assured, Godard formed his own production company, Anouchka Films, in the hope of a more sympathetic reception.

Angry Young Men:
British New Cinema

For most of the 1950s, wrote Vincent Canby, "the British seem to have relied almost solely on bright, sophisticated comedy, supplemented by an occasionally brittle whodunit or two, to tap the U.S. market. Now they are shipping us, along with Alec Guinness, Peter Sellers, and Terry Thomas, that sort of frankly probing adult drama which could not be manufactured here under existing Production Code rules."[1] Canby was referring to the latest British New Cinema hit, Karel Reisz's *Saturday Night and Sunday Morning*, which starred Albert Finney. It was not the first such British import. The first was Jack Clayton's *Room at the Top*, which opened at the Fine Arts on March 30, 1959. It was followed by Tony Richardson's *Look Back in Anger* in September—just as the first batch of French New Wave films were about to arrive. Although *Saturday Night and Sunday Morning* did not arrive until April 1961, it ushered in a new production trend that included Richardson's *A Taste of Honey* and *The Loneliness of the Long Distance Runner* in 1962 and Bryan Forbes's *The L-Shaped Room*, Lindsay Anderson's *This Sporting Life*, and John Schlesinger's *Billy Liar* in 1963.

The British New Cinema grew out of the Free Cinema documentary movement, the Angry Young Men writers, and the English Stage Company. Founded in 1956 by journal-based film critics Lindsay Anderson, Tony Richardson, and Karel Reisz, the Free Cinema movement got its name from a series of short documentary programs presented at London's National Film Theatre between 1956 and 1959. Supported in part by the British Film Institute, which offered modest grants to aspiring filmmakers, the young critics started out making short documentaries about "ordinary people" at work and play in "modern cities, with their jazz clubs, night life, seaside resorts, factories, and markets."[2]

Lindsay Anderson articulated the aspirations of the group in an article for *Variety* written after a visit to Cannes in 1958. Anderson complained to reporter Gene Moskowitz that "conventionalism and pussyfooting in treating pressing problems of the day" are the main faults of British cinema. "Other countries are making timely films, but not Britain. Producers hide behind tired cycles of folksy comedies and public school–type heroic war films. The social and political changes in Britain [since 1945] have rarely been pictured." Anderson was convinced that the time was right to introduce films in England with both social commentary and viable box office potential. Moreover, he was "convinced, by noting the great advances of other countries, that the two can be correlated and must soon be in Britain if the English film is not to disappear altogether."[3]

Moving into feature films, British New Cinema directors adapted the novels and plays of a new generation of writers dubbed "Angry Young Men" by the media. The group comprised "working-class" writers like John Braine, John Osborne, Alan Sillitoe, and David Storey, among others. Distant cousins of America's Beat Generation writers, these novelists and playwrights spoke "for a large group that hitherto had virtually no voice of its own—the so-called 'working-class intellectuals,' men who had been given new teeth and a free education and nowhere to go."[4] Disaffected by the British welfare state, complacency in the arts, and "the clichés and vested power of upper middle-class values and culture," these writers set out to destabilize the status quo, to militate against any and all institutions of the new welfare state.[5]

A defining event of the British New Cinema was the premiere of John Osborne's play *Look Back in Anger* on May 8, 1956. Osborne's bitter attack on the British establishment "marked a watershed in the history of modern drama," according to British theater historian Martin Esslin, who described the premiere: "The opening night audience was shocked by the new tone, the colloquialism of the language and the violence of the leading character. Never before had one heard the hero of a play in an English theater rant against womankind in such an ungentlemanly manner. . . . Within the space of a minute every language taboo of the English stage was flouted. And more than that: a vulgar, ungentlemanly type, representative of the really disrespectful stratum of the population—outside even the confines of the well-behaved, lower middle class or the working class—had been put in the center of the stage. This Jimmy Porter was the spokesman of a new class, a new language and, above all, a new generation."[6] Directed by Tony Richardson, an Oxford University graduate who began his career in 1953 as a television director for the BBC, the play ran for 252 performances in London and another 408 on Broadway. It was produced by the English Stage Company, which Richardson managed with actor-director George Devine.

The notoriety and profits from the London and Broadway runs enabled Richardson and Osborne to form Woodfall Films in 1958, which became the principal sponsor of the British New Cinema. From the start Richardson and Osborne agreed that all Woodfall films would adhere to the same aesthetic and production principles that had been identified with both the Angry Young Men and Free Cinema movements: "realistic" films that dealt with subjects and themes than had not previously been seen in the British cinema, within a production context that placed artistic control in the hands of creative personnel. The new look of these films would be "the streets, the factories and towns, houses and backyards of grim, modern, industrialized England."[7]

The type of film Woodfall intended to produce required a new breed of actor. Clive Barnes described the latter as "rougher, tougher, fiercer, angrier and more passionately articulate than their well-groomed predecessors. . . . No longer from the playing fields of Eton, they have swarmed up from the local grade schools. No longer speaking the 'how-now-brown-cow' tones of B.B.C. refinement, they usually boast of a rich assortment of provincial accents. . . . They are radicals—not so much in a political as an emotional sense. The parts they play, the image they present is frequently iconoclastic. Their personalities erupt rather than emerge and they are, to a greater or lessor extent, against authority. Their popularity . . . is given an added fillip by their representing some ethos of the time."[8] The new actors that came to the fore included Albert Finney, Alan Bates, Richard Harris, and Tom Courtenay.

Continental Distributing, the art film subsidiary of the Walter Reade theater chain, was the main distributor of these films. Walter Reade Jr., the head of the company, acquired the pictures by putting up partial financing in return for U.S. distribution rights. (Unless otherwise noted, the films discussed in this chapter were released by Continental.) Reade faced the daunting task of finding a constant stream of suitable films for his art houses. Investing in the British New Cinema had certain advantages. For one thing, the films did not require English subtitles. For another, given the fact that these writers were familiar to many art house patrons, the films would have name recognition. Lastly, the adult subject matter and conventional plot structure made them easy sells to theaters, including commercial houses.

Romulus's Entry

Jack Clayton's *Room at the Top*, the movie that introduced the British New Cinema to the United States, was, to quote Alexander Walker, the "first important [British] film to have as its hero a youth from the post-war working class." Oddly, the film did not originate with Woodfall but rather with John and James Woolf, brothers whose London-based company, Romulus Films, produced *The African Queen*, *Moulin Rouge*, and other critically acclaimed Anglo-American films during the early 1950s that were "successfully geared to the international box office." The brothers "had no connection to Woodfall or the Free Cinema movement," according to Walker; they simply were quicker to take advantage of what they perceived as a new trend in the contemporary British literary scene.[9]

Room at the Top was adapted by Neil Paterson from John Braine's first novel about Joe Lampton, "a young man of extremely humble background, who cynically and cruelly plots his way to wealth and position." It starred Laurence Harvey as "the opportunistic youth" and France's Simone Signoret as "an older woman whom he loves but abandons to marry an heiress."[10] Jack Clayton had previously directed only one short film, *The Bespoke Overcoat*, which won an award at the Venice Film Festival. *Room at the Top* had broken box office records in England and was Britain's entry for the 1959 Cannes Film Festival. "One reason why British have gone potty over *Room*," said *Newsweek*, "is that it is the first top-drawer British pic in a long time which presents English life as it is lived today rather than during England's finest hour or back in medieval times. . . . England enters the realm of topical films of social significance. It is an estimable debut."[11]

American critics also went "potty" over the film. Writing in the *New York Times*, A. H. Weiler said, "The cynical, disenchanted and footloose post-war youths of England, who justifiably have been termed 'angry,' never have been put into sharper focus than in *Room at the Top*. The British-made import . . . glaringly spotlights them in a disk of illumination that reveals genuine drama and passion, truth as well as corruption. Although it takes place 3,000 miles away, it is as close to home as a shattered dream, a broken love affair or a man seeking to make life more rewarding in an uneasy world." In contrast to Osborne's hero, who "merely shouted . . . fiery protests against class distinctions and other contemporary English inequities," noted Weiler, Braine's hero was a multidimensional figure, "a type of schemer . . . born to poverty in a North Country manufacturing town but determined to catapult himself out of a world he never made or wanted. . . . Joe is a calculating, shrewd and realistic campaigner,

Laurence Harvey and Simone Signoret in Jack Clayton's *Room at the Top* (1959)

yearning for wealth and the opportunity to rid himself of low-caste stigma through marriage with the heiress to a great fortune." Lampton pays for his acquisition of wealth and status when he is forced to reject the "touchingly wise married woman" with whom he has fallen in love. The resulting portrait is of a "man in whom all conscience has not been killed. He is a hero without medals and one mourning defeat when he should be enjoying victory."[12]

Stanley Kauffmann and others were quick to note that the climb-to-the-top structure of the film was old hat and could be found in novels, plays, and films going all the way back to Stendahl's *The Red and the Black*. According to Kauffmann, "*Room at the Top* is basically no more contemporary a story than *Tono-Bungay*." Nor did he feel that Joe Lampton was the best example of "the Angries' quandary: that of the Red Brick University graduate struggling in a society where he is educated above his class origins and further frustrated in a small country that lacks sufficient opportunities for an increasing number of overeducated young men. Joe is neither 'overeducated' nor democratic. He is an adventurer who yearns for power, not equality, and he has before him the example of his future father-in-law—a Yorkshireman married to a Mayfair type." Nevertheless, "as a drama of human drives and torments told with maturity and penetration, it is a rare event among English-language films."[13]

Arthur Knight admired the film because it avoided the conventional moralizing usually associated with the Production Code. *Room at the Top* "is bound to revise our concept of what that word [adult means] as applied to the screen. Not because it uses most of the four- and many of the five-letter words that adorn contemporary literature, although this has something to do with it. But more importantly, because it incorporates the point of view, the frankness, above all the veracity of the contemporary novel. There has been no attempt to 'lick' John Braine's acrid book to conform to movie-morality. Its characters swear, curse, connive, commit adultery like recognizable (and not altogether unlikable) human beings. And the effect is startling. One feels that a whole new chapter is about to be written in motion picture history."[14]

Assessing the acting, Stanley Kauffmann said, "Those who have seen Laurence Harvey may not credit that he gives, as Joe, a performance of subtlety and color, springing from inner resources one would not have suspected in him and, in any event, would not have believed he knew how to use. Equipped with a Midlands accent, Harvey fuses persuasively his feelings of revenge for centuries of peasantry behind him, for personal slights suffered, and the discovery in himself of emotional reaches that make his calculated victory hollow." As the older woman, "Miss Signoret is so heart-breakingly effective in the role that it is inconceivable without her. . . . Clayton has got from her a rich, sophisticated performance, saturated with the musk of femininity—a fatalistic sexual pilgrim's progress from attraction to passionate love to death."[15]

Pauline Kael noted that *Room at the Top* "helped bring adults back into movie houses. This was partly because of the superb love scenes, and partly, no doubt, because of the unusually blunt dialogue."[16] After a run of thirty-three weeks at the Fine Arts, the film went on to become one of "few to break the foreign production barrier in the U.S. by landing a whole batch of playdates in commercial, bigger capacity first-runs," reported *Variety*.[17] It grossed $1.6 million in rentals in 1959 and another $1 million in 1960. Simone Signoret won an Oscar for Best Actress and Neil Paterson for Best Writing (Adapted Screenplay).

The Woodfall Films

Look Back in Anger, Woodfall's entry into the British New Cinema, marked Tony Richardson's feature film debut. It starred Richard Burton as Jimmy Porter, the role he originated on the London stage, and Mary Ure as his wife, Alison, a role she played in London and New York. Burton's presence in the film required Woodfall to seek an additional source of financing, which Warner Bros. put up in return for U.S. distribution rights. Expecting to attract a crossover audience,

Warner launched the film with little fanfare on September 15, 1959, at the Forum, a Times Square house, and at Walter Reade's Baronet, on Manhattan's East Side.

Despite the presence of Burton in the cast and the "pre-sold" quality of the controversial play, *Look Back in Anger* received a uniformly hostile reception. American film critics just could not understand exactly what or who Jimmy Porter was ranting against.[18] *Variety*, which had first crack at the film, said it "concerns an ex-college student who runs a confectionary push-cart in a market, plays trumpet and goes out of his way to humiliate his wife and friends. His wife leaves him and he has an affair with her best friend. The girl leave him and he snuggles up again with his wife after she has lost their baby." *Variety* then went on to say, "Somewhere along the line the film has lost its way. Jimmy Porter . . . is an angry young man but there are few indications of why he is angry or for what he is striving. He emerges as a selfish, incredibly rude, almost psychopathic [*sic*] who hardly ever sparks off a mood that engenders pity or understanding."[19]

Bosley Crowther characterized Burton's character as "a conventional weakling, a routine crybaby who cannot quite cope with the problems of a tough environment and, so, vents his spleen in nasty words." Crowther noted the "hard, crisp documentary" look of the film and how the "dismal atmosphere" and the "prevalence of social stagnation" might explain why "our young man" is frustrated. In the end, Crowther faulted *Look Back in Anger* for having no program and no solution to Jimmy Porter's problem. His rebellion is "blind and irrational."[20]

Time agreed: "On the screen [Osborne's play] suffers from imprecision: as Jimmy's troubles fester, Playwright Osborne never seems to know quite where to probe for the core of the boil, often strikes wildly at life itself, implicitly blaming society and government for failings that could only originate in the soul. *Look Back in Anger* might have been a sounder achievement if Jimmy were just healthy enough to arouse more fear, less pity." He needs not an audience but a "a doctor, for he looks back not so much in anger as in madness."[21]

Room at the Top was still running strong at the Fine Arts. In a follow-up piece, Crowther took stock of the first two British New Cinema entries. Crowther saw nothing really new in the "Angry Young Men" as dramatic characters. "The snarling young hero" in *Look Back in Anger* "is really not very much different from an old-fashioned ranter at fate who is the way he is because he hasn't got the gumption to face up to things. He may be the victim of a troubled childhood, of his environment, of any number of things. But he was with us long before the new expression was conveniently applied to him." Nevertheless Crowther thought it remarkable that the directors of both *Look Back in Anger* and *Room at the Top* "had never before these pictures directed a feature-length film. . . . This strikes us as vastly significant and much to be considered by the producers of American movies who are worrying about the future of the screen. For here are two vivid demonstrations of power being put into films largely through the exercise of vigor and freedom in directorial hands. It is notable that both of these pictures have a clear, hard, naturalistic look and are conspicuously uncluttered with familiar compositional and editing clichés. . . . The coincidence of these two pictures . . . with the rise of a group of young directors labeled the 'new wave' in France . . . shocks one into a realization that we have really nothing to compare in the way of young directors and fresh talents in American films."[22]

Woodfall hit its stride with Karel Reisz's *Saturday Night and Sunday Morning,* which opened at the Baronet on April 3, 1961. Adapted by Alan Sillitoe from his first novel, it marked Reisz's feature film debut and introduced Albert Finney as Arthur Seaton, a "scoundrelly" Nottingham factory worker whose slogan in life was, "Don't let the bastards grind you down. That's one thing you learn. What I'm out for is a good time. All the rest is propaganda." The film was a "stupendous success" in London and made an international star of Albert Finney in his first major role.

Time ran a profile on the twenty-four-year-old Finney that heralded him as "the second Olivier." Specifically, "Like Olivier, Finney is immensely versatile But he has none of the smooth gloss of the classical acting tradition. He is relentlessly naturalistic, and his technique seldom shows on the surface." The profile implied that Finney was not that different from "the rough and un-educated Arthur Seaton, who fairly hums with the joy of doing wrong. . . . He seldom spends more than two nights in the same flat, chain-smokes, sometimes has kippers and champagne for breakfast."[23]

Finney's engaging performance made him palatable to most American re-viewers. Bosley Crowther saw Arthur Seaton as a "comforting relief from the devious, self-pitying rogues and weaklings we have seen in a lot of modern-day films." Arthur Seaton, he said, is "a tough, robust, cheeky factory worker [who] gripes about his low pay and harsh foreman and spends his Saturday nights drinking beer in the pub. Sure, he is skeptical and surly, sarcastic and rebellious toward certain things, [but] he has confidence and a quiet determination. He can stand on his two feet in this world."[24]

Stanley Kauffmann considered *Saturday Night and Sunday Morning* "one of the best of the movement . . . the only one that faces certain emotional im-plications for the present-day working class." Arthur Seaton, "is not out of Dreiser or Lawrence or John Braine, surging upward." He is "a proletarian,

Albert Finney and Rachel Roberts in Karl Reisz's *Saturday Night and Sunday Morning* (1961)

consciously trapped in his class, both exultant in and exasperated by the improvement of his lot over his dad's. Better factory conditions and full employment and the National Health Service have given him armor against poverty and the boss's threat of discharge; but he is shrewd enough to see that these benefits have sapped the dynamism of the working class, made them relatively resigned, and, in a sense, put gilded locks on the class barriers. Naturally he is not against the improvement per se; he is against the implicit attitude, on the part of both workers and bosses, that now they ought to be content with their lot."[25]

The film was deemed immoral by the Legion of Decency and received a "Condemned" rating. Arthur Seaton carries on an affair with the wife of a co-worker (Rachel Roberts) and is quite willing to help her get an abortion when he gets her pregnant. Arthur seemingly gets off easily when Roberts decides not to go through with the abortion and "resolves instead to tell her husband and face the consequences." Arthur receives a vicious beating from the husband's pals but emerges from the incident relatively unscathed.[26] However, Arthur is made to "pay" for his transgressions when he decides to settle down and get married. As Edith Oliver in the *New Yorker* described it, "Toward the end, we see him on a hilltop with his fiancée. Hooked at last, he angrily throws

Dora Bryan and Rita Tushingham in Tony Richardson's *A Taste of Honey* (1962)

a stone at a housing development and tells his girl what he thinks he has let himself in for—the life of his parents all over again, staring blankly at television every evening, 'dead from the neck up.'"[27] *Saturday Night and Sunday Morning* ran for twenty-seven weeks at the Baronet and enjoyed long runs in major cities around the country. While it did not quite measure up to *Room at the Top* at the box office, it became the second most successful British New Cinema import in the United States.[28]

Woodfall scored another hit with Tony Richardson's *A Taste of Honey*, which was based on Shelagh Delaney's hit play about a lonely teenage girl left to shift for herself in a Manchester slum by her alcoholic mother. Delaney was eighteen when she wrote it. To increase the film's chances of winning acceptance in the United States, Richardson produced the play on Broadway first. It opened at the Lyceum on October 4, 1960, and starred Joan Plowright as Jo, the teenager, and Angela Lansbury as her mother. The New York production, like its London predecessor, "drew theatregoers like flies" and won the New York Drama Critics Circle award in 1961.[29]

To play the part of Jo in the film, Richardson picked Rita Tushingham, a beginning acting student in the Liverpool Repertory Company, from among two thousand applicants. Commenting on the choice, *Variety* said, "Miss Tushingham has nothing of the conventional box office prettiness about her. She plays with no makeup, her hair is untidy, her profile completely wrong by all accepted standards, but her expressive eyes and her warm, wry smile are haunting. . . . She brings a vitality to her role which clearly suggests a new successful entry into Britain's growing stable of fresh, exciting talent."[30] Richardson chose Dora Bryan to play the mother; Paul Danquah, the "Negro sailor who loves her and leaves her—pregnant"; and Murray Melvin, Jo's shy young gay friend. Working with a budget of $350,000, Richardson collaborated with Delaney on the screenplay and shot his film on locations in the north of England. "As a result," said Hollis Alpert, "the film has turned out to be virtually the revolutionist's handbook of non-studio moviemaking. No neat, prettied-up sets, and, more important, in this case, no well-known stars of the kind that are supposed to beget, automatically, $2,000,000 worth of financing."[31]

A Taste of Honey opened at the Paris Theatre on April 30, 1962. Critics agreed that Richardson's film adaptation was even better than the Broadway play. *Time* called it "a heady pint of bitter drawn from that always-sputtering bung of discontent, the British working class. . . . In her first film script, touched up by Director Tony Richardson, the angry young ma'am displays dramatic drive, concussive humor, a barmaid's ear for dialogue, a slum kitten's shrewdness about people and motives, a melancholy flair for the poetry of wasted lives."[32] Crowther liked the film because it had no actual villains: "Not even society is blamed for the pitiful and poignant little crises that occur as it valiantly unfolds. . . . Shelagh Delaney—bless her!—does not have a trace of rancor in her." He was also glad to see that the characters "are not mean or cruel or vicious people who slatter about in the slums. . . . [U]nderneath they are mere children with hearts that yearn for reassuring affection and dispositions that take delight in childish joys." Lastly, Crowther praised "everyone who had a hand or a role in this film"—particularly Rita Tushingham, "the supple little actress who plays the sassy, spunky girl as if she were a lustrous bit of childhood wrapped in a coil of barbed wire."[33] At Cannes in 1962 Tushingham and Melvin received the Best Actress and Actor awards.

Tony Richardson's *The Loneliness of the Long Distance Runner* marked the end of Woodfall's working-class pictures. Adapted by Alan Sillitoe from his short story, the film introduced Tom Courtenay, the "latest in the modern wave of young British actors who rely on ability rather than in conventional good looks," commented *Variety*. Sillitoe's Angry Young Man is Colin Smith, a rebellious and disaffected youth from a tawdry Midlands home, who is arrested for robbery and sentenced to a Borstal reformatory. There he discovers his talent as a long distance runner and "is selected to represent the Borstal in a long distance race against a public school team. It is the ambition of the governor (Michael Redgrave) to win the cup for Borstal."[34]

The film opened at the Baronet on October 8, 1962. Losing patience with the trend, Crowther stated that the angry young man "is simply a heedless social rebel." He was particularly irked by the concluding scene: "What does this truculent youngster do when the race is run—the race for which he has so sternly, stoically and solitarily trained? He stops a hundred yards from the finish, when he is comfortably ahead, and lets all the other runners beat him. That's how defiant he is. Precisely what is proved by this conclusion that Alan Sillitoe has given to the film . . . is left to the startled viewer to analyze."[35] Richardson introduced flashbacks in the film to suggest why Colin "thumbs his nose at the system"—to no avail.

Time was more perceptive: "In the end, given the chance to win his freedom by winning a big race for the greater glory of the Guv'nor, the lad leads the way right up to the finish line—and stops. Why? Because he suddenly makes up his mind that if he has to play the game according to the rotten inhuman rules laid down by The Establishment, he would rather not play at all." Yet even this reviewer had to admit: "Unfortunately, the hero is too palpably prolier-than-thou, his case is too obviously rigged."[36]

Stanley Kauffmann attempted to place Crowther's question in an historical perspective: "The social paradox of England has been that the mother of parliaments, of Magna Carta and slave emancipation, has treated its own working class with the ruthlessness of a Russian boyar. . . . Many thousands of people still living in England have known circumstances that would make a Southern sharecropper's lot seem almost enviable." Kauffmann continued: "The 'new' English working man feels almost as frustrated and antagonistic as ever. He has an indoor toilet now, a telly, and sufficient food, but his remoteness from whatever his job, his sense of being exploited, his feeling that he has had little chance for worldly advancement or spiritual connection are virtually as strong as ever." Kauffmann disliked the film's questionable attitude—"the proletarian concept of 'them' and 'us.' Everything about 'them' is wrong and everything about 'us' is right or excusable. It is the self-pity of diluted Marxism, the assumed martyrdom that made American audiences in the thirties root for a worker-hero no matter how much of a slob he was."[37] *The Loneliness of the Long Distance Runner* ran for only six weeks at the Baronet.

The Concluding Films

The British New Cinema had run its course by 1963. Three films concluded the trend, Bryan Forbes's *The L-Shaped Room*, Lindsay Anderson's *This Sporting Life*, and John Schlesinger's *Billy Liar.* They sustained the trend through product variation. *The L-Shaped Room* contained a Hollywood star, Leslie Caron, who was known to most moviegoers as the charming gamine of *An American in Paris* and *Gigi.* The film was based on a popular novel by Lynne Reid-Banks (who had no connection to the Kitchen Sink group). Miss Caron was offcast as a young Frenchwoman in London who "has a brief affair resulting in pregnancy. Rejecting the idea of an abortion, she decides to live it out on her own. And, in the loneliness of her L-shaped room in a seedy tenement, she finds a new hope and purpose in life through meeting others who, in various ways, suffer their own loneliness and frustration," as *Variety* put it.[38] "In contrast with many of the tough films coming from Britain these days," said Crowther, *The L-Shaped Room* has "a chin-up tolerance of the Establishment AND the Kitchen Sink."

The L-Shaped Room was produced by James Woolf and released by Columbia Pictures, which sent Miss Caron on a grueling "jet-age" tour of the United States to promote it. It opened at the Fine Arts on May 27, 1963. Crowther liked the film because Miss Caron gave "a stunning, mature performance" and because the story "doesn't go in for kicking and snarling against The Misery of It All or The Powers That Be. It accepts the bedbugs and the social station. It concerns the status of the heart."[39] *Time* described the plot as "frayed from use and old age" but admitted that *The L-Shaped Room* "shrugs off these shortcomings to become a beautiful and refreshing film." The review concluded: "A larger share goes to Leslie Caron, [who] plays not a girl who 'got into trouble' but a young woman of remarkable dignity."[40]

An independent venture by producer Karel Reisz and director Lindsay Anderson, *This Sporting Life* was based on the novel by David Storey about "a Yorkshire mine worker, Frank Machin, who claws his way up from the cold loneliness of the mine shaft to the cheers and wealth of success on the rugby field." It came to the United States after having won two top honors at Cannes in 1963—the International Film Critics award and the Best Actor award for Richard Harris, the star. The film was distinctive because it borrowed a subjective editing technique from Alain Resnais to interweave the story of Frank Machin's tortured life as a rugby star with his futile attempt to win the affection of a young widow (Rachel Roberts), a woman paralyzed with grief over the death of her husband.

Weiler thought the flashbacks made the story more lucid, whereas Andrew Sarris thought they confused it: "The player-victim is hauled off to a dentist and under the ether begins remembering episodes from his past life. In a series of oppressively elliptical close-up sequences, the audience is thrust back into the beginning of a bizarre sexual conflict between the hero and his landlady, a repressed widow whose husband probably committed suicide. The only trouble with the second plot is that it has no discernible connection with the first. Two unrelated plots, one sexual and one social, would almost be a refreshing change of pace from the cliches of commitment perpetuated in the British cinema ever since the commercial breakthrough of the bedridden *Room at the Top*."[41] *Time* agreed: "The story makes more sense on paper than it does on film. Like a mirror smashed to splinters, the plot fractures into flashbacks, and the spectator spends half his time putting the pieces together. He spends the rest of the show trying to understand the principal characters."[42] *This Sporting Life* opened at the Little Carnegie on July 16, 1963. It ran for seventeen weeks but never approached the commercial success of Reisz's *Saturday Night and Sunday Morning*.

Billy Liar was released on December 16, 1963, at the Baronet, bringing the trend to a close in the United States on a different note. Based on the hit West End comedy of the same name by Keith Waterhouse and Willis Hall, it starred Tom Courtenay, a funeral parlor clerk with a vivid imagination who dreams of escaping his ignorant, provincial family and boring job by imagining himself a famous novelist, a great lover, and a benevolent dictator of a country called Ambrosia. Billy dreams of escaping to London yet lacks the courage to break out of his rut until his girlfriend, Liz, played by Julie Christie, tries to entice him to hop on a train with her bound for London. "Escaping to London is a snap,' she says. 'You just buy a ticket and get on a train—that's all you do." "In a bitter climax, laughter gives way to self-knowledge, to quiet defeat," said *Time*. "While Liz heads for London alone, Billy saunters back toward the cold but certain comforts of home—and the loyal troops of Ambrosia fall into step behind him."[43] Crowther said that the only thing that "saves this picture from being just one more of those angry-young-man British dramas—is [Billy's] fertile ability to dream, to weave fantasies of himself as various heroes accomplishing bold and glamorous deeds."[44] Having grown weary of the trend, critics probably agreed with John McCarten's assessment: "I suspect that most of us have begun to feel a certain resistance to any more studies, either comic or tragic, of the rebellious young folk currently yearning and groaning in the streets and dance halls and semidetached houses of those grim cities in the coffin-shaped industrial heart of England."[45]

The Second
Italian Renaissance

Every few years, the center of gravity of serious moviemaking shifts from one country to another. Today it is dramatically clear Italy is producing some of the most extraordinary films since that country's own postwar neorealistic movement. Three directors—Federico Fellini, Michelangelo Antonioni, and Luchino Visconti—are the leaders of this renaissance." They have taken "a hard look at the contemporary world and have returned a unanimous report of moral shipwreck." This assessment appeared in *Newsweek* and was prompted by the release, within weeks of each other, of Antonioni's *L'Avventura*, Fellini's *La Dolce Vita*, and Visconti's *Rocco and His Brothers* in New York in 1961. Comparing the Italians to France's New Wave directors, the article insisted that "these Italian critics of society are new neither to the world nor to the movies. Their heroes are adults, and they themselves are members of what has been begun to seem a vanishing breed: The rebel who is also mature."[1] At the time Fellini was forty-one, Antonioni forty-eight, and Visconti fifty-five.

All three had established reputations in Europe, but only Fellini was a familiar art house name. *L'Avventura* was Antonioni's sixth feature and the first to be shown theatrically in New York. If filmgoers had heard of Visconti, it might have been because of *Bellissima*, which had a brief run in 1953. It was described by Eugene Archer as "a bitter comedy starring Anna Magnani about an ambitious mother who tries to get her homely daughter into the movies."[2]

Fellini as Precursor

Fellini arrived on the art house scene in 1956, when three of his films—*The White Sheik*, *I Vitelloni*, and *La Strada*—were released almost back to back. They were his first solo efforts as director. Previously Fellini had worked with Roberto Rossellini on the screenplays of *Open City* and *Paisan* and had played the part of The Stranger in *The Miracle*. His international reputation as a director was established at the Venice Film Festival, which awarded the Silver Lion to *I Vitelloni* and *La Strada* two years in a row.

La Strada was acquired first. It was the initial buy of Richard Brandt's Trans-Lux Distributing, the new subsidiary of the former Trans-Lux newsreel chain, which was in the process of converting to foreign films. *La Strada* was a calculated choice; the picture had proven itself at the box office in Europe and contained two familiar Hollywood faces, Anthony Quinn as Zampano and Richard Basehart as Matto (The Fool). A veteran Hollywood character actor, Quinn was the better known, having appeared in over fifty films and winning an Oscar for Best Supporting Actor in *Viva Zapata!* in 1952. Basehart started out on Broadway, winning the New York Drama Critics Circle award in 1945 for his leading role in *The Hasty Heart*. He made a name for himself in the movies as a psychopath in Alfred Werker's *He Walked by Night*, an Eagle-Lion film noir produced in 1948. Both actors had moved to Italy in the 1950s to seek new opportunities. *La Strada* had one more thing going for it—Giulietta Masina as Gelsomina. *Variety* had reported from Venice that Miss Masina, Fellini's wife, was "one of Italy's best performers [and] easily steals show with her clownish mimicry."[3]

The White Sheik (*Lo Sceicco Bianco*), not *La Strada*, was the first Fellini film to reach the market. It was released by Janus Films in association with Mario de Vecchi, who presented the film. De Vecchi was one of the producers of *I Vitelloni*, which had also been acquired by Janus Films. It's therefore likely that de Vecchi arranged the distribution of the two films once Trans-Lux made its move.[4] *The White Sheik* opened on April 25, 1956, at the 55th Street Playhouse but died almost immediately after Crowther dismissed "the naive and farcical adventures of a honeymoon couple in Rome," played by Alberto Sordi and Brunella Bovo, as a "practice swing."[5]

La Strada opened on July 16, 1956, at the 52nd Street Trans-Lux. (The voices of the Americans were dubbed into Italian and the initial release was subtitled.) A Dino De Laurentiis–Carlo Ponti production, *La Strada* was greeted by A. H. Weiler of the *New York Times* as "a tribute both to [Fellini] and the Italian neo-realistic school of film-making." The simple story of Zampano, a brutish circus strongman, and Gelsomina, his dim-witted assistant, "is a modern picaresque parable. Like life itself, it is seemingly aimless, disjointed on occasion and full of truth and poetry. Like the principals, it wanders along a sad and sometimes comic path while accentuating man's loneliness and need for love." Weiler added that Americans might be turned off by the film since it "offers neither a happy ending so dear to the escapists nor a clear-cut and shiningly hopeful plot. Suffice it to say that his study is honest and unadorned, strikingly realistic and yet genuinely tender and compassionate. *La Strada* is a road well worth traveling."[6]

Arthur Knight described the film as "Italian Realism Refreshed," likening it to "a modern morality play, set along the fringes of our urban society." In terms of its structure, "*La Strada* has no story. Its structure, like its title, suggests the straight line of the highway, beginning at the seaside by day, ending at the seaside by night. . . . What Fellini is saying through his parable-like yet human people is the echo of John Donne's 'No man is an island.' But Fellini says it in the poetry of film—images created with the haunting clarity of a Cartier-Bresson photograph."[7]

Critics especially admired the acting. Giulietta Masina was compared favorably to the great movie pantomimists in the tradition of Chaplin, Barrault, and Marceau. Robert Hatch noted that although Anthony Quinn and Richard Basehart were familiar faces, their "work as the brute and the zany is as different from their usual screen competence as flying is from crawling on all fours. Quinn's rough mastery of his crude little show (breaking chains and a debased fragment of *commedia dell'arte*), his bull rage in the face of perplexity or new circumstances, and Basehart's inhuman agility and asexual glee are pantomime creations of [a] high order."[8] *La Strada* received the inaugural Academy Award for the Best Foreign Language Film as well as a top award from the New York Film Critics Circle. The Screen Directors Guild, in a "'vigorous protest' against the 'failure' of the Academy of Motion Picture Arts and Sciences" to consider Fellini for the best direction Oscar, established an annual award for best direction in 1957 and named Fellini the first recipient.[9]

La Strada played a full year at the Trans-Lux. Richard Brandt reported that the film had been seen by more than 290,000 persons, "who deposited nearly $390,000 at the 560-seat theatre's box office." He also reported that it was slated to play the Loew's neighborhood circuit in Greater New York in a dubbed version and was already booked in another thousand theaters around the country. Eventually Brandt hoped to get as many as five thousand bookings for the film.[10]

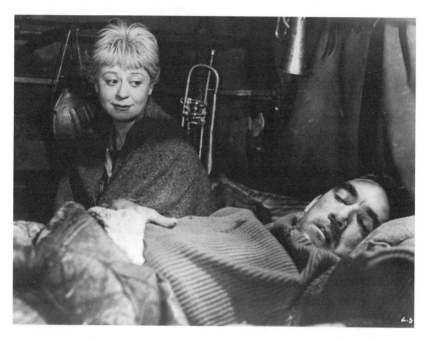

Giulietta Masina and Anthony Quinn in Federico Fellini's *La Strada* (1956)

I Vitelloni opened at the 55th Street Playhouse on October 23, 1956, four months into *La Strada*'s run. Crowther considered it a social problem film: "A presumably irritating problem in post-war Italy—that of lazy, parasitic sons of good middle-class families—is explored by Federico Fellini with a sense of its tragi-comic character." Fellini takes "a vigorous whiplash to the breed of over-grown and over-sexed young men who hang around their local poolrooms and shun work as though it were a foul disease. . . . The weakness of this picture is that it reaches a weak conventional end. The bawdy hero forsakes his infidel-ities when his wife runs away from him, and the philosophical brother pulls himself together and leaves town to find a job. It seems as though Signor Fellini simply got tired and called it off."[11]

Taking a slightly different tack, *Time* described the film as "a murderous satire" and analyzed the title as follows: "The title means 'the big calves' in Ital-ian,' but it is perhaps most idiomatically translated as 'the slobs.' The slobs in question are the sons of some middle-class families in a small city in Italy. In body they are full-grown males, but at heart they are just big bambini." *Time* went on to praise the authenticity of the film: "The nimbleness, the knowing-ness, the irony, the sharp observation of small-town life in all this has hardly been surpassed on the screen . . . It is one measure of Fellini's superiority to most of his neorealist colleagues in the Italian film industry that he does not trouble his head, or his audiences, with social problems as such; on the reactionary assumption (which horrifies his Communist critics) that societies are made up of people, Fellini simply makes pictures about people's problems."[12]

Fellini now began to receive the auteur treatment by critics. For example, a profile by Robert F. Hawkins in the *New York Times* identified Fellini as one of the "handful of Italian writers" who collaborated with Roberto Rossellini and "helped begin the Italian film renaissance with the film *Open City.*" After working "hand in hand with Rossellini for several years," Fellini struck out on his own as a director. Hawkins asserted that "Fellini's films are frankly autobiographical in many details, as if the director were bent on serializing parts of his life in his work." *I Vitelloni*, for example, "is also the story of his own life since it mirrors his restless youth in a small town, followed by his escape from his companions' routine life to the big city." Hawkins went on to specify Fellini's unique contribution: "To the neo-realist film in general, Fellini has brought a distinct new poetical note, his particular, bittersweet kind. His films are life interpreted within realistic settings, not merely mirrored, and his story developments are flights of fancy—often jarring to audiences expecting the usual." He described Fellini the man as "a tall, heavy-set adoptive Roman of 36, with a strong, expressive face, a healthy smile, an errant crop of hair, and a good-natured temper on the set." As a working artist, "Fellini has the respect of the man who has come up through the ranks. He neither wears nor affects any typical director's get-ups, or sports suspendered trousers and rolled-up sleeves. A perfectionist, Fellini often runs up a fair number of takes. He knows the effect wanted, waits for it." Nowhere in the profile did Hawkins mention Fellini's producers, Carlo Ponti and Dino De Laurentiis, who financed his two recent films, or his collaborators—screenwriters Ennio Flaiano and Tullio Pinelli, cinematographer Otello Martelli, and composer Nino Rota.[13]

Cabiria (Le Notti di Cabiria), the next Fellini film to reach the United States, was released by Lopert Pictures and opened at the Fine Arts on October 28, 1957. It starred Giulietta Masina as an "over-optimistic prostitute" who dreams that someday the ideal man will "give her true love and a wedding ring."[14] The decision to capitalize on Miss Masina's success in *La Strada* was likely made by Dino De Laurentiis, *Cabiria*'s producer. To execute it, Fellini again collaborated with screenwriters Flaiano and Pinelli, cinematographer Martelli, and composer Rota.

Miss Masina won the Best Actress award at Cannes for her performance. As a result, her name appeared over Fellini's in larger type in the ads. The attempt was to convince filmgoers that *Cabiria* was "Even Better than *La Strada!*" A cover story by Arthur Knight in the *Saturday Review* praised Fellini and his wife for transforming "a subject that is so often merely sordid into a film that glows with the affirmation of life. Like *La Strada*, *Cabiria* is deeply moving, reality shaped with an artistry rarely found in films today. But it moves with such quick humor and it ends on a note of such spiritual exaltation that one loses all sense of the fact that this is a picture about pimps, prostitutes and dope pushers. It emerges rather as a film of hope, regeneration, love and self-respect." In Knight's opinion, the picture confirmed Fellini's status as an auteur: "At thirty-six, Federico Fellini is without question Italy's greatest film artist today."[15]

Cabiria ran for three months at the Fine Arts and enjoyed an added boost after winning the Oscar for Best Foreign Language Film—the second year in a row for Fellini. However, winning the award was no great feat. *Cabiria* was the only nominee that had been released commercially in Los Angeles prior to the balloting. A rave review from Philip K. Scheuer in the *Los Angeles Times* cinched it. Scheuer described *Cabiria* as "a strange and wonderful kind of motion picture, one which transcends the sordidness of its theme to rise to a kind of reaffirmation of faith in the human spirit."[16]

The Vanguard

L'Avventura debuted at Cannes in May 1960 and caused "a ruckus," reported Cynthia Grenier. In the course of the screening, the crowd "starting hooting, whistling, and stamping during an explicitly filmed, steamy love scene that took place as the actress rolled about in the grass near some railroad tracks. Other people, deciding they understood what the director was getting at, started shouting back and *L'Avventura* ended with almost no one looking at the screen." On closing night, the awarding of a Special Jury Prize to *L'Avventura* for its "new cinematographic language and plastic beauties" was "unmercifully catcalled."[17]

L'Avventura arrived in the United States at the Beekman on April 4, 1961. It was released by Janus Films. To prepare American audiences for Antonioni's kind of cinema, it brought the director to New York for the launch. He was accompanied by Monica Vitti, the star of the film, and was "girded for battle." Antonioni began his interview with the *New York Times* by saying, "I expect a barrier of incomprehension, even hostility. But I am told that the reception of Ingmar Bergman's films, and *Hiroshima Mon Amour* may have paved the way for my kind of cinema." He then explained that "eroticism is the disease of our age . . . our method of substituting action for thought. It corresponds, in another way, to the universal trend toward adolescent violence—to the cinema's tendency toward action for its own sake, toward plot and movement in preference to ideas." Antonioni declared that "my film is a deliberate act of defiance — an attempt to demonstrate that neither plot nor dialogue is as important as the underlying motivation — the personality of the individual artist." *L'Avventura*, he said, "begins with one protagonist, Anna, a neurotic brunette who disappears on a barren Mediterranean island. Her lover, Gabriele Ferzetti [Sandro], and her best friend, Monica Vitti [Claudia], search for her, and in the process become lovers themselves. Midway through the film the blonde dons a brunette wig and subconsciously transforms herself into the vanished girl. You never find out what happens." Monica Vitti added, "That's the one question the audience isn't supposed to ask. It isn't important. What is important is that Anna was carrying two books before she disappeared — the Bible and F. Scott Fitzgerald's *Tender Is the Night*. One suggests our concern with morality — the other was a literary experiment in which the heroine disappears half way through the book and is replaced by another protagonist." Antonioni concluded: "I want the audience to work. I ask them to see the film from the beginning and devote their full attention to it, treating it with the same respect they would give a painting, a symphony, a novel or any work of art. I treat them with the same respect by inviting them to search for their own meanings, instead of insulting their intelligence with obvious explanations. When the viewer participates directly in the search, the film becomes an intellectual adventure, a mystery on many levels — for the personages, for myself, and for the audience as well."[18]

Not everyone took Antonioni's advice to heart. More than a few critics found the film little more than a shaggy-dog story. The game of analysis revolved around the question, "What happened to the missing girl?" Bosley Crowther, who apparently was in no mood for an intellectual adventure, complained, "Watching *L'Avventura* is like trying to follow a showing of a picture at which several reels have got lost. Just when it seems to be beginning to make a dramatic point or to develop a line of continuity that will crystallize into some sense, it will jump into a random situation that appears as if it might be due perhaps three reels later and never explain what has been omitted. At least, that's how it strikes us." Crowther then posed the question he wasn't suppose to ask: "What has happened to this poor young woman? Has she committed suicide? Has her lover stuffed her in a cozy crevice? Signor Antonioni never explains. He just keeps us there on that ugly island for what seems an interminable length of time while the party and police hunt for the body. Then he suddenly jumps the scene to Sicily, where the lover and another young woman in the party somehow meet on strangely disagreeable terms."[19] Edith Oliver of the *New Yorker* was equally baffled: "I had no notion what was going on."[20]

Monica Vitti and Gabriele Ferzetti in Michelangelo Antonioni's *L'Avventura* (1961)

Hollis Alpert came to Antonioni's defense. In response to the question, "What happened to the girl?" Alpert said, "No one knows, and no one—including the audience—ever finds out the answer. What Antonioni presumably considers more important is the curious relationship that develops between the fiancé and the other girl, who alternate between a search for the missing girl and the unwilling but strong passion for each other. All this takes time, much time, but if you're willing to allow Antonioni his own way, you may find yourself fascinated." Alpert went on to explain that Antonioni's vision "of his indolent characters is bleak, and this sense of bleakness is conveyed on film in what I can only call poetic terms. Noticeable is an awareness of landscape and atmosphere: the rocky barrenness of the volcanic island, the white silence of a town in Sicily, the passionless formalities and intrigues that occur in an elegant villa. All seems muted, even the emotions of the characters." Commenting on the narrative style of the film, Alpert declared, "Antonioni would . . . appear to have thrown aside usual film conventions in the development of his story; adopting instead an avant-garde novelist's approach. He is deliberately not so much undramatic as antidramatic. His people, aware enough on a superficial level, seem prisoners of deeper forces set in motion by the disappearance of the girl." Alpert concluded his review with the following advice: "Be prepared for a moody, strange film that requires from its audience an adventurous spirit, along with the willingness to recognize the fact that Antonioni is less concerned with telling a story than with communicating a personal vision, a task that is the most difficult any film director can set for himself."[21]

Stanley Kauffmann, Dwight Macdonald, and Andrew Sarris, among others, were essentially in agreement, with each adding something different to Antonioni's defense. For example, Sarris said: "Every shot and bit of business in *L'Avventura* represents calculation of the highest order. The characteristic Antonioni image consists of two or more characters within the same frame not looking at each other. They may be separated by space, mood, interest, but the point comes across, and the imposing cinematic theme of communication is brilliantly demonstrated."[22]

Variety correctly predicted that *L'Avventura* would "probably find tough box office going."[23] *L'Avventura* exasperated the New York critics and much of the public. Moreover, it was eclipsed by the arrival of *La Dolce Vita* two weeks after opening. The setback was only momentary. In January 1962 *L'Avventura* was chosen as one of the ten best films of all time by a poll of seventy international film critics conducted by the British Film Institute. A little later, Dwight Macdonald reported, "Everywhere I go people begin talking about one film — Antonioni's *L'Avventura*. Their feeling about it is intense and personal; they have discovered a movie that is unlike any other they have seen, one that comments on modern life in the intimate, subjective terms that hitherto have been found only in books. They—that isn't we—compare notes on each scene, argue about the significance of details. I know of no movie that has stimulated so much interesting talk. A kind of Antonioni underground is forming, analogous to the early devotees of Joyce and Eliot."[24]

La Dolce Vita had also played in competition at Cannes in May 1960, and it too caused a ruckus. During the screening, reported Crowther, the audience was "violently mixed in its sentiments," and when Fellini went up to receive the Golden Palm, "boos and whistles outweighed the light fusillade of conventional applause."[25]

La Dolce Vita premiered on April 19, 1961, at the Henry Miller. Announcing the upcoming release, the *New York Times* stated, "After the premiere of *La Dolce Vita* in Italy more than a year ago, one man offered his comment on the movie by spitting at its maker, Federico Fellini. Life has been stormy—and sweet—for *La Dolce Vita* ever since. Amidst the almost hysterical demands that it be banned in Italy as 'an incitement to evil, crime and vice,' it has become the greatest box-office success in the history of Italian movies. Starting soon, New Yorkers will be able to see Fellini's bold, bitter images of decadence and immorality among Rome's upper crust and judge for themselves: work of art or mere sensation."[26] Produced by Giuseppe Amato and Angelo Rizzoli at a cost of $1.6 million, *La Dolce Vita* was one of the most expensive Italian films ever made—and, as it turned out, the longest, with a running time of nearly three hours. Amato—whose producing credits included *Shoe Shine*, *The Bicycle Thief*, and *Umberto D*—took on the project when Dino De Laurentiis rejected Fellini's script as "too chaotic, depressing and realistic."[27] Amato secured the financing from Angelo Rizzoli, the Milanese industrialist and book publisher, who had his doubts but stayed with it to its completion.

La Dolce Vita was acquired by Astor Pictures, the former Poverty Row distributor that had branched out into foreign film distribution under new owners. Both *La Dolce Vita* and *Rocco and His Brothers* were its first foreign film acquisitions. To obtain the U.S. rights to the two films, Astor paid $625,000 for *Dolce*, "the highest amount that had ever been offered for a film import" and $350,000 for *Rocco*, which struck "industryites . . . as sheer folly," reported *Variety*.[28]

Astor gave *La Dolce Vita* a hard sell, presenting it as a road show in a legitimate theater, complete with reserved seats, special prices, and an intermission. By the time it opened, Astor had taken in nearly $300,000 in advance ticket sales and had lined up 162 play dates in theaters across the country.[29] The rush was likely fanned by the pre-release publicity. Take, for example, Robert Neville's article in *Harper's* a year earlier, which described *La Dolce Vita*'s "remarkable impact" in Europe. Fellini's "fresco representing life today" in Rome "contains a wide assortment of the characters of the city: playboys, priests, whores, housewives, princes, pederasts, painters, press agents, existentialist singers, lawyers, matinee idols, aristocrats. Not, on the whole, a very wholesome lot. The protagonist is a young newspaperman named Marcello, whose central beat is the café-lined Via Veneto, spawning place of scandals and haunt of what the Eternal City calls 'snobility.' He specializes, it seems, in gossip." Neville goes on to say that "*La Dolce Vita*, in effect, consists of both the events Marcello covers and the stories in which he inadvertently finds himself a participant. . . . Perhaps the most daring episode of the film is that in which a rich young nymphomaniac persuades Marcello to make love to her on a prostitute's bed. The most effective episode of the film, however, and essentially the most shocking, takes place at the free-for-all aristocrat's party in a real castle outside Rome." In effect, "The episodes put together become a sort of catalogue of the sybaritic ills that infest the society." Neville suspects that "Fellini has not had to look hard for erotic stories. Practically all his highly sexed raw material for *La Dolce Vita* has been culled directly from the front pages of newspapers of the last decade." As a final comment Neville states that *La Dolce Vita* was "the first popular film to

Marcello Mastroianni and Anita Ekberg in Federico Fellini's *La Dolce Vita* (1961)

bring pederasty out into the open. Homosexuals appear throughout the film. Obviously Fellini believed they were an integral part of the local scene, and, in fact, the film makes clear the extent to which the institution of pederasty has gained respectability during the last ten years."[30]

Bosley Crowther judged the film a work of art and gave it a rave review, claiming that it deserves "all the hurrahs and the impressive honors it has received. For this sensational representation of certain aspects of life in contemporary Rome . . . is a brilliantly graphic estimation of a whole swath of society in sad decay and, eventually, a withering commentary upon the tragedy of the over-civilized."[31]

Hollis Alpert also gave it a rave. *La Dolce Vita* "begins with a white figure of Christ being carried by helicopter over the roofs of Rome to the Vatican [and] ends with a monstrous, formless fish being stared at on the sand at Ostia. During the intervening three hours, Fellini gives us a mordant vision of contemporary decay, a swirl of corrupt pleasure in which his journalist hero eddies until he is lost in soulless emptiness. Call it an indictment, a warning if you like, but it is also the most fascinating three hours of cinema turned out in recent years, a culmination of the Italian realistic approach, the most brilliant of all movies that have attempted to portray the modern temper."[32]

Alpert was especially impressed with the acting. In particular he singled out "Anita Ekberg, hitherto not known for high acting gifts, who, as the American star, is every movie star who ever fell for Rome. She dances at a nightclub, in the ancient ruins of the baths of Caracalla, wades deliriously in the Trevi fountain, sends Marcello on a late-night search for milk for a kitten she has just found, [and] is glassily conscious of her fleshly endowments." "Most impressive of all," he said, was Marcello Mastroianni as the newspaperman, "an actor of the highest sensitivity, his face a continual mirror of feeling and comment on the material of Fellini."[33]

Dwight Macdonald's verdict was "mere sensation." "It is a sermon against upper-class corruption," he said, "but one that exploits its gamy subject matter as much as it exposes it. Our own Cecil B. De Mille was expert at this. But of course what Federico Fellini has that De Mille didn't have is an interest in human beings—and a sophisticated technique."[34] *Time* agreed: "For all its vitality, the film is decadent, an artistic failure. The creator thinks the film 'puts a thermometer to a sick world,' but it may be that he has simply taken his own temperature. A good deal of the picture is out-and-out sensationalism, smeared on with a heavy hand to attract the insects; and Fellini's selection of café society as a central symbol of evil is vulgar and naive."[35]

La Dolce Vita was a huge success. It played a total of eighteen road show engagements in key cities around the country before it went into wider release. It was shown with subtitles and booked into commercial theaters that had never booked a subtitled film before, which led *Variety* to conclude that *La Dolce Vita* would become "the yardstick by which all future subtitled foreign imports would be judged."[36] The film eventually grossed $19.5 million at the box office, ranking number two on *Variety*'s All-Time Foreign Language Films.

Rocco and His Brothers (*Rocco e i suoi fratelli*) opened on June 27, 1961, at the Beekman. It, too, had generated controversy at the Venice Folm Festival in 1960. The cause, reported Grenier, was "a rape scene in the mud, which easily exceeded that of Bergman's *Virgin Spring* for graphic detail, and an intensely violent murder during which audiences involuntarily gasp as each of the fifteen-odd knife blows sink into the woman's body . . . Cries, screams, and shouts went up; women fainted; men stood, waved fists, delivered speeches against Visconti; his defenders fought in the aisles with the detractors."[37] To tap the double audience, Astor booked the film into the Pix, a Times Square grind house, in addition to the Beekman.

Renato Salvatori and Annie Girardot in Luchino Visconti's *Rocco and His Brothers* (1961)

The second part of Visconti's Sicilian trilogy, which began with *La Terra Trema* in 1948, *Rocco and His Brothers* told the story of a widow and her five five sons, who migrate from a poverty-stricken village in Sicily to the industrial north of Milan. It starred Alain Delon, Renato Salvatori, Annie Girardot, and Katina Paxinou. *Rocco* originally had a running time of over three hours. For its New York launch, Astor cut it down to 149 minutes.

Crowther said that *Rocco and His Brothers* could "stand alongside the American classic, *The Grapes of Wrath*. . . . In essence, it is a story of what happens to people when they are displaced from one environment to another, from one old familiar way of life to a new and strange and, in this instance, potentially corrupting realm. It is a universal drama, as old as civilized man and as modern in massive repetition as the flow of Puerto Ricans to New York." Comparing the sociological themes of *Rocco and His Brothers* and *La Dolce Vita*, "the main difference is that the condition that makes it possible for society to corrupt in *Rocco and His Brothers* is the change of environment. The people in *La Dolce Vita* are accustomed to where they are; their fibers are deteriorated by deliberate exposure to satiety. But the people in *Rocco* are innocent victims of displacement and climactic change. They are truly piteous human beings who are the playthings of a fate of migration." Crowther viewed the rape scene as "the ultimate expression of the brutalizing change that has occurred, the fatal manifestation of corruption of character. And from this point on, the deterioration and resolution of the family's fate are as surely marked in developing incidents as they are in a Greek tragedy."[38]

Stanley Kauffmann disagreed. "Its theme is the corruption of simple folk by modern city life. . . . But how does the city corrupt them? At the end one brother is a successful boxer, another is joyously married, a third blissfully betrothed and the Alpha Romeo employee he wants to be, and the child is loved by all. Only one brother, Simone, has gone bad, and he brought his egotistical sneakiness with him from the happy homeland."[39] Nearly all the critics were put off by the rape. Dwight Macdonald said that the scenes of violence reminded him "unpleasantly of the shower-bath murder in *Psycho*; they seemed to correspond not to the requirements of the work of art, but to some neurotic need in the artist—or perhaps his sense of the exploitability of such a need in the audience."[40]

Time gave the most damning review, calling *Rocco and His Brothers* "an interminable, sprawling, jerkily cut and overpraised melodrama." Visconti "still concerns himself with peasants and is old-guard. *Rocco* keeps all the bench marks of Italian neo-realism—the urine-streaked tenement walls, the fields full of rubble, the endless squawk of language ('Ecco! Ecco! Basta! Basta!')," but "the acting is pointlessly, if deliberately, melodramatic; the murderer needlessly apes a silent-film villain—slack jaw, rolling eyes and all. Whole episodes are unprofitably murky. . . . A question at the core of the film—whether corrosive city is preferable to deadening land—is never convincingly asked, although *Rocco* is supposed to end with its answer."[41]

By the time *Rocco and His Brothers* hit second-run houses, an additional half hour had been sliced away, reducing Visconti's carefully graded structure "to a formless series of violent climaxes. As a result, it proved a commercial failure."[42]

Sustaining the Trend

Antonioni sustained the renaissance almost single-handedly in 1962, with the release of *The Night* and *Eclipse*, the second and third installments of his planned trilogy. After *L'Avventura*'s hostile reception at Cannes, Antonioni's fortunes improved on the festival circuit when *The Night* won the Golden Bear at the Berlin Film Festival in 1961. Even Crowther was more receptive. *The Night* (*La Notte*) starred Marcello Mastroianni and Jeanne Moreau, with Monica Vitti in a supporting role. It was released by Lopert Films, the new art film subsidiary of United Artists. Because of its thematic similarity to *La Dolce Vita*, Lopert waited until Fellini's film had played itself out before releasing Antonioni's film on February 19, 1962, at the Little Carnegie.

"At least, Michelangelo Antonioni lets us know what he's about in his new film," said Crowther. "He is coolly cataloguing with his camera the wealth of telltale things that occur in the course of an afternoon and evening in the life of an Italian novelist's wife as she comes to the dismal conclusion that her husband no longer loves her, that she no longer loves him and she wishes he were dead. Where Signor Antonioni was elusive, if not obscure, in tracing a dramatic line in *L'Avventura*, his controversial film of last year, he is absolutely explicit in tracing the line in this." Having said that, Crowther concluded, "Whether one finds it stimulating or a redundant bore will depend, we suspect, in large measure upon the subtle attunement of one's mood."[43]

Hollis Alpert focused on Antonioni's style. *The Night* "is here to prove that the style of *L'Avventura* was no accident, and that Michelangleo Antonioni has his personal and accomplished way of telling a film story." Alpert then demonstrated how Antonioni's techniques did away with conventional dramatic emphasis and substituted an abstract quality that suggested "an estrangement between the people and their backgrounds." He pointed to his editing methods in particular: "If there is a technical trick involved, it would seem to lie in Antonioni's editing methods. He trades on the filmgoer's conditioning to the usual cuts, fades, and dissolves, and consciously disturbs accustomed rhythms, which is tantamount to doing away with dramatic emphasis. When a particular scene has made its point [Antonioni] does not immediately cut away to something else, but allows the scene to remain on the screen for a time. . . . The spectator may uncomfortably wonder why the story doesn't continue. On the other hand, he can find himself forced into a deeper involvement than might otherwise have been possible." Alpert concluded, "There is no doubt that this gifted Italian director is using the screen medium in a new way for his own purposes. His bent is reflective and literary. Like some of the newer novelists, he is exploring the vaguer reaches of unhappiness, and it is undeniably fascinating to watch his people wander sadly, beautifully, in their intelligent anguish."[44]

Nevertheless, most critics thought *The Night* was a comedown after *L'Avventura*. *Time* complained that the picture "moves too slowly, lasts too long (two hours), and demands too much intellectual attention to command a mass audience. Even moviegoers who liked *L'Avventura* will probably find *The Night* black and cold; it has a basilisk intensity that turns the heart to stone."[45]

The fact that *Eclipse* (*L'Eclisse*) had received a Special Jury Prize at Cannes did little to quash such criticism. It was released by Times Films on December 20, 1962, at the Little Carnegie and Murray Hill theaters. Alpert described

Eclipse as continuing Antonioni's inquiry into "the nature and possibility of love in our time." Monica Vitti as Vittoria was described as "an artistically inclined young woman" who embodies "imprisoned sentiments." She "leaves a man she doesn't love, and leaves another she does love," a stock broker played by Alain Delon, who is "equally imprisoned in his world of money and speculation." Alpert had "some misgivings" about the film: "This third time around we are more ready for him, more aware of his gloomy preoccupations, and somehow less affected." In particular, he found the performance of Monica Vitti "more studied than the work she had done in the past, and even a trifle self-conscious."[46]

Yet Antonioni's reputation endured. *Time*'s celebrated cover story asserted that Antonioini "has done only three pictures [the trilogy] that really matter, but they matter a lot; any one of them would suffice to establish him as one of the finest stylists in the history of cinema."[47] *Red Desert* (*Il deserto rosso*), Antonioni's first color film and the winner of the Golden Lion at the Venice Film Festival in 1964, garnered even greater acclaim. *Red Desert* was released by Rizzoli Films, the new art film subsidiary of Angelo Rizzoli's media empire, and opened on February 8, 1965, at the Beekman. *Time* described *Red Desert* as "at once the most beautiful, the most simple and the most daring film yet made by Italy's masterful Michelangelo Antonioni, a director so prodigiously gifted that he can marshal a whole new vocabulary of cinema to reiterate his now-familiar themes."[48] Stanley Kauffmann agreed: "With Michelangelo Antonioni's *Red Desert*, the art of film advances. This masterly creator has, in all his films shown here, opened new possibilities. Now, with his first use of color and with other elements, he further enlarges our vision of what a film can be and do."[49]

Despite Antonioni's innovative use of color, critics again found fault with his unrelieved pessimism and the performance of his leading lady, Monica Vitti, who played another "alienated modern woman," this time in the bleak industrial landscape of Ravenna. For example, Andrew Sarris complained, "I have the feeling that Antonioni would rather curse the discoloration of modern life than distort his contrived decor with one small candle of flickering hope. I can no longer accept Antonioni's assertion that the modern man fails to communicate, simply because Antonioni refuses to allow his players any garden-variety expressiveness to invade their incommunicado faces. Much of Antonioni's meaningful manner is derived from staring at a rock so long that mere opacity comes to equal profundity." Sarris went on to say, "I must confess that I have had it with Monica Vitti as a stand-in for Everyman or even Everywoman. In fact, Miss Vitti's excessive solemnity engenders in me at times the giddy illusion that I am watching Barbra Streisand adrift in an industrial documentary."[50]

Luchino Visconti concluded his Sicilian trilogy with *The Leopard* (*Il Gatto-pardo*). The notoriety surrounding *Rocco and His Brothers* enabled Visconti to secure financing from 20th Century-Fox for his most ambitious undertaking to date: the filming of Giuseppe di Lampedusa's famous novel about Sicily at the time of the Risorgimento (the movement to unify Italy led by Garibaldi). With an international cast headed by Burt Lancaster, Alain Delon, and Claudia Cardinale, *The Leopard* met with a glorious reception in Italy and won the Golden Palm at Cannes in 1963. *Variety* said, "*The Leopard* comes to the screen . . . munificently outfitted and splendidly acted by a large cast dominated by Burt Lancaster's standout stint in the title role. It must also be added that, at nearly 3½ hours, the film is way overlong. Several sequences fail to trenchantly move forward the story."[51]

The Leopard was presented at Cannes in an Italian-language version. The version 20th Century-Fox released on April 17, 1963, at the Plaza contained an English-language soundtrack and was forty-five minutes shorter. In this version Burt Lancaster spoke his own English dialogue, as did Claudia Cardinale, while the other actors had their voices dubbed into English. Fox feared that American audiences would not want to hear the Hollywood star speaking Italian, but almost everyone disliked the decision. Crowther, who had once argued that dubbing would increase a foreign film's chances of reaching a broader audience, disliked Lancaster's regular voice and delivery: "Got up in side-burns and tall coats, plug hats and canes, the American star gives a physically forceful presentation of the massive, imperious man [upon] whom the mood of melancholy descends most heavily at the ball. He is mighty in moments of anger, harsh in his sarcastic bursts and amazingly soft and sympathetic when the call is for tenderness. But unfortunately Mr. Lancaster does have that blunt American voice that lacks the least suggestion of being Sicilian in the English-dialogue version shown here."[52]

Critics faulted other things about the film. Andrew Sarris thought it was a mistake to shorten the film for American consumption: "A bad film can never be improved by cutting simply for length, and a good film can only be harmed. Careless scissors only increase tedium, because the meaningful links are severed and the plot dribbles out in all directions."[53] Stanley Kauffmann thought that Burt Lancaster, "my fellow alumnus of DeWitt Clinton High School in the Bronx, is badly miscast as the scion of an ancient aristocratic line."[54] *Newsweek* agreed, saying, "Thanks largely to the direction, Burt Lancaster looks as if he were playing Clarence Day's 'Father' in summer stock, Claudia Cardinale appears rather more common than necessary, and Alain Delon is reduced to the barely noticeable niceness of a good headwaiter."[55]

Fellini followed up *La Dolce Vita* with *8½*. Explaining the meaning of the title, Hollis Alpert said, "From 1950 until the present, [Fellini] has made seven films of feature length and three that he terms 'halves.' Perhaps nonplussed for a title, he has added all these together and simply called his latest *8½*."[56] Fellini's "portrait of the artist as a middle-aged man" starred Marcello Mastroianni, Claudia Cardinale, Anouk Aimée, and Sandra Milo. It was released by Joseph E. Levine's Embassy Pictures and opened the company's "shiny new" Festival Theater, located at 6 West 57th Street, on June 25, 1963. The 546-seat movie theater extended the art house district around the Little Carnegie to the east into the commercially fashionable part of the Fifty-seventh Street corridor between Fifth and Sixth Avenues.

Levine, it will be recalled, made his initial fortune distributing the Japanese horror film *Godzilla* in 1956. He made another fortune distributing the Italian "sword and sandal" film *Hercules* in 1959. Beginning in 1961, he branched out into art films by linking up with Carlo Ponti to release a series of vehicles built around Sophia Loren. By the time *8½* was produced, Levine had become the leading distributor of Italian films in the United States.

A "masterpiece," declared Dwight Macdonald, calling it "the most brilliant, varied and entertaining movie I've seen since *Citizen Kane*. Like *Kane*, it deals with large topics like art, society, sex, money, ageing, pretense and hypocrisy—all that Trollope wrote about in *The Way We Live Now*."[57] Most other critics agreed.

Since Marcello Mastroianni played a film director who is suffering from a creative block, critics naturally concentrated on the so-called autobiographical elements in the film. Crowther felt that "there isn't the slightest question that the basic nature of the hero corresponds almost precisely to the nature of Mr. Fellini as we have found it to be. . . . It is interesting, therefore, to discover that his hero is a rampant egotist, a highly self-centered individual with a bit of a sadistic streak."[58] *Newsweek* qualified this view by stating that "if *8½* is autobiographical, it is not an autobiography. It is, beyond doubt, a work of art of the first magnitude, dealing with the raw material of experience and the way an artist adjusts to it." *Newsweek* went on to note that Dante, Joyce, Stevens, Pirandello, and other writers had created autobiographical works.[59] Fellini, however, made it difficult to accept such easy comparisons, for he was quoted as saying, "I've never read *Ulysses*. I've never seen *Last Year at Marienbad*. I don't know anything about Proust, and I have only seen one film by Bergman." Guido is just a man who finally accepts his own confusion and doubts and sees "that this chaos is the real force out of which his creativity comes."[60]

Guido's own confusions and doubts were manifested in daydreams that captured the interest of critics. Here is how Kauffmann described the opening sequence: "The film opens in a silent dream, as the director suffocates in a traffic-jammed car while impassive faces in other cars watch or don't watch. He floats up through the sun roof into the sky, and in a perspective like that of Dali's *Crucifixion*, we look down past his leg along a kite-rope attached to it, held by a man on a beach. He crashes—and wakes in his hotel bed." Crowther was taken by the harem scene: "One of the most delightful fabrications is a wild and robust fantasy in which the director sees himself as the master of a harem of all the women he has known (or desired) ordering them to do his bidding, slapping them with a whip, receiving their utter adulation in a state of complete harmony."[61] The ending generated the most talk. As *Time* described it, a caravan takes Guido's party "to an eerie Cape Canaveral set for the film, which is to be a science-fiction movie. Reporters badger Mastroianni once more, and he crawls under a table and shoots himself. This clears his head once and for all, and in a moment of revelation he sees that the way to turn chaos into creativity is to stop brooding about the hobgoblins of his dreams and to start working on a film about the real people who surround him. *8½* is at least a wildly pictorial electroencephalogram, at best a fascinating ride down Fellini's stream of unconsciousness."[62]

Although not as successful at the box office as *La Dolce Vita*, *8½* did quite well, grossing $10.5 million at the box office and ranking number five on *Variety*'s All-Time Foreign Language Films. In addition, *8½* won an Oscar for Best Foreign Language Film, the top prize at the 1963 Moscow Film Festival, plus many other honors.

Fellini answered *8½* with *Juliet of the Spirits* (*Giulietta degli spiriti*), "probably the most eagerly awaited picture of the year," said Sarris. "The Venice and New York Film Festivals panted for it in vain, and now Fellini has been given the Great Director treatment in New York by a local ad agency hired by the Rizzoli interests."[63] *Juliet of the Spirits* opened simultaneously on November 3, 1965, at three New York theaters—the RKO 58th Street, the RKO 23rd Street, and the new Embassy on Broadway at 46th Street—so optimistic was Rizzoli about the film's commercial chances.

The film had a lot going for it. It was Fellini's first color feature and a vehicle for his wife, Giulietta Masina, the star of *La Strada* and *Cabiria*. Describing Fellini's use of color, Andrew Sarris said, "Fellini has drenched the screen with lurid reds to denote sensuality, pale whites for purity and dull blacks for churchly repression. Every last costume counts in Fellini's color scheme, and every last fabric seems to have been invented for the film. If *The Red Desert* is a mobile painting, *Giulietta of the Spirits* is a moving mass of watercolors."[64]

Critics were quick to point out the parallels to *8½* . For example, Stanley Kauffman said, "This film is its female counterpart—*Hers* to hang next to *His.* The age of the two protagonists is about the same—the moment of realization that all is not to be realized." Yet he went on to say that "*Juliet* is pallid as written and, to make it worse, the person of Giulietta Masina (who is Mrs. Fellini) contributes much less to this character and portrayal than Marcello Mastroianni supplied in the other film. Her fantasies and fantastic adventures seem unrelated to her—they seem neither to spring from her nor to affect her or us as they are meant to: she just plods modestly through. There is this rather dull, reticent, little woman, and then there are these vaguely interesting, unconventional cinematic shenanigans."[65]

The critics mostly agreed. Sarris went on to say, "Like so many other films of our time, *Giulietta of the Spirits* is a dazzling dead end, and I am thinking of Alain Resnais' *Last Year at Marienbad,* Jean-Luc Godard's *The Married Woman,* Ingmar Bergman's *All These Women,* and Michelangelo's *The Red Desert.* These are all films that try to get by almost entirely on directorial personality without any dramatic core, and I don't think this is the way the cinema can go. I preferred Fellini's art in the days of *[I] Vitelloni* and *La Strada* when he was still telling little stories with great themes than now when he is exploring great themes with hardly any story at all."[66]

The De Sica–Loren Collaborations

A series of pictures directed by Vittorio De Sica arrived in the United States concurrently with the second Italian renaissance. Constructed as vehicles for Sophia Loren, they were produced by Carlo Ponti and released by Joseph E. Levine's Embassy Pictures. De Sica's directorial career had declined after *Umberto D.* The commercial failure of this masterpiece had made him unbankable. To sustain himself, he focused more on his acting career and directing other people's pet projects. Under Ponti's tutelage, Loren had become a huge international star. In the United States she made her first appearance on the cover of *Life* magazine, which labeled her "Europe's No. 1 Cover Girl" and described her as the "popular successor to Gina Lollobrigida."[67] Given a Hollywood contract in 1955, Loren played opposite America's most popular movie idols in such films as Stanley Kramer's *The Pride and the Passion* (1957), Delbert Mann's *Desire Under the Elms* (1958), and Martin Ritt's *The Black Orchid* (1958). Although she won the Best Actress award at Venice in 1958 for her performance in Ritt's film, in Ponti's opinion she had yet to reach her full potential. *Two Women* provided her with that opportunity.

Sophia Loren and Eleanora Brown in Vittorio De Sica's *Two Women* (1961)

The Loren vehicles comprised *Two Women, Yesterday, Today and Tomorrow*, and *Marriage Italian Style*. *Two Women* (*La Ciociara*) opened at the Sutton on May 8, 1961, about a month after the release of *L'Avventura* and *La Dolce Vita*. The story has it that when Ponti showed Levine the sequence from the uncompleted film in which the Loren character and her daughter (Eleanora Brown) are raped in a church by advancing Allied troops during World War II, Levine snapped up the distribution rights for a hefty $300,000 and told Ponti that Loren was going to win an Oscar.[68] Levine launched *Two Women* with a two-page ad in the *New York Times*, which displayed a photo of Loren, "her dress ripped, kneeling in the dirt and weeping with rage and grief."[69] The critics focused mainly on her acting. Crowther noted that Loren's role was "a sharp change of pace . . . from the generally slick and frivolous roles she has played during the last several years in American movies." In *Two Women* "the beauty of Miss Loren's performance is her illumination of a passionate mother role. She is happy, expansive, lusty in the early phases of the film, in tune with the gusto of the peasants, gentle with her child. But when disaster strikes, she is grave and profound. When she weeps for the innocence of her daughter one quietly weeps with her. The child is played with luminous sweetness and dignity by Eleanora Brown and the Frenchman, Jean-Paul Belmondo (the thug of *Breathless*), is mildly amusing as the timid young man."[70]

Variety wondered about the rape scene: The "unremitting horror" of the film, cresting with the "marathon debauching [of the two women] by a band of Moroccan soldiers [is] so bleak that audiences are apt to puzzle for a philosophic point."[71] Crowther provided an explanation: "Evidently, the purpose of this suddenly tragic account . . . is to represent the disaster of those people—and, indeed, of Italy—who thought the war was a matter of playing it cozy and making do. The indication of Allied soldiers committing the devastating rape is the ultimate bitter dramatization and comment on the tragedy of war."[72]

After completing a six-month run at the Sutton, Levine released a dubbed version of the film in eighty-five RKO theaters throughout the Greater New York area. It was paired with Basil Deardon's *Man in the Moon*, starring Kenneth More—"a fun picture," as the ads had it. Loren dubbed her own voice into English, which made for a "first rate dubbing job," according to *Variety*.[73] Levine then waged a successful publicity campaign, which resulted in Loren winning the 1961 Academy Award for Best Actress—the first for a foreigner in a foreign film. Immediately following the awards ceremony, Levine re-released the film in commercial theaters. The film's box-office take marked the beginning of a lucrative collaboration between producer Carlo Ponti, his protégée Sophia Loren, director Vittorio De Sica, and Joseph E. Levine's Embassy Pictures.

Yesterday, Today and Tomorrow and *Marriage Italian Style* paired Sophia Loren with Marcello Mastroianni and did even better at the box office. The pairing resulted in part from Levine's investment in Pietro Germi's *Divorce Italian Style* (*Divorzio all'italiana*), which he released in 1962. Named best comedy of the year at Cannes in 1962, *Divorce Italian Style* arrived in the United States at the crest of a wave of Italian national self-satires that included Vittorio De Sica's *Gold of Naples* in 1957 and Mario Monicelli's *Big Deal on Madonna Street* in 1960. *Variety* described *Divorce Italian Style* as a "comedy with grotesque and satirical overtones" that just might "turn into a sleeper." *Divorce* provided a tongue-in-cheek solution "to unhappy couples unable to divorce under Catholic Italian law: kill your spouse—but make sure that your deed is recognizably in defense of your and your family's honor. In which case, under article 587 of Italian law, the murderer is penalized only 3 to 7 years in jail; no more, sometimes less."[74] Crowther said that Mastroianni "surpasses himself as a comedian in *Divorce Italian Style*. [Germi] gets out of Mr. Mastroianni a performance that hangs in one's mind as one of the most ingenious and distinctive comic characterizations that has lately been. Not since Charlie Chaplin's beguiling Verdoux have we seen a deliberate wife killer so elegant and suave, so condescending in his boredom, so thoroughly and pathetically enmeshed in the suffocating toils of a woman as Mr. Mastroianni is here. His eyelids droop with a haughtiness and ennui that are only dispelled when he looks with a gaze of lecherous longing at his teenage cousin, whom Stefania Sandrelli plays."[75] After playing at the Paris for nearly a year—breaking the house record of thirty-eight weeks set by Bardot's *And God Created Woman* in 1958—*Divorce Italian Style* broke through to the popular audience.

The vehicles Ponti fashioned for Loren and Mastroianni were based on familiar Italian stereotypes. In *Yesterday, Today and Tomorrow* (*Ieri, oggi, domani*), a three-part omnibus film, Loren played "a Roman call girl, a society woman in Milan and a black-marketeer in Naples who is eternally pregnant. In each episode she matches love and wits with Marcello Mastrioianni, Italy's greatest male star."[76] Embassy Pictures opened the film on March 17, 1964, at the Festival, an art house, and at the Loew's Tower East, a regular theater. It did better at the box office than *Two Women* and won an Oscar for Best Foreign Language Film, De Sica's third such award.

Embassy Pictures opened *Marriage Italian Style* (*Matrimonio all'italiana*) at the same two theaters on December 20, 1964. Brendan Gill suggested that the film "must be forgiven its title, which crudely seeks to gain an extra dollar or two by associating itself with the very successful *Divorce Italian Style* of several seasons ago." Gill further explained that "the two pictures have nothing in common except their leading man Marcello Mastroianni, who, after all, is the leading man in nearly all the Italian pictures that make their way to these shores."[77] Based on a play by the celebrated Neapolitan writer Eduardo De Filippo, *Marriage Italian Style* "relishes every step of a slut's progress from a bawdyhouse to a legal bed," said *Time*. "Though *Marriage* occasionally creaks like a piece of stage machinery, Director De Sica cunningly transforms its back street romance into an earthy, exuberant paean to virtue."[78]

By art house standards, the Loren vehicles were huge box office hits, grossing $7.2, $9.3, and $9.1 million, respectively, ranking number ten, seven, and eight on *Variety*'s All-Time Foreign Language Films. Although they were released in Italian with subtitles and initially played in art houses, they had conventional plots and crossed over easily into commercial exhibition—*Two Women* in a dubbed version and the two others subtitled. However, there was a downside in that they helped confuse the terms "art film," "foreign film," and "foreign film market." As Vincent Canby explained in 1964, the terms "came into existence 15 or 20 years ago to define a situation which no longer exists. Many people today, for example, persist in calling any film that is subtitled an 'art' film, no matter how commonplace the subject matter, theme and treatment. Others will point to the success of a Sophia Loren picture as a significant triumph for all 'foreign' films, even though Miss Loren had a previously established name . . . in many Hollywood pics before her first big Italo success *Two Women* this side."[79] Films like these also prompted art house managers to avoid booking offbeat product and hold out for the sure thing, a trend that gained momentum during the 1960s and hastened the demise of independent foreign film distribution.

Veteran Italian filmmakers Antonioni, Fellini, and Visconti represented the vanguard of the second Italian renaissance. By 1960 the Italian film industry had weathered the inroads made by television in Italy and once again ranked second to Hollywood in production and exports. As a result of the boom, new talents found their way into the industry and further strengthened the renaissance. Among the young directors who gained prominence during the 1960s and enriched the U.S. art film market were Bernardo Bertolucci, Vittorio De Seta, Ermanno Olmi, Pier Paolo Pasolini, and Francesco Rosi. Credit for introducing them rested mainly with the New York Film Festival.

Auteurs
from Outside the Epicenter

his history has thus far focused mainly on what *Time* called "the epicenter
of the new cinema," namely, Western Europe. This chapter deals with
filmmaking from "secondary concentrations of film production," which include Spain, India, Japan, Soviet Russia, the Eastern bloc, and beyond.[1] Imports from such countries faced stiff resistance from exhibitors. "If you're an
indie trying to find an outlet for an Indian, Japanese, Argentine or Polish feature film," said Vincent Canby in *Variety*, "you're going to have a hard time
lining up the all-important New York booking. And if you have a Spanish, Nor-
wegian, Brazilian, Hungarian, Yugoslav or some other such film you might as
well give up entirely if you base your hopes on the experience of the last two
years. No pictures of these nationalities had played a New York art house in the
entire 1960–61 season."[2] Films outside the epicenter were handled by Thomas
J. Brandon, Edward Harrison, and a few other venturesome distributors. They
found outlets for their releases at the Fifth Avenue Cinema, a 273-seat house
operated by the Rugoff chain in Greenwich Village, or at the New Yorker and
Bleecker Street revival houses, run by Dan Talbot and Lionel Rogosin, respectively. Beginning in 1963, their efforts were aided by the New York Film Festival, which became the main port of entry for such pictures. The festival was
organized just in time to counter the growing commercialization of the art film
market and programmed films that normally would have had difficulty finding
theatrical exhibition.

Luis Buñuel

Luis Buñuel, the Spanish filmmaker and founder of surrealist cinema best known for *Un Chien Andalou* (1929) and *L'Age d'Or* (1930), returned to the scene in 1952 with the release of *Los Olvidados*, a Mexican film Buñuel made in 1950. It was a total surprise since nothing important had come from Buñuel since he had fled Spain during the civil war. Buñuel spent most of World War II in Hollywood dubbing films for the Latin American market. Thereafter he moved to Mexico and worked for producer Oscar Dancigers making mostly melodramas and comedies for Spanish-language movie houses.

Los Olvidados captured a top prize at Cannes in 1951. It was first shown in New York later that year in Spanish at the Cinema 48.[3] There it caught the attention of Arthur Mayer and Edward Kingsley, who re-released it in March 1952 at the Trans-Lux with subtitles and a new title, *The Young and the Damned*. Arthur Knight noted that "an unbelievable number of Mexican-made films cross the border every year. Most of them we never hear of. Untitled and unsung, they quickly pass into the oblivion provided by some 400 Spanish-language houses spread across the country."[4] Buñuel's film, however, was unlike anything that had come before. Inspired by Vittorio De Sica's *Shoe Shine*, *The Young and the Damned* was shot in the slums of Mexico City using nonprofessional actors to portray homeless adolescents who prey on the disadvantaged. According to Knight, it was "definitely not a film for the sensitive stomach." The film contained "scenes of violence and depravity" that were justified. "They all spring from incidents uncovered and vouched for by Mexican educational and penal authorities" [and are] by no means exclusive to Mexico. They hold equally true for any industrial center, where poverty is rampant and children go uncared for and unloved."[5]

Crowther disliked the film because Buñuel did not offer a solution to the social problem: "[He] simply has assembled an assortment of poverty-stricken folk—paupers, delinquents, lost children, and parents of degraded morals—and has mixed them altogether in a vicious and shocking melange of violence, melodrama, coincidence and irony."[6] *Time* leveled a similar criticism, concluding its review, "*The Young and the Damned* sometimes seems as one-dimensional and as far short of the truth as a lurid propaganda poster."[7] *The Young and the Damned* had only a limited run in the United States.

Buñuel's fans had to wait ten years for his next picture, *Viridiana*, which was released at the Paris Theatre on March 19, 1962. Kingsley-International, Columbia's art film subsidiary, acquired the film after it won the Golden Palm

Fernando Rey and Silvia Pinal in Luis Buñuel's *Viridiana* (1962)

at Cannes the year before. Buñuel made the film in Spain at Franco's invitation. The government gave him carte blanche and selected *Viridiana* to represent Spain at Cannes. Somehow the film got into the festival without first being submitted to the Spanish censors. After seeing what Buñuel had wrought, the government banned it. Kingsley made much of the scandal. Its publicity noted that *Viridiana* "contained an orgy sequence in which a group of depraved beggars strike a sustained pose resembling da Vinci's painting of 'The Last Supper'." Its ads made sure to remind people that *Viridiana* was "Banned in Spain!" The film, which starred Silvia Pinal and Fernando Rey, told the story of "a young novice who leaves her convent to learn about the world, and is gradually corrupted by the evil she encounters."[8]

Reviewers considered *Viridiana* an allegory of "conditions in contemporary Spain." Like *Los Olvidados*, which, said *Time*, "opened people's eyes to the horrors of poverty in the Mexican slums [*Viridiana*] . . . attempts to open people's eyes to the evils of sentimental piety and morbid tyranny in Franco's Spain. . . . The girl is obviously intended to personify what is false in Spanish Pietism; the uncle signifies the sickness of the ruling classes. He is a quixotic solitary, indolent in the grand Spanish manner; he secretly preens himself in corsets worn many years before by his wife, who died on their wedding day. . . . Buñuel indulges in no sentimentality about 'the masses.' Rabble is rabble to him; the mob is a beast with many heads that destroys both good and evil, that overwhelms humanity with animality. Nevertheless, Buñuel seems to believe that revolution is necessary in Spain, that only a revolt of the masses can dissolve its calcified structure."[9]

Crowther, who also interpreted the film as a "guarded criticism of social conditions in Spain," added, "It is an ugly, depressing view of life. And, to be frank, about it, it is a little old-fashioned, too. His format is strangely literary; his symbols are obvious and blunt, such as the revulsion of the girl toward milking or the display of a penknife built into a crucifix. And there is something just a bit corny about having his bums doing their bacchanalian dance to the thunder of the 'Hallelujah Chorus'."[10]

Viridiana nontheless proved a big commercial success. There followed "a kind of Buñuelian *âge d'or*," said Vincent Canby, a decade of "extraordinarily rich moviemaking of the sort that most fine, idiosyncratic directors—probably unfortunately—pass through before they're 50."[11] Buñuel's next film, *The Exterminating Angel*, was chosen to open the first New York Film Festival in September 1963, and he remained a festival favorite thereafter.

Satyajit Ray

In its survey of international cinema, *Time* noted: "In India there is Satyajit Ray, 42, a onetime commercial artist in Calcutta who has proved himself one of cinema's greatest natural talents. In the last five years, six of Ray's films have been released in the U.S., and every one of the six swells with the fullness of life and glows with the light of the spirit. His first three pictures (*Pather Panchali, Aparajito, The World of Apu*) made up a trilogy that speaks a thousand volumes about life in India and stands as the supreme masterpiece of the Asian cinema. . . . They are beautiful to look at and musical to be with. They are quiet films, as all deep things are quiet. They are not in a hurry to happen, they take time to live. They experience life, they experience death. Nothing human is alien to them. They are works of love."[12]

New Yorkers saw their first Ray film in April 1955, when *Pather Panchali* was shown during the Indian Exhibition at the Museum of Modern Art. "There it was seen and applauded by a number of serious movie fans," said Crowther, "whose educated endorsement made it a natural for the international film festivals."[13] The distributor who introduced Ray to the art film market was Edward

Harrison. He had started out in the business by distributing Japanese films but then switched to Ray following the MoMA screening. After acquiring the rights to *Pather Panchali* in 1955, Harrison distributed nearly all of Rays's films in the United States until his death in October 1967. Because *Pather Panchali* had been submitted by India as its entry for the 1956 Cannes Film Festival, Harrison decided to hold off on the New York premiere until after the results of the competition were known. Although *Pather Panchali* won a Special Jury Prize for Best Human Document at Cannes and brought international recognition to the director, Harrison was unable to find first-run art house in New York willing to screen it.

Undeterred, Harrison acquired the distribution rights to *Aparjito*, the sequel, which won the Golden Lion at Venice in 1957. The San Francisco Film Festival invited Harrison to submit the film for its inaugural competition in 1957, but he sent *Panther Panchali* instead, which took the top prize. Harrison subsequently released it commercially at the local Vogue Theater, where it ran for months. He next entered *Pather Panchali* in the first Vancouver Film Festival, where it took the top prize in August 1958. In September he introduced Satyajit Ray in person, plus his two films, at the Robert Flaherty Seminar in Brattleboro, Vermont. Harrison finally found a theater in New York willing to screen *Pather Panchali*—the Fifth Avenue Cinema—where it opened on September 22, 1958. It ran for six months, breaking the house record. Thereafter the Fifth Avenue Cinema would serve as the regular venue for the Apu trilogy.[14]

Pather Panchali, which translates as "Song of the Little Road," presented "a series of closely observed, sensitively recorded incidents that happen to a humble family living in wretched poverty in a small Benares village," said Arthur Knight. The family "consists of a charming but impractical father, a sensitive mother, and a 10-year-old boy, Apu, who has curiosity enough to kill nine cats." Knight described the film as "a documentary, but with none of the rigors that the word so often implies. It is a human documentary, a rich and often beautiful, often poignant introduction to people we need to know more about."[15] *Time* called it a masterpiece: "*Pather Panchali* is perhaps the finest piece of filmed folklore since Robert Flaherty's *Nanook of the North*. It is a pastoral poem dappled with the play of brilliant images and strong, dark feelings, a luminous revelation of Indian life in language that all the world can understand."[16] Crowther described it as "one of those rare exotic items, remote in idiom from the usual Hollywood film that should offer some subtle compensations to anyone who has the patience to sit through its almost two hours."[17]

Aparjito, whose title translates as "The Unvanquished," reached the United States in 1958 by way of the second San Francisco Film Festival, which selected

Soumitra Chatterjee and Sharmila Tagore in Satyajit Ray's *The World of Apu* (1960)

Ray as best director at the event. *Aparajito* opened in New York on April 28, 1959, succeeding *Panther Panchali*. "Although sequels are almost axiomatically inferior to the original," said Arthur Knight, "this one is, if anything, stronger than its predecessor. Where the first film drew in no less than five major characters, *Aparajito* centers solely on Apu and his relation to his mother during his adolescent years. . . . Where the first film presented the little family living in virtual isolation in a remote village, here Apu is set down in teeming Benares and in Calcutta. As a result, there is not only a firmer structural unity to *Aparajito*, but a clearer line of development, a wider canvas."[18]

The World of Apu (*Apur Sansar*), the conclusion of the trilogy, opened on October 4, 1960. In the words of A. H. Weiler, it tells of Apu's "happy marriage to an Indian girl, played by the great-granddaughter of the famed poet Rabindrinath Tagore, as well as her tragic death in childbirth. Although Apu renounces the child and becomes a wanderer, he ultimately returns to assume the responsibilities of fatherhood."[19] In the opinion of *Time*, "As a piece of craftsmanship, *The World of Apu* is the finest film of the three. Director Ray, who had never turned a camera before he started shooting PP, began his trilogy with incredible strokes of beginner's luck, but he ends it with deliberate mastery of the medium. He has superb control of his camera. His images are continuously beautiful, but never obtrusive; they rise out of the story as naturally as thoughts rise out of the pool of Vishnu—there is nothing arty in Ray's art. By the same token his actors act, not with the usual bombinations of Oriental drama, but as though the camera had found them alone and simply living; and they live, as few characters in pictures do, real lives that swell to the skin with pain and poetry and sudden mother wit."[20]

Despite the fact that Ray had a cult following, few theaters were willing to book his films. The Apu trilogy generated less than $100,000 in rentals in 1960.[21] Fortunately, the modest box-office returns affected Ray not at all. He was a complete filmmaker: he wrote the scripts, composed the scores, and designed the sets. To produce his films, he used mostly nonprofessionals in terms of cast and crew. As he told one reporter, "The relatively low budgets of all my pictures (an average of $60,000 whether in black-and-white or color) allow my producers to amortize their investments in all my films on the Bengali market only, without ever thinking about the rest of India, the Bombay audience or overseas release."[22]

Ray's growing stature enabled Harrison to secure uptown venues for his next two releases, *Devi* and *The Music Room. Devi* opened at Don Rugoff's new Cinema II on October 7, 1962. The publicity described it as "a tale about a happy young girl of a rich family whose life changes tragically when the people of her region come to believe she is an incarnation of the goddess Kali."[23] *The Music Room* (*Jalsaghar*), which Ray produced in 1958 after completing the first two parts of his Apu trilogy, opened at the Carnegie Hall Cinema on October 15, 1963. The publicity described it as a fable about "the decline of a once-wealthy aristocrat who clings to feudal ways in a changing India."[24] Both films received appreciative reviews and enjoyed modest runs.

Beginning in 1964, the principal venue for Rays's new films was the New York Film Festival. *The Big City* (*Mahanagar*) concluded the second festival and received a warm reception from Bosley Crowther, who described the film as "another of his beautifully fashioned and emotionally balanced contemplations of change in the thinking, the customs and the manners of the Indian middle-class."[25] Nevertheless the film languished for three years before it was released commercially on June 29, 1967, at the 55th Street Playhouse, where, reported Crowther, it "died a death it didn't deserve."[26]

Ray's subsequent films barely made a dent in the market, leading Vincent Canby to observe in 1972 that "if it weren't for the New York Film Festival, few of Satyajit Ray's post Apu trilogy films would ever have been seen in this country." Canby meant this as "a comment on the American public's movie-going tastes, which are actually no worse than anybody else's." Among the reasons he gave was that a "Ray film doesn't demand our immediate attention in the way that a Buñuel or a Bergman or a Godard does." For one thing, "a Ray film carries no guarantee to shock. Its characters are too involved in one form or another of daily survival to fret about metaphysical matters. It won't outrage us." For another, the "rhythm of his films . . . is so regular as almost to lull us to sleep in a place (a movie theater) where custom has taught us to expect a continuing succession of alarms of varying tones and volumes." Lastly, "Ray's vision of Indian life . . . is anything but exotic or sensuous. His male characters, especially, seem at first somewhat timid, dressed in their occidental clothes that hang on them like the hand-me-downs from someone else's civilization."[27]

Akira Kurosawa

Taking stock of Kurosawa's *Rashomon*, *The Magnificent Seven*, and *Ikiru* in 1960, Arthur Knight concluded that "Kurosawa must be compared to Ingmar Bergman. Not that there is any particular spiritual affinity between the mystic Swede and the hyper-realistic Japanese," he added. "But Bergman has emerged as the symbol of the individualistic director, the complete filmmaker who originates a story that is meaningful to him and illuminates it through his own special handling of the camera and sound track. Kurosawa is no less personal, even to the extent of building, like Bergman, his own stock company of actors—notably Takashi Shimura and Toshiro Mifune—and working, when possible, with a sympathetic cameraman, Takeo Ito."[28] Kurosawa assumed more control over his work in 1959, when Toho, his home studio, set up a separate production unit for him, the Kurosawa Production Co. Although Kurosawa could now make films as he saw fit, the question as to how to overcome audience resistance remained unresolved.

Several theories have already been offered to explain the low turnout for Japanese films in the United States. In Kurosawa's case, it's appropriate to add that of film historian Jay Leyda. In his review of Donald Ritchie's book *The Films of Akira Kurosawa*, Leyda blamed Kurosawa himself, who, continuing the tradition of D.W. Griffith and John Ford, "(using great art to make popular films), is no more willing to be articulate about himself as an artist than they have been. Often, when this book uses his own words, they seem to be disdainful of his art, to fling a long arm toward the screen—'There is what I have to say.' And the world's film critics hesitate to accept his films on the highest level."[29]

Kurosawa might have gotten a warmer reception with better distribution. Unlike Bergman, who had just one principal distributor to promote his films—Janus Films—Kurosawa had many. *Rashomon* and *The Magnificent Seven*, it will be recalled, were distributed by two Hollywood companies—RKO and Columbia, respectively—and were handled as costume-action pictures in an attempt to get them into commercial theaters. *Ikiru* and several early Kurosawa's pictures were presented by Tom Brandon as part of a one-man Japanese film festival to reveal the range of styles in Kurosawa's oeuvre. The experiment was confined to the Little Carnegie and proved a failure. Kurosawa's plight led Stanley Kauffmann to complain, "We keep reading about the activity of Akira Kurosawa . . . who is one of the finest film artists alive, and keep hoping to see more of his work. But with him, as with many foreign directors, it is as if each of his films were put in a rudderless boat, shoved out from home, and left to the winds of commercial chance to bring it to us."[30]

At least eight of Kurosawa's films were released commercially in New York during the 1960s. The first arrivals—*Throne of Blood*, *The Hidden Fortress*, and *The Lower Depths*—were made in the 1950s and opened within months of each other, beginning in November 1961. Tom Brandon handled *Throne of Blood* and *The Lower Depths*, while New Yorker Films handled *The Hidden Fortress*. They played briefly at the Fifth Avenue Cinema, the New Yorker Theater, and at the Bleecker Street Cinema, respectively, under the banner of "overlooked" features by noted foreign directors. At the New Yorker *Hidden Fortress* played on a double bill with a revival of Roger Vadim's second film, *No Sun in Venice*, a romantic thriller that contained an improvised score by the Modern Jazz Quartet. Kurosawa became better known in this country when *Yojimbo*, his second independent production, was presented at the Carnegie Hall Cinema on October 15, 1962. (Its premiere followed the seven-month run of Alain Resnais's *Last Year at Marienbad*.) It was released by Seneca International, an arm of Seneca Productions, a short-lived New York film producer. *Yojimbo*, its one-and-only release, ran for nearly four months at the Carnegie, representing Kurosawa's biggest commercial success of the decade.

Since Kurosawa's films were based on Western sources, critics naturally compared his adaptations to the originals and evaluated Toshiro Mifune's interpretation of the leading roles accordingly. *Time*'s review of *Throne of Blood* (*Kumonosu-jô*) began: "No doubt about it now: Japan's Akira Kurosawa must be numbered with Sergei Eisenstein and D. W. Griffith among the supreme creators of cinema." It described Kurosawa's "resetting of Macbeth among the clanking thanes and brutish politics of 16th century Japan [as] a visual descent into the hell of greed and superstition, into the gibbering darkness of the primitive mind. It is a nerve-shattering spectacle of physical and metaphysical violence, quite the most brilliant and original attempt ever made to put Shakespeare in pictures." The review said Kurosawa's intention "is plainly to hack off the Gothic foliage of Shakespeare's fancy and compress his tale into that traditional form of Japanese theater known as noh." "It added that Kurosawa's Macbeth "is no reflective and susceptible villain, 'too full o' the milk of human kindness.' He is a sweat-simple soldier, as physical as his horse, and he is played with tremendous thrust and mien by Toshiro Mifune, who is surely the most prodigiously kinetic cinemactor [*sic*] since Doug Fairbanks."[31]

Hollis Alpert was similarly impressed with *Yojimbo*, Kurosawa's adaptation of American westerns like *Shane* and *High Noon*, "both of which portrayed a lonely man doing battle with evil forces in town." He described *Yojimbo* as "an eastern-western on a similar theme" and noted that "Kurosawa has, in effect, taken a familiar tale of violence and made from it a magnificent ironic parable: for Sanjuro, symbol of force and power that he is, becomes a plague on both houses. This extra dollop of significance helps give the film its glow of distinction."[32]

Stanley Kauffmann was especially taken with Toshiro Mifune's acting, particularly his performance as Sanjuro, which won the Volpi Cup at the Venice Film Festival. Mifune played an unattached samurai who wanders into a village and sells his services to rival gangs. What ranks *Yojimbo* "above most of the better Westerns is not its script but its execution," said Kauffmann. "*Shane* and *The Gunfighter* had Alan Ladd and Gregory Peck in their leading roles. This has Toshiro Mifune. Mifune's versatility (the true sort, a range of imagination and resource, not trick voices and make-ups) continues to impress. The animalistic brigand (*Rashomon*), the bumptious faker (*The Seven Samurai*), the lithe lover (*The Lower Depths*), among others, are supplemented now by this contained, amused, self-reliant swordsman."[33]

Crowther, on the other hand, showed little appreciation for any film in the group. For example, he considered *Throne of Blood* a cultural oddity. "If you think it would be amusing to see *Macbeth* done in Japanese, then pop around to the Fifth Avenue Cinema," he said, "For a free Oriental translation of the Shakespearean drama is what this is, and amusing is the proper word for it. . . . We label it amusing because lightly is the only way to take this substantially serio-comic rendering of the story of an ambitious Scot into a form that combines characteristics of Japanese No theatre and the American Western film. Probably Mr. Kurosawa . . . did not intend it to be amusing for his formalistic countrymen, but its odd amalgamation of cultural contrasts hits the occidental funny bone."[34]

Kurosawa's next releases—*The Bad Sleep Well, Sanjuro,* and *High and Low,* representing his first, third, and fourth independent projects—were distributed in the United States by Toho and premiered at the company's new Manhattan showcase, the Toho Cinema, beginning in January 1963. Toho acquired the latter by leasing the 299-seat D.W. Griffith Theater, just off Times Square. To create a proper ambience for its presentations, Toho decorated the theater in the Japanese style and dressed the attendants in kimonos. Tea was available in the lounge and was served in the traditional Japanese manner.

Crowther, for a change, liked *The Bad Sleep Well* (*Warui yatsu hodo yoku nemuru*), a social problem film in modern dress. He described it as "an aggressive and chilling drama of modern-day Japan, exposing a fringe of 'big business' in the forthright manner of an American gangster film," adding that "if all the future imports in this theater are as forceful and engrossing as this one . . . local film fans are due for a lot of excitement and the popularity of the project should be assured."[35] However, now it was Stanley Kauffmann who seemed befuddled: "*The Bad Sleep Well,* is not good. . . . It is so remote in every way from the mainstream of his work that, except for the opening sequence and the presence of some of his 'stock company,' there is no internal reason to believe that Kurosawa did it. It could have been made by any experienced, tamely imaginative director of films or television. . . . The picture's one reward is in seeing Toshiro Mifune young, handsome, and sprucely double-breasted."[36]

Sanjuro (*Tsubaki Sanjûrô*), the sequel to *Yojimbo,* was released in May. Mifune played "another scraggly samurai," said *Time.* "As in *Yojimbo,* he drifts into a village torn by civil war. . . . But in *Yojimbo,* an angry allegory of contemporary civilization, both parties to the dispute were vicious villains. In *Sanjuro,* there are the good guys and there are the bad guys. The hero joins the good guys and leads them to victory. In the process Mifune demonstrates anew that he sure does swing a mean katana. In one scene he slaughters 27 men in 30 seconds. . . . Moviegoers who missed *Yojimbo* will assuredly find *Sanjuro* a bloody good show."[37]

High and Low (*Tengoku to jigoku*) opened in November. A film whose actors wear contemporary dress, like *The Bad Sleep Well,* it was based on the Ed McBain novel *King's Ransom.* Like the earlier film, it received mixed reviews. Crowther described it as "one of the best detective thrillers ever filmed. . . . Here is one import—for suspense fans and students of moviecraft—that simply must be seen. . . . The result is a sizzling, artistic crackerjack and a model of its genre, pegged on a harassed man's moral decision, laced with firm characterizations and tingling detail and finally attaining an incredibly colorful crescendo of microscopic police sleuthing. Crime, believe us, doesn't pay in Yokohama."[38] Kauffmann remained befuddled: "I have no satisfactory idea why, at this stage of his career, he wanted to make it. . . . It is just the story of a kidnaping, with some of the light psychological and social trim now in vogue in detective novels. We see how the police finally find the kidnaper. That is all. . . . *High and Low* begins, drives on, ends. No more; no resonance of any kind, if we disregard the jacket-blurb guff about Good and Evil on every mystery story. I would like to know why—apart from the pleasure of my asking it—why Kurosawa wanted to make it."[39]

The Toho Cinema closed on June 7, 1965, following a twenty-eight-month trial period. During its short life, the theater introduced more than thirty pictures, principally from the studios of Toho Films. According to Ryu Yasutake, the manager, the theater fulfilled its announced purpose of determining the range of American tastes for Japanese films. Crowther provided another explanation for the closing: "It found the local interest in contemporary films from Japan too feeble and unreliable to warrant its going on. And it wasn't as though it hadn't offered some exciting and picturesque films. . . . It was just that the New York public appears to have grown indifferent to Japanese films."[40]

Kurosawa's last releases of the decade, *I Live in Fear* and *Red Beard*, premiered at the New York Film Festival in 1963 and 1965, respectively. They were not released commercially until 1967 and 1968, respectively, the former by Tom Brandon and the latter by Frank Lee International, a San Francisco-based distributor that handled mostly Hong Kong fare for the Chinatown circuit.

I Live in Fear (*Ikimono no kiroku*), a 1955 production, was described by *Time* as "an eerie and comminatory meditation on the life of man in the shadow of the Bomb."[41] Brandon presented the film in January 1967 at the conclusion of his three-week Kurosawa retrospective at the Fifth Avenue Cinema. Crowther explained why the commercial release took so long: "It is one of the weakest of the great Japanese director's works," he concluded. "Aiming, it seems, to tell a story of an aging man's fears of the hydrogen bomb and his consequent obsessive endeavors to get his family to move with him to a farm in Brazil, it dwindles off into a talky, tedious recounting of the family's bickering with the old man, who is obviously a crank at the beginning and is totally mad at the end."[42]

Red Beard (*Akahige*) had won the Volpi Cup at the Venice Film Festival for Toshiro Mifune's performance in the title role. Reviewing the film at the festival, Crowther said that *Red Beard*, "which had been touted as one of the top attractions at the 12-day show, . . . turned out to be an over extended and highly sentimental account of how a gruff old Japanese doctor in a charity clinic about 100 years ago teaches and directs a young intern to see and understand the hardships and ironies of life." Crowther expected the film to be reflective of nineteenth-century Japan. Instead, "it is reflective mainly of the patterns and cliches of an American television show on the order of Dr. Kildare or Ben Casey, played in Japanese settings and costumes."[43]

Time was more appreciative: "As for plot, *Red Beard* could be Dr. Gillespie, and the intern Dr. Kildare: the story is that simple. But where his hero is a physician, Kurosawa is a metaphysician. Going beneath the bathos, he explores his characters' psychology until their frailties and strengths become a sum of humanity itself. Despite his pretensions, the young doctor is as flawed—and believable—as his patients. If Red Beard himself is a heroic figure, he is nonetheless cast in a decidedly human mold: gruff and sometimes violent—as when he forcibly takes the girl from her captors—he keeps the clinic open by such inglorious expedients as coercion and extortion. Kurosawa seems to share with Red Beard the knowledge that the price of compassion is often compromise."[44]

Frank Lee International released the film at the 55th Street Playhouse, which had given itself over mostly to Hong Kong kung fu and Japanese samurai fare. *Time* reported that *Red Beard* "is being presented at a special foreign-language theater with only a whisper of publicity. Thus, filmgoers across the country may once again miss a masterpiece by one of the world's great film makers."[45]

Soviet Films

A series of Soviet films reached the United States beginning in 1959, the result, in part, of a U.S.-Soviet film exchange. It occurred during a thaw in the cold war, when Nikita Khrushchev instituted a de-Stalinization process in 1956 and tensions between the U.S.S.R. and the United States eased somewhat. The first cultural exchange involved the Bolshoi Ballet and the New York Philharmonic. The film exchange, which restored the prewar film ties between the two countries, promised to be just as popular. Under the terms of the original agreement, which was negotiated through the State Department, the Russians and the major American film companies agreed to distribute around ten of each other's pictures the first year. Since the Soviet offerings were unknown quantities, the majors decided to draw lots to divvy up the films for distribution.

Soviet films had regularly been shown in Russian at the Cameo Theater, located on Eighth Avenue off Times Square. They were of the type *Time* described as "Boy meets tractor. Boy loses tractor. Boy gets tractor."[46] For the exchange, the Soviets offered up prizewinners from international film festivals. Mikhail Kalatozov's *The Cranes Are Flying* (*Letyat zhuravli*), the winner of the Golden Palm at Cannes in 1958, was the first. To celebrate the start of the program, the organizers arranged a joint premiere. On November 10, 1959, *Cranes* opened in Washington, D.C., at the Dupont Theatre and Delbert Mann's

Alexei Batalov in Mikhail Kalatozov's *The Cranes Are Flying* (1959)

Marty, which had won an Oscar for Best Picture in 1956, opened in Moscow. *Cranes* was distributed by Warner Bros. and opened in New York on March 21, 1960, at the Fine Arts. Crowther praised it for extolling love and peace: "Believe it or not, it is a picture about two young people romantically in love—in love with each other, that is, not with a tractor or the Soviet state. And its theme, which evolves in the agony of their being separated by war (the fellow is killed at the front, as it finally turns out), is poignantly and powerfully pro-peace."[47] *Time* felt that *Cranes* "probably matters less as a work of art than as a revelation of the modern Russian mood. It adds, for one thing, to the mass of evidence that the nation that leads the world in rocketry is still inspired by the romantic ideals of 19th century 'servants' literature.' The film also suggests that there has been some relaxation of the puritanical morality of the revolution: the heroine errs, but is forgiven at the fade. And there is even a mild suggestion that people in Russia sometimes get tired of the canned ideas they are continually fed—the party's production slogans and political cant ("Fascist beasts") come in for some sly kidding. So do the professional women, the emancipated amazons of Marxist society. But one *Cranes* does not make a summer."[48]

The other Soviet offerings included Grigori Chukhrai's *Ballad of a Soldier,* Sergei Bondarchuk's *Fate of a Man,* and Georgi Daneliya and Igor Talankin's *A Summer to Remember.* Although the Russians expected their films to receive regular commercial distribution, they played mostly in art houses. The U.S.-Soviet film exchange ended abruptly in early 1963 when the majors opted out of the arrangement, claiming they were losing money on the films. U.S. distributors subsequently negotiated directly with the Soviet government to acquire films. Two noteworthy Russian films reached the United States in this manner: Andrei Tarkovsky's *My Name Is Ivan* and Sergei Bondarchuck's *War and Peace.*

My Name Is Ivan (Ivanovo detstvo) was released by Sig Shore International on June 27, 1963, at the Murray Hill. It was Tarkovsky's first feature-length film and had won the Golden Lion at the Venice Film Festival in 1962. Shore International originally distributed foreign films to TV. In 1958 it went into theatrical distribution and released a dubbed version of Aleksandr Ptushko's *The Sword and the Dragon,* an enormously popular children's fantasy based on Russian folktales. *My Name Is Ivan,* Shore's only other theatrical release, was described by Bosley Crowther as an antiwar film about "an orphan boy [Kolya Burlaiev] who serves the army by reconnoitering behind the enemy lines." Crowther noted that "a keening cry of sadness seems to come from the Russian film. . . . It is a cry not so much of sorrow for the agonized 12-year-old lad. . . . It is more a cry of anguish for all youngsters lost in World War II, for youths whose lives were exhausted in hatred, bloodshed and death." The film, moreover, "has an uncommon personal quality, a concentration such as we didn't used to get in Soviet films," said Crowther. "Here the entire consideration of the story and the camera approach of the director . . . is the personal experience of the boy and the few people around him. It is the boy's behavior in action, his manliness under fire, the let-down, when he comes back from spying and then the dreams that haunt his restless sleep and the edginess of his contacts with other soldiers that make the substance of the film." Crowther concluded that "beauty, poetry and sadness are certainly lodged in its brief dramatic span, to be seized and embraced by anybody who will give a compassionate mind to it."[49]

War and Peace (Voyna i mir) was released by Walter Reade's Continental Distributing and had its American premiere on April 28, 1968, at the De Mille Theater, located on Seventh Avenue and 47th Street. Bondarchuk's adaptation of the Leo Tolstoy novel was financed by the Soviet government at a cost of $100 million. "Filmed as an epic in praise of the glories of the Russian soldiers and people," according to Richard L. Coe it took five years to make and was released as a four-part widescreen feature that ran more than seven hours.

The roles of Natasha, Pierre, and Andrei were played by Lyudmila Savelyeva, Sergei Bondarchuck, and Vyacheslav Tikhonov, respectively. The Walter Reade Organization paid the Soviet government $1.5 million for the U.S. rights. To market it, Reade "spent the cost of a major film" dubbing the film into English, preparing a set of titles to introduce all the principal characters, and making suitable color prints that could be used in American projectors.[50] For the American premiere the film was edited down to a little over six hours and presented in two parts, with the intermission lasting two and a half hours. The invited audience consisted of government and film-industry leaders as well as diplomats and society members, each of whom paid $125 per ticket to attend the benefit screening. For the continuing run at the De Mille, tickets were sold on a reserved-seat basis "at the highest admission scale ever set for a movie"— from $5.50 to $7.50. The previous high for films was $6 for *Funny Girl*.[51]

The dubbing was a major irritant. Penelope Gilliat complained, "The decision to tack on alien voices seems madness. . . . Robbing an actor of his voice and substituting the sound of another man going through a translation in a vacuum, in the doomed hope of matching foreign lip movements, is like taking away Fontyn's arms and pasting on the flippers of a bored penguin."[52] Renata Adler, Bosley Crowther's successor at the *New York Times*, stated, "It proves once and for all, on the grandest possible scale, the futility of dubbing." She considered the film to be "a vulgarism and a failure" and labeled it "a full-length animated Classic Comic."[53]

Time gave it a more considered review. It agreed that *War and Peace* "has escaped greatness, except in cost and length. . . . The movie is awesome in war and pusillanimous in peace. . . . Cavalries plunge and break in tidal waves; columns of infantry writhe to the horizon and beyond; choruses of cannons shout like narrow mouths of hell in a series of vivid instants that recall the trancelike battle paintings of Uccello. With a knowing artist's eye, the director composes vignettes reminiscent of the harshness and heartbreak of Goya etchings. Again and again, the dolor and grandeur of Russia's convulsive struggle with Napoleon provide a panorama truly worthy of Tolstoy." *Time* went on to say that in the book "the war was only the background framing the twin heroes, Prince Andrei Bolkonsky and his friend Pierre Bezukhov, who represent the two faces of the aristocracy. . . . It is in the telling of their lives that the film fails. Pierre and Andrei are at best only shallow, literal representations of Tolstoy's rich characters. To portray Natasha's giddiness, Savelyeva never walks when she can dash, never smiles when she can give shiny-eyed grins that reduce her to a caricature coquette." In the end, "after all the excesses and errors, considerable power abides. Tolstoy's book may not have been reliable as history or wholly satisfactory as fiction; yet it achieved, in the words of Tolstoy's biographer, Henri Troyat, 'the majesty of a second Genesis.' Bondarchuk's film catches part of that majesty by showing Mother Russia dressed in the 19th century's bloodstained finery, overshadowing her doomed, noble children. She, and she alone, is worth two trips to the movie house."[54] *War and Peace* received an Oscar and the New York Film Critics Circle prize for Best Foreign Language Film.

Andrzej Wajda

Meanwhile, the thaw in the cold war instituted by Nikita Khruschev had spread to Communist Eastern Europe. In 1956 protests by Polish workers led to a brief period of liberalization when, wrote Arthur Knight, "artists and intellectuals learned the unaccustomed taste of freedom—a freedom that extended even to the filmmakers in the state-supported studios."[55] New Yorkers were introduced to the New Polish Cinema beginning in May 1960, when the Museum of Modern Art presented a series of recent Polish films. Nearly all were made after 1956 and "dealt with one big traumatic theme—World War II and its moral and spiritual repercussions," according to Cynthia Grenier.[56] Two of those films, Andrzej Wajda's *Kanal* and *Ashes and Diamonds*, found commercial distribution.

A member of the first generation of Polish films directors, Wajda graduated from the Lodz Film School in 1952. After serving his apprenticeship under the prominent Polish filmmaker Aleksandr Ford, Wajda made his first feature, *A Generation*, in 1954, representing the first part of his "War Trilogy" about Polish resistance in World War II. *Kanal* and *Ashes and Diamonds*, produced in 1957 and 1958, respectively, comprised the final two parts of the trilogy. Released within weeks of each other in May 1961, they "startled moviegoers with their black intensity," said *Time*.[57] *Kanal*, the winner of a Special Jury Prize at Cannes in 1957, established the young Pole's international reputation. It was distributed by J. Jay Frankel and played briefly at the New Yorker Theater beginning on May 9, 1961. Frankel was a twenty-four-year-old importer who had originally specialized in distributing Russian films, among them *Ballad of a Soldier* and *A Summer to Remember*. *Kanal* told of the humiliating defeat of Polish resistance fighters, who hid in the sewers to escape the German Wehrmacht during the final days of the disastrous Warsaw uprising of 1944. The actual uprising resulted in the killing of an estimated 370,000 Poles by the Germans and the virtual destruction of the city. *Ashes and Diamonds*, the winner of the Golden Lion at the Venice Film Festival in 1959, featured Zbigniew Cybulski, who became known as the Polish James Dean. It was distributed by Janus Films and opened at the Fifth Avenue Cinema on May 29, 1961. Bosley Crowther saw the film as "a melancholy recapitulation on the political and social chaos at the end of the war."[58] It told the story of Maciek, a young resistance fighter in a provincial town, who is ordered to assassinate an incoming Communist Party functionary, a deed he is loathe to perform on the first day of peace.

Wajda's baroque visual style generated the most comment, both positive and negative. Stanley Kauffmann described *Kanal*'s sewer sequences as follows: "The sense of trudging for hours hip deep in slime is so well conveyed that even your olfactory nerve is suggestively stimulated."[59] *Time* admired the "memorable metaphors" in *Ashes and Diamonds*, such as "the mad, drunken celebration of victory to Chopin's Polonaise in A Major; the ironic reflection of V-E day fireworks in a stagnant pool, beside which the Communist boss lies dead; the lovers in a ruined church, its Christ figure splintered and dangling upside down in the foreground; Maciek setting fire to each glass of vodka on a bar and delivering weird incantation to old, dead loves; his girl drenched in sunlight while Maciek—in the death throes on a dank rubbish heap—whimpers and twitches like a wounded rabbit."[60]

On the negative side, the acting in both films drew criticism. Crowther found the acting of *Kanal* overbearing. He interpreted the film as "a symbolic story of . . . the way Polish freedom crumbled and died in World War II," but added that the telling of it might have been "a little more endurable" if the action had been "directed and played in a coldly realistic and sharply representational way. But Mr. Wajda has put it in a rather lofty heroic style, with the soldiers striking poses, popping their eyes and flinging themselves into passionate moods. The sewer fumes with caldron-like vapors, hollow sounds rumble down the walls, weird, maniacal music echoes behind it all."[61] Of the acting in *Ashes and Diamonds*, Stanley Kauffmann noted: "The film combines the worst of two widely different artistic styles. On the one hand it is full of unsubtle character actors in unsubtle character parts (the pompous young secretary, the drunken old editor), all contributing tiresome little cameos in pseudo-Moscow-Art-Theater tradition. On the other hand the hero, complete with dark glasses, is out of the lowest stratum of diluted American realism: taciturn, sexy, soulful, tough, brutal, a rebel without a Dean. . . . The youth kills his man as fireworks go off symbolically in the sky. His own death at the end is stupidly contrived and is protracted so long that I thought he was going to stumble on into another film where he would make his first entrance wounded."[62]

Even the plots came in for criticism. Like the *Time* review of *Ashes and Diamonds*, Arthur Knight admired Wajda's "skillfully composed" images. However, "as Wajda follows his hero across the twelve crowded hours to his doom, one senses first a superficiality in many of the encounters, then a contrivance in the episodes, and finally comes the reluctant recognition that cinematic effects are perhaps even more important to the director than his characters' emotions. In the end, it is Zbigniew Cybulski, as Maciek, who holds the film together, not Wajda."[63] Despite mixed reviews, *Ashes and Diamonds* ran for nearly two months at the Fifth Avenue Cinema. Taking a second look at the director, Crowther said Wajda showed promise of becoming "the Ingmar Bergman of Poland or, at least, a one-man Polish 'new wave.' Anyhow, we want to see more of his films."[64]

During the 1960s, Czechoslovakia, Yugoslavia, and Hungary also enjoyed brief periods of liberalization, which resulted in successive "new waves" from these countries. Most of these films would enter the United States by way of the New York Film Festival and enrich the city's film culture. Like all entries from outside the epicenter, they were considered hard sells, of which only a few would reach the art house.

Part Three

Changing Dynamics

12

Enter Hollywood

Lured by Brigitte Bardot, Columbia Pictures entered the art film market in a serious way beginning in 1957; by 1966 the majors dominated the market, having absorbed nearly the entire pantheon of European auteurs with sweet deals offering total production financing, directorial freedom, and marketing muscle. These auteurs included Michelangelo Antonioni, Luchino Visconti, and Federico Fellini of Italy; Tony Richardson, Joseph Losey, and Karel Reisz of Great Britain; and François Truffaut, Jean-Luc Godard, Louis Malle, and Eric Rohmer of France.[1]

Hollywood's motives were transparent. Foreign films—especially those that depicted sex in ways forbidden by the Production Code—were attracting customers, and the majors wanted a part of the business. The majors also wanted to exploit the European pop culture scene—particularly Swinging London fashions and music—to attract young adults. The core audience for foreign films during the 1960s now comprised America's "cinephile" generation—university students born during the late 1930s and 1940s—who had joined an estimated four thousand college film societies by 1968. As obvious as these motives appear, taking on art films was basically a conservative move that enabled the majors to cover all the bases in a period of rapid cultural, political, and social change. This chapter describes the first phase (1957–66) of Hollywood's entry into the market. It covers a period of relative industry stability during which the majors still adhered—albeit reluctantly—to the tenets of the Production Code.

Hollywood's venture into art films has to be seen as part of the American film industry's postwar efforts to reestablish its hegemony over international distribution. It accomplished this by releasing its huge backlog of pictures

227

made during the war, adopting a united front to combat protectionism, and shifting production overseas to take advantage of European film subsidies—a phenomenon known as runaway production. International distribution also meant investing in European filmmakers and marketing foreign films in the United States. The two went hand in hand and had the goal of discovering and absorbing new talent wherever it could be found.

Hollywood's heaviest overseas investments were targeted to European production centers in Rome and London. Rome had much going for it. The city was within easy reach of colorful scenery, it had an abundance of trained extras, and it had up-to-date studios. Films made in Rome, which became known as "Hollywood on the Tiber," could easily be tailored for American tastes. Such films included Mervyn LeRoy's *Quo Vadis?* (MGM, 1951), William Wyler's *Roman Holiday* (Paramount, 1953); Jean Negulesco's *Three Coins in the Fountain* (20th Century-Fox, 1954), Joseph L. Mankiewicz's *The Barefoot Contessa* (United Artists, 1954), King Vidor's *War and Peace* (Paramount, 1956), Anthony Mann's *Trapeze* (United Artists, 1956), William Wyler's *Ben-Hur* (MGM, 1959), Joseph L. Mankiewicz's *Cleopatra* (20th Century-Fox, 1963), David Lean's *Doctor Zhivago* (MGM, 1965), and John Huston's *The Bible* (20th Century-Fox, 1966).

As foreign markets opened up, Hollywood signed coproduction pacts with top-ranked producers—starting with Goffredo Lombardo, Dino De Laurentiis, and Alberto Grimaldi—and financed or participated in the financing of Italian pictures intended for international distribution. Such ventures were typically bi- or tripartite productions between Italy, France, and Germany and were released in the United States dubbed for mainstream consumption. They usually teamed up American male actors with Italian stars such as Sophia Loren, Gina Lollobrigida, Verna Lisi, Monica Vitti, and Silvano Mangano. What kinds of films did the majors produce? Every conceivable kind—peplums, romantic comedies, continental dramas, biblical epics, spaghetti westerns, sex comedies, crime comedies, and melodramas.

A similar story can be told about London. By the 1960s the majors were financing nearly all the important pictures produced in Great Britain each year. The films from "Hollywood on the Thames" include the James Bond and Pink Panther series (United Artists), David Lean's *Lawrence of Arabia* (Columbia, 1962), Fred Zinnemann's *A Man for All Seasons* (Columbia, 1966), Lewis Gilbert's *Alfie* (Paramount, 1966), Silvio Narizzano's *Georgy Girl* (Columbia, 1966), Stanley Kubrick's *Dr. Strangelove* (Columbia, 1967) and *2001: A Space Odyssey* (MGM, 1968), Michelangelo Antonioni's *Blow-Up* (MGM, 1967), Franco Zeffirelli's *Romeo and Juliet* (Paramount, 1968), and Joseph Losey's *Secret Ceremony* (Universal, 1968), to name a few. Vincent Canby noted in 1962 that the ever-growing

"American investment in British production has made it almost impossible to define a 'British' film."[2]

The Little Three Move In

Columbia Pictures and United Artists, former members of the Little Three, were the first Hollywood companies to make the move. As was previously mentioned, Columbia led the charge in 1957 by hiring Kingsley-International to handle the distribution of the Brigitte Bardot pictures, beginning with *And God Created Woman*. The decision allowed Columbia to circumvent a Motion Picture Association of America (MPAA) rule forbidding a member company from distributing any picture that lacked a Production Code seal or carried a C rating by the Legion of Decency—both of which *And God Created Woman* had against it.

United Artists followed Columbia's lead in 1958 by acquiring Lopert Films, another prominent independent distributor, to serve as its art film subsidiary. Lopert's first release was Marcel Camus's *Black Orpheus*, which helped usher in the French New Wave in 1959. Lopert served the same purpose as Kingsley-International had in 1960 when it released Jules Dassin's *Never on Sunday*, a low-budget Greek-American import, without a Production Code seal and with a C rating from the Legion of Decency. A clash-of-cultures film set in the Greek seaport of Piraeus, *Never on Sunday* (*Pote tin Kyriaki*) told the story of Homer Troy (Jules Dassin), a middle-aged American tourist from Connecticut and a student of Greek civilization, who attempts to "improve" Ilya (Melina Mercouri), a carefree, warm-hearted prostitute, by persuading her to abandon the pleasures of the body for the pleasures of the mind. According to *Time*, Ilya obliges him at first but eventually "she also discovers that when nature is denied, [the] spirit suffers too. The film ends with a blare of strumpets as the heroine leads a rousingly hilarious red-light revolution and the luckless hero sails home sadder but wiser." *Time* adds, "Dassin's satire is obviously directed at the U.S., but his touch is light and his affection for the object of his satire unmistakable. Unlike his hero, Dassin is not trying to save anybody. He merely wants to suggest that the missionary mentality, which he believes to be an American complex, is at best childish and at worst ineffective. The idea is scarcely original, but Dassin expresses it in a wonderful rush of animal spirits and earthy humor."[3]

Lopert released *Never on Sunday* at the Plaza on October 18, 1960. It ran there for more than a year before going into general release. To overcome the potential handicap of the C rating, United Artists marketed the film in upscale suburban theaters, which were immune to any backlash from local pressure groups. Whether or not to dub was another consideration. In the original release

Melina Mercouri and Jules Dassin in Dassin's *Never on Sunday* (1960)

Homer and Ilya speak to each other in English, whereas when Ilya addresses the other local characters, it is in Greek. As Arthur Knight explained, there was a good reason for this: "Dassin *arranged* his film as a multilingual experience, with the difference in languages exploited to emphasize differences in culture and temperament. He clearly recognizes the color values of a native tongue; it contributes as much to the milieu as the graceful native dances and the lilt of the native bouzoukia music. To translate this, to dub it, would mean a loss not merely of flavor; but most of the humor and most of the point of the film."[4]

United Artists wished to take no chances, however, and used a dubbed version for the suburban run. The strategy paid off. *Never on Sunday* eventually grossed over $4 million in rentals to rank alongside *And God Created Woman* as a crossover hit. Manos Hadjidakis's bouzouki theme, which became one of Europe's top tunes, won an Oscar for Best Original Song.

What motivated these two companies? The United Artists that dominated the art film market of the 1960s was a far cry from the company once owned by Charlie Chaplin and Mary Pickford. A distribution company for independent producers from the start, United Artists teetered on the verge of bankruptcy after the war until a new management team took control in 1951 and transformed it into an industry leader. It accomplished this by doing what United Artists had never previously been able to do, namely, supply production financing to attract top free-lance producers, directors, and stars. The plan required it to distribute a full roster of films each year, which would generate enough revenue from distribution fees to cover its operating costs and create a cushion to offset any production losses. Once the company reached breakeven in any given year, everything else it collected from film rentals was considered profit, including the returns from such low-grossing pictures as art films. Stated another way, United Artists operated on a "tonnage" basis, meaning that, in the words of David Londoner, "distribution overhead is essentially fixed and that incremental product put through above break-even carries a disproportionately high profit contribution.[5]

Although Columbia Pictures pursued a similar goal, it was motivated by a different cause. Primarily a B film producer, Columbia found itself in a precarious position after the war as demand for its second-tier product declined. Lacking the resources to move into A films on an exclusive basis, Columbia took the offensive by opening its doors to independent producers, venturing early into television production, and going into foreign film distribution.

After the Bardot craze had subsided, Columbia placed a bet on Jean-Luc Godard—described in the *New York Times* as "one of the most offbeat and controversial of the young French directors"—by giving him a multiple-picture contract. The deal was struck in 1963. It provided Godard with small budgets ranging between $100,000 and $120,000 per film, with no strings attached. Columbia vice president Stanley Schneider defined the agreement with Godard as making films "at a price," which meant that Godard's budgets had "to bear a realistic relation to the probable returns" in the U.S. art film market.[6] The caveat was typical of the multiple-picture contracts the majors were giving foreign film directors around this time. Columbia undoubtedly realized that Godard's chances of producing a crossover hit were slim, but it could hope for another *Breathless*, which had been a favorite with college students. Meanwhile, Columbia's investment was more than safe since Godard's films regularly returned their investments in his home market. The filmmaker was now assured of steady financing—as long as he stayed within his preapproved budgets—and he had a single distributor—a Hollywood major at that—to seal his commercial fate.

Columbia's pact with Godard resulted in three pictures: *The Married Woman* (1965), *Band of Outsiders* (1966), and *Masculine Feminine* (1966).[7] They were released by Royal Films, Columbia's new in-house art film subsidiary, which had been formed in 1962 following the death of Edward Kingsley. Columbia decided to lead off with Godard's second film, *The Married Woman* (*Une Femme mariée*), starring Macha Meril. The reasoning behind this choice may have been that the film could be exploited as "a French drama of infidelity" and stood the best chance of success at the box office. "The Married Woman" was Godard's original title for the film, but he changed it to "A Married Woman" for its French release at the insistence of the French censors because it was thought that the original title commented on French womanhood in general.

Columbia "boldly" restored the original title for U.S. release in 1965 and secured Walter Reade's classy Baronet on Manhattan's Upper East Side—across the street from Bloomingdale's—for an August 16 premiere. Columbia's ads posed the question "Husband or Lover?" together with a close-up photo of a man's hand resting on a woman's bare knee. The woman's left hand partially covers the man's and has a wedding ring on it. The banner stated, "She Loves Two Men . . . She Is Married to One."[8]

Bosley Crowther warned that "if Godard isn't careful he's going to shoot his way out of the avant-garde—out of the idolatrous affection of all those cinema buffs who go for movies that are formless and obscure." The structure of the film was unusual but was" fairly easy to understand." Godard's theme—"modern woman is adrift without [moral] charts or bearings on a sea of methodical sex"—had contemporary relevance.[9] (Crowther named the film among his "Ten Best" of 1965.) Brendan Gill called it "the best Godard I have ever seen . . . immaculately photographed and with an exquisite spareness of speech and deed." The film is "a nearly perfect study of what it is to be young and in love and incapable of behaving for more than a few minutes at a time in a sensible fashion, much less in a conventionally honorable one."[10] *Time* called the film "a sociological tract on the mechanization of modern middle-class sex."[11] *The Married Woman* ran for seven weeks at the Baronet. Encouraged by early box office returns, Royal lined up several commercial theaters in the metropolitan area for the general release and took out large ads in the *Times*—but the picture died.

Royal released *Band of Outsiders* (*Bande à part*) in March 1966, nearly two years after it opened in Paris and a year and a half after it premiered at the New York Film Festival. According to the festival program, *Band of Outsiders* "is in some ways a return by director Jean-Luc Godard to the world of *Breathless*—the world of the outsiders, the fringe people." It starred Anna Karina, "a wistful young girl who encounters a pair of larcenous criminals, Sami Frey and Claude Brasseur."[12] Critics concentrated on Godard's portrait of disaffected youth. For example, Robert Hatch noted that "first with *Breathless*, now with

Band of Outsiders . . . Godard is compiling a dossier on the somnambulist generation. . . . They remind me of 19th-century romantic heroes and heroines, wasting from consumption into ethereal purity. Godard's people are in a decline of fantasy. The disease is authentic enough and it is international. Walk through Greenwich Village any night, and you will pass stragglers from Lee's Confederate Army, outriders from Brando's motorcycle gang, Edwardian dandies and Chekhovian students, Japanese revolutionaries and transvestites beyond counting."[13]

Pauline Kael claimed that "Godard's style, with its nonchalance about the fates of the characters, . . . is an American teenager's ideal. To be hard and cool as a movie gangster yet not stupid or gross like a gangster—that's the cool grace of the privileged smart young." She went on to say, "Jean-Luc Godard intended to give the public what it wanted. His next film was going to be about a girl and a gun. 'A sure-fire story which will sell a lot of tickets.' And so, like Henry James' hero in *The Next Time*, he proceeded to make a work of art that sold fewer tickets than ever."[14]

Masculine Feminine (*Masculin-féminin*) premiered at the 1966 New York Film Festival in tandem with Godard's *Pierrot le Fou*. Starring Chantal Goya and Jean-Pierre Léaud, it was another foray into the Parisian youth culture of the 1960s. According to the festival program, "Godard himself has described his film as concerning 'the Children of Marx and Coca-Cola,' the generation who have just turned 20. His left-wing young hero finds it hard to adjust to the fact that his girl friends don't care about Vietnam; they're only interested in James Bond."[15]

Masculine Feminine played to a capacity house at the festival and opened the following day at the Little Carnegie, the first time in the festival's four-year history that one of its selections went immediately into commercial release to take advantage of the festival buildup. Royal promoted the film as "a movie happening! Jean-Luc Godard's swinging look at youth and love in Paris today!" Crowther picked up on this when he remarked, "It gives a pretense of being a study of the mores of Parisian youth. . . . But this is just the pretense of the picture. Mainly it seems to be a movie happening, in which Mr. Godard can play whimsical and sometimes comical stunts, not leading to any clear conclusion as to the stability of youth. . . . From lengthy and tedious conversations between his fellow and his girl about themselves, he will jump to scenes of youngsters demonstrating in the streets against Vietnam. In the middle of the random flow of the story, he stops for a lengthy interview with a girl who holds the screen for the entire shot, sitting casually on the windowsill. . . . But it adds up to entertainment of only the most loose and spotty sort."[16]

Time called the film a "cubistic jigsaw-puzzle picture of the go-go generation," adding that "like most Godard movies *Masculine Feminine* is hard to watch and hard to stop watching. Time and again Godard shows that he is a great bad director. Great because he is superbly endowed with what Sergei Eisenstein called 'the film sense,' bad because he is so painfully lacking in common sense."[17] Brendan Gill deplored the film: "*Masculine Feminine* is more talk than plot. . . . I have to admit that the picture has slipped through my mind as through a sieve, but I *think* the main parts were played by Jean-Pierre Léaud and Chantal Goya."[18] Although Royal devised some interesting strategies to broaden Godard's appeal, the average moviegoer remained unfazed by such efforts. Godard's core audience remained the so-called Godardians.

Columbia Pictures later financed and distributed Jacques Demy's first American film, *The Model Shop* (1969), François Truffaut's *Bed and Board* (1971), and Eric Rohmer's *Claire's Knee* (1971) and *Chloë in the Afternoon* (1972). In addition, Columbia distributed Leopoldo Torre Nilsson's *The Terrace* (1963), Jack Clayton's *The Pumpkin Eater* (1964), Francesco Rosi's *Salvatore Giuliano* (1964), Roman Polanski's *Repulsion* (1965), and Luchino Visconti's *Sandra* (1966), among others.

United Artists moved more aggressively into the art film market. *Never on Sunday* naturally paved the way for additional Greek-American coproductions. In 1962 Lopert released two very different films based on classic Greek myths: Jules Dassin's *Phaedra* and Michael Cacoyannis's *Electra*. Both were financed by United Artists. *Phaedra*, a modern retelling of the Greek myth, capitalized on Miss Mercouri's new status as an international star. Showing off her talent as a tragedienne, she played "the wife of a wealthy Greek shipowner (Raf Vallone) who falls passionately in love with her stepson (Anthony Perkins) and subsequently commits suicide after her stepson rejects her and her husband denounces her."[19] Like *Never on Sunday*, *Phaedra* was shot on location, in this case on the beautiful Greek island of Hydra, which may have been familiar to moviegoers who had seen Jean Negulesco's *Boy on a Dolphin* a few years earlier.

Lopert released *Phaedra* in an English-language version simultaneously at the Plaza and in fifteen theaters in the Greater New York area. To bolster the launch, it brought Miss Mercouri to New York. As reported in the *New York Times*, "Mercouri arrived on the Queen Mary Tuesday in a shower of rose petals dropped onto the ship from a helicopter (a gesture of affection from local Hellenes as well as promotion for her new film) and accompanied by a wardrobe of Christian Dior clothes. She will wear them in a series of personal appearances connected with *Phaedra*. . . . In it she plays a wealthy shipbuilder's wife who falls in love with her stepson. The woman is, among other things, a

Dior customer and the movie has a scene filmed in the Paris couture home."[20] *Phaedra* did only so-so business despite some good reviews. As A. H. Weiler commented, "*Phaedra* may be ageless but despite its solemn dedication and modernity this version sometimes is as close to the tearful sagas of afternoon television as it is to the work of the titans who created it."[21]

Electra (*Ilektra*) was played in ancient dress and was released in a subtitled version. It starred Irene Papas as the daughter of King Agamemnon, who emerges from exile to avenge her father's murder by her mother, Clytemnestra, and her lover, Aegisthus. Crowther described Cocayannis's adaptation as "a worthy screen rendering of a classic Greek drama" that transmutes "the gold of verbal poetry from one to another art form." Here is how Bosley Crowther described Irene Papas's performance: "The inner fires of Electra are also made eloquent by the heroic appearance and performance of Irene Papas in this role. Seldom has a face or conveyance of the human figure so beautifully depicted the nature and the passion of a character as do Miss Papas here. Her eyes and the gestures say quite as much as the few words — the comparatively few words — she has to utter in expressing her grief and pain."[22] Shot in stark black and white on locations in Greece, *Electra* was a modest box office success given its production cost of only $70,000.

United Artists next sought out French New Wave directors with commercial potential, in particular Philippe de Broca and Louis Malle. With UA financing, de Broca made two comedy-adventure vehicles for Jean-Paul Belmondo, *That Man From Rio* (1964) and *Up to His Ears* (1966). Distributed by Lopert they were both box office hits. In *That Man from Rio* (*L'Homme de Rio*), a James Bond spoof, wrote *Variety*, "Belmondo is an airline pilot who becomes involved in a wild adventure that takes him from Paris to Rio, and the Amazon, in order to help his archaeologist fiancee (Françoise Dorleac) search for stolen treasure. . . . Belmondo sways on the ledges of high buildings, has fights on scaffoldings, is almost eaten by an alligator, has to jump out of a plane and has many fights. It is all done with invention, speed and knowhow."[23] Crowther described it as "more reckless than James Bond's adventures, more ridiculous than what happens in *It's a Mad, Mad, Mad, Mad World* . . . Obviously, Mr. De Broca has schooled himself so joyously in the comedy styles of Mack Sennett, Harold Lloyd and the films of Pearl White that he fairly pants to imitate them when he brings actors and camera face to face. He bubbles with improvisations of crises that tangle fun and thrills, and he sparks with cliff-hanging situations that have to be seen to be disbelieved."[24] The New York Film Critics Circle named *That Man From Rio* Best Foreign Language Film of 1964. *Up to His Ears*, which repeated the same formula, teamed Belmondo with Ursula Andress.

De Broca subsequently made *The King of Hearts* (1967), a witty antiwar film starring Alan Bates.

Louis Malle, which *Time* described as "the most wide-ranging of the French New Wave auteurs," was known in the United States for such films as *The Lovers* and *Zazie* and for the Brigitte Bardot vehicle *A Very Private Affair*. United Artists put up over $2 million for Malle's *Viva Maria!* (1966), which united French cinema's two grandes demoiselles, Brigitte Bardot and Jeanne Moreau, in a "lusty musical comedy." Bardot and Moreau are members "of a music-hall caravan touring the donkey trails south of the border at the turn of the century. One night, by accident, they invent the striptease and their fame sweeps Mexico; another night, also by accident, they become the appassionatas of a revolution, and lead peons by the hecatombs to glorious death."[25]

UA arranged for Bardot to visit the United States for the first time to promote the film. Upon her arrival at John F. Kennedy International Airport, she gave a twenty-minute news conference. Here is how Vincent Canby reported the event: "Following the airport formalities, the actress slipped back into her black and white striped coat and, accompanied by a 10-car motorcade, road to the Plaza hotel in a bubble-top limousine supplied by the Ford Motor Company. The car, once used by former President Dwight D. Eisenhower, is bulletproof, but the only shooting yesterday was done by photographers in nearby cars."[26] UA released the film simultaneously at the Plaza in a subtitled version and at the Astor in a dubbed version. Following the opening, Miss Bardot flew to California for the Hollywood premiere.

Variety wrote, "Here is a film that measures up to its advance publicity. It has the wit, scope and color for both arty and playoff or regular first run chances. It strikes the right note of larger than-than-life adventure, uses sex in a delicious, rather than leering or over-exploited manner and deftly pays homage to the Yank films of this kind in its stable, good natured succession of gags, leavened with some frisky but never blue French humor."[27]

Taking a contrary position, Robert Hatch said, "Louis Malle, who apparently intended his picture as a lusty musical comedy, spoils the chance by overdoing all his effects, straining for a synthetic naivete and never implying what he can make explicit. Perhaps having persuaded the Mlles. Moreau and Bardot to appear on the same screen, he felt compelled to back up this redundancy of provocation with the maximum noise and confusion. The result is a film of heartless monotony: all those little men in white pajamas, straw hats and crossed cartridge belts from the murals of Rivera dying in the long grass because the girls are tired of doing the cancan. The use of violence in a musical wants a deft touch: one should not, for instance, impale a man with a billiard cue or allow the bullets to be seen cutting across a back; such details spoil the air of gaiety. And what sort of humor sends Brigitte Bardot off in a closed wagon with three middle-aged cafe types, to return in the morning, sprung with exhaustion and murmuring that love is indeed a marvelous occupation?"[28] *Viva Maria!* grossed around $1.5 million at the box office—a success by art house standards but a disappointment for UA, which had hoped for a crossover hit.

UA had invested heavily in British productions since the 1950s to meet its quota requirements and to take advantage of British film subsidies. Many of these films produced in British studios "were sometimes indistinguishable in look and tone" from the films produced in Hollywood, said Alexander Walker.[29] Beginning in 1962, UA began investing in strictly British films that reflected the contemporary pop culture scene. That same year the company struck two significant deals, the first with producers Albert R. Broccoli and Harry Saltzman for a James Bond film and the second with director Tony Richardson for an offbeat picture based on Henry Fielding's eighteenth-century novel *Tom Jones*.

Tom Jones was too risqué for a Production Code seal and was released through Lopert Films, UA's art film subsidiary. Pitching the film to UA's top management, David Picker—who was being groomed for a top executive position in the company—had said, "This is Albert Finney starring, Tony Richardson directing the John Osborne screenplay. . . . This is ribald, bawdy, Hogarthian; it jumps from bed to bed, from adventure to misadventure—it could be great fun. It does have, of course, its serious overtones, but essentially it is a wild caricature of times in England in the seventeen hundreds. Made by these picture-makers, I see this as a potentially important world-wide grosser."[30] The stellar cast included Susannah York, Hugh Griffith, Dame Edith Evans, Diane Cilentro, Joan Littlewood, and Joyce Redman. Michael MacLiammoir, the great Irish stage actor, delivered the wry voice-over narration. And John Addison, the classical music composer, supplied the jaunty harpsichord-driven score.

Although *Tom Jones* broke house records all over England, in the United States conditions were different. American moviegoers were unfamiliar with the title and the supporting cast. Moreover, they generally disliked British costume pictures. UA therefore decided go slow and treat *Tom Jones* as an art film. It opened at the Cinema I on October 7, 1963, and received rave reviews. *Time* said, "Britain's Tony Richardson has made the novel into an absolutely magnificent movie. The film is a way-out, walleyed, wonderful exercise in cinema. It's also a social satire written in blood with a broadaxe. It is bawdy as the British were bawdy when a wench had to wear five petticoats to barricade her virtue. It is as beautiful in EastmanColor as England is in spring. And it is one of the funniest farces anybody anywhere has splattered on a screen since Hollywood lost the recipe for custard pie."[31]

Rather than capitalizing on all this publicity by going wide with the picture, UA continued with its hard-to-get policy. *Tom Jones* ran at the Cinema I on an exclusive basis for a month, after which it opened in a single theater in Los Angeles. UA had the sophisticated audience in its pocket; the tactic was to build word-of-mouth to attract general audiences in the hinterlands. It was not until Christmas that the picture played other metropolitan areas—a total of eighteen theaters in twelve cities. And it was not until spring, when *Tom Jones* won Oscars for Best Picture and Best Director, among others, that UA opened the film wide. By the end of its run, *Tom Jones* had grossed over $16 million in rentals, making it one of the top non-road show releases up to that time.

UA rewarded Richardson with a multiple-picture contract following the Academy Awards ceremony. It agreed to finance Richardson's personal projects as well as projects by his Woodfall associates. The contract was nonexclusive, which meant that if UA passed on a proposal, Richardson could set up it up elsewhere. He did exactly that with *The Loved One*, which he took to MGM. Woodfall, meanwhile, produced a series of three low-budget pictures under the supervision of Oscar Lewenstein, a founding member of the English Stage Company and Richardson's associate producer on *Tom Jones*. The three films were Desmond Davis's *Girl with Green Eyes* (1964), Peter Yates's *One Way Pendulum* (1965), and Richard Lester's *The Knack . . . and How to Get It* (1965). They were released by Lopert Films.

Of the group, *The Knack*, which was based on Ann Jellicoe's hit play, had the most going for it. Lester had become a star of sorts after directing the Beatles' hit film *A Hard Day's Night* in 1964. Moreover, the Off-Broadway production of Jellicoe's play, directed by Mike Nichols, was still running in New York. The film starred Rita Tushingham as a naive country girl who arrives in London in search of the YWCA and stumbles into a house occupied by two bachelors, one of whom has "quite a knack in the art of making it successfully with girls." The youths were played by Ray Brooks and Michael Crawford. Where Jellicoe's play was confined to one room onstage, for the film Lester added sight gags, freeze-frames, and other tricks that, said *Time*, "are diverting at first but finally smack of gimmickry."[32] *The Knack* won the Golden Palm at Cannes in 1965 and did substantial business in Great Britain. During its New York run the picture set a house record at the Plaza, leading UA to think it had another *Tom Jones* on its hands, but outside the art house circuit interest in the film dropped off.

UA later financed and distributed François Truffaut's *Stolen Kisses* (1969) and *The Wild Child* (1970), plus two big crossover hits from Italy, *Fellini's Satyricon*

(1970) and Bertolucci's *Last Tango in Paris* (1972). In addition, it distributed four films by Ingmar Bergman: *Persona* (1967), *Hour of the Wolf* (1968), *Shame* (1968), and *The Passion of Anna* (1970).

Universal Pictures and Allied Artists, two other companies formerly consigned to the lower rungs of Hollywood, entered the art film market in 1966. As was previously noted, Universal had a brief fling with art films after the war when it handled J. Arthur Rank's pictures. Following the collapse of Rank's motion picture empire, Universal avoided art films until 1966, when it invested in an ambitious program of British films targeted at young adults. Universal had recovered from the postwar slump by 1962, when it was acquired by MCA, the most powerful talent agency in the business and the leading producer of network television programming. MCA was forced by the Justice Department to jettison its talent agency in order to complete the merger, after which it concentrated on film and television production. British popular culture demonstrated great commercial promise in the 1960s, leading Universal to back a range of films in all price brackets. As a group they were typically based on offbeat literary properties by popular or critically acclaimed British writers and directed by a group of auteurs with international reputations, like Charlie Chaplin, François Truffaut, Karel Reisz, and Joseph Losey. Most played in commercial theaters and, without exception, were critical and box office failures. The Universal pictures that played the art house circuit include François Truffaut's *Fahrenheit 451* (1967), Peter Watkins's *Privilege* (1967), Albert Finney's *Charlie Bubbles* (1968), and Peter Hall's *Work Is a Four-Letter Word* (1968).[33]

Fahrenheit 451, Truffaut's first English-language film, attracted the most interest. Inviting Truffaut to make his next film in London, Universal might have wanted to co-opt a European auteur the way MGM had done when it brought Antonioni to London to make *Blow-Up* the previous year. According to *Time*, *Fahrenheit 451*, which starred Oskar Werner and Julie Christie, was based on Ray Bradbury's "allegory of a totalitarian state where books are burned, not read, and preserved only in the minds of a *maquis* of secret *litterateurs*."[34] Hollis Alpert said that the circumstances of working under Universal's auspices in London was "presumably not congenial" for Truffaut and consequently "the film came out constrained, rather dull, almost pompously literary."[35] Crowther began his review as follows: "If François Truffaut were trying to make literature seem dull and the whole hideous practice of book-burning seem no more shocking than putting a blow-torch to a pile of leaves, he could not have accomplished his purpose much better than he unintentionally has in his first picture made in English, *Fahrenheit 451*. Holy smoke! What a pretentious and pedantic production he has made of Ray Bradbury's futuristic story."[36] Most reviewers agreed that it was an offbeat and potentially interesting entry, but that the film was too cold and intellectual and made for dreary entertainment.

Although Allied Artists entered the market late, it succeeded in releasing several noteworthy pictures, among them Claude Lelouch's *A Man and a Woman* (1966), Luis Buñuel's *Belle de Jour* (1968), and Claude Chabrol's *La Femme infidèle* (1969). Formed in 1946 as a subsidiary of Monogram Pictures, Allied Artists was designed to be Monogram's ticket out of Poverty Row by producing quality features, such as William Wyler's *Friendly Persuasion* (1956) and Billy Wilder's *Love in the Afternoon* (1957). Allied's films were praised by the critics but failed at the box office. Continued losses in the 1960s forced Allied to cease production completely in 1965. To remain in business, it resorted to pickup deals and acquired Lelouch's *A Man and a Woman* after it shared the top prize at Cannes in 1966. In 1967 Allied was acquired by Kalvex, a drug distributor, which sold off the old Monogram studio and stepped up the importing and coproduction of foreign films as an interim measure until regular production could be resumed.

Although Lelouch had made six features and many television shorts in France, he was unknown in the United States before *A Man and a Woman* (*Un Homme et une femme*). The first big commercial success to come out of the French New Wave, *A Man and a Woman* starred Jean-Louis Trintignant and Anouk Aimée. Backed by a musical score by Francis Lai, it told a simple romantic story: "A widowed racing car driver with a child meets a widowed script-girl with a child and *voila*! It's love!"[37] The picture ran for more than a year at the Paris Theatre and went on to gross $6 million at the box office, ranking number four on *Variety*'s All-Time Foreign Language Films. At the Academy Awards it won Oscars for Best Foreign Language Film and Best Original Screenplay.

A Man and a Woman was disdained by the critics but suffered no ill effects at the box office. *Time* posed the question, "Will the widow forget her old love for the sake of the new? Trying to answer the question, Director Claude Lelouch, 28, composes some stylish scenes and tosses in enough cinematic tricks borrowed from older New Wave directors—abrupt switches from black-and-white to color, for example—to have won this year's Cannes Festival Grand Prix. But his does-she-or-doesn't-she story, banal to begin with, sounds like nothing so much as an existentialist 'Dear Abby' column in which sentiment has melted into sentimentality."[38] Pauline Kael also complained about the look of the film. "Lelouch is his own cinematographer and he never lets us forget it," she said. "The people have exciting photogenic occupations: stunt-man, script-girl, racing-car driver. They take their kids on photogenic boats, for walks on wintry beaches. The actors don't have to do anything because the gamboling camera supplies all the moods for them. Anouk Aimée is blankly mysterious

Anouk Aimée and Jean-Louis Trintignant in Claude Lelouch's *A Man and a Woman* (1966)

and glamorous, like Joan Crawford as the Mona Lisa. Both the men, Jean-Louis Trintignant and Pierre Barouh, are oddly like a teen-age girl's dream boyfriend—he may be a daredevil to the world but with her he's real sweet. Lelouch throws a nimbus of mist around everything: he makes everything pretty. Maybe *A Man and a Woman* is drawing such long lines of customers because all this gauzy enchantment makes it a good make-out movie—which is the best thing to be said for it."[39] *A Man and a Woman* earned most of its profits in a dubbed version playing in commercial theaters.

The Big Five Follow

Former members of the Big Five moved into art films more cautiously. Initially they were more concerned than the struggling Little Three about "tarnishing their reputations by becoming affiliated with Code-less and Legion of Decency–condemned films in the domestic market," according to *Variety*.[40] Being more conservative, they released fewer foreign films and concentrated mainly on "Euro-American" films. As defined by Peter Lev, the Euro-American film attempts "a synthesis of the European art film and the American entertainment film" with the goal of breaking into the mainstream market. The films are directed by European filmmakers and contain American stars, who speak English or perform in foreign-language films that are dubbed into English. The films utilize "specific qualities of the European art film (ambiguity, originality, personal style, emphasis on character over plot, connection to other arts)." They also utilize "specific qualities of the American entertainment film (stars, genres, presold subjects, spectacle, action)." In the end, the film "is in some way a meeting of European and American cultures."[41]

Four examples of Euro-American films have thus far been mentioned in this chapter: UA's *Never on Sunday*, *Phaedra*, and *Viva Maria!* and Universal's *Fahrenheit 451*. They were launched like regular art films and premiered in first-run New York art houses to establish a reputation. Subsequently they went into general release and played in commercial theaters. *Fahrenheit 451* was released in English. *Never on Sunday* was released in a subtitled version and then dubbed for the suburban run. *Viva Maria!* was released simultaneously in two versions, subtitled for the first-run art house engagement and dubbed for the Broadway commercial run. Subsequently it went into general release in a dubbed version. During this period Fox and MGM each released a Euro-American film of note: Michael Cacoyannis's *Zorba the Greek* (1964) and Michelangelo Antonioni's *Blow-Up* (1966), respectively.

Cacoyannis originally pitched *Zorba the Greek* to United Artists, but the company passed on it. He had better luck with the project after Anthony Quinn agreed to play the title role. With the latter's help he secured financing from Darryl Zanuck at 20th Century-Fox. Zanuck apparently had high hopes for the picture because he put up $800,000—three times more than UA had spent on *Never on Sunday*.

Zorba was based on the novel by Nikos Kazantzakis and, like *Never on Sunday*, contrasts two character stereotypes: Anthony Quinn's Zorba, the quintessential ethnic—an uneducated, aging, lusty peasant—who is totally committed to life no matter what it holds, and Alan Bates's Basil, the prim and proper Englishman, who "takes refuge from life in literature."[42] Zorba's famous lines addressed to the Englishman include: "I got hands, feet, head, they do the jobs, who the hell am I to choose?" . . ."You think too much, that is your trouble, clever people and grocers they weigh everything." . . ."In work you are my man, but in things like playing and singing. I am my own." In supporting roles Irene Papas played the "doomed widow, a role without dialog," while Lila Kedrova played "the aging courtesan with all stops out, always halfway between laughter and tears," according to *Variety*.[43] *Zorba* was shot in black and white on location on the Greek island of Crete and contained a musical score by Mikis Theodorakis. Like *Never on Sunday*, the principal dialogue was in English.

Alan Bates and Anthony Quinn in Michael Cacoyannis's *Zorba the Greek* (1964)

Zorba opened at the Sutton on December 17, 1964. "Quinn *is* Zorba" the ads proclaimed. Quinn dominated the picture, giving the best performance of his career. Stanley Kauffmann wrote that "he makes the tough, juicy, dancing, dallying old man flare across the screen, and his warmth convinces us that this man lived before we met him and will continue afterward. This performance is all that holds the film together."[44] Bosley Crowther described Quinn's Zorba as possessing "all the energies and urges of the great ones of history and myth. He is Adam in the Garden of Eden, Odysseus on the windy plains of Troy. He is a little bit of Nijinsky and a good bit of Tom Jones."[45]

Quinn was nominated for an Academy Award but lost out to Rex Harrison in *My Fair Lady*. However, *Zorba* came away with three Oscars: Best Supporting Actress (Lila Kedrova), Best Art Direction (Vassilis Fotopoulos), and Best Cinematography (Walter Lassally). Fox originally released the film through its art film subsidiary, International Classics, but after the Oscar ceremonies the company took over the distribution for the commercial release.

Blow-Up, Antonioni's portrait of "Swinging London," was produced for MGM by Carlo Ponti, one of MGM's most active collaborators in the international market during the 1960s. It was only natural for Ponti to want to exploit the hip London scene, and he persuaded Antonioni to try his hand at it. MGM, which was attempting to shed its stodgy, conservative image, supplied the financing and gave Antonioni a three-picture contract as well.

A construct of the media, "Swinging London" received its greatest hype in a *Time* cover story by Piri Halasz: "In this century, every decade has had its city. Today it is London, a city steeped in tradition, seized by change, liberated by affluence, graced by daffodils and anemones, so green with parks and squares that, as the saying goes, you can walk across it on the grass. In a decade dominated by youth, London has burst into bloom. It swings; it is the scene."[46] (*Time* was oblivious to the slang meaning of "grass.") Woodfall's *The Knack* was a harbinger of the "Swinging London" production trend, which included John Schlesinger's *Darling* (1965), Karel Reisz's *Morgan!* (1966), Lewis Gilbert's *Alfie* (1966), and Silvio Narizzano's *Georgy Girl* (1966). These commercial ventures reached the United States within eighteen months of each other, beginning in August 1965. *Darling* and *Morgan!*, the first arrivals, were independent ventures distributed by Embassy and Cinema V, respectively. *Alfie* and *Georgy Girl* were produced and distributed by Paramount and Columbia, respectively. *Blow-Up* arrived in December 1966, "at the end of a series of movies that had made everyone over-familiar with even the phrase 'Swinging London' and heartily sick of it," said Alexander Walker.[47]

Blow-Up starred David Hemmings in a role modeled after the trendy London fashion photographer David Bailey.[48] To attract the youth audience MGM described the picture's milieu as "set against the world of fashion, dolly girls, pop groups, beat clubs, models, parties, and above all, the 'in' photographers who more than anyone have promoted the city's new image." To attract the art house set, MGM reported Antonioni's response to the question whether the picture would be clear or ambiguous as "Definitely ambiguous."[49] To attract the mainstream audience, MGM stressed the mystery plot, calling it "vintage Antonioni with a Hitchcock twist." Covering all its bases, MGM hyped the orgy scene with the groupies and released the picture through a subsidiary, Premier Productions, without a seal instead of cutting it to conform to Production Code standards. *Life* magazine helped the cause by publishing full-page photographs of the scenes which "lost *Blow-Up* the Seal."[50] Pressing home the point, MGM gave Vanessa Redgrave star billing and displayed the now famous photo of her standing with her crossed arms covering her bare breasts in its ads. David Hemmings, who was in practically every shot, received co-star billing with Sarah Miles, who had a small role.

Blow-Up opened on December 18, 1966, at the Coronet. Andrew Sarris raved, "Michelangelo Antonioni's *Blow-Up* is the movie of the year, and I use the term 'movie' advisedly for an evening's entertainment that left me feeling no pain (or Antoniennui) whatsoever. . . . [N]o other movie this year has done as much to preserve my faith in the future of the medium. If you have not yet seen *Blow-Up*, see it immediately before you hear or read anything more about it."[51] *Time* echoed his remarks: "*Blow-Up* will undoubtedly be by far the most popular movie Antonioni has ever made. It has Vanessa Redgrave, an actress who may well become the Garbo of the '60s, and what's more it has Vanessa in (almost) topless form. It has Actor Hemmings in a grincingly accurate portrait of the sort of squiggly little fungus that is apt to grow in a decaying society. And it has color photography (by Italy's Carlo Di Palma, who shot Antonioni's *Red Desert*) that often does for the bricks of London what Guardi did for the stones of Venice."[52]

Blow-Up went into general release within weeks of its New York premiere. As Stanley Kauffmann observed, the film "was seen here more widely and more quickly than, for instance, *La Dolce Vita* for at least two reasons: it was made in English and it was distributed by a major American company. There are other reasons, less provable but probably equally pertinent: its mod atmosphere, its aura of sexuality, and, most important, its perfect timing. The end of a decade that had seen the rise of a film generation around the country was capped with a work by a recognized master that was speedily available around the country."[53] *Blow-Up* was named best film of the year and Antonioni best director by the newly organized National Society of Film Critics. It also won the Golden Palm at Cannes in 1967, plus many other awards. Produced as a cost of $1.8 million, *Blow-Up* took in close to $20 million at the box office in the United States.

Later examples of Euro-American films financed by the majors include: Luchino Visconti's *The Damned* (Warner, 1969) and *Death in Venice* (Warner, 1971); *Fellini Satyricon* (United Artists, 1969); and Bernardo Bertolucci's *Last Tango in Paris* (United Artists, 1972).

The Dubbing Controversy Revisited

The big box office returns of the Euro-American films led Bosley Crowther to revisit the dubbing controversy since he was convinced that foreign films needed to be dubbed into English if they were to get wider circulation in the United States. International coproduction has made dubbing "as common-place in Europe as the musical scoring of films."[54] Coproductions—which involved the financial, artistic, and technical participation of two or more countries—were made with multilingual casts and were typically shot with the actors speaking in their mother tongues. This method of shooting resulted in a polyglot sound track. In postproduction the spoken dialogue would be recorded by dubbing actors in the languages of the coproducing countries and released in separate versions for the two coproducing markets. "The dialogue you hear," said Crowther, "is as frankly controlled and manufactured, arbitrarily determined and arranged, after the shooting as is the music or the sound effects. And the basic choice of the language in which the film will appear is entirely up to the producer."[55] The choice of language for the U.S. market would naturally be English.

"Dubbing is here to stay," proclaimed Crowther. "Therefore it seems that the wise course for all those who stubbornly protest against the barbarity of the practice is to urge and insist that it be done with all the skill and respect for the substance of the story that is available in the dubbing craft." Crowther went on to say that most first-run New York theaters will continue showing the "so-called 'original' versions of foreign-language films. But don't think that you'll be seeing (or hearing) a non-dubbed film. It will simply be a question of which dubbed version you will be seeing."[56] Crowther lost the argument again, but the dubbing controversy contributed to the general confusion over the terms "art film," "foreign film" and "foreign film market."

Changing Dynamics

Hollywood's entry into art film distribution contributed to a wave of new construction and remodeling that had added nine first-run art houses in Manhattan by 1962. The expansion followed the changing demographics of the city. After the demolition of the Third Avenue El and the construction of new luxury apartments on Manhattan's Upper East Side, Rugoff Theatres built the Cinema I and Cinema II, a double-decker movie complex on Third Avenue, across from Bloomingdale's. The first art houses to be built in the city in ten years, the Cinema I was located on the main level and seated 750; the Cinema II, located on the lower level, seated 250. The concentration of so many luxurious theaters on the Upper East Side now replaced "Times Square as the prime area for motion picture exhibition in New York," said Stuart Byron.[57] The revitalized neighborhood around the new Lincoln Center for the Performing Arts spurred the construction of the Lincoln Art and Embassy's Festival Theater, which served as the gateway to the New Yorker Theater and other revival houses on upper Broadway between 57th and 107th streets. Aging neighborhood houses were remodeled and transformed into art houses in sections of town being transformed by new housing initiatives. They included the Murray Hill on East 34th Street, the Loew's Tower East on Third Avenue at 72nd Street, and the Kips Bay on Second Avenue at 31st Street.

Manhattan now had close to forty first-run art houses and was overbuilt. As Bosley Crowther noted, "The number of first-class films—or even second-class films—that are suitable to the requirements of these theaters is limited. . . . [T]here are simply not enough top pictures to keep this number of theaters happily fed."[58] Art house managers therefore started booking U.S. domestic product. For example, in 1964 *Variety* reported that Columbia's *Dr. Strangelove*, Fox's *What a Way to Go*, and the independently produced *One Potato, Two Potato* had enjoyed long runs at such prestigious art houses as the Baronet, the Sutton, and the Embassy, respectively.[59]

Observing this trend, Cy Harvey of Janus Films concluded that "the art film market as we have known it is over." In the 1950s "several hundred theaters round the country could, and did, play truly offbeat product and, because of low overhead, made a profit." But rising overhead expenses and advertising costs were forcing art houses to reject smaller foreign films in favor of the sure thing. Harvey said the pictures made by the Indian director Satyajit Ray and others like him "would have to find American outlets via the then-burgeoning 16mm market of film clubs, university film societies, and the like."[60] And now that Hollywood had become a player, the sure thing was beyond the reach of independent distributors. The majors upset the old market by putting up complete financing to acquire new films—like Louis Malle's *A Very Private Affair* and *Viva Maria!*—and by offering top dollar for interesting imports. As a result, foreign film producers demanded higher prices for their films, "prices which often seemed unrealistic to the small distributors or which they could not afford."[61]

Unwilling to adjust to changing conditions, Embassy Pictures dropped out of art film distribution in April 1964 and signed a production pact with Paramount to make crowd pleasers. Irvin Shapiro, who distributed *Breathless*, became a sales agent. Other small distributors "pulled gracefully out of the market entirely or went precipitously into bankruptcy." Still others turned to the so-called peripheral markets in search of films. Nevertheless, as *Variety* noted, "as new filmmakers were discovered, the majors seduced them as well with a host of benefits such as financial remuneration and the promise of production continuance if they clicked."[62]

By the mid-1960s, only two prominent independent art film distributors remained, Continental Distributing and Cinema V. As was previously noted, Continental was formed in 1954 by the Walter Reade Organization as a cooperative venture to provide production financing in return for distribution rights. Cinema V was formed in 1963 by Donald Rugoff as the distribution arm of his art house chain. Rugoff was also prepared to enter into coproduction deals, if necessary, to acquire new films. Cinema V distributed a small but eclectic array of foreign films, among them Karel Reisz's *Morgan!* (1966), Bo

Widerberg's *Elvira Madigan* (1967), Milos Forman's *The Fireman's Ball* (1968), Costa-Gavras's *Z* (1969), Dusan Makavejev's *WR: Mysteries of the Organism* (1971), and Vittorio De Sica's *The Garden of the Finzi-Continis* (1971).

Competition over quality foreign films suitable for first-run exhibition contributed to the growth of revival houses in the city. Going into the 1960s, there were three Manhattan repertory theaters; at the end of 1971 there were at least eleven. Many catered to the growing "cinephile" generation in the city. The New Yorker, Thalia, and Symphony Space were located on upper Broadway, near Columbia University. The Bleecker Street Cinema and the Elgin were located in Greenwich Village, close to New York University. The Thalia, the oldest in the group, was operated by Martin and Ursula Lewis and had been presenting a "Summer Film Festival" every year since 1943. The films were predominantly foreign and were shown as twin bills that changed daily. The Bleecker Street Cinema was operated by Lionel Rogosin, who launched the theater in 1961 with a ten-week season of old foreign movies under the auspices of Brandon Films.

Arguably the most beloved independent art house in the city was the New Yorker. It was operated by Dan Talbot, a former story editor and movie critic. When Talbot's friend Henry Rosenberg acquired this moribund 900-seat neighborhood house for his Spanish-language chain, Talbot convinced Rosenberg to let him manage it as an experiment. Talbot realized that the theater was situated in a neighborhood that was attracting "young marrieds in the arts and professions." The New Yorker soon became a beloved local institution. "Now the theater's guest book bears names such as poet W. H. Auden (who requested more Marilyn Monroe movies), Bud Abbott (who asked for more Abbott and Costello movies), Arthur Miller and Gloria Swanson," said *Newsweek*.[63]

Starting out, Talbot said, "the only policy we have [at the New Yorker] is not to have any policy. We show old films, new films, foreign or American films. Just so long as they're good. And don't call us an 'art house.' I hate the term."[64] After the founding of the New York Film Festival in 1963, the New Yorker gradually became a first-run art house and specialized in showing what Bosley Crowther called "marginal" foreign films. By that he meant films that had arrived in New York without a distributor and that had been given a single screening at the festival.[65] Talbot had a dual purpose in presenting premieres. Like all independent houses, his New Yorker Theater operated on a slim profit margin. He was therefore anxious to capitalize on the word of mouth and free publicity generated by the festival. As the theatrical market for art films declined in the late 1960s, Talbot sought to acquire festival entries for his New Yorker Films, which serviced the college and university nontheatrical market.

Premiering the films at his theater could generate favorable press coverage and enhance the value of his holdings.

Foreign film distribution was a sideline for the majors. However, as the "tonnage" thesis reveals, even low-profit films could contribute to the bottom line. The majors used the art film market as a convenient way to connect with promising young auteurs, to cater to the college crowd, and to add panache to their rosters. By forming art film subsidiaries, the major were able to release films prohibited by the Production Code. They thus had the best of both worlds. When the industry jettisoned the Production Code, the majors no longer needed their art film subsidiaries, which they soon dismantled. From the very beginning companies were occasionally willing to back so-called uncommercial auteurs under certain circumstances. A case in point is Columbia's three-picture deal with Jean-Luc Godard. More often, however, the majors preferred backing projects with crossover potential, such as Euro-American hybrids. A first-run art release was just a ploy to establish a film's reputation before sending it out to commercial theaters. Hollywood's involvement in the art film market raised expectations among art house managers and foreign film producers, which would soon bring the era of independent foreign film distribution to a close.

13

The Aura
of the New York Film Festival

To create a film festival worthy of New York City, the board of Lincoln Center for the Performing Arts invited Richard Roud, an American scholar, to replicate his success as the director of the London Film Festival.[1] To manage affairs while Roud traveled the international festival circuit in search of films, Amos Vogel, the founder of Cinema 16, was brought in as administrative director. Unlike the big three international film festivals—Cannes, Venice, and Berlin—the New York Film Festival, like its London model, would be noncompetitive. As Vincent Canby explained, "Competitive festivals are required to show films that have not yet been released outside the country of origin, which considerably limits the number of the possible entries of quality, so much so that competitive festivals today, as a matter of course, present a lot of films 'out of competition,' either because the films have already been released abroad or because the producer doesn't want to be embarrassed when his film doesn't win a prize." By opting out of the awards business, "the people who run the New York Film Festival . . . vastly increase the number of films from which they can make their selections. The New York festival can show anything, new or old, as long as the film demonstrates some sort of importance, artistic or historical, in the minds of the members of the selection committee."[2]

The festival was launched on September 10, 1963, and was an immediate success. Twenty-one films were shown over ten days in Lincoln Center's Philharmonic Hall, which seated 2,700, and most were sellouts.[3] Luis Buñuel's *The Exterminating Angel*, Mexico's entry at Cannes in 1962 and the winner of the

International Critics Prize, opened the event. It was followed by an eclectic mix of films that included Leopoldo Torre Nilsson's *The Terrace* (Argentina), Masaki Kobayashi's *Harakiri* (Japan), Alain Resnais's *Muriel* (France), Roman Polanski's *Knife in the Water* (Poland), and Ermanno Olmi's *The Fiancés* (Italy). The festival also presented Joseph Losey's British drama *The Servant*, and Adophas Mekas's American independent effort *Hallelujah the Hills*. Concurrent with the festival, the Museum of Modern Art (MoMA), a co-sponsor, presented a series of older films that had never been released in the United States, among them Kenji Mizoguchi's *Sansho the Bailiff,* Akira Kurosawa's *I Live in Fear,* Luchino Visconti's *La Terra Trema,* and Max Ophüls's *Lola Montes.*

The audience mainly consisted of young people aged twenty-five years and under, whom Vogel considered the "true tastemakers of the festival." This audience "is not a Times Square film audience. It does not hanker after bikini-clad starlets; it fails to be excited by the ordinary. Instead, passionate and opinionated and vociferous, it testifies at the Festival to its commitments by applause, hisses and unswerving presence. These are the people who discuss film at their parties, read the new film magazines, loyally attend art and repertory theaters and are often found at the more specialized museum showings or midnight conclaves."[4] To ease the concerns of distributors, who feared the damage a negative review at the festival might do to their films, the New York newspapers adopted a no-reviewing policy the first year and confined themselves to reporting festival news.

According to Eugene Archer, who filed daily reports for the *New York Times,* the festival favorites "in terms of audience response and over-all post mortem comments" were *Knife in the Water, The Servant, Muriel,* and *The Fiancés. Knife,* Polanski's first feature and the winner of the Critics Award at Venice in 1962, had made the twenty-nine-year-old director famous. A member of the second generation of Polish filmmakers working under the direction of the Lodz Film School, Polanski conceived the idea for this psychological drama and was allowed by the Polish Ministry of Culture to make it on his own terms. The festival response led *Time* to use a portrait of the young student and the wife portrayed in the film on the cover of its issue celebrating cinema as an international art. *Time* described the plot as "a Polish thriller as sharp as a knife and as smooth as water. Director Roman Polanski . . . puts two lusty men and one busty woman aboard a small sailboat, throws them a knife, and for the next 90 minutes lets the tension build."[5] *The Servant* marked the return of Joseph Losey, the blacklisted American director, to the United States after a twelve-year exile. Losey's first collaboration with playwright Harold Pinter, *The Servant,* which starred Dirk Bogarde, "offered a penetrating dissection of British society" comparable to *La*

Jolanta Umecka and Zygmunt Malanowicz in Roman Polanski's *Knife in the Water* (1963)

Dolce Vita's dissection of Italian society. Losey told Eugene Archer that *The Servant* "was the first picture he had been able to make 'without interference' during his European career, and the first to be presented intact as he had filmed it."[6] *Muriel*, Resnais's first color feature, starred Delphine Seyrig of *Last Year at Marienbad* fame and "set last night's audience astir with heated discussions about its importance and possible interpretation. Almost everyone agreed that it was impossible to understand after a single viewing," according to Archer.[7] *The Fiancés*, Olmi's second feature, which employed "a complicated flashback technique to tell a moving story of a pair of lovers separated by economic necessity," so impressed Janus Films that it immediately acquired the film for distribution, along with Olmi's first feature, *Il Posto*, and set about to establish Olmi as "an American box-office attraction."8

The founding of the New York Film Festival served as the perfect antidote to Hollywood's presence in the art film market. Appraising the impact of the inaugural festival, Hollis Alpert said, "There is no question that the festival had a valid reason for being. It emphasized the profound interest in serious filmmaking all over the world; it gave public showing to a great many films, short and long, that might not otherwise have achieved theatre exhibition in this country; it introduced several new film-making talents; it demonstrated the wide range of current experimentation in film-making; and it permitted us to see the directions taken by the film-making units of communist and socialist countries."9

Knife in the Water (*Nóz w wodzie*) was the first festival entry to be released commercially. It had been acquired prior to the festival by Kanawha Films, a new distribution company founded by Archer King, a Broadway producer and talent agent. The film initially opened at the Beekman on October 28, 1963, and eventually grossed over $100,000 in rentals—a modest success by art house standards. It also picked up an Oscar for Best Foreign Language Film. However, only a minority of festival films were released commercially. Such films were typically handled by a new generation of small, independent outfits— Altura Films International, Sigma III, Pathé Contemporary, Cinema Ventures, and Kanawha, to name a few—and, like *Knife in the Water*, had been picked up for distribution after attracting attention at one of the big international film festivals. Functioning outside the Hollywood orbit, the festival presented only a few studio releases, among them Bernardo Bertolucci's *The Conformist* (Paramount, 1971), Luis Buñuel's *The Discreet Charm of the Bourgeoisie* (20th Century-Fox, 1972), Bertolucci's *Last Tango in Paris* (United Artists, 1973), and François Truffaut's *Day for Night* (Warner, 1973). Such films were typically acquired by the majors via production-financing deals.

Once established, the festival served as a pre-release showcase of sorts for distributors. Crowther commented on this function in 1967 when he puzzled over how the Czech New Wave would ever get the wide distribution it deserved. In the postwar period "it was possible to get an art theater and open a foreign film, such as *The Bicycle Thief* or *La Strada*, for a few thousand dollars. But today, in order to get a popular theater . . . an importer must make a percentage arrangement that is as high as 90 per cent favorable to the theater, and then he must put at least $10,000 into an advertising campaign. Furthermore, the critical and public reactions toward films so launched are becoming more and

more demanding." He then added, "The present costly system of all-out premieres for foreign films . . . is one reason why the showing of a film at the New
York Film festival is accepted by a foreign producer or his American importer
as a chance to get a line on a film. If it gets a good response at Lincoln Center,
it has a better chance for propitious release. But even a good response is by no
means an assurance of success or even release."[10] What follows are some of the
highlights of the festival in the decade after its founding, with the focus on those
films that went into commercial distribution and enriched the market.

Luis Buñuel

Buñuel's *The Exterminating Angel* (*El angel exterminador*), the opener at the first New
York Film Festival, received mixed reviews. It took four years before it was acquired by Altura Films. According to Hollis Alpert, the film "seemed to many
hardly the best choice for opening the festival, since it was not the director's
best, and remained rather leadenly cryptic to the end."[11] Nevertheless Buñuel
became a festival regular. The festival went on to present *Diary of a Chambermaid*
in 1964, *Simon of the Desert* in 1966, and two "farewell" films Buñuel made after
his sixty-seventh year—*Tristana* in 1970 and *The Discreet Charm of the Bourgeoisie* in
1972. Conspicuously absent from this group is *Belle de Jour*, Buñuel's greatest
box office success, which was acquired by Allied Artists after winning the
Golden Lion at the Venice Film Festival in 1967 and placed directly into commercial release the following spring.

Buñuel's "farewell" films, arriving in the wake of *Belle de Jour*, performed
the best. *Tristana*, a French/Spanish coproduction, played out of competition at
Cannes in 1970 because Buñuel refused to have his film connected to the
Franco government, which had requested this. As described by Vincent Canby,
"Tristana is a sad, sweetly enigmatic girl (Catherine Deneuve) who is raped by
her guardian, Fernando Rey, and who then lives on to watch him die as an old
and broken man, whose wooden leg is propped against his bed."[12] *Tristana*
found no takers among the majors despite the presence of Catherine Deneuve,
the star of *Belle de Jour*, in the title role. Canby himself may have discovered the
reason: "In the context of the license of today's cinema, the movie looks positively prudish, even though it tells a story of tremendous, everpresent sexuality.
When Tristana is raped by Don Lope, it happens behind closed doors, out of
the eye of the camera."[13] It was not until the New York Film Festival chose
Tristana to close the 1970 program that it was picked up for distribution by
Maron Films, a newcomer specializing in horror films like *Godzilla* and *Gargan-
tua*. Maron released it the day after the festival closed at the Lincoln Art, where

it received excellent reviews. For example, *Newsweek* said, "*Tristana* shows the old anarchist's genius at its purest, most incandescent. . . . It's all there—his unique facility for shifting from dream to reality, his mellowing anticlericalism, his symbolism (which Buñuel would deny) and of course his preoccupation with those peculiarly human perversions of the flesh. . . . What Buñuel says here about evil, individual and social, he distills to the level of human relationships, with all their complexities, obscurities and concrete realities."[14] *Tristana* ran for nearly three months at the Lincoln Art.

The *Discreet Charm of the Bourgeoisie* (*Le Charme discret de la bourgeoisie*) played at the 1972 festival courtesy of 20th Century-Fox, which released it soon after it closed at the Little Carnegie. Buñuel's film continued his critique of the French monied class, only this time in the form of a light comedy. With a cast headed by Fernando Rey, Delphine Seyrig, and Stéphane Audran, the film presented "a small group of chic, upper-crust Parisians who spend most of the film trying, unsuccessfully, to dine together. Every time they sit down at the table, peculiar things happen: an Army arrives, the hosts disappear, or perhaps a curtain goes up and the guests find themselves on stage in a play whose lines they don't know."[15] This was Buñuel's most accessible work. The presence of Fernando Rey in the cast, immediately following his appearance as the crafty dope smuggler in William Friedkin's *The French Connection* (1971), undoubtedly increased the film's commercial appeal. Vincent Canby named *The Discreet Charm of the Bourgeoisie* the best feature film of the year. It went on to win an Oscar for Best Foreign Language Film and top awards from the National Society of Film Critics.

The French New Wave

Throughout this period the New York Film Festival favored French films, and no other French director received more attention than Jean-Luc Godard. Arguably the most popular filmmaker among hard-core cinephiles, Godard was the darling of the festival. From 1964 to 1972 the festival presented fifteen paired Godard films courtesy of Richard Roud, who considered Godard "one of the most important artists of our time, worthy of comparison with Joyce and Vermeer."[16] Festival audiences agreed, and Godard's films always played to capacity houses. Nevertheless, sellouts at the festival did little to convert skeptical art house managers, who considered Godard box office poison.

As was previously noted, Godard's *A Woman Is a Woman* and two of his Columbia releases—*Band of Outsiders* and *Masculine, Feminine*—premiered at the festival between 1964 and 1966. Godard's other festival films dating from his first period of filmmaking include *Alphaville* (1965), *Pierrot le Fou* (1966), *Made in U.S.A.* and *Les Carabiniers* (1967), *Two or Three Things I Know About Her* and *Weekend* (1968), and *Le Gai Savoir* (1969). Godard's festival films from his Dziga-Vertov period include *Vent d'est* (1970) and *Letter to Jane* and *Tout va bien* (1972). Conspicuously absent from this group is Godard's *La Chinoise*, a 1967 film distributed by Leacock/Pennebaker outside the festival. Besides Columbia, Godard's principal distributors were Pathé Contemporary, which released *Alphaville*, *Pierrot le Fou*, and *Made in U.S.A.*, and New Yorker Films, which released *Les Carabiniers*, *Two or Three Things I Know About Her*, and the Dziga-Vertov films.

Alphaville, winner of the Golden Bear at Berlin, opened the 1965 festival. It starred Anna Karina and Eddie Constantine in what the festival program described as "Alphaville. Or, Tarzan versus I.B.M. (this was the original title). Better still, Jean-Luc Godard meets science fiction, or best of all, the first successful incursion of pop art into the cinema."[17] Pathé Contemporary opened it at the Paris on October 25, 1965. Phillip T. Hartung, writing in *Commonweal*, neatly summed up the critical reception: "Of all the so-called New Wave directors, Godard more than any other, divided reviewers into advocates and detractors. It seems to me that after his interesting start in *Breathless*, Godard has gone steadily downhill. His cinema technique is bright and stimulating, but the content of his movies and his in-jokes (mostly references to other films and their makers) are becoming more and more self-indulgent; and he probably doesn't give a damn what reviewers think. He still has his followers."[18]

Pierrot le Fou, which starred Jean-Paul Belmondo and Anna Karina, was a bigger hit in France than *Breathless*, but it was not released commercially until Pathé Contemporary opened it in January 1969 at the 72nd Street Playhouse. Pathé's decision to acquire the film was probably motivated by the box office success of Bo Widerberg's *Elvira Madigan* in 1967 and Franco Zefferelli's *Romeo and Juliet* in 1968, both of which concerned doomed lovers. Andrew Sarris claimed that *Pierrot le Fou* was the first Godard film he had ever had to stand in line to see. (It had a six-week first run.) "As a genuinely lyrical expression of love," he wrote, "Godard's *Pierrot le Fou* is worth a thousand anemically academic *Elvira Madigans* and a million mendaciously swirling and swishing *Romeo and Juliets*." Sarris especially admired Jean-Paul Belmondo's performance: "He gives Pierrot more charm, dignity, and resignation than Godard himself alone is capable of, and the jokes that worked in those churlish jests that haven't worked since, work once more."[19]

In 1967 the festival paired Godard's *Made in U.S.A.*, his latest film, with *Les Carabiniers*, dating from 1963. Bosley Crowther chided these choices: "Both are patently poor pictures—the first a talky, symbolic, obscure, comic-strip kind of lampoon of the United States and the latter a simply sophomoric farcical blast against war. It's time for the festival people to use some judgment about Mr. Godard."[20] *Les Carabiniers* was acquired by Dan Talbot's New Yorker Films and was simultaneously released on April 25, 1968, at the New Yorker Theater and Bleecker Street Cinema, where it ran for about three weeks in each. Talbot's decision may have been influenced by the hoopla surrounding the opening of Sergei Bondarchuck's *War and Peace*. Robert Hatch, writing in the *Nation*, viewed Godard's treatment of war as "exactly opposite to that used by the Russians. . . . He deploys two men and two women, interpolates some old combat footage, and films the whole thing in the style of an underground movie made on the city dump."[21] Joseph Morgenstern, writing in *Newsweek*, said, "If you will forgive this film a little . . . you will never forget it. Along side the new *War and Peace* it is incomparably puny, yet makes its points with startling clarity. . . . Very much like *Dr. Strangelove*, it sets its own uncompromisingly comic terms and sticks to them. It deflates war, but also deflates itself with an acute sense of proportion and settles wisely for small pertinence instead of universal triviality. War always was too important to be left to the movies."[22] Renata Adler added *Les Carabiniers* to her "Ten Best" list: "Not characteristic of Godard's style, this tight, spare, inspired fable shows that Godard can do just about anything anyone else can do, and do it better. Among other things, it is one of the strongest anti-war films ever made—without resorting in any way to sentiment."[23]

In an effort to win more converts to Godard, in early 1968 Richard Roud curated a retrospective of his films at the Museum of Modern Art. The event accompanied the publication of Roud's book on the director. According to Craig Fischer, Godard's films were shown in chronological order and alternated with "a group of films that have influenced Godard or that provide amusing and suggestive contrasts to his own work."[24] The screenings were jammed and generated a lot of press. Although most critics conceded that Godard was arguably "one of the most important artists of our time," they were quick to point out that the filmmaker had little regard for his audience. Eugene Archer, writing in the *New York Times*, complained, "This prodigious ex-enfant terrible is an audience hater. . . . His films are often sheer torture to the eye and ear. Even worse—it is almost impossible to like his heroes and harder still to care what happens to them."[25] Raymond Sokolov explained that "Godard's stories are uneven and hard to follow, because they are just as dislocated and loose-ended as modern life itself. The director's job, according to Godard, is to juxtapose significant aspects of the disarray." Nevertheless, Sokolov conceded that Godard would remain a tough sell and quoted fellow New Wave director Claude Chabrol, who said, "Godard couldn't give a good goddam about the public. The appreciation of young film people is enough for him, and they dig his intellectual mixture of theater and fact."[26]

The 1968 festival presented three Godard films, *Two or Three Things I Know About Her* and *Weekend*, produced in 1967, and *One Plus One*, which was finished just in time for the event. *Weekend* was immediately placed into release at the 72nd Street Playhouse by Grove Press on September 30, 1968. The festival program described *Weekend* as "a tough and hard-hitting denunciation of contemporary French society. Using that idol of French sex films, Mireille Darc, as a typically depraved young bourgeoise, Godard mixes documentary, fiction and fantasy to give us an apocalyptic picture of the present and the very near future."[27] *Weekend* contained a series of set pieces reminiscent of Luis Buñuel's satires of bourgeois society, and is best remembered for the tour-de-force tracking shot of an interminable traffic jam on a narrow country road. According to *Time*, "This chilling sequence—perhaps the finest single scene that Godard has ever filmed—is only the beginning [of the violence]. During the couple's repeatedly interrupted trip, which lasts for the rest of the movie, wrecked automobiles, hideously dismembered bodies and senseless violence meet them at every turn."[28] "Apart from the admirable set pieces," said Sarris, "*Weekend* tends to disintegrate into witless bourgeois-baiting and coy Pirandellianism. Godard has destroyed the notion of beginning, middle, and end by shooting everything in existential sequence, so that his films do not so much end as stop. The disadvantage of this approach even for Godard is becoming increasingly apparent. Godard seldom has any kick left for the last lap. His best scenes are likely to be in the middle or the beginning or whatever day of shooting he felt up to it."[29] *Weekend* ran a respectable two months at the Playhouse.

One Plus One was picked up for distribution by New Line Cinema, a fledgling company founded by Robert Shaye in 1967. Godard's first English-language film, *One Plus One* was shot in London and featured the Rolling Stones. To drum up interest among college students, New Line ran it three times at Hunter College a month before the commercial release at the Murray Hill on April 26, 1970. At the latter New Line presented two versions of the film—the director's and the producer's. As Roger Greenspun explained, "If you go on Monday, Wednesday, Friday or Sunday, you will see Godard's film, which is properly known as *One Plus One*. On other days, you will see a film popularly advertised as *Sympathy for the Devil*, which exactly resembles *One Plus One*, except that in the latter part of the last reel a complete version of the song 'Sympathy for the Devil,' which the Rolling Stones have been rehearsing and recording in cuts throughout the film, is played on the soundtrack . . . The changes and additions are the work of the producer, Iain Quarrier."[30] This ploy kept *One Plus One* running for about a month.

Two or Three Things I Know About Her (*Deux ou trois choses que je sais d'elle*) was picked up for distribution by Dan Talbot and opened at the New Yorker Theater on April 29, 1970, no doubt to piggyback on the publicity surrounding the commercial release of *One Plus One*. The festival program described *Two or Three Things* as "a sociological essay in the form of a novel written, not with words, but with notes of music. Its subject is nothing less than the whole Paris region (the 'her' of the title), its protagonist a young housewife (Marina Vlady) who resorts to occasional prostitution to make ends meet. But prostitution is only a pretext for the expression of Godard's view on the larger social picture."[31] The film ran a brief two weeks at the New Yorker.

After *Weekend*, Godard ceased making "bourgeois movies for bourgeois producers." "From now on," he said, "there will be nothing but revolutionary movies made in revolutionary situations with revolutionary performers for revolutionary audiences."[32] Although the Dziga-Vertov films at the festival were eventually picked up for distribution by New Yorker Films, they reached audiences "of an ever dwindling number of supporters," according to Canby.[33]

The festival presented the following three films by Alain Resnais: *Muriel* (1963), *La Guerre est finie* (1966), and *Je t'aime, je t'aime* (1970), representing his third, fourth, and fifth features, respectively. Although all three found commercial distribution, only *La Guerre est finie* was favorably received by the critics. *Muriel* was released by Lopert Films a month after the festival closed and quickly died, unable to recover from Bosley Crowther's scathing review, which began, "Perhaps there are those who can follow the scattered clues in the devious mystery that Alain Resnais has thrown together in his new French film" and went downhill from there.[34]

La Guerre est finie used a novelistic approach to tell its story. According to Brendan Gill, it was "as conventionally 'written' as *The Forsyte Saga*."[35] It starred Yves Montand as an aging Spanish revolutionary, based in Paris, who works with the Spanish underground to bring down the Franco government. *La Guerre est finie* had achieved a certain notoriety at Cannes when France, under pressure from Spain, withdrew it from competition. Honored as the best foreign film at the 1966 festival, it was released by Brandon Films at the Beekman in February 1967 and garnered excellent reviews. Perhaps the most inspired appreciation came from Andrew Sarris, who considered it "in some ways the most satisfying movie Resnais has made. . . . We are no longer concerned with the pretentious counterpoint of love and the Bomb, past and present, illusion and reality. . . . We are obsessed instead with the doubts and fantasies of Diego. Through his mind passes what we know and feel about the heritage of the Old Left, that last, desperate camaraderie commemorated in kitchens and cemeteries as old comrades grapple with the old rhetoric they are doomed never to forget and the new reality they are doomed never to understand. . . . The meaning is in the title. The war is over and Resnais . . . makes no attempt to reconstruct the agonies of antiquity with old newsreels. The ultimate tragedy of the Spanish Civil War is that all its participants are either dead or thirty years older. Spain still exists as a geographical entity, but it has been repopulated with an indifferent generation. Tourists swarm through Madrid and Barcelona while old Bolsheviks haul pamphlets into Seville. The New Left sneers at the Old Left. But it doesn't matter as long as one man can keep faith in the midst of uncertainty."[36] Crowther added it to his "Ten Best" list and the New York Film Critics Circle named it Best Foreign Language Film. Nevertheless a surprised Crowther reported that the film "never got off the ground."[37]

Claude Chabrol, a former *Cahiers du cinéma* critic and one of the original founders of the French New Wave, initially enjoyed some success in the United States with the release in 1959 of *Le Beau Serge* and *The Cousins*, only to be overshadowed by Godard and Truffaut. During the 1960s Chabrol made "a series of witty, perverse, ravishingly beautiful exercises in love, murder, guilt and expiation, most of which star Stéphane Audran," wrote Canby, but Chabrol found no takers for such films in the United States until 1968, when the festival presented *Les Biches*.[38] *Les Biches*, which translates as "The Does," was described in the festival program as "a triangle story set in St. Tropez involving a Lesbian photographer (Stéphane Audran), an undecided young Bohemian (Jacqueline Sassard), and a highly seductive young architect (Jean-Louis Trintignant). Being a typical Claude Chabrol film, it mixes way-out humor with tragedy, psychological subtlety with a disregard for conventional plotting."[39] The film had been acquired by Jack H. Harris Enterprises, a producer/distributor of sci-fi horror films best known for *The Blob* (1958), a cult classic that became a huge box office success. Harris promoted *Les Biches* in ads as "A Deviate *Dolce Vita*" and it became Chabrol's comeback film.

Chabrol's next production, *La Femme infidèle*, was acquired by Allied Artists and placed directly into commercial release at the Little Carnegie on November 9, 1969. Roger Greenspun, a *New York Times* film critic and a Chabrol champion, hoped that the film "would establish [Chabrol] with audiences who may at last be open to what makes his vision strange and wonderful." Another star vehicle for Audran, *La Femme infidèle* "tells the story of a happy family that is somewhat upset when the husband murders his wife's lover but ultimately finds a yet richer harmony in the wife's new respect for her husband's initiative and prowess. In concept and prowess, it is a film so calmly and thoughtfully perverse that it can have been born only in the unique cinematic imagination of Claude Chabrol."[40] Vincent Canby named the film to his "Ten Best" list and felt compelled to add, "It's a disquieting commentary on the state of movie tastes that this film should have had only a short, unspectacular first-run here."[41]

The festival showed *Le Boucher* in 1970. Immediately following its closing MoMA presented a Chabrol retrospective consisting of fourteen films, most of which had rarely if ever been seen in this country, among them *Les Bonnes Femmes* and *This Man Must Die*. The exposure helped. *Le Boucher* was picked up by Cinerama Releasing and began a three-month commercial run at the 68th Street Playhouse beginning in December 1971. Naming the film to his "Ten Best" list, Canby described *Le Boucher* as the story of a "small-town school mistress of marvelously unlikely chic (Stèphane Audran) who can't quite bring herself to love the local butcher (Jean Yanne) enough to save him from his private compulsions. The frame is bizarre, but the emotions are real and the two lead performances are most engaging and witty. This is one of Chabrol's most elegant and sorrowful films."[42]

Eric Rohmer, another founder of the French New Wave, remained pretty much unknown in the United States until *My Night at Maud's* was presented at the 1969 event. Editor in chief of *Cahiers du Cinéma* before turning to filmmaking in the early 1960s, Rohmer set out to produce six "contes moraux," or moral tales. As defined by Vincent Canby, "Each is a variation on a single situation: a man who is in love with one woman meets and spends some time with another woman, whom he finds supremely attractive, but with whom he does not consummate the affair."[43] As described by Melton S. Davis, *My Night at Maud's* (*Ma nuit chez Maud*), the third installment, is "narrated by its main character, an introspective, puritanical engineer played Jean-Louis Trintignant. Marooned by a snowstorm, the engineer takes refuge in Maud's apartment. Maud (Françoise Fabian), an attractive divorcee, tries to seduce him, but the engineer, who is a strict Catholic with Jansenist leanings, declines. The two pass the night discussing predestination, atheism, and Pascal's *Pensées*."[44] Andrew Sarris praised the film for its "talk, civilized talk. . . . [I]t seems so long since we have heard the sounds of real people on the screen. . . . Jean-Louis Trintignant and Françoise Fabian are especially remarkable as creatures of a sensibility so refined as to make them virtual outcasts from today's anything-for-a thrill cinema."[45] Vincent Canby noted, "To my way of thinking, it's the first new film to be seen at the current New York Film Festival that achieves with elegance and eloquence the goals it has set for itself."[46] The rave reviews persuaded Pathé Contemporary to acquire the film and to open it the following spring at the 68th Street Playhouse, where it enjoyed a fourteen-week run and provided a refreshing change from the glut of sex movies on the market.

Rohmer suddenly became a valuable property. Jack Weiner, head of European production for Columbia Pictures, reportedly was shown a twelve-page outline of *Claire's Knee* and immediately offered to finance it.[47] Columbia later agreed to finance Rohmer's final installment, *Chloë in the Afternoon*. *Claire's Knee (Le Genou de Claire)* went directly into commercial release and opened at the 68th Street Playhouse, the home of *Maud*. Shot in color near Annecy in the Haute-Savoie, *Claire's Knee* starred Jean-Claude Brialy, a thirty-five-year-old diplomat on holiday who develops a "mad, pure, undefined passion" for a young woman's right knee. To play the pivotal role of Claire, Rohmer selected Laurence de Monaghan, a newcomer to movies. Canby claimed that *Claire's Knee* "comes very close to being a perfect movie of its kind, something on the order of an affectionate comedy of the intellect that has no easily identifiable cinema antecedents except in other films by Mr. Rohmer. . . . It is a product of a literary sensibility, and it grows out of a literary tradition, but it is, first and foremost, a superlative motion picture."[48] Rohmer's film enjoyed a long run at the Playhouse and went on to win the Best Film award from the National Society of Film Critics, among other honors.

Chloë in the Afternoon (L'Amour l'après-midi) was selected to open the 1972 festival. The program notes called it a "worthy successor to *Maude* and *Claire*. But the tone is different, for our hero is married and wants both the joys of domesticity and the excitement of continually falling in love. Suddenly, with the eruption into his life of Chloë—a hippy version of Maude—things begin to get out of hand."[49] *Chloë* starred Bernard Verley and Zouzou, a French model who introduced the Twist to Paris. She had never acted in a major movie before. Columbia released the film the day after the festival premiere, again at the 68th Street Playhouse, but it failed miserably. Although Vincent Canby included *Chloë* in his "Ten Best" list, Richard Schickel contended that Rohmer's "six tales meant to illustrate the same moral are at least four too many" and described *Chloë* as the "last and least" of the group."[50] Pauline Kael called it "about as forgettable as a film can be."[51]

The first Truffaut film to be shown at the festival was *The Wild Child*. This was the fourth film Truffaut had made under contract with United Artists, coming after *The Bride Wore Black* (1968), *Stolen Kisses* (1969), and *Mississippi Mermaid* (1970). The first three pictures were commercial failures in the United States and UA had apparently given up on the filmmaker—that is, until *The Wild Child* received unanimous praise from French critics and broke box office records in Paris. *The Wild Child (L'Enfant sauvage)* opened the 1970 festival and was released commercially the following day at the Fine Arts. It told the real-life story of Jean Itard, a young doctor living in southern France in the eighteenth

François Truffaut and Jean-Pierre Cargol in Truffaut's *The Wild Child* (1970)

century, who attempts to civilize a "retarded" boy discovered living in the woods. Truffaut himself played the part of Itard and Jean-Pierre Cargol the part of Victor, the "black-eyed gypsy boy." Canby remarked that the film "looks almost as if it had been designed to answer those critics who have been finding all of Truffaut's post–*Jules and Jim* films either too romantic or too charming—both quite superficial qualities (but never the true substance of Truffaut) that have been rigorously suppressed in *The Wild Child*." Noting the film's resemblance to *The 400 Blows*, Canby observes that "where the first film had to do with the making of a boy into a man, *The Wild Child* is about nothing less than the evolution of beast into human, a really epic theme that Truffaut obstinately refuses to emphasize in any showy or sentimental way."[52] *Variety* was similarly impressed with the maturity of Truffaut's approach: "There are no forced dramatics, no morbidity or exploiting this basic theme of man's essence and what he becomes if left 'uncivilized.' Themes of adaptability, social or antisocial behavior, are given a microcosm treatment of great insight that could have this appealing to youthful as well as older audiences." The reviewer felt that "United Artists deserves a bow for backing this unusual, offbeat film made in black and white."[53]

The festival went on to present *Two English Girls* in 1972 and *Day for Night* in 1973. Having grown dissatisfied with UA's handling of his pictures, Truffaut turned to Columbia and Warner Bros., respectively, for financing. *Two English Girls* (*Les Deux Anglaises et le continent*), Truffaut's first color feature, was based on a Henri-Pierre Roché novel, just like *Jules and Jim*, "but this time Truffaut reverses the situation with Jean-Pierre Léaud and two English actresses as the corners of this pre–World War I triangle. Charming, sympathetic, and ironic, this is that rarity of rarities, a genuinely romantic film, a picture about feelings, a eulogy of life," said the festival program notes.[54] It was released by Janus Films, the company that distributed *Jules and Jim*, four days after the festival premiere at the Fine Arts. *Two English Girls* received a hostile critical reception in Paris, which apparently led Columbia to offload the U.S. distribution rights. Vincent Canby described *Two English Girls* as "a film of such beautiful, charming and comic discretion that it isn't until the end that one realizes it's also immensely sad and even brutal, though in the nonbrutalizing way that truth can sometimes be."[55]

Day for Night (*La Nuit américaine*) opened the 1973 festival. The program notes proclaimed, "This is Truffaut's long-awaited valentine to the cinema—a movie about the making of a movie—and perhaps his most endearing work to date. While there may be occasional storms of temperament on the set of his film-within-a-film, the emotional climate of *Day for Night* is as warm and sunny as the Riviera locations where it was shot."[56] With a cast comprising Jacqueline Bisset, Jean-Pierre Léaud, Jean-Pierre Aumont, Valentina Cortese, and Truffaut himself, *Day for Night* went on to win numerous honors, including awards from the New York Film Critics Circle and the National Society of Film Critics and an Oscar for Best Foreign Language Film. When *Day for Night* opened in Los Angeles shortly before the Academy Awards ceremony, Charles Champlin, writing in the *Los Angeles Times*, predicted, "I will be astonished if, when this appears on Wednesday morning, the Oscar [for best foreign language film] has not gone to François Truffaut's *Day for Night*. His homage to the movies and all those who make them is beyond question the warmest, liveliest, funniest, slyest, most revealing and most deeply affectionate ever paid, and I can hardly imagine a Hollywood heart remaining unmelted."[57]

Japanese Films

The New York Film Festival promoted Japanese cinema from the start and regularly included at least one Japanese film on its roster. These included Masaki Kobayashi's *Harakiri* (1963), Hiroshi Teshigahara's *Woman in the Dunes* (1964),

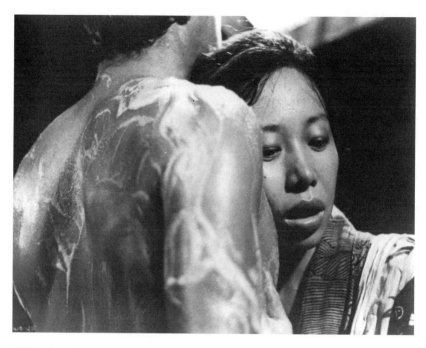

Eiji Okada and Kyoko Kishida in Hiroshi Teshigahara's *Woman in the Dunes* (1964)

Akira Kurosawa's *Red Beard* (1965), and Kon Ichikawa's *The Burmese Harp* (1966). They were all released commercially but, with one exception, made little headway in the market.

The exception was *Woman in the Dunes* (*Suna no onna*). The winner of the 1964 Special Jury Prize at Cannes, the film was based on the Kôbô Abé novel and contained an original musical score by the noted Japanese composer Toru Takemitsu. In the form of a parable, it told the story of a young teacher, an amateur entomologist (Eiji Okada, the star of *Hiroshima Mon Amour*), who travels to a remote beach to collect specimens and accepts an offer from local villagers to spend the night with a young widow (Kyoko Kishida) in a hut at the bottom of a sand pit. In the morning the ladder that took him down is gone and he becomes imprisoned with the woman, whose sole task is to keep sand from filling up the hole. Crowther described it as "a strongly allegorical, strangely engrossing film . . . packed with a bewitching power and poetry."[58] *Time* called it "a cinema masterpiece. Deep, original, strange. . . . Again and again he tries [to escape and] again and again he fails. Slowly, through long years of suffering, he learns to relinquish his will, to accept his fate. In the end, serene as a sage, he fathoms a great mystery of life: a man is not free unless his will is free, but if his will is free it does not matter if his body is bound."[59]

Robert Hatch was captivated by the camerawork. The film was shot virtually in its entirety inside and outside the confines of a wooden hovel in a sand pit. "The ramshackle, slowly collapsing house is a magic box of startling angles, intriguing textures and stimulating frames for action," he said. "And the sand, which he uses with small regard for its natural behavior, creeps and floods, rages and insinuates, peels and crumbles. It is sand with volition—a substance of authentic horror. Mr. Teshigahara mixes styles with the same insouciance that he manipulates sand. The basic manner is hyper-realism, as much respect being shown to the patina on an old tea kettle as to the expression of the hero's face in agony."[60]

Pathé-Contemporary, the distributor, had not obtained a theater booking for the film at the time of the festival, but the positive reviews got it into the Cinema II the following month. Arthur Knight and Hollis Alpert stated, "Symbolic and stylized, *Woman in the Dunes* is a microcosmic allegory of the human condition, with sex given all the prominence it deserves. It was the rarest of films, an artistic and commercial success."[61]

Young Italian Cinema

As Amos Vogel pointed out, the giants of the second Italian renaissance—Antonioni, Fellini, and Visconti—had become the middle generation of filmmakers by the mid-1960s. Meanwhile a new generation of directors came to the fore and created what became known as Young Italian Cinema. They did not comprise "a school with fervent aims," nor did they exhibit the stylistic flourishes of the French New Wave.[62] Nevertheless these young filmmakers—the group included Ermanno Olmi, Bernardo Bertolucci, and Pier Paolo Pasolini—were influenced by postwar Italian neorealism and used film as a political tool to address the numerous unresolved problems of contemporary Italy. Credit for introducing Young Italian Cinema to the United States largely rests with the New York Film Festival.

In its effort to establish Olmi as "an American box-office attraction," at the end of the 1963 festival Janus opened *Il Posto* at two theaters, the Cinema II and Fifth Avenue Cinema, and changed the title to *The Sound of Trumpets*. Winner of the Italian Film Critics Award at the Venice Film Festival in 1961, it told the story of a young Milanese (Alessandro Panseri) who gets "a job for life" with a big corporation. "The praise, plus its festival prizes, was enough to make one wary, but the news is good," said Stanley Kauffmann. It "proves to be a delicate,

Alessandro Panseri in Ermanno Olmi's *The Sound of Trumpets* (1963)

piercing work with a quality that is precious in films: it is personal . . . the protest is Olmi's, not his characters'. The boy and the girl accept the state of things completely. . . . It is Olmi who is sad and angry. He sees that the 'Detroit' syndrome is especially poignant in Italy, not because it has a long tradition of personal freedom (it hasn't) but because it has a long tradition of personality."[63] Strangely, the film "died dismally" in the words of Crowther.[64]

Janus released *The Fiancés* the following January at the Cinema II. Crowther described it as "a sort of poetic exposition of the loneliness and nostalgia of . . . a young bachelor who takes a job on what appears to be a power-plant construction project in a remote part of Sicily, leaving his widowed father and his girl friend in northern Italy." As an experiment, the Rugoff theater charged no admission on opening day and attracted crowds. "The viewers were predominantly young people and film connoisseurs," reported Crowther. "By midafternoon, the line for *The Fiancés* paralleled that of *Tom Jones* at the adjacent Cinema I."[65] Nevertheless the experiment failed. *The Fiancés* ran only two weeks, leading Dwight Macdonald to remark, "When the art-cinema public in a city like New York stays away from movies of this quality and stands in line four-deep month after month for *Tom Jones*, there's something wrong somewhere."[66]

In 1964 the festival introduced Bernardo Bertolucci by screening his second feature, *Before the Revolution*. Richard Roud called it the kind of film that "justifies the festival." A low-budget venture written and directed by Bertolucci in 1964, when he was twenty-three, *Before the Revolution* (*Prima della rivoluzione*), based on Stendhal's novel *The Charterhouse of Parma*, is about a young man (Francesco Barilli) who revolts against his respectable middle-class family, dallies with communism and abstract philosophy, and falls in love with his beautiful, unhappy young aunt (Adriana Asti). "Viewing life in such romantic terms is the special province of a very young director," observed Eugene Archer, "but Mr. Bertolucci has approached his story with such deep feeling that its full implications are communicated. This is a young man's film, but it has large social references. Cinematically, it is also filled with references to the best modern directors in Italy and France. Knowledgeable viewers can detect strong influences from Roberto Rossellini and Alain Resnais in Mr. Bertolucci's sophisticated style."[67]

In 1966 the festival presented Bertolucci's first feature, *The Grim Reaper*, which was produced in 1962. It was followed by *Partner* (1968), *The Spider's Stratagem* and *The Conformist* (1970), and *Last Tango in Paris* (1972). *The Conformist* (*Il conformista*) was financed by Paramount Pictures and provided Canby with evidence that "good movies, at least some good movies, can find an audience." However, he noted with dismay that "some Paramount executives didn't even know the company owned [the film] at the time it was shown at the New York Film Festival last September."[68] Paramount's financing allowed Bertolucci to make what he described as "a kind of big commercial blockbuster [that] mixed sex, suspense, spying, intrigue, murder, politics in the form of Mussolini-vintage fascism, and the excellent baroque detail of consummate filmmaking to form a devastating, bitter vision of the Fascist psychosis."[69] *The Conformist* opened at the Little Carnegie on March 22, 1971. Canby considered it "a superior chronicle film that equates the rise and fall of Italian Fascism, from the early 1920s until 1943, with the short, dreadful, very romantic life of Marcello (Jean-Louis Trintignant), a young man for whom conformity becomes a kind of obsession after a traumatic homosexual encounter in his youth."[70] Critics particularly admired its visual style. "Based on a novel by Alberto Moravia, the film reproduces the Italy and France of the 1930s with almost operatic splendor; no recent film has been so visually lush or stylistically exhilarating," said *Time*.[71] After playing at the Little Carnegie for three months, Paramount released the film wide in the Greater New York area. The National Society of Film Critics named Bertolucci Best Director of the year.

In 1966 the festival presented two films by Pier Paolo Pasolini, *Accatone* and *The Hawks and the Sparrows*. This controversial and provocative young Italian filmmaker was by no means an unknown in the United States. In fact, Pasolini was a celebrity. On February 17, 1966, Pasolini's *The Gospel According to St. Matthew* (*Il vangelo secondo Matteo*) opened at the Fine Arts and became the movie "sleeper" of the season. The film had been greeted "with insults, both verbal and vegetable, rotten eggs and scurrilous pamphlets" at the Venice Film Festival in 1964, reported Melton S. Davis. "That a convinced Marxist should have turned out a movie on the life of Christ . . . was thought to be the height of presumption." But a half hour into the film, "the theater was completely still, and at the movie's end, the applause was unanimous, the critics ecstatic. Before the festival was over, the film had garnered more awards than any other shown."[72] Walter Reade's Continental Distributing acquired the U.S. rights to the film.

The film was shot on location in the south of Italy using nonprofessional actors. Crowther admired Pasolini's choice of Enrique Irazoqui, "a young Spanish student," in the role of Jesus: "The Jesus we see is no transcendent evangelist in shining white robes, performing his ministrations and miracles in awesome spectacles. He is a young man of spare appearance, garbed in dingy, homespun cloaks, moving with quiet resolution across a rugged and dusty countryside, gathering his tough-faced disciples from toilers he meets along the way and preaching his words of exhortation to crowds of simple, sullen peasants and sprawling children." "This is a drama of a leader among a people who are poor and ignorant," said Crowther. "Mr. Pasolini has worked it by pursuing the naturalistic style and by the assiduous and tangible avoidance of all the Bible story clichés." The music, too, is anything but cliché, he added. "It has a distinct eclectic range, from Bach's 'St. Matthew Passion' to 'Missa Luba,' a Congolese mass sung to African instruments and rhythms. . . . [T]hese are just further surprises in a most uncommon film."[73]

The New York run attracted people from nearly every walk of life—"family groups, school groups and religious groups"—in addition to "the regular art-theater crowd and the young way-outniks, in beards and tight pants—two types of moviegoers who usually wouldn't be caught dead at religious pictures like *The Greatest Story Ever Told* or *Ben-Hur*," said Sheldon Gunsberg, a Walter Reade executive.[74] Endorsements by major Roman Catholic and Protestant publications generated bookings in all the major cities. Continental predicted that the picture would gross more than $3.5 million, exceeding the record *Room at the Top* set for the company.[75]

Pasolini's two festival films were quite different. According to the festival program notes, *Accatone*, Pasolini's debut feature, "is set in the outskirts of Rome with its prostitutes, pimps, and drifters; the lyrical freshness of this look at the 'other Italy' keeps the film from ever becoming sordid. Pasolini has succeeded in ennobling his characters and materials as did De Sica and Rossellini before him. It is both a modern tragedy and an indictment of the affluent society—in Italy, or anywhere else."[76] *The Hawks and the Sparrows* (*Uccellacci e uccellini*), produced in 1966, starred the famous Italian clown Toto, who won a special prize at the Cannes Film Festival. The festival called it "a delightful fable: a man and his son on the road of life, the strange and wonderful things that happen to them. . . . For many, the appeal of the film will be the care-free wayout atmosphere; for others its confrontation of the message of Pope John XXIII with other points of view. In every way, an astonishing film."[77] The two films were released by Brandon Films, *Accatone* at the 72nd Street Playhouse in 1967 and *The Hawks and the Sparrows* at the Fifth Avenue Cinema in 1968.

In 1967 the festival opened with Gillo Pontecorvo's *The Battle of Algiers* (*La battaglia di Algeri*), winner of the Golden Lion at Venice in 1966. It came to the festival courtesy of Rizzoli Films. Pontecorvo had been enlisted to make this film by Saadi Yacef, a survivor of the Algerian independence movement, who played himself onscreen in a starkly realistic reenactment of the struggle for independence by the Algerian National Liberation Front from 1954 to 1960. Pontecorvo's film showed French soldiers torturing Algerian terrorists, which the French delegates at Venice considered "an insult to France." Despite the latter's demand that the film be withdrawn from the festival, the management held firm.[78]

The Battle of Algiers played to a capacity audience at Philharmonic Hall, following which Pontecorvo was greeted with a standing ovation. Reviewers admired the film because it was "freed from all propaganda and sentimentality." According to *Time*, "At film's end, it is the French who win, blasting into bits the final survivors of the once-widespread revolutionary council. An epilogue, however, acknowledges that history later proved too much for the French, who granted Algeria its independence and moved out. Pontecorvo's achievement is in making that epilogue understandable simply by showing the Arab faces of Algiers—intense, fierce-eyed men and women cold-blooded enough to blow up a restaurant full of innocents to prove a point, courageous enough to undergo the most inhuman tortures rather than betray their comrades."[79]

The day after it was shown at the festival, *The Battle of Algiers* opened at the Cinema II, where it burnished its reputation as the greatest film ever made about terrorism. Joseph Morgenstern, writing in *Newsweek*, reported that at the Cinema II "many young Negroes cheered or laughed knowingly during each terrorist attack on the French, as if it were a textbook and a prophecy of urban guerrilla warfare to come. It could be that, but its obvious intent was illumination, not incitement to riot. The makers of matches cannot be blamed if the whole world is on a short fuse."[80]

New Waves from Eastern Europe

The loosening of political and cultural controls in the U.S.S.R. instituted by Nikita Khrushchev's de-Stalinization program stimulated new waves of filmmaking throughout Eastern Europe. The first occurred in Poland, which allowed Andrzej Wajda and the Polish school to flourish briefly during the early 1960s. Soon filmmaking centers were being established in the former Czechoslovakia, Yugoslavia, and Hungary as well. Although the movements peaked by 1968, within a short space of time an enormous body of creative work was introduced to the U.S. art film market courtesy of the New York Film Festival and MoMA.

Polanski's *Knife in the Water* was the first film from the Polish school to be presented by the festival. After making the picture, Polanski departed Poland for London, where he teamed up with the Polish-born film producer Gene Gutowski to make two commercial ventures, *Repulsion* (1965) and *Cul-de-Sac* (1966), both intentionally shocking studies of violence and sexual pathology that established Polanski as a master of horror and the grotesque. The two pictures led to a Hollywood contract.

The festival's second Polish discovery was Jerzy Skolimowski. A member of the second generation of Polish filmmakers working under the direction of the Lodz Film School, Skolimowski had collaborated with Polanski on the script for *Knife on the Water* before directing and starring in his first two features, *Identification Marks: None* and *Walkover*. In 1965 the festival presented the pair, which were dismissed by Crowther as "distractingly random and incoherent studies of a youth before his induction into the army and then 10 years later, when he is trying to land a job."[81] They were released by New Yorker Films in 1968 and 1969, respectively. In 1967 the festival presented Skolimowski's third and fourth features, *Bariera* and *Le Départ*. The festival program notes described *Bariera* as "a gentle fantasy of youthful romance in the 'new' Poland, influenced by Godard and Fellini. . . . The new generation is torn between the memories of socialist idealism and the anticipation of capitalist opportunism, but Skolimowski's lovers find their own magic in the monumental wreckage of society."[82] *Le Départ* was a French film Skolimowski made in Brussels. It starred Jean-Pierre Léaud and won the Golden Bear at the 1967 Berlin Film Festival. Howard Thompson wrote that "this free-wheeling, inventive comedy of a youth obsessed with fast autos has been put together with fresh, deceptive simplicity that makes it a joy to watch."[83] *Le Départ* was picked up by Pathé Contemporary and released in April 1968 at the Murray Hill. Despite a big buildup targeted at young adults, it had a limited run and was considered a forgettable film of 1968.

The Czech new wave was led by a small group of young directors working within the state-run film industry, among them Ján Kadár, Elmar Klos, Milos Forman, Jirí Menzel, Jan Němec, Věra Chytilová, and Ivan Passer. Most attended the Czech film school, the Film Academy of Theatrical Arts (FAMU), and rejected the official state socialist-realist aesthetic, producing eclectic, technically skillful, and highly assured features that won international acclaim.

Ján Kadár and Elmar Klos's *The Shop on Main Street* (*Obchod no korze*), the first Czech new wave film to arrive, premiered at the 1965 festival and "knocked us out of our chairs," said Crowther. Starring Ida Kaminska, the doyenne of Warsaw's Yiddish theater, and Josef Króner, it told a simple story about the growing affection between an aged Jewish proprietress of a modest button shop on the main street of a small town, and a dim-witted carpenter who is appointed "Aryan manager" of her business in Nazi-occupied Czechoslovakia. "The climax comes with a roundup of Jews for the concentration camps," said *Time*. "Should Tono [the carpenter] risk hiding his friend or force her to join the frightened crowd in the square? The end is a moving, ironic illumination of the small-scale greed and failure of nerve that enabled the Nazis to triumph over so many free men."[84] *Newsweek* described the performances of the two principals as "miraculous" and stated that codirectors Ján Kadár and Elmar Klos were "masters of the medium. Their taste is almost flawless. . . . Grotesquely charming as the situation may be at the outset, it is never sentimentalized."[85] Crowther considered it "one of the most arresting and devastating pictures I've seen from Europe or anywhere else in several years. The effectiveness of it is clearly in the honesty and simplicity with which it reckons with a great moral issue on the level of small human beings."[86]

The Shop on Main Street was released on January 24, 1966, at the 34th Street East by Prominent Films, a small New York firm that represented Marie Desmarais, a Canadian, who had acquired the North American rights to this offbeat picture at Cannes. Desmarais originally paid $2,000 for the rights but later made a preemptive bid to seal the deal when the Czech government informed her that it could not proceed as planned because it had received a better offer from another company. Desmarais decided to handle the distribution in the United States herself, "with Prominent Films taking care of the actual sales." Vincent Canby considered it a big gamble since the film would have to sell a lot tickets to break even.[87] The gamble paid off. *The Shop On Main Street* won the Oscar for Best Foreign Language Film—a first for Czech films—and went on to gross more than $3 million at the box office.[88]

Milos Forman's *Loves of a Blonde* (*Lásky jedné plavovlásky*) opened the 1966 festival and was another big hit. The festival program notes described the picture as follows: "The blonde in question is Czech, incurably romantic, and slightly dizzy. After a night with a touring young jazz musician, she decides this must be love and takes off to Prague to find him. What she finds instead are his scandalized parents screaming, 'What does this girl want with our son the musician?'"[89] *Time* enthused, "*Loves of a Blonde* is a boy-meets-girl comedy so fresh and unassuming that 34-year-old Writer-Director Milos Forman appears to have put it together without quite realizing the strength of his perceptions. The seeming simplicity conceals extraordinary skill: Forman observes small human aspirations very precisely, then borrows the style of a documentary to carve out a comic slice of life in swift, easy strokes." The *Time* reviewer was not alone in remarking on the "classic comic episodes," such as the dance-hall sequence that pits Andula and "the man-hungry girls against a trio of loutish army Lotharios. One furtively removes his wedding ring, only to see it go spinning crazily off among dancing feet." Another such episode was the "film's bittersweet climax in Prague, where the boy's parents forcibly separate their wayward son from his unexpected guest by dragging him off to their own bed for a riotous family quarrel."[90] Crowther described these incidents as "comedy of the grandest sort. Human comedy, I think they call it."[91] *Loves of a Blonde* was also presented by Prominent Films, which released it a month after the festival closing at the Sutton. The film went on to gross more than $1 million at the box office.

The audience response to these films convinced the film departments of Lincoln Center and MoMA to co-sponsor a "Festival of New Czechoslovak Cinema" in June 1967. Comprising twelve features never previously shown in the United States, the festival sold out every night. Penelope Gilliatt's verdict was succinct: "Amazing and unforgettable; the knife is often on the bone. A group of serious and gifted people are suddenly expressing themselves through film as naturally as, say, the writers of the Spanish Civil War did through poetry."[92] Three of the films—Jirí Menzel's *Closely Watched Trains*, Věra Chytilová's *Daisies*, and Zbynek Brynych's *The Fifth Horseman Is Fear*—were presented by Carlo Ponti, the Italian producer. Ponti apparently acted as their sales agent and arranged with Sigma III, a relatively new distribution company founded by Leonard S. Gruenberg, to handle them.

Closely Watched Trains (*Ostre sledované vlaky*), Menzel's first feature, opened on October 15, 1967, at the Festival Theater and fared the best. It tells a coming-of-age story about a callow youth (Vaclav Neckar), the second assistant stationmaster at an unimportant railway junction during the Nazi occupation, who aspires to loose his virginity and become a ladies' man like his superior. Like *The Shop on Main Street*, the film begins as a folk comedy and ends on a somber note when the young man is killed while sabotaging a German supply train.

Like the other film, said Crowther, it is a "picture that tacitly implies a rueful
and lingering contrition for the behavior of some Czechoslovaks during the
war—a subtle sort of sardonic comment on the slowness with which they became aware of the annihilating menace of those arrogant, closely watched
trains and the casualness with which they pulled themselves together and did
something about them in the end."[93]

Joseph Morgenstern, writing in *Newsweek*, raved: "Nothing can prepare you
for the special pleasures of this gentle masterpiece, and nothing should. It
moves along with the gravely comic deliberation of a cuckoo clock. . . . Any improvement in Vaclav Neckar's performance as Milos would be unimaginable,
and any flaws in Jiří Menzel's direction are unimportant. He has sprinkled
every scene with a magical mixture of stardust and coal dust. He has worked at
a level of taste, imagination, simplicity and delicacy that should compel re-
spectful attention of every director in America and put most of them deeply to
shame."[94] *Closely Watched Trains* won the Oscar for Best Foreign Language
Film—the second for a Czech film—and became another box office hit.

The thaw that allowed the Czech new wave to blossom ended abruptly in
August 1968, when President Alexander Dubček's liberal vision of "socialism
with a human face" was shattered by direct Soviet military intervention. The
Soviet invasion spelled the end of the Czech new wave and marked an end—or
temporary halt—in the careers of many of its finest directors. As a result, the
New York Film Festival took on even greater significance for the group. In 1968,
barely a month after the Soviet invasion, the festival presented three Czech
films in succession: Jiří Menzel's *Capricious Summer*, Jan Němec's *Report on the
Party and Its Guests*, and Milos Forman's *The Firemen's Ball*. Forman's and
Němec's films had been banned by the former regime headed by Antonin
Novotny, but Dubček had lifted the ban on the films before the invasion.

The Firemen's Ball (*Horí, má panenko*) brought the audience to its feet and
was the hit of the 1968 festival. The festival program notes observed that
"behind this brilliantly warm, funny and self-contained anecdote about a small
town firemen's ball, with its reluctant beauty queens, its stolen lottery presents,
its tiny status wars, lies a bitter allegory about the state of things in pre-July
Czechoslovakia."[95] The film had been acquired by Donald Rugoff's Cinema V,
which released it immediately following the festival at the Cinema II. Critics
read all sorts of allegorical or hidden meanings into the film. For example, *Time*
said, "The film has lived through three Czechoslovak eras, and its meanings
has changed accordingly." In pre-Dubček Czechoslovakia, it could be seen as
"a delicious parody-fable of Slavic bureaucracy. . . . After the coming of
Dubček, it could be enjoyed as broad comedy as well as trenchant comment.

With the Russian occupation, the farce is suddenly open to newer and darker interpretations—of men too weak and ill-equipped to fight, while liberty and hard-won independence are stolen or reduced to ashes."[96] Nevertheless the film died at the box office. Andrew Sarris offered the following explanation: "I suppose part of the problem is the inevitable backlash against overpraise of the Czech cinema as a whole. Also, the local left seems somewhat embarrassed by any reminders that there is a country called Czechoslovakia somewhere in the center of Europe. It would be much easier for everyone if the Czechs would stop whimpering and go away. Then our own hated America could resume its rightful role as the sole oppressor of mankind."[97]

The Hungarian films presented by the festival included Miklós Jancsó's *The Roundup* (1966) and *The Red and the White* (1968), plus István Szabó's *Father* (1967). All three were released commercially. In 1967, immediately after the close of the festival, Continental Distributing released Szabó's *Father (Apa)*, winner of the Grand Prix at the Moscow Film Festival, at the Little Carnegie. Bosley Crowther described it as "a beautiful and tender account of a young man's recollections of his dead father" from the time of the young man's "boyhood, when he imagined his father as a great wartime resistance hero, to his maturity, when these illusions were slightly disabused." Crowther added, "There is one brilliant metaphor in it that tersely and tellingly states the political confusions of the Hungarians in the postwar years. The young hero is acting as an extra in a film that is being made about the tragic war years. He is playing one of a mob of Jewish prisoners trudging along heavily and weakly under the prodding of Nazi guards. Suddenly, the film's director decides he needs another guard—a blond one with an arrogant appearance. He pulls the hero out of the mob, gives him a gun and exchanges his Star of David armband for one with a swastika. Now he's a Nazi. It's as simple and senseless as that."[98] *Father* was one of many critically acclaimed foreign films of 1967 that never got off the ground.

Jancsó's *The Red and the White* and the *Roundup* were released within a month of each other in 1969 by Brandon Films and Altura Films at the Fifth Avenue and Carnegie Hall Cinemas, respectively. "Both reveal a savage irony and a cold, implacable loathing for war—and for the species that causes it," said *Time*.[99] The festival program notes described *The Red and the White (Csillagosok, katonák)* as a "beautifully photographed, stylized drama of the Russian civil war in which neither Reds nor Whites are heroes and only war is evil."[100] *Time* explained that "propaganda was not Hungarian Director Miklós Jancsó's aim. Instead, he views the war as a lethal chess game in which his camera alternates from side to side, until war becomes a force beyond control of the combatants.

The Red and the White becomes the tortured landscape of a country's soul through a series of ironic contrasts: biplanes flying above horsemen, love scenes interrupted by violence, military bands trumpeting gaily after the executions of wounded soldiers."[101]

The festival's program notes described *The Roundup* (*Szegénylegények*) as "a fantastically diabolical trap set by the Austrian Army to round up the last of the Hungarian insurgents" after the Kossuth Rebellion of 1848.[102] In the opinion of Vincent Canby, "[Jancsó] is a director of exquisite humanism. . . . The narrative line threads from one incident to another with a kind of Brechtian impartiality. . . . [The movie] is so full of cruelty and grief that is made bearable only by the eloquence of its images. . . . It is a movie of awesome contrasts, not only of visual tones, but also of feelings and sounds. . . . It is, I think, as close to being a true epic as any film made by a contemporary movie-maker."[103]

Films from Yugoslavia were introduced in 1967, with the presentation of Dragoslav Lazic's *The Feverish Years* and Dusan Makavejev's *An Affair of the Heart*. In 1968 the festival presented Vastroslav Mimica's *Kaya, I'll Kill You*. However, it was not until November 1969, when MoMA presented a series of twelve recent Yugoslav films, that the new cinema began to be fully appreciated. Roger Greenspun's review of the series described the "national cinema as attractive (though not as revolutionary) as any to emerge since the French New Wave 19 years ago." He singled out three films—Kresimir Golik's *I Have Two Mummies and Two Daddies*, Dusan Makavejev's *Innocence Unprotected*, and Ljubisa Kozomara and Gordan Milhic's *Crows*—as having "the look and feel of achieved maturity."[104]

Makavejev emerged as the most controversial and iconoclastic of the group when the festival presented his *WR: Mysteries of the Organism* in 1971. Makavejev's signature collage style juxtaposed historical footage with fictional scenes and scatological situations. Of course, it was those scatological elements that made the films easy to sell. *Mysteries of the Organism* was entered in the countercultural festival at Cannes and "electrified" everyone at the midnight screening of the film. Cynthia Grenier reported that a standing-room-only audience "cheered and screamed and applauded for a good quarter of an hour" at 2 o'clock in the morning.[105] The festival's program notes said that Makavejev "takes as his point of departure the career of Wilhelm Reich. Beginning as a documentary, fictional scenes are inserted telling of a Yugoslav girl who preaches Reich's theories of socialism through more and better orgasms. . . . Note: This film is bound to offend practically everybody."[106]

Mysteries of the Organism had been acquired by Cinema V, which released it commercially at the Cinema II on October 14, 1971, a day after it was screened at the festival. Rugoff launched the film by throwing a party for Makavejev at the Plaza Hotel and backed the film throughout its run with a provocative and controversial ad campaign. One such ad contained a photo of a young woman eating a banana whose caption read, "If you saw what she's seeing, you'd see . . . ," which was followed by blurbs from reviews. According to Justin Wyatt, Makavejev's treatment of Reich's sexual theories "so enraged some Reichians that they sought (unsuccessfully) to get an injunction against its showing,"[107] which no doubt helped the box office.

Bo Widerberg

Commercially the most successful independent release presented by the New York Film Festival during this period was Bo Widerberg's *Elvira Madigan* in 1967. (The most successful studio release presented by the festival was *Last Tango in Paris* in 1973.) *Elvira Madigan* was distributed by Cinema V and opened at the Cinema II on October 31, 1967. A leading Swedish novelist and film critic, Widerberg attracted attention when he published a collection of essays in 1962 entitled *Vision in the Swedish Cinema*, which denounced Swedish film— and Ingmar Bergman in particular—as rarified and oblivious to everyday contemporary issues. Widerberg turned to directing in 1962. *Elvira Madigan*, his fifth feature, starred Pia Dagermark, who received the best actress award at Cannes, and Thommy Berggren. It recounts the legend of a married army officer in eighteenth-century Sweden who deserts his regiment and family to run off with a beautiful circus artist. As Arthur Knight explained, "Their life together, while idyllic, is clearly doomed. The man is shunned by his friends, cut off by his family, and hunted by the police. Together, he and Elvira flee to Denmark, but here poverty and privation take their toll. Not even starvation, however, can shake their love and it is the strength of this love that brings about their final tragedy." Knight praised Widerberg for making "all of this as painfully immediate as a stab in the heart, yet as beautiful and controlled as the Mozart piano concerto that supplies an anachronistic but singularly appropriate accompaniment to his film."[108]

Crowther commented, "Exquisite is only the first word to describe this exceptional film. . . . [S]o brash and immature are the lovers, so confident and gay are they at first, and then so shaken and helpless are they as their idyll is remorselessly dissolved, that they do bear a wistful resemblance to some of the florid young people of today who might hold with the young man in this story that 'a blade of grass is all the world.'"[109] Stanley Kauffmann offered a dissenting opinion: "These two lovers are stupid. What is obvious to the viewer [is that] this pair have neither any plan nor any sense of what they are getting into. They are just dumb. Their fate has some pathos because they have been happy

Pia Dagermark in Bo Widerberg's *Elvira Madigan* (1967)

and they do end up dead, but our impatience with them spoils the intended tragic fall. All the breathtaking long shots across quiet meadows, the prospects through waving grass, seem wasted on two ninnies."[110] *Elvira Madigan* obviously struck a chord with young lovers because the film grossed over $10 million at the box office, to rank number six on *Variety*'s All-Time Foreign Language Films. Stated another way, *Elvira Madigan* probably grossed more at the U.S. box office than all of Ingmar Bergman's films up to that time.

This survey does not do justice to the range of films shown at the festival that never found commercial release or timely exposure outside the festival. As the next chapter reveals, the art film market went into decline beginning in 1967, just as the festival was taking hold. The entry of Hollywood into the market and the rising costs of doing business convinced art house managers nationwide to reject the offbeat in favor of the sure thing. By 1973 the market had collapsed. Critics sometimes questioned the decisions of the selection committee and occasionally faulted the festival for its continued loyalty to certain auteurs. Yet it cannot be doubted that the New York Film Festival functioned as a keeper of the flame by showcasing international talent and providing foreign film directors with an opportunity to crack the American market. New York City film culture would have been the poorer without it.

Collapse

Reminiscing about the art film scene of the 1960s, Andrew Sarris remarked: "No one on either side of the Atlantic—or Pacific—wants to admit it today, but the fashion for foreign films depended a great deal on their frankness about sex. At a time when the Hollywood censors imposed twin-bed strictures on American movies, foreign films were daringly adult. Once the censors began to depart, in the late '60s, Hollywood was free to supply the ooh-la-la factor—and without subtitles."[1] As the title of Sarris's article suggested, foreign films had lost their cachet.

Hollywood in Transition

A seismic shift in American culture during the 1960s led to the dismantling of movie censorship. For over three decades a triad of controls had regulated content: (1) governmental censorship boards (2) organized religious pressure, and (3) industry self-regulation. Governmental censorship effectively ended in 1965 when the Supreme Court handed down a decision involving the Danish film *A Stranger Knocks*, which declared that the statutes governing the New York Board of Censors were unconstitutional. No longer would films have to be submitted to the state agency to secure a license for public exhibition. Because of New York City's strategic importance as the port of entry for foreign films, the decision had an immediate impact on the entire art film market. Thereafter almost anything could be shown as long as it was not obscene. According to the Motion Picture Association of America (MPAA), the industry trade association, the obscenity law was in "a hopeless mess" in the courts.[2]

Organized religious pressure declined as well. In 1966 the Legion of Decency renamed itself the National Catholic Office for Motion Pictures and adopted a new stance. Instead of advocating picketing and boycotts of films deemed offensive to the church, it decided to support "worthy films and a widespread educational campaign to develop a new appreciation of the medium among Catholic laymen."[3]

Beginning in 1966, industry self-regulation went by the boards when the MPAA, under the leadership of its new president, Jack Valenti, replaced the old Production Code with a more liberal version that allowed the organization to affix the "Suggested for Mature Audiences" label to Hollywood films judged unsuitable for children. In 1968 the MPAA did away with the Production Code altogether and instituted a full-scale rating system, the Code and Rating Administration that classified films according to their suitability for different age groups. The ratings included an X, which prohibited those under seventeen from gaining admission to the movie and gave Hollywood producers license to deal with themes and subjects designed specifically for adult audiences. Valenti justified the changes by claiming that "films can't live in a vacuum. They relate to the temper of the times, the postures of today."[4]

The impact of this new freedom on Hollywood was immediate. As *Time* put it, "Hollywood has at long last become part of what the French film journal *Cahiers du Cinéma* calls 'the furious springtime of world cinema,' and is producing a new kind of movie." Freed from the shackles of the Production Code, the New American Cinema, as it was dubbed, "assimilated the cinematic techniques of the French New Wave" and began to treat "once-shocking themes with a maturity and candor unthinkable even five years ago."[5]

Time singled out Arthur Penn's *Bonnie and Clyde*, a revisionist gangster film set in the Depression, which starred Warren Beatty and Faye Dunaway, as exemplary of the trend. Released by Warner Bros. in August 1967, "*Bonnie and Clyde* stirred up a battle among movie critics that seemed to be almost as violent as the film itself." Bosley Crowther, it will be recalled, was so offended by the violence in the film that he reviewed it—negatively—three times and ultimately resigned his post as chief film critic of the *New York Times*. Taking a fresh look at the film, *Time* said, "Undeniably, part of the scandal and success of *Bonnie and Clyde* stems from its creative use of what has always been a good box-office draw: violence. But what matters most about *Bonnie and Clyde* is the new freedom of its style, expressed not so much by camera trickery as by its yoking of disparate elements into a coherent artistic whole—the creation of unity from incongruity. Blending humor and horror, it draws the audience in sympathy toward its anti-heroes. It is, at the same time, a commentary on the mindless daily violence of the American '60s, and an esthetic evocation of the past." *Time* observed that an audience now existed in America for "the intellectually demanding, emotionally fulfilling kind of film exemplified by *Bonnie and Clyde*." It also observed that a new generation of movie executives in Hollywood would ensure that such movies "can and will be made."[6]

Young production chiefs like Richard Zanuck (aged thirty-four) at Fox, David Picker (thirty-six) at United Artists, and Robert Evans (thirty-seven) at Paramount came into their own as a result of a recession that hit the industry in 1969. In that year the majors suffered more than $200 million in losses. To compete with television, studios had placed their bets on blockbusters and big-budget musicals like *My Fair Lady* (Warner Bros., 1964), *Mary Poppins* (Disney, 1964), and *The Sound of Music* (20th Century-Fox, 1965) to reach a mass market. But by 1969 the era had come to a close. As Charles Champlin of the *Los Angles Times* put it, "The movies entered the 60s as a mass family entertainment medium in trouble and they leave them as a mass but minority art form, important and newly influential, wildly divergent and addressed to many divergent audiences. . . . Moviegoing as a national habit is over except among the young and unmarried (or the young and married but childless) segment of the population. And even this young audience is, like everyone else who goes to movies at all, enormously selective and discretionary."[7] The young production chiefs saw a way out of the dilemma by focusing "on what seemed to be the two only surefire target areas left in the business—the so-called youth market and the sex-ploitation field."[8]

Youth films hit the market in 1969.[9] The list includes Larry Peerce's *Goodbye, Columbus* and Haskell Wexler's *Medium Cool* from Paramount; John Schlesinger's *Midnight Cowboy* and Arthur Penn's *Alice's Restaurant* from United Artists; Dennis Hopper's *Easy Rider* from Columbia; Frank Perry's *Last Summer* from Allied Artists; and Robert Downey Sr.'s *Putney Swope* from Cinema V. *Midnight Cowboy* and *Easy Rider* were big commercial hits. *Midnight Cowboy* appealed to the "youth" audience through its journey into American culture and the national psyche, its depiction of the disintegrating American city, and its attitude toward sex and drugs. A Jerome Hellman–John Schlesinger production, *Midnight Cowboy*, based on a novel by James Leo Herlihy, was directed by Schlesinger and starred Dustin Hoffman in his first role since *The Graduate*. Jon Voight made his screen debut as Joe Buck, a young Texan who travels north by bus to Manhattan to seek his fortune as a gigolo but, in the words of Vincent Canby, winds up "a half-hearted 42nd Street hustler whose first and only friend is a lame, largely ineffectual con artist."[10] *Midnight Cowboy*'s rancid portrait of New York's Times Square earned it an X rating. Nominated for seven Academy Awards, it won an

Oscar for Best Picture—the only time an X-rated picture won the award. John Schlesinger won for Best Director and Waldo Salt for Best Adapted Screenplay. Produced at a cost of $3.2 million, *Midnight Cowboy* grossed $18 million in rentals in the United States.

Easy Rider, a low-budget independent venture produced by Peter Fonda and Dennis Hopper, did even better and earned a reputed $60 million worldwide. Fonda and Hopper starred as two hippie bikers who score big on a drug deal in Los Angeles and head for New Orleans in time for the Mardi Gras, "a search for freedom thwarted by that streak of ingrained, bigoted violence in the U.S. and their own hangups," as *Variety* put it.[11] Stephen Farber observed that *Easy Rider*'s "importance is not as a work of art but as a cultural document that expresses—more by instinct than design—many of the feelings of today's youth. The film is so phenomenally popular because it is so completely in tune with its college and teenage audience—the movie-makers and the movie-goers share identical fantasies and anxieties."[12] By 1970 almost everyone had jumped on the *Easy Rider* bandwagon, wrote Mel Gussow, "making low-budget movies with non-names, directed at (and often, by) young people. . . . Drugs, desertion, Vietnam, race, sex, ecology—no subject seems too contemporary or too controversial."[13]

Sexploitation films hit the market in 1970. For most of the 1960s Audubon Films, Sigma III, Grove Press, and other independents had the sexploitation market almost to themselves. They distributed such films as Mac Alberg's *I, a Woman*, Lars Magnus Lindgren's *Dear John*, Mai Zetterling's *Night Games*, and Vilmot Sjöman's *I Am Curious (Yellow)*. Following the release of Grove Press's *I Am Curious (Yellow)*, the majors entered the game and the market was soon flooded with "sex spoofs, sex satires, sex dramas and sex melodramas," with no end in sight.[14] Within a year erotic films from the major studios rivaled what was being shown in grind houses. Michael Sarne's *Myra Breckinridge* and Russ Meyer's *Beyond the Valley of the Dolls* from Fox were thought to have pushed the boundaries as far as they could go.

Nevertheless a lucrative pornographic film industry soon emerged, signaled by the release in 1972 of *Deep Throat*, a hard-core feature starring Linda Lovelace. The film grossed over $3 million in six months and played in seventy theaters across the country. According to Ralph Blumenthal, in New York, at the New World Theater on West 49th Street, the picture attracted an average of five thousand people a week, "including celebrities, diplomats, critics, businessmen, women alone and dating couples, few of whom, it might be presumed, would previously have gone to see a film of sexual intercourse, fellatio and cunnilingus."[15] For the record, the New World Theater, under its old name, had introduced New Yorkers to Rossellini's *Open City* and other great European postwar films.

Art Film Market Trends

During this period of transition, the majors continued to release a few foreign films each year that dominated the market. Like always, they put their money on proven auteurs and promising new talent. Without exception, the filmmakers came from Western Europe. Independent distributors, led by Continental Distributing and Cinema V, relied on films from Eastern Europe or from film-makers in Western Europe deemed too experimental or too offbeat for popular tastes. Such films were almost always shown first at the New York Film Festival.

The target moviegoer for the majors and independents alike remained the young adult under thirty. The buying power of these individuals was enormous, and they were frequent moviegoers. However, discovering what appealed to this audience was another matter. The 1960s witnessed the rise of political activism, the hippie movement, and a social revolution involving the sons and daughters of the American middle class. Where this counterculture was heading no one could easily predict.

The art film market remained healthy through 1966. In that year more than eight films grossed $1 million or more in rentals—a first. They included *Dear John*, *The Shop on Main Street*, *The Gospel According to St. Matthew*, *Viva Maria!*, *Juliet of the Spirits*, and *A Man and a Woman*.[16]

In 1967—the year in which Norman Jewison's *In the Heat of the Night*, Mike Nichols's *The Graduate*, and Arthur Penn's *Bonnie and Clyde* were released—conditions changed. For every unanticipated smash hit "a half dozen reason-ably expected winners have languished and fallen by the wayside," reported Crowther. The disappointments included Ingmar Bergman's *Persona*, Carlos Saura's *The Hunt*, Alain Resnais's *La Guerre Est Finie*, and István Szabó's *Father*.[17]

Ingmar Bergman's *Persona*, the first disappointment of the year, deserves a closer look. It was distributed by United Artists, which had acquired the world-wide distribution rights to Bergman's films from Svensk Filmindustri in 1967. Presumably Janus's contract with Svensk for exclusive rights to Bergman's films had expired when Bergman became director of the Royal Dramatic Theater of Stockholm in 1963. Now that Bergman decided to resume his work as a film-maker, Svensk turned to UA, hoping that a Hollywood major could find a larger market for his films. United Artists sealed the deal after *Persona* opened in Stockholm in October 1966. Hailed by Werner Wiskari as a "film about intense personal loneliness," *Persona* seemed to confirm the new direction Bergman

took in 1963 with *The Silence*, "a dramatization of the ugliness of human relations when the only contact is physical."[18]

Persona was released on March 6, 1967, at the Festival. UA's ad described
the plot as follows: "Liv Ullmann and Bibi Andersson, as a mentally disturbed
actress and a psychiatric nurse, develop a strange love-hate relationship in Bergman's new movie." The ad emphasized the physical resemblance of the two
women by showing a composite photo containing half of each woman's face as
interlocking pieces of a jigsaw puzzle. Following the opening, the ad included
review blurbs that focused on Bibi Andersson's erotic monologue: "There is a
bizarre sexual encounter with two boys on a beach done with remarkable simplicity and dignity (*NYT*)"; "[Bergman] has followed the Swedish freedom into
the exploration of sex (*N.Y. Post*)"; "Bergman proves that a fully clothed woman
telling of a sexual experience can make all the nudities and perversions that his
compatriots have been splattering on the screen lately seem like nursery school
sensualities (*World Journal Tribune*)."[19] *Persona* played for a month at the Festival
but subsequently died.

UA went on to release *Hour of the Wolf* and *Shame* in 1968—which completed the so-called Island Trilogy—and *The Passion of Anna* in 1970. Like *Persona*, they starred Liv Ullmann, the newest member of Bergman's acting company, a stage actress Bergman had met in Norway. The National Society of
Film Critics heaped awards on these films. Making no distinction between domestic and foreign films, the society named *Persona* Best Film of 1968 and *The
Shame* Best Film of 1969. It named Bergman Best Director four times—for *Persona, Hour of the Wolf, Shame*, and *The Passion of Anna*—and Bibi Anderson Best
Actress for *Persona* and Liv Ullmann Best Actress for *Hour of the Wolf*. The box
office returns on these films were another matter. *The Shame* generated only
$163,000 in rentals and to get that UA spent $111,000 on advertising, which essentially put the film in the red for the company.[20] By the time *The Passion of Anna*
came out, UA's display ad simply stated that "man is the king of beasts. . . ." UA
was hemorrhaging money in 1970, the result of the industrywide recession, and
seemingly had given up on the director.

The box office winners of 1967 included *Closely Watched Trains* and *Elvira
Madigan*, plus Joseph Strick's *Ulysses* and Philippe de Broca's *King of Hearts*.
Ulysses's claim to fame, according to *Variety*, was that "for the first time in the
history of motion pictures, perhaps, the case for obscenity lies not in what is
seen on the screen but what is heard on the soundtrack . . . . Visually, there's
little in the film to offend most adult viewers. . . . The obscenity is in the speech,
the ear is besieged with suggested phrases, propositions, descriptions, and re-
grets of lost opportunities. Even inanimate objects are used to comment—a

Barbara Jefford and Milo O'Shea in Joseph Strick's *Ulysses* (1967)

cuckoo clock berates Bloom with its chirp of 'cuckold, cuckold, cuckold.' Some of the dialog is offensive in its very wording."[21] What audiences heard was the word "fuck" from Barbara Jefford in the role of Molly Bloom.[22] Strick's adaptation of James Joyce's novel was produced by Walter Reade Jr. and released by Continental Distributing. Banned in the United States from 1922 to 1933 for its scandalous language, Joyce's novel is set in Dublin and uses a stream-of-consciousness technique to depict one day (June 16, 1904) in the lives of three people: Stephen Dedalus, a young poet-teacher; Leopold Bloom, a middle-aged Jewish ad salesman; and Bloom's "erogenous wife Molly," played by Maurice Roeves, Milo O'Shea, and Barbara Jefford, respectively.[23] Strick condensed Joyce's massive novel to 140 minutes of screen time and shot the picture in contemporary Dublin locations to keep down costs.

Continental designed a fast play-off for the film, allegedly to give "the blue-noses" as little time as possible to hold up the film's release. The plan was to release the film simultaneously in sixty-five theaters around the country for three-day runs at advanced admission prices.[24] In New York City *Ulysses* opened on March 14, 1967, at the Beacon Theater, located on Broadway at 75th Street. Due to the "unprecedented audience response and critical acclaim," the film was re-released the following week at the Trans-Lux 85th Street on a reserved-seat basis. During the initial release the picture grossed $800,000 at the box office, which approximated the production cost of the film.[25]

Crowther included *Ulysses* in his "Top Ten" films of 1967 and described it as "a faithful and brilliant screen translation of Joyce's classic novel, done with taste, imagination and cinema artistry. Most notable and commendable are the candor and clarity with which Joyce's ribald language and erotic images are presented to achieve understanding and the rhythm and ring of poetry."[26] *Time* said, "For those who have the patience and the intellectual equipment to read it, the novel is something very like a revelation; the film is not much more than a titillating tale like the Gospel according to Joyce."[27]

De Broca's *King of Hearts*, an offbeat item from United Artists, introduced a series of antiwar films to the market that included: Richard Lester's *How I Won the War* (1967), Tony Richardson's *The Charge of the Light Brigade* (1968), and Ingmar Bergman's *Shame* (1968) from United Artists; Jean-Luc Godard's *Les Carabiniers* (1968) from New Yorker Films; and Richard Attenborough's *Oh! What a Lovely War* (1969) from Paramount. The Vietnam War was a nightly feature on the evening news, and if these films did not directly mention the conflict, their messages must have implied some connection—or so it was presumed. *King of Hearts* (*Le Roi de coeur*) fared the best. Based on an original idea, the film is set in World War I and contains a haunting score by Georges Delerue. Alan Bates, a British soldier, is sent to a deserted French village to defuse a time bomb left behind by the retreating Germans. He discovers that the town has been claimed by the inmates of the local insane asylum, who hail him as the "King of Hearts." Vincent Canby gave away the ending of the film in the very first sentence of his review: "In the last scene of *King of Hearts* . . . Alan Bates stands at the gate of a madhouse, seeking permanent asylum from the real world. He is holding a bird cage and is stark naked." Canby explained that de Broca had "seized on a theme . . . that, briefly stated, is that the certified insane of the world are a lot less lunatic than the madmen who persist in making lunatic war."[28] A box office failure in France, *King of Hearts* originally received mixed reviews in the United States but went on to become a cult favorite in the 1970s, when it was invariably paired with *Harold and Maude* in repertory theaters. The film eventually grossed $5.7 million at the box office, ranking number thirteen on *Variety*'s All-Time Foreign Language Films.

Shame and *Les Carabiniers*, the two low-budget entries, received rave reviews—if little else. Pauline Kael considered *Shame* a masterpiece: "The film is set a tiny step into the future—1971—we feel we have already known this time. . . . This is just degrading, ordinary old war, and it takes a while before we realize that Bergman has put us in the position of the Vietnamese and all those occupied peoples we have seen being interrogated and punished and frightened until they can no longer tell friend from enemy, extermination from liberation."[29] As was previously noted, Renata Adler included *Les Carabiniers* in her "Top Ten" list, calling it "one of the strongest anti-war films ever made— without resorting in any way to sentiment."[30]

The big ticket items—*How I Won the War*, *The Charge of the Light Brigade*, and *Oh! What a Lovely War*—were critical and box office failures. All three were British productions and dealt with past wars—World War II, the Crimean War, and the Great War, respectively—and exposed "the follies of the upper classes." As Pauline Kael put it, "Their explanation of war is the British equivalent of the adolescent *Mad*-magazine approach: wars are made by the officers, who are homicidal imbeciles interested only in personal position and indifferent to the death of their men."[31]

The box office winner of 1968 was Luis Buñuel's *Belle de Jour*. The film's draw was Catherine Deneuve as Séverine, a sexually repressed housewife who works part time as a prostitute in a high-class brothel, where she accepts only the most fantastic and perverse clients. As Arthur Knight put it, "It would be difficult to imagine any actress more entrancingly right in this pivotal role than Catherine Deneuve. With her blond, wide-eyed beauty and patrician elegance, she seems wholly credible, immune to the sordid life into which she plunges herself."[32] Based on a Joseph Kessel novel, *Belle de Jour* was produced by Robert and Raymond Hakim and received the Golden Lion at the Venice Film Festival in 1967. As described by Knight and Alpert in their "Sex and the Cinema" series for *Playboy*, "Buñuel, characteristically, has decorated the basic story with innumerable fetishistic allusions (including a necrophilic suggestion of inter-course in a coffin) and expanded it with dream sequences that illustrate the heroine's pathological need for degradation and shame. As the film progresses, the dreams and reality become nightmarishly intertwined—but through it all, the blonde Catherine Deneuve (whose *nom de brothel* is Belle de Jour) remains ravishingly, radiantly beautiful."[33] An Allied Artists release, *Belle de Jour* was Buñuel's greatest commercial success, grossing $8 million at the box office in the United States and ranking number ten on *Variety*'s All-Time Foreign Language Films.

The disappointments of 1968 included Jean-Luc Godard's *La Chinoise* and François Truffaut's *The Bride Wore Black*. *La Chinoise* was the second release by Leacock/Pennebaker, an independent distributor founded in 1963 by cinema verité documentarians Richard Leacock and D. A. Pennebaker. The company made it big distributing its first film, *Don't Look Back*, Pennebaker's documentary about Bob Dylan's 1965 tour of England. Released in 1967, it broke all existing box office records for theatrical documentaries. *La Chinoise* seemed to anticipate the events of May 1968 in Paris's Latin Quarter, when leftist student demonstrators battled riot police in a demand for "greater student control of university administration and, in general, the violent overthrow of the 'capitalist establishment.'" It follows a group of university students on summer holiday who hole themselves up in an apartment belonging to one of their parents and proceed to turn the elegant quarters into a Maoist cell. The leader of the cell is Véronique, a philosophy student at the Sorbonne, who is played by Anne Wiazemsky, the granddaughter of Nobel laureate François Mauriac and Godard's future wife.

To lay the groundwork for *La Chinoise*'s New York premiere, the company sent Godard on a national speaking tour of college campuses. The timing couldn't have been better. The tour coincided with a monthlong Godard retrospective at MoMA. The prestigious series generated a lot of publicity and enabled the curious to chart the development of Godard's art. While on the tour, Godard answered questions at each stop and was greeted like a rock star. Although the turnout may have been what Leacock had hoped for, Godard was disillusioned by the political apathy he discerned in the young audiences and departed for France after visiting only four campuses.

For the New York launch on April 3, 1968, Leacock rented the Kips Bay Theater in Manhattan on a "four wall" basis. Renting the theater signified either that the exhibitor was reluctant to book the film or that the distributor was willing to take a calculated risk and collect the bulk of box office receipts should *La Chinoise* attract a following. The critics were evenly divided. Those who liked the film applauded Godard for his sympathetic treatment of the young radicals. For example, Robert Hatch said, "Godard works well with young people as though he liked being with them, and they must like him, for they let down their guards as though he were not around."[34] Pauline Kael compared Godard's treatment of youth in *La Chinoise* to that of F. Scott Fitzgerald's, "in that [Godard] loves beautiful, doomed youth."[35]

Those who disliked the film damned Godard as a technically proficient opportunist. For example, Stanley Kauffmann said, "When he made *Breathless* almost ten years ago, postwar nihilism was 'in' with youth, so it was 'in' with him; *Breathless* was nihilistic. . . . Today the cognate youth-group is politically activist, so *La Chinoise* is Maoist. . . . [T]he impression grows and persists that Godard is congenitally a bootlicker of young boots."[36] Renata Adler used the film to pen a diatribe against the entire youth movement: "It is not really foreseen in any philosophy of history that a group of middle-class young people, against whom the system has done no injustice whatsoever—whom the system was actually educating for positions of power—should want to bring the system down for fun. The gratuitous personal act has long been famous in literature, but it took the age of movies to bring us the gratuitous political movement."[37] *La Chinoise* ran for a month at the Kips Bay and reopened briefly at the 8th Street Playhouse and Brandt's Regency, but it never measured up to *Breathless* in popularity.

Hollywood nevertheless saw a trend in the making and began investing in student-protest films as early as 1968, when Paramount backed Lindsay Anderson's *If . . .*, a British entry and the second student-protest film to reach the United States. *If . . .* starred Malcolm McDowell as the leader of a group of nonconformists at a posh English boy's school who stage an armed revolt against the archaic customs and authoritarian spirit of the institution. Anderson stated that the attack against the school was "a metaphor for a much wider evil which the public school system promotes and preserves."[38] It opened at the Plaza on March 9, 1969, and went on to win the Golden Palm at Cannes, after which it enjoyed a successful commercial run.

Deciding that American youth wanted to see movies about their own experiences, Hollywood studios released a number of student-protest films in 1970, among them Stuart Hagmann's *The Strawberry Statement* and Michelangelo Antonioni's *Zabriskie Point* (MGM) and Richard Rush's *Getting Straight* (Columbia). None of these films performed well at the box office. In fact, *Zabriskie Point* was a financial disaster, grossing a mere $900,000 during an embarrassingly brief theatrical run, as well as a huge disappointment for MGM, which had invested more than $7 million in the picture. A seismic shift had occurred among the young. Student interest in radical politics and the "hippie temptation" had cooled. As a result of the Kent State shootings and the Vietnamization of the ongoing Vietnam War, by 1971 student interest in movies about revolution had shriveled to almost zero.

Truffaut's *The Bride Wore Black*, another casualty of the times, took in a mere $32,000 in rentals in 1968. As was noted earlier, UA's relationship with Truffaut began in 1968. Although his *Fahrenheit 451* had earlier been a disappointment for Universal, UA was more than willing to finance and distribute his subsequent films, which normally performed well in his home market. Moreover, he had published a book-length interview with Alfred Hitchcock in 1967, which generated a lot of favorable publicity and made him even more attractive to young cinephiles. *The Bride Wore Black* (*La mariée était en noir*), an *hommage* to the master of suspense, starred Jeanne Moreau as a "determined widow" who methodically murders the men responsible for her fiancé's death. In an effort to explain its poor box office performance, Andrew Sarris wrote: "*The Bride Wore*

Lena Nyman and Börje Ahlstedt in Vilgot Sjöman's *I Am Curious (Yellow)* (1969)

Black has been reviewed as if it were a filmed sequel to Truffaut's book on Alfred Hitchcock. But it isn't. Whereas Hitchcock is basically a genre director, Truffaut's temperament is closer to the sprawling humanism of Renoir. Of course, no director can memorize the life's work of another director without picking up a few tricks and ideas along the way. . . . Truffaut breaks the rules of the genre without abandoning the genre, and thus teeters precariously between Hitchcock and Renoir without committing himself entirely to either."[39]

The year 1969 represented the high-water mark for foreign films: Vilgot Sjöman's *I Am Curious (Yellow)* and Costa-Gavras's *Z* broke out of the art film ghetto to attract crossover audiences, ranking numbers one and three, respectively, on *Variety*'s All-Time Foreign Language Films. However, as Vincent Canby observed the same year, they were anomalies: "It's a disquieting commentary on the state of movie tastes that [*La Femme infidèle*] should have had only a short, unspectacular first run here."[40] *I Am Curious (Yellow)* (*Jag är nyfiken— en film i gult*) attracted attention for being "as explicit as one can get in or out of a stag film."[41] Ostensibly about "the social, political and sexual journey of a young Swedish woman," the film was produced for $160,000 by Sandrews, an exhibitor-financed studio in Stockholm that had turned out Alf Sjöberg's *Miss Julie*, Bergman's *Sawdust and Tinsel*, and Mai Zetterling's *Night Games*, as well as other uninhibited Swedish films.[42]

I Am Curious (Yellow) was distributed by Grove Press, a newcomer to the business, which put up a $100,000 advance plus 30 percent of the distribution gross for the U.S. rights. Grove also agreed to cover all the advertising expenses and legal fees, which turned out to be a fairly expensive proposition.[43] The film failed to get through U.S. Customs because it left "nothing to the imagination, including acts of fornication," according to Assistant U.S. Attorney Arthur Olick.[44] Grove president Barney Rosset took legal action to secure its release. He then invited Andrew Sarris, Bosley Crowther, Amos Vogel, Stanley Kauffmann, and other prominent film critics to view the film at a private screening in the hope that they would be willing to serve as friendly witnesses in the case. The critics agreed not to reveal anything about the film until the hearings. A federal district court refused to order the release of the film and the case went to trial in May 1968. The jury, consisting of seven men and five women, deliberated for three hours and found the film obscene. Grove appealed the decision. In the interim it published a paperback version of the shooting script containing over 250 illustrations, "many of the sort that usually come in plain brown wrappers." In November 1968 a federal appeals court ruled that *I Am Curious (Yellow)* was protected by the First Amendment and could be shown uncut.[45]

Simultaneously released on March 10, 1969, at Grove's own downtown Evergreen Theater and at the Cinema Rendezvous, *I Am Curious (Yellow)* opened on a reserved-seat basis at advance ticket prices. *Time* issued the following warning to its readers: "Viewers who expect a titillating kind of 1,001 Scandinavian Nights will be disappointed. For all its well-publicized explicitness, *Yellow* is not much more erotic than the Fannie Farmer cookbook."[46] Vincent Canby reported that when he attended the opening at the Rendezvous in the early afternoon, "the crowds were large, mostly middle-aged and ruly. This week's landmark film doesn't seem to be unhinging the populace. Nor is it likely to. *I Am Curious* is a good, serious movie about a society in transition, told in terms of recording devices—pads and pencils, posters, cinéma vérité interviews, tape recordings and the fiction film. In an interesting—although not terribly revolutionary—way, it attempts to be a total movie." He went on to say the scenes "in which Lena and Börje effect sexual congress in a tree, on a balustrade in front of the royal palace . . . and in other locations, indoors and out, are explicit, honest and so unaffectedly frank as to be nonpornographic—that is, if to be pornographic means to be offensive to morals. . . . By acknowledging the existence of genitalia and their function in the act of love, the movie salvages the depiction of physical love from the scrap heap of exploitation, camp and stag films. A full-length portrait of Lena, the troubled, liberated woman, simply could not exist without these scenes."[47]

I Am Curious (Yellow) grossed over $20 million at the box office, which secured its top ranking on *Variety*'s All-Time Foreign Language Films for twenty-three years. *Variety* later reported that, "ironically enough, following *I Am Curious Yellow*'s legal victory, a significant number of art house cinemas in America became porn theatres to cash in on the boom that these Swedish films indirectly kick-started."[48] *I Am Curious (Blue)*, the sequel, was released on May 20, 1970. By the time it reached the United States, the court battle surrounding *I Am Curious (Yellow)* was over and the market for such fare had changed.

Z, a modern thriller, continued the vogue of the political film introduced by Alain Resnais's *La Guerre est finie* in 1966 and Gillo Pontecorvo's *The Battle of Algiers* in 1967. *Z* was turned down by every major studio before winning the Special Jury Prize at Cannes in 1969. Finally, Donald Rugoff acquired the film for release through his Cinema V distribution company. It was Rugoff's individual attention and promotion that made it one of the year's biggest hits.

An Algerian-French coproduction, *Z* was based on the 1963 assassination in Salonika of Greek pacifist leader Gregarios Lambrakis by right-wing goons and the official investigation of that crime by an uncompromising magistrate. After a military coup d'état, almost everyone connected with the assassination was conveniently "rehabilitated." It starred Yves Montand as Lambrakis, Irene Papas as his wife, and Jean-Louis Trintignant as the government investigator. *Z* was banned in Greece by the presiding junta. Born Constantin Gavras in 1933 in Athens, Costa-Gavras moved to Paris at war's end and took up filmmaking. According to Jospeh Morgenstern, to make *Z*, his third feature, Costa-Gavras teamed up with scenarist Jorge Semprún, cinematographer Raoul Coutard, and composer Mikis Theodorakis to present a story "in the form of a traditional police thriller. The result is absolutely breath-taking."[49]

Z opened at the Beekman on December 8, 1969. Stanley Kauffmann was particularly impressed with Coutard's camerawork: "The physical impression that this film gives is that it is hurrying to record certain facts before they are covered over. Motion is of the essence. Costa-Gavras's camera tracks and dollies almost constantly, yet without dizzying us . . . because all the motions are tightly linked to the impulses of the characters or of the audience. We *insist* that the camera move as it does, so the tracking both feeds and stimulates our concern."[50]

The *Time* review saw allusions to the Kennedy assassination in the film. "In its advocacy of the conspiracy theory of government, *Z* provides echo chambers

of horror. The series of stop-motion pictures of the Deputy's death revives involuntary memories of the Zapruder film. The coincidence of alleged complic-
ities recalls the farther shores of Jim Garrison's New Orleans fantasies. But essentially Z is grinding its ax not for politicians but for politics. Tyranny is always
better organized than freedom; beneath the idea of order—in Eastern Europe,
says the film, as well as in Greece—truly anarchic forces are loosed upon the
world. The Greek letter Z is a symbol for 'he still lives.' In this case, Z refers to
the murdered Deputy. But it is also the spirit of revolt against a stifling government that has banned, in addition to miniskirts, Twain, Chekhov, Beckett, and
of course, Z. As a work of art, Z can live without Greece. The question is, can
the Greeks truly live without Z?"[51]

After opening at the Beekman on December 8, 1969, Z went on to win the
Oscar for Best Foreign Language Film and the top awards from the New York
Film Critics Circle and the National Society of Film Critics. It grossed close
to $16 million at the box office, ranking it number three on *Variety*'s All-Time
Foreign Language Films. According to Stuart Byron, much of the box office
success was the result of dubbing. Rugoff paid $400,000 for the picture, one of
the highest amounts ever paid for a French film. In the hope of reaching the
mainstream market, Rugoff spent an additional $260,000 to prepare an English
version. As Byron noted, "It is difficult to describe to anyone not in the industry
what spending that much to dub a movie means; most films come through
sounding so dreadful because they take at most three weeks to dub and even
now cost at most $40,000. Z, it could be said, was the *Cleopatra* of dubbing jobs."
Rugoff's investment clearly paid off since "some two-thirds of the gross was
earned by the dubbed version."[52]

The majors scored a single foreign film hit in 1970 with *Fellini Satyricon*, a
United Artists release. It came to UA by way of Italian producer Alberto Grimaldi, who started out in the business producing low-budget action films, including Sergio Leone's "spaghetti" westerns. Produced at a cost of $3 million,
Fellini Satyricon premiered at the Venice Film Festival in September 1969 and re-
affirmed Fellini's stature as a major artistic talent. (UA affixed Fellini's name to
the film's title to differentiate it from Gian Luigi Polidoro's controversial 1968
version of *Satyricon*. It also bought the distribution rights to the Polidoro film to
keep it off the market.) Based on Petronius's chronicle of Nero's Rome, it follows the adventures of two young students, Encolpius and Ascyltus. According
to Fellini, the young heroes were supposed to represent the youth of today.
"Mankind remains ever the same," he said. Encolpius and Ascyltus "are half
bourgeois provincials, half beatniks, such as we can see in our times on the
Spanish Steps in Rome, or in Paris, Amsterdam and London. . . . [They] go

from one adventure to another—even the most reckless—without the slightest remorse, with the natural innocence and splendid vitality of two young animals."[53] Fellini cast unknowns for the leads. To play Encolpius, he chose Martin Potter, a twenty-four-year-old Englishman, whose "blond good looks reminded him of Antonius, lover of the emperor Hadrian."[54] To play Ascyltus he chose Hiram Keller, who spent nine months in the Broadway production of *Hair*.

To attract the young adult audience, UA arranged an American tour for Fellini prior to the launch on March 11, 1970, at the Little Carnegie. The first stop was Los Angeles, where Fellini participated in a symposium at the American Film Institute. From there he headed east, stopping in major cities for press and television interviews. The climax of the tour was a midnight screening of the film after a rock concert at Madison Square Garden.

Vincent Canby described *Fellini Satyricon* "as nothing less than a quintessential Fellini film, a magical mystery tour that [Fellini] likes to describe, with some accuracy, as a science fiction film projected into the past, instead of the future."[55] Andrew Sarris interpreted the film as a metaphor for the 1960s: "The mindless vanity, gluttony, lust, cruelty, and superstition that stalk every frame of *Satyricon* would seem to have a counterpoint (sans toga and tunica) in the Romans who now infest the Via Veneto and Cinecitta. Rome, like all the other citadels of Western Civilization in the Age of Aquarius may bear at least a superficial resemblance to the Rome of Nero's time." However, Sarris added: "Unfortunately, *Satyricon* arrives in America at a time when the screen indulges its sensationalism even as it denounces it, and Fellini's chaste treatment of amoral antics may thereby seem too tame in the context of contemporary permissiveness."[56] Pauline Kael was similarly unimpressed: "I think it's a really bad movie—a terrible movie. . . . If it were put to members of the foreign-film audience rationally, probably few of them would identify the problems in the world today with fornication and licentiousness, or with the loss of faith in a divine authority."[57] Although the film undoubtedly returned its $3 million negative cost—and then some—it clearly did not measure up to UA's expectations.[58]

By 1970 advertising and promotion costs had risen to the extent that even the majors were reluctant to spend the money on a New York launch for foreign films when the chances of breaking even were slim. As Vincent Canby later reported, "An executive at Columbia Pictures estimates that it costs his company an average of $180,000 to put a foreign-language film into release in this country. 'Most of the time,' he says, 'it just isn't worth it.' . . . For the big distributing companies it is a poor gamble to spend $180,000 on the outside chance of earning $300,000 or $400,000."[59] He could have pointed to *Investigation of a Citizen Above Suspicion*, Elio Petri's political parable starring Gian Maria

Volonte, which Columbia released in 1970. Despite receiving fine reviews and winning the Oscar for Best Foreign Language Film, it did only so-so business, providing Canby with further evidence that Americans were becoming less interested in quality foreign films.[60]

By 1970 art houses were rejecting subtitled films, instead preferring sexploitation films or "'arty" American movies like Bob Rafelson's *Five Easy Pieces* (1970), Mike Nichols's *Carnal Knowledge* (1971), Stanley Kubirck's *A Clockwork Orange* (1971), and Peter Bogdonovich's *The Last Picture Show* (1971). Dan Talbot, the head of New Yorker Films, noted, "'Ten years ago you had an art house movement in America. There were close to 600 art houses around the country that devoted themselves largely to foreign films. There's been a tremendous decline. They've declined from 600 to very close to zero. They've gone over to the commercial product.'"[61] *Film Daily Year Book*, the bible of the film industry, had taken stock of the situation as early as 1969 and decided to drop the separate art theater category from its theater listings.[62]

Conditions like these convinced United Artists, Columbia, and Universal to close their art film subsidiaries in 1970. That same year Sigma III, Pathé Contemporary, Trans-Lux, and other independents closed up shop as well. Continental Distributing lasted until 1974, while Cinema V hung on until 1979, when Rugoff lost control of his company. The majors continued to back those foreign filmmakers whose films were popular in their home markets, such as Bernardo Bertolucci's *The Conformist* (Paramount, 1971), Eric Rohmer's *Chloë in the Afternoon* (Columbia, 1972), Luis Buñuel's *The Discreet Charm of the Bourgeoisie* (20th Century-Fox, 1972), and François Truffaut's *Day for Night* (Warner Bros., 1973). To this list should be added Luchino Visconti's *The Damned* (1969) and *Death in Venice* (1971), which were released by Warner Bros. in dubbed versions and placed directly into mainstream exhibition.

In the early 1970s exceptional films from independent distributors that went straight into theaters included Vittorio De Sica's *The Garden of the Finzi-Continis* from Cinema V (1971) and Ingmar Bergman's *Cries and Whispers* from New World (1972), both of which were released subtitled. De Sica's *The Garden of the Finzi-Continis* (*Il giardino dei Finzi-Contini*), an adaptation of Giorgio Bassani's novel, describes how two elegant Jewish families in Ferrara, Italy, were brutally crushed by the fascists. It starred Dominique Sanda, Lino Capolicchio, and Helmut Berger. De Sica said he made the film "as an act of atonement and as a warning," adding that "we were all guilty [of] the systematic murder of Italian Jews" during the days of Mussolini. "That period was the blackest page in the history of mankind. Yet, today in Italy there are many fascists—young people who do not believe what it was like then. And, unfortunately, there are many old people who have forgotten."[63] De Sica's two most recent films—*A Place for Lovers* (1969) and *Sunflower* (1970)—had generally been regarded as commercial fluff, but *The Garden of the Finzi-Continis*, having won the Golden Bear at the Berlin Film Festival in 1971, restored his international reputation. As *Time* put it, "Now, after more than a decade of indifferent and impersonal work, De Sica has returned to form. If *The Garden of the Finzi-Continis* does not fully rival *The Bicycle Thief* and *Umberto D*, it is good enough to stand comparison with them. *Garden* is a quietly touching, achingly human requiem for the passing of a social order—one of those rare films that can make effective personal drama out of political chaos."[64] The surprise hit of the year, it won the Oscar for Best Foreign Language Film—De Sica's fifth such honor—and grossed $6 million at the box office, with a ranking of number twelve on *Variety*'s All-Time Foreign Language Films.

Cries and Whispers (*Viskningar och rop*), another surprise hit, was bypassed by the majors, who were in no mood for taking risks. Roger Corman's New World Pictures, best known for its low-budget exploitation films, picked it up for around $150,000 and then spent almost $80,000 on promotion. Naming it to his "Ten Best" list, Canby said the film was "about the tormented lives of three sisters, set in a Swedish manor house at the turn-of-the-century. . . . One sister (Harriet Andersson) is dying of cancer slowly and painfully, attended by her two other sisters (Liv Ullman and Ingrid Thulin) and by her loving woman-servant (Cari Sylwan). They talk, argue, dream and despair in sequences that end in dissolves to a screen that is blood red, the primary color of the film. The meanings are sometimes ambiguous, but the effects are magnificent and moving, and the focus is so sharp the film seems to have the clarity of something seen through a high fever."[65] *Cries and Whispers* won four awards from the New York Film Critics Circle, including best film, and earned $1.2 million in 803 theaters around the country—the most a Bergman film had earned since *The Silence* in 1964. To place the returns in perspective, Canby noted that *Five Easy Pieces*, an "arty" American film, had played 6,000 theaters and earned $9 million.[66]

A huge box office hit, *Last Tango in Paris* (*Ultimo tango a Parigi*) was thought at the time to signal a revival of the art film market. *Tango* had all the ingredients of a crossover hit: an American star who had just scored a comeback in *The Godfather*, a highly esteemed European director, and an erotic story. To test the waters before the commercial release, UA arranged a single screening of the film on October 14, 1972, the closing night of the New York Film Festival. "That date," said Pauline Kael in her lengthy rave review in the *New Yorker*, "should become a landmark in movie history comparable to May 29, 1913—the night 'Le Sacre du Printemps' was first performed in music history." Kael went on to say that "Bertolucci and Brando have altered the face of an art form."[67]

To prepare for the New York opening, UA took the self-imposed X rating for the picture rather than submit it to the Code and Rating Administration. Adopting a "tough to see" policy, UA scheduled *Last Tango* to open in only one theater, the 561-seat Trans-Lux East. Tickets were to be sold on a reserved-seat basis for five dollars each (which, coincidentally, was the going price for porn films). Showings would be limited to two per day midweek and three on weekends.

UA's buildup began on December 24, when it placed a two-page ad in the Sunday edition of the *New York Times* that reprinted Kael's rave review in its entirety. The spread cost $32,000, but UA would not have to spend much more to promote the picture. A week before the opening, *Time* magazine featured a portrait of Brando on its cover with "Sex and Death in Paris" emblazoned across the top. Entitled "Self-Portrait of an Angel and Monster," the cover story was illustrated with photos of Brando and Maria Schneider making love in the

Maria Schneider and Marlon Brando in Bernardo Bertolucci's *Last Tango in Paris* (1973)

nude. It posed the question, "Is the movie basically pornography with an over-lay of philosophic angst—or pornography of a peculiarly vulgar type since it features one of the world's most famous actors capering up there on the screen?"[68] Three days after the opening, the *New York Times* reprinted an interview with Schneider in which she revealed that she had left home at fifteen, had her first affair at sixteen, earned four thousand dollars in Bertolucci's film, and admitted to having had twenty female lovers and fifty male lovers.[69]

Last Tango opened on February 7, 1973. Art versus pornography was the issue that dominated the reviews. Robert Hatch said, "I would not call it por-nography at all. . . . Bertolucci's concern for his characters is manifestly much warmer and much more humane than mere preoccupation with their physical exploits."[70] Stanley Kauffmann said that *Tango* was physically fake "where porno is not." He added that although "the publicity has carefully suggested that you can actually see Brando "'do it,' you can't. You never see him fully nude, though Schneider frisks about in her pelt. (When I told a lecture audi-ence that they wouldn't see Brando's organ, the ladies groaned.) Nonetheless the atmosphere of hard sex is there."[71]

New York's Trans-Lux East remained the sole exhibition outlet for *Tango* for nearly eight weeks. UA then opened it in a second theater, the 602-seat Fine Arts in Los Angeles. A month later UA opened the picture in thirty-three key cities nationwide on a "four-wall" basis, whereby the company in effect rented the theaters and instituted a hard-ticket policy. UA adopted this strategy be-cause it wanted to control every facet of the promotion. *Last Tango* did not open wide until July, six months after the New York premiere.

Last Tango grossed $40 million at the box office domestically and $60 million overseas. A confluence of unusual circumstances had made the film a huge commercial success. Nevertheless, it did not rekindle interest in foreign films on the part of the American film majors. Nor did it become a landmark, leading to an adult art cinema, as Pauline Kael had predicted. As Vincent Canby pointed out, *Last Tango* was not your "average, run-of-the-mill foreign-language film. For one thing, less than half of it was shot in a foreign language. For another, it's a Marlon Brando spectacle. Although it was directed by Bertolucci . . . *Last Tango* is hardly more foreign than *On the Waterfront* or *The Godfather*."[72]

Having survived a three-year recession, the majors were back in the black by 1973. Experience had proven that sex was not the "magic ingredient for box-office success," as was once thought. Jonas Rosenfeld, a Fox vice president, stated flatly that the X-rated *Myra Breckinridge* and *Beyond the Valley of the Dolls* proved to be "absolute disasters" for the company. He noted that "the whole country has undergone a remarkable reversal in taste."[73] Local newspapers and theater chains nationwide were refusing to advertise or play X-rated product. As a result, Fox and other companies ceased producing such pictures.

After 1970 it no longer made commercial sense for the majors to release X- or even R-rated films. The former rating prevented those under seventeen years of age from being admitted to a film, while the latter kept out those under seventeen unless they were accompanied by an adult. According to James H. Nicholson, president of American International Pictures, "Youngsters in their middle and late teens are the most valuable part of audiences today . . . and producing films to exclude them is financial suicide."[74] In 1970 two rather pedestrian pictures—Paramount's *Love Story* and Universal's *Airport*—broke box office records and were heavily attended by the under-thirty age group. When Paramount's *The Godfather* broke the all-time box office record in 1972, a new course for Hollywood had been set. The majors stuck to the tried and true and produced their films mostly on their home turf.

In 1974 Vincent Canby observed that "the market for foreign-language films, which in the late 1950s and early 1960s seemed so exciting to us and so financially rewarding to the entrepreneurs, has more or less collapsed in the midst of the so-called arts explosion. . . . The unhappy truth of the matter is that American movie audiences today seem to be far less interested in good foreign films than they have been at any time since the immediate post-World War II years."[75]

Epilogue

Although the art film market has endured, it has done so on a diminished scale. It returned to its roots during the 1970s and functioned as a niche business operated mainly by small, independent outfits. During the 1950s foreign films accounted for as much as 7 percent of the total U.S. box office each year, whereas since 1970 they have accounted for around 2 percent on average.[1] Every year one or two foreign films achieve the status of an art house blockbuster in the United States, while several others do enough to turn a small profit. As *Variety* once noted, "Successes have followed failures; surprise hits have emerged and anticipated bonanzas have turned into financial disasters."[2] Art house hits from the later 1970s on *Variety*'s All-Time Foreign Language Films to 2000 (see appendix) include Lina Wertmüller's *Swept Away* (1974), Jean Charles Tacchella's *Cousin, Cousine* (1975), Just Jaeckin's *The Story of O* (1975), and Edouard Molinaro's *La Cage aux folles* (1978). The record set by Vilgot Sjöman's *I Am Curious (Yellow)* in 1969 as the highest-grossing foreign film in the United States was not broken until 1993, when Alfonso Arau's *Like Water for Chocolate*, a Miramax release, passed the $20 million mark.

In New York City the "ferocious economics" of art film exhibition forced Dan Talbot to sell his New Yorker Theater to the Walter Reade chain in 1973. In 1977 the Walter Reade chain filed for bankruptcy and reorganized itself into a mainstream commercial theater chain.[3] In 1979 Donald Rugoff lost his movie houses and his Cinema V distribution company in a stockholders battle, following which the chain went mainstream.[4] During the 1980s the number of theaters in the United States that regularly showed foreign films declined steadily, succumbing to real estate pressures, home video, and the trend among large

301

theater chains to convert single-screen "art" or "revival" houses into more profitable multiplexes showing new Hollywood fare.

Although foreign films regularly open in New York City, most receive only brief limited releases. A few make it to Los Angeles and other big cities. These films have had to compete with British independent imports and American independent movies for playing time in a constricted market. Rising costs of prints and advertising, dwindling coverage in local newspapers, a shrinking cohort of dedicated viewers, and declining interest in film culture among college students are other factors working against them. The growth of two new outlets for feature films during the 1980s—pay television and home video—with voracious appetites for programming of all types, was supposed to provide a shot in the arm for foreign films. However, a picture has to generate name recognition in the theatrical release before it can profit from the ancillary markets. Since foreign titles usually have minuscule ad budgets and receive minimal distribution, most lose out on these opportunities. Subtitles also work against them, and every so often the question whether "to dub or not to dub" resurfaces. Dubbing remains an incendiary issue and has not been considered a viable option.

Winning a coveted Oscar for Best Foreign Language Film translates into longer runs and greater takes at the box office, but the award does not guarantee a bonanza. Surveying the Oscar winners for Best Foreign Language Film from 1986 to 1993, *Variety* reported that the post-award percentage jump in box office performance ranged as high as 2000 percent. However, in terms of the actual dollar take, the grosses ranged from a low of $260,000 for the 1991 winner (*Journey of Hope*, Switzerland) to a high of over $13 million for the 1989 winner (*Cinema Paradiso*, Italy). Five of the eight winners in this period grossed less than $5 million.[5] In other words, "For most of Europe's art-house distribs," according to Derek Elley, "Oscar's added-value b.o. clout is questionable. Most film execs believe that a pic will make it on its own worth, and will often have played most territories before the Academy bestows its favors. And if a film is a downer in subject matter or flops the first time around, Oscar won't get it back on its feet."[6]

Still, there is money to be made in the specialty market, and scores of companies have panned for gold. Independent distributors had the market pretty much to themselves until 1979, when United Artists created a classics division to handle foreign and American independent releases. Columbia, 20th Century-Fox, and Universal followed suit soon thereafter. The lure was the growth of pay television and home video. UA and Columbia, with sizable libraries of foreign films, were the first to cash in. But their new releases (mostly pickups) had difficulty breaking into theaters. Only François Truffaut's *The Last Metro* (1981) and Jean-Jacques Beineix's *Diva* (1982), released by UA Classics, attracted much attention. Operating a classics division made little sense financially for the majors, and within a few years they again retreated from the art film market.

During the 1980s the preeminent foreign film distributor was Orion Classics, a division of Orion Pictures. A mini-major, Orion Pictures was founded in 1978 by the disgruntled management team that had formerly run UA. In 1985 Orion hired the management team that had formerly run UA Classics to run its new classics operation. By building relationships with promising and proven auteurs and demonstrating an uncanny ability to pick up inexpensive sleepers at international film festivals, Orion Classics briefly dominated the field. Its release included: Akira Kurosawa's *Ran* (1986); Claude Berri's *Jean de Florette* and *Manon of the Spring* (1987); Louis Malle's *Au Revoir les Enfants*, Wim Wenders's *Wings of Desire*, Gabriel Axel's *Babette's Feast*, and Pedro Almodóvar's *Women on the Verge of a Nervous Breakdown* (all 1988); Jean-Paul Rappeneu's *Cyrano de Bergerac* (1990); and Agnieszka Holland's *Europa, Europa* (1992). All made it to *Variety*'s All-Time Foreign Language Films. *Cyrano*, which starred Gérard Depardieu, was the top money earner, and *Babette's Feast* won an Oscar for Best Foreign Language Film.

Clearly not a bad record by art house standards, Orion Classics was actually done in by its parent company, which declared bankruptcy in 1991. Orion Pictures made it big in 1986 when three of its releases—Oliver Stone's *Platoon*, Woody Allen's *Hannah and Her Sisters*, and *Hoosiers*—received eighteen Academy Award nominations (more than any other studio) and captured the biggest share of the theatrical market the following year. The company had two more big hits, Kevin Costner's *Dances with Wolves* (1990) and Jonathan Demme's *Silence of the Lambs* (1991). *Dances with Wolves* won seven Oscars, including Best Picture, and *Silence of the Lambs* swept the top five Academy Awards, but the success of these movies were unable to offset Orion's costly failures.

During the 1990s the mainstays of the foreign film market were Miramax, the Samuel Goldwyn Company, and Sony Pictures Classics. The three companies at first relied on pickups and then branched out into production to guarantee a steady flow of marketable films—or at least that was the hope. The goal was to build a library of titles that would have a long shelf life in DVD and on cable following the theatrical run. Foreign films played only a marginal role in their operations, but as a group the three companies breathed life into the market year after year.

Founded by brothers Harvey and Bob Weinstein in 1979, Miramax remained on the fringes of independent film distribution until 1989, when three of its films drew critical and commercial attention. Jim Sheridan's *My Left Foot*, an offbeat Irish picture starring a then relatively unknown Daniel Day-Lewis—who won the Oscar for Best Actor—grossed nearly $15 million at the box office.

Steven Soderbergh's *sex, lies and videotape*, a low-budget American independent venture, won the Golden Palm at Cannes and grossed nearly $25 million. And Giuseppe Tornatore's *Cinema Paradiso*, an Italian pickup, won an Oscar for Best Foreign Language Film and took in $13 million to become the highest-grossing art film of 1990.

From 1989 to 1992 Miramax collected an unprecedented four Best Foreign Language Film Oscars for Bille August's *Pelle the Conquerer* (1988), Giuseppe Tornatore's *Cinema Paradiso* (1990), Xavier Koller's *Journey of Hope* (1991), and Gabriele Salvatore's *Mediterraneo* (1992). Later in the decade Miramax picked up two more Best Foreign Language Film Oscars for Jan Sverák's *Kolya* (1997) and Roberto Benigni's *Life Is Beautiful* (1998). The latter, the top money earner of the group, set a new record for foreign films in the United States, grossing over $57 million at the box office and far surpassing *Like Water for Chocolate*'s take. Miramax also released the Japanese director Masayuki Suo's hit *Shall We Dance?* (1997), which took in an impressive $9.7 million.

Miramax's success in marketing foreign films became legendary. The Weinsteins were not above reediting pictures to make them more accessible to American audiences. Moreover, they were masters at generating free publicity. Placing a picture in distribution, they were also quick to react to newfound opportunities. For example, after the initial reviews for *Like Water for Chocolate* came in, Miramax opened the picture beyond the usual art house circuit to include Spanish-language theaters in Latino neighborhoods—a remarkable market penetration for a foreign film.[7] To give the picture an added boost, Miramax generated an elaborate cross-promotional campaign that tapped Mexicana Airlines, Mexican restaurants and radio stations, plus the food, travel, book review, and entertainment sections of newspapers.[8]

Miramax nevertheless played it safe. To guard against the volatility of the art film market it released primarily English-language productions. In an effort to further protect itself, in 1992 Miramax branched out into the genre market and formed Dimension Pictures, a subsidiary specializing in horror and action pictures—the kinds of films that could profitably be sold to home video, TV, and foreign markets. Nevertheless Miramax's future would always remain tenuous as long as it specialized in pickups. It needed to go into production to nurture talent and develop properties. To accomplish this, the Weinsteins sold their company to Disney in 1993. As part of the buyout, Disney acquired Miramax's library of over two hundred English-language and foreign films and agreed to finance the development, production, and marketing of Miramax's movies. With Disney's backing, Miramax placed its bets mainly on American independent ventures, which resulted in a string of Oscar-winning crossover hits that included Quentin Tarantino's *Pulp Fiction* (1994), Anthony Minghella's *The English Patient* (1996), Gus Van Sant's *Good Will Hunting* (1997), and John Madden's *Shakespeare in Love* (1998). Miramax was the success story of the 1990s. Its total domestic box office gross rose from $53 million in 1990 to over $327 million in 1999. At one point the Dimension label accounted for as much as 45 percent of the take.[9]

In 2005 the Weinsteins and Disney went their separate ways. The brothers had always bridled under Disney's staid corporate culture, and when Disney refused to release Michael Moore's controversial antiwar film *Fahrenheit 9/11*, the break was inevitable. Disney bought out the brothers and they left to form a new venture called the Weinstein Company. With the backing of Goldman Sachs, they laid plans to go head to head with the majors by producing star-driven vehicles with larger budgets and by diversifying into nonfilm-related businesses.

The Samuel Goldwyn Company, headed by the son and namesake of the famous Hollywood independent producer, was founded in 1980 as a distributor for the Samuel Goldwyn library of Hollywood classics. The company at first expanded into art film distribution, then into television production and syndication, motion picture production, and finally into exhibition.

As a motion picture distributor, Goldwyn was best known for its British pictures, such as Bill Forsyth's *Gregory's Girl* (1982), a quirky youth comedy set in Scotland; Richard Eyre's *The Ploughman's Lunch* (1985), a scathing satire of former prime minister Margaret Thatcher's England during the Falklands skirmish; and Kenneth Branagh's hit Shakespearean adaptations *Henry V* (1989) and *Much Ado About Nothing* (1993). Goldwyn released at least one foreign film every year. Coline Serreau's *Trois hommes et un couffin*, which Goldwyn released as *Three Men and a Cradle* (1985) to mixed reviews, was remade by Disney as *Three Men and a Baby* (1987). It grossed $168 million at the box office and helped spawn a cycle of American remakes of French films. The cycle included Luc Besson's *La Femme Nikita*, which Goldwyn released in 1991. It was remade by Warner Bros. as *Point of No Return* (1993) and as an English-language television series. Besson's action thriller made it to *Variety*'s All-Time Foreign Language Films, as did two other Goldwyn releases, Ang Lee's *The Wedding Banquet* (1993) and *Eat Drink Man Woman* (1994), the second and third installments, respectively, of what Lee described as his "Father Knows Best" trilogy.

Goldwyn did not expand into other facets of the business until it was well established as a motion picture distributor. As always, the company played it safe. For example, the 1991 acquisition of the 125-screen Landmark Theaters chain of art houses in California, Washington, and Minnesota was motivated by the idea that if Goldwyn pictures stumbled, the company could make some money from whatever hits were playing in the art film circuit.

However, the company overplayed its hand. In 1994 it posted a $20 million loss. Brought down by the debt load from its Landmark theater chain acquisition and a string of costly film and TV failures, the company was put up for sale. In December 1995 Goldwyn was acquired by Metromedia, an international telecommunications business headed by John W. Kluge, the owner of Orion Pictures. Unable to meld the film and television libraries of Goldwyn and Orion into his business, Kluge sold the two companies to Metro-Goldwyn-Mayer in April 1997. As of this writing, Landmark Theaters, which had been spun off earlier, remains the largest art house chain in the country. It is jointly owned by Mark Cuban and Todd Wagner through their 2929 Entertainment enterprise.

Sony Pictures Classics was formed in 1992 by Sony Pictures Entertainment, the Japanese media giant and parent company of Columbia Pictures and Tri-Star Pictures. Lured, in part, by the prestige of being connected with quality films and by the profit potential of the occasional crossover indie hit, Sony simply hired the same management team—Michael Barker, Tom Bernard, and Marcia Bloom—that had run the defunct Orion Pictures Classics. The majors followed suit. As was previously noted, Disney acquired Miramax in 1993, while the others formed specialty divisions—Fox Searchlight in 1994, Paramount Classics in 1998, and Universal Focus in 2002.

Sony Pictures Classics was most committed to foreign films. The company released a diverse slate of sixteen to twenty pictures a year and stuck to a basic game plan. Operating autonomously with a lean and committed staff, the company "carried the flag for modest-grossing foreign-language fare, arthouse films, and quirky personal offerings," according to *Variety*. Co-presidents Baker and Bernard were regarded as savvy pickup artists who shunned bidding wars and paid only what the market would bear for acquisitions. "Other companies look for home runs," said Barker, whereas "we just go for singles and doubles."[10]

Starting off, however, Sony Pictures Classics hit a home run. *Howards End*, a Merchant-Ivory production based on the E. M. Forster novel of the same name and starring Emma Thompson, earned more than $25 million in over one thousand play dates and picked up three Academy Awards, among them the Oscar for Best Actress. Sony Pictures Classics' second release, Régis Wargnier's *Indochine*, starring Catherine Deneuve, won the Oscar for Best Foreign Language Film of 1992 and was the first of five such awards won by the company. The others were Fernando Trueba's *Belle Époque* (1994), Ang Lee's *Crouching Tiger, Hidden Dragon* (2000), Florian Henckel von Donnersmarck's *The Lives of Others* (2007), and Stefan Ruzowitsky's *The Counterfeiters* (2008). *Crouching Tiger,* the martial arts fantasy, set a new record for foreign films by surpassing $128 million—the first Chinese film to become a worldwide blockbuster.

Barker and Bernard had a long-standing relationship with Pedro Almodóvar and released his *All About My Mother* (1999), *Talk to Her* (2002), *Bad Education* (2004), and *Volver* (2006)—all hits—with *Volver* leading the pack at $13 million. Sony Pictures Classics also released such international hits as Walter Salles's *Central Station* (1998), Tom Tykwer's *Run Lola Run* (1999), Wolfgang Becker's *Goodbye Lenin!* (2004), Michael Haneke's *Caché* (2005), and Vincent Paronnaud and Marjane Satrapi's *Persepolis* (2007).

Sony Pictures Classics entered into coproduction agreements from the start and then branched out into production in 1999. Subtitled films originally comprised two-thirds of Sony's annual slate; more recently the proportion has dropped to a third. The increased emphasis on in-house productions can be seen as a defensive measure to ensure access to theaters in a market that continues to devalue foreign films. Today, Sony Pictures Classics' library comprises over three hundred titles that remain viable on DVD.

The prospects for foreign films in the U.S. theatrical market are dire, and nothing on the horizon suggests that conditions will improve. In a piece she wrote for the *New York Times* entitled "The Decay of Cinema," Susan Sontag defined cinephilia of the type that existed among young people in the 1960s as something special: "It was born of the conviction that cinema was an art unlike any other: quintessentially modern; distinctively accessible; poetic and mysterious and erotic and moral—all at the same time. Cinema had apostles (It was like religion.) Cinema was a crusade. For cinephiles, the movies encapsulated everything. Cinema was both the book of art and the book of life."[11] Sontag blamed the decay of cinephilia on the "ferocious economics" of the movie business, which led Hollywood to favor "the blockbuster over the low-budget film." However, as we have seen, cinephilia was waning well before the blockbuster trend of the 1980s at a time when Hollywood was still into foreign films. Cinephilia exists to this day. It is a mild sort that is experienced by an older age cohort, which Dan Talbot has described as "an elite, college-educated, well-traveled group [that is] very determined."[12] Drawn to foreign films with humanistic impulses, this group will attend local film festivals and the occasional museum film retrospective but cannot be relied on to sustain a local art house. These people are not frequent filmgoers. Their needs are met mostly by DVDs. True, watching movies even on large-screen TVs cannot match the experience of "going to the movies," but for those of us who attended college in the late 1950s and early 1960s the easy availability of foreign films on DVD today is indeed a wonder to enjoy. It's a good option to have.

Appendix

Variety's All-Time Foreign Language Films to 2000

Title	Country	Year	Distributor	Box Office*	Director
Crouching Tiger, Hidden Dragon (*Wo Hu Zang Long*)	Hong Kong / Taiwan / U.S.	2000	Sony Pictures Classics	$128.0	Ang Lee
Shall We Dance? (*Shall we dansu?*)	Japan	2000	Miramax	9.7	Masayuki Suo
Run Lola Run (*Lola rennt*)	Germany	1999	Sony Pictures Classics	7.2	Tom Tykwer
Life Is Beautiful (*La Vita è Bella*)	Italy	1998	Miramax	57.6	Roberto Benigni
The Red Violin (*Le Violon rouge*)	Canada / Italy / U.K.	1998	Lion's Gate	10.0	François Girard
Central Station (*Cental do Brazil*)	Brazil / France	1998	Sony Pictures Classics	5.6	Walter Salles
The Dinner Game (*Le Dîner de cons*)	France	1998	Lion's Gate	4.0	Francis Veber
The Boys (*Les Boys*)	Canada	1997	Cinépix	4.8	Louis Saïa
Kolya	Czech Rep.	1996	Miramax	5.8	Jan Sverák

Table continued on next page

*Annual domestic box office gross in millions of dollars.

309

Title	Country	Year	Distributor	Box Office*	Director
Antonia's Line (*Antonia*)	Belgium / Neth. /U.K.	1996	First Look	4.2	Marleen Gorris
The Postman (*Il Postino*)	Italy/ France / Belgium	1994	Miramax	21.8	Michael Radford
Eat Drink Man Woman (*Yin shi nan nu*)	Taiwan	1994	Goldwyn	7.3	Ang Lee
The Wedding Banquet (*Hsi yen*)	Taiwan / U.S.	1993	Goldwyn	6.9	Ang Lee
Farewell My Concubine (*Ba wang bie ji*)	China / Hong Kong	1993	Miramax	5.2	Kaige Chen
Like Water for Chocolate (*Como agua para chocolate*)	Mexico	1992	Miramax	21.7	Alfonso Arau
Belle Époque	Spain / Portugal / France	1992	Sony Pictures Classics	6.0	Fernando Trueba
Indochine	France / Vietnam	1992	Sony Pictures Classics	5.7	Régis Wargnier
Mediterraneo	Italy	1991	Miramax	5.8	Gabriele Salvatores
Nikita (*La Femme Nikita*)	France / Italy	1991	Goldwyn	5.0	Luc Besson
Cyrano de Bergerac	France	1990	Orion Classics	8.0	Jean-Paul Rappeneau
Europa Europa (*Hitlerjunge Salomon*)	Germany / France / Poland	1990	Orion Classics	5.6	Agnieszka Holland
Tie Me Up! Tie Me Down! (*¡Átame!*)	Spain	1990	Miramax	4.1	Pedro Almodóvar
Cinema Paradiso (*Nuovo Cinema Paradiso*)	Italy / France	1988	Miramax	12.0	Giuseppe Tornatore
Women on the Verge of a Nervous Breakdown (*Mujeres al borde de un ataque de nervios*)	Spain	1988	Orion Classics	7.5	Pedro Almodóvar

Title	Country	Year	Distributor	Box Office*	Director
Babette's Feast (*Babettes gæstebud*)	Denmark	1988	Orion Classics	5.2	Gabriel Axel
Wings of Desire (*Der Himmel über Berlin*)	West Germany / France	1988	Orion Classics	4.9	Wim Wenders
Au Revoir les Enfants	France / West Germany	1987	Orion Classics	5.3	Louis Malle
Manon of the Spring (*Manon des sources*)	France / Italy / Switzerland	1987	Orion Classics	4.7	Claude Berri
My Life as a Dog (*Mitt liv som hund*)	Sweden	1986	Skouras	10.1	Lasse Hallström
Jean de Florette	France / Switzerland / Italy	1986	Orion Classics	5.5	Claude Berri
The Decline of the American Empire (*Le Déclin de l'empire américain*)	Canada	1986	Cineplex Odeon	4.7	Denys Arcand
Ran	Japan / France	1985	Orion Classics	7.3	Akira Kurosawa
Emmanuelle	France	1984	Columbia	11.5	Just Jaeckin
Fanny and Alexander (*Fanny och Alexander*)	Sweden / France / West Germany	1982	Embassy	7.4	Ingmar Bergman
Das Boot	West Germany	1981	Triumph	11.6	Wolfgang Petersen
Diva	France / U.K.	1981	United Artists Classics	6.5	Jean-Jacques Beineix
La Cage aux folles II	France / Italy	1980	United Artists	5.8	Edouard Molinaro
La Cage aux folles	France / Italy	1978	United Artists	17.7	Edouard Molinaro
Madame Rosa (*La Vie devant soi*)	France	1978	Atlantic	5.2	Moshé Mizrahi
The Story of O (*Histoire d'O*)	France / West Germany	1975	Allied Artists	10.0	Just Jaeckin

Table continued on next page

Title	Country	Year	Distributor	Box Office*	Director
Cousin, Cousine	France	1975	Libra	8.6	Jean-Charles Tacchella
Swept Away _(Travolti da un insolito destino nell'azzurro ma re d'agosto)_	Italy	1974	Cinema V	6.0	Lina Wertmüller
The Garden of the Finzi-Continis _(Il Giardino dei Finzi-Contini)_	Italy / West Germany	1971	Cinema V	6.0	Vittorio De Sica
_Z_	Algeria / France	1969	Cinema V	15.8	Costa-Gavras
I Am Curious (Yellow) _(Jag är nyfiken — en film i gult)_	Sweden	1967	Grove Press	20.2	Vilgot Sjöman
Elvira Madigan	Sweden	1967	Cinema V	10.1	Bo Widerberg
Belle de Jour	France / Italy	1967	Allied Artists	8.0	Luis Buñuel
A Man and a Woman _(Un Homme et une femme)_	France	1966	Allied Artists	14.3	Claude Lelouch
King of Hearts _(Le Roi de coeur)_	France/ Italy	1966	Lopert	5.7	Philippe de Broca
Yesterday, Today and Tomorrow _(Ieri, oggi, domani)_	Italy / France	1964	Embassy	9.3	Vittorio De Sica
Marriage Italian Style _(Matrimonio all'italiana)_	Italy / France	1964	Embassy	9.1	Vittorio De Sica
Dear John _(Käre John)_	Sweden	1964	Sigma 3	8.8	Lars-Magnus Lindgren
_8½_ _(Otto e mezzo)_	Italy	1963	Embassy	10.4	Federico Fellini
Two Women _(La Ciociara)_	Italy / France	1961	Embassy	7.2	Vittorio De Sica
La Dolce Vita	Italy / France	1960	Astor	19.5	Federico Fellini

Source: Variety, February 21–27, 2000.

Notes

Unless otherwise indicated, citations in the notes are to film reviews. Citations to reviews and articles in the *New York Times* (*NYT*) and the *Los Angeles Times* (*LAT*) are to ProQuest Historical Newspapers: New York Times (1851–2005) and to ProQuest Historical Newspapers: Los Angeles Times (1881–1985), respectively. Those in *Time* are to the Time Archive, 1923 to the present (www.time.com/time/magazine/archives). Those in *Variety* are to *Variety Film Reviews* (*VFR*) (New York: Garland, 1983–). Citations to reviews by James Agee, Pauline Kael, Stanley Kauffmann, Dwight Macdonald, and Andrew Sarris are to the respective collected film reviews listed in the bibliography.

Introduction

1. Thomas M. Pryor, "The Personal History of Roberto Rosellini," *NYT*, January 23, 1949; *Open City* ran until November 23, 1947, at the World and was followed by Luigi Zampa's *To Live in Peace*; "Rome's New Empire," *Time*, July 14, 1952.

2. *VFR*, February 27, 1946.

3. Bosley Crowther, *NYT*, February 26, 1946.

4. *Newsweek*, March 4, 1946, 86.

5. James Agee, *Nation*, April 13, 1946, 443.

6. Ibid.

7. *VFR*, December 12, 1945.

8. John McCarten, *New Yorker*, March 2, 1946, 81.

9. "A Religion of Film," *Time*, September 20, 1963.

10. Quoted in Hy Hollinger, "Foreign Pix Gain by Racy Take," *Variety*, June 30, 1954, 7.

11. Genêt, "Letter from Rome," *New Yorker*, February 5, 1949, 77.

12. "Rome's New Empire," *Time*, July 14, 1952.

13. Genêt, "Letter from Paris, *New Yorker*, August 13, 1960, 91–92.

14. Hollis Alpert, "New Wave: Orpheus in Rio," *Saturday Review*, December 19, 1959, 12–13.

15. Hollis Alpert, *Saturday Review*, April 22, 1961, 33.

16. Eugene Archer, "Artful Odyssey of an Aristocrat," *NYT*, August 18, 1963.

313

17. Addison Verrill, "Hard Going in U.S. for Foreign Films," *Variety*, January 5, 1972, 31.

18. Quoted in Paul Gardner, "Foreign Films, Popular in U.S. in 60s," *NYT*, October 4, 1973.

19. Andrew Sarris, *Village Voice*, March 30, 1967.

20. "Arties 'Sink or Swim' with N.Y. Times," *Variety*, November 6, 1957, 5.

21. Ernest Callenbach, "U.S. Film Journalism—A Survey," *Hollywood Quarterly* 5 (1950–51): 359–61.

22. Stanley Kauffmann, "A Life in Reviews," *New Republic*, December 1, 1958, 118–19.

23. Stephen Koch, "The Cruel, Cruel Critics," *Saturday Review*, January 26, 1970, 14.

24. Kauffmann, "A Life in Reviews," 118–19.

25. Laurence Goldstein, "Special Screening," *New York Times Book Review*, May 15, 1966.

26. Dwight Macdonald, "After Forty Years of Writing about Movies," *Esquire*, July 1969, 80.

27. John Simon, "Let Us Now Praise Dwight Macdonald," *Commonweal*, October 17, 1969, 68–70.

28. Emanuel Levy, ed., *Citizen Sarris, American Film Critic* (Lanhan, Md.: Scarecrow Press, 2001), 239, 78–79. See Andrew Sarris, "Notes on the Auteur Theory in 1962," *Film Culture* 27 (Winter 1962–63): 561–64; Andrew Sarris, "The American Cinema," *Film Culture* 28 (Spring 1963): 1–51.

29. Pauline Kael, "Circles and Squares," *Film Quarterly* 16 (Spring 1963): 12–26.

30. Andrew Sarris, "The Auteur Theory and the Perils of Pauline," *Film Quarterly* 16 (Summer 1963): 26–33.

31. Emanuel Levy, "The Legacy of Auteurism," in Levy, *Citizen Sarris*, 86.

32. Stuart Byron, "A Critic's Own Brand of Cinéma Vérité," *New York Times Book Review*, September 27, 1970.

33. Ben Yagoda, *About Town: The New Yorker and the World It Made* (New York: DaCapo Press, 2001), 351.

34. Quoted in Hollis Alpert, "The Movies and the Critics," *Saturday Review*, December 26, 1964, 12.

35. Emanuel Levy, "Sarris, Kael, and American Movie Culture," in Levy, *Citizen Sarris*, 250.

36. Edward Murray, *Nine American Film Critics* (New York: Ungar, 1975), 117–18.

37. Wilfrid Sheed, "The Good Word: Kael vs. Sarris vs. Simon," *NYT*, March 7, 1971.

Chapter 1. Antecedents

1. Tony Guzman, "The Little Theatre Movement: The Institutionalization of the European Art Film in America," *Film History* 17 (2005): 261–84.

2. Barbara Wilinsky, *Sure Seaters: The Emergence of Art House Cinema* (Minneapolis: University of Minnesota Press, 2001), 50.

3. Bosley Crowther, "New Link in Art-Theater Chain," *NYT*, June 24, 1963.

4. "Foreign Films Over Here," *Variety*, December 29, 1931, 13.

5. Mordaunt Hall, *NYT*, October 13, 1930.

6. *Time*, October 3, 1932.

7. *VFR*, September 27, 1932.

8. Quoted in Douglas W. Churchill, "Hollywood on the Wire," *NYT*, September 1, 1935.

9. Mordaunt Hall, *NYT*, April 3, 1933.

10. Mordaunt Hall, "A Wireless Operator's Hoax," *NYT*, April 16, 1933.

11. Ibid.

12. Bosley Crowther, "End of a Golden Age," *NYT*, November 10, 1940; Noel Meadow, "French Pictures Gain in Popularity," *NYT*, June 8, 1947.

13. Frank S. Nugent, *NYT*, June 19, 1936.

14. Herman G. Weinberg, "The Funny Business of Picking Hits," *NYT*, May 12, 1940.

15. Frank S. Nugent, *NYT*, September, 23, 1936.

16. Bosley Crowther, *NYT*, May 8, 1951.

17. Frank S. Nugent, *NYT*, September 14, 1937.

18. *VFR*, September 15, 1937.

19. Lillian Nadel," War Films Round Out Long Cycle," *NYT*, September 11, 1938.

20. Frank S. Nugent, *NYT*, September 13, 1938.

21. *VFR*, January 1, 1937.

22. "Film Censors Reversed," *NYT*, September 16, 1939.

23. Frank S. Nugent, *NYT*, October 3, 1939.

24. Frank S. Nugent, *NYT*, February 27, 1940.

25. Harry T. Smith, "'Talkies in All Tongues," *NYT*, July 5, 1936.

26. Thomas M. Pryor, "The Soviet Fadeout," *NYT*, February 11, 1940.

27. *Time*, February 8, 1932.

28. Pryor, "The Soviet Fadeout."

29. *Time*, January 28, 1935.

30. Richard Griffith, "Finance: Where Are the Dollars?," pt. 2, *Sight & Sound* (January 1950): 40.

31. *VFR*, October 17, 1933.

32. Mordaunt Hall, *NYT*, October 13, 1933.

33. Mordaunt Hall, *NYT*, February 15, 1934.

34. *VFR*, February 20, 1934.

35. Scott Higgins, "London Films: United Artists and Exhibitor Resistance, 1933–1940" (research paper, Department of Communication Arts, University of Wisconsin–Madison, n.d.).

36. Frank S. Nugent, "Rene Clair's Debut—In English," *NYT*, January 19, 1936.

37. Richard Griffith, "Finance: Where Are the Dollars?," pt. 1, *Sight & Sound* 18 (December 1949): 14.

Chapter 2. Italian Neorealism

1. Thomas M. Pryor, "Foreign Films Become Big Business," *NYT*, February 8, 1948.

2. Robert F. Hawkins, "In Rome the People Are the Movie Stars," *New York Times Magazine*, September 21, 1952.

3. Andre Sennwald, *NYT*, December 28, 1935.

4. Tag Gallagher, *The Adventures of Roberto Rossellini: His Life and Films* (New York: DaCapo, 1998), 159. *Time* reported that "Geiger had bought the exclusive U.S. rights for $13,000"; see "Rome's New Empire," *Time*, July 14, 1952.

5. *VFR*, February 27, 1946.

6. Arthur Mayer, *Merely Colossal* (New York: Simon & Schuster, 1953), 233.

7. "Art, Exploitation Audiences Bait for TV; Only Sex Lures 'Em Back," *Variety*, July 23, 1952, 18.

8. Laura Wittern-Keller and Raymond J. Haberski Jr., *The "Miracle" Case: Film Censorship and the Supreme Court* (Lawrence: University Press of Kansas, 2008), 73.

9. Bosley Crowther, "The Case of Burstyn," *NYT*, December 13, 1953.

10. Arthur Mayer, "A Critic for All Seasons," *NYT*, December 10, 1967.

11. Bosley Crowther, "The Strange Case of 'The Miracle,'" *Atlantic Monthly*, April 1951, 35–39.

12. Bosley, Crowther, "The Miracle Happens," *NYT*, June 1, 1952.

13. *Time*, September 8, 1947.

14. Robert F. Hawkins, "Rossellini's New Rival," *NYT*, January 1, 1950.

15. Thomas M. Pryor, *NYT*, August 27, 1947.

16. *Time*, September 8, 1947.

17. Philip T. Hartung, *Commonweal*, October 12, 1947, 529.

18. Bosley Crowther, "The Tragic Muse," *NYT*, September 14, 1947.

19. Ibid.

20. Lux's first film tailor-made for Anna Magnani's was Luigi Zampa's *Angelina* (*L'onorevole Angelina*), which was released by President Films on April 5, 1948, and played at the Avenue Playhouse.

21. Bosley Crowther, *NYT*, November 25, 1947.

22. John McCarten, *New Yorker*, November 22, 1947, 127.

23. Mayer, *Merely Colossal*, 233.

24. Richard Griffith, "European Films and American Audiences," *Saturday Review*, January 13, 1951, 54.

25. Al Hine, "Italian Movies," *Holiday*, February 1954, 11.

26. Bosley Crowther, "Ultimate Irony of War," *NYT*, April 11, 1948.

27. *VFR*, February 11, 1948.

28. Crowther, "Ultimate Irony of War."

29. Robert Hatch, *New Republic*, March 29, 1948, 31.

30. "Dubbing a Foreign Pix Is Still a Moot Point," *Variety*, April 19, 1952, 13.

31. Hugh Barty King, "Seven Americans," *Sight & Sound* 15 (Autumn 1946): 83; *Time*, April 19, 1948.

32. Mayer, *Merely Colossal*, 233.

33. Bosley Crowther, *NYT*, December 13, 1949.

34. John Mason Brown, *Saturday Review*, January 7, 1950, 30.

35. *Cue*, December 17, 1949, 24.

36. John Mason Brown, *Saturday Review*, January 7, 1950, 32.

37. "Evil Minded Censors," *Life*, March 13, 1950, 40.

38. Thomas M. Pryor, "Front Runner in Foreign Film Sweepstakes," *NYT*, December 3, 1950.

39. Bosley Crowther, *NYT*, December 13, 1950.

40. "McCaffrey, Warned of Injunction," *NYT*, December 30, 1950.

41. "'Miracle' Banned Throughout City," *NYT*, December 27, 1950.

42. Bosley Crowther, *NYT*, December 13, 1950.

43. "Spellman Urges 'Miracle' Boycott," *NYT*, January 8, 1951.

44. "NY Regents Board Limits 'Miracle' Testimony to Burstyn and Lopert," *Variety*, January 31, 1951, 18.

45. "Freedom of Film," *Newsweek*, June 9, 1952, 91.

46. Pryor, "Front Runner in Foreign Film Sweepstakes."

47. Kevin Heffernan, "Censorship and the Art Film: The Production Code, Market Conditions, and Strategies for Distribution, 1951–1960" (research paper, Department of Communication Arts, University of Wisconsin–Madison, 1993).

48. Quoted in Arnaldo Cortesi, "De Sica on 'Miracle in Milan,'" *NYT*, December 9, 1951.

49. *Time*, December 17, 1951.

50. "Rome's New Empire," *Time*, July 14, 1952.

51. Bosley Crowther, "Plenty for All," *NYT*, December 23, 1951.

52. *Time*, December 17, 1951.

53. Manny Farber, *Nation*, January 19, 1952, 65–66.

54. Bosley Crowther, "The Face of Age," *NYT*, November 13, 1955.

55. Bosley Crowther, *NYT*, November 8, 1955.

56. "Imports' U.S. Problem," *Variety*, May 21, 1952, 7.

57. *Time*, September 8, 1947.

58. Genêt, "Letter from Rome," *New Yorker*, February 5, 1949, 89.

59. "Storm Over Stromboli," *Time*, February 20, 1950.

60. Jane Cianfarra, "RKO Ponders 'Stromboli,'" *NYT*, January 15, 1950.

61. Ibid.

62. Bosley Crowther, *NYT*, February 16, 1950.

63. *Time*, February 27, 1950.

64. Ibid.

65. Bosley Crowther, "L'Affaire 'Stromboli,'" *NYT*, February 19, 1950.

66. Phillip T. Hartung, *Commonweal*, October 6, 1950, 632.

67. *VFR*, November 16, 1949.

68. Robert Hatch, *New Republic*, October 9, 1950, 30.

69. John McCarten, *New Yorker*, September 30, 1950, 61.

70. Al Hine, "Italian Movies," *Holiday*, February 1954, 11.

71. Bosley Crowther, *NYT*, September 19, 1950.

72. "The New Italian Movie Industry," *Newsweek*, August 31, 1953, 67.

73. "Italian Film Invasion," *Life*, October 20, 1952, 112.

74. Arthur Knight," Italian Realism Refreshed," *Saturday Review*, June 30, 1956, 23.

Chapter 3. British Film Renaissance

1. Bosley Crowther, "British Films," *NYT*, April 8, 1945.

2. Ibid.

3. Bosley Crowther, "Displays of Acting." *NYT*, June 25, 1950.

4. Robert Hatch, *New Republic*, March 10, 1947.

5. The exceptions, Carol Reed's *The Fallen Idol* and *The Third Man*, were backed by Alexander Korda's London Films and released in the United States by the Selznick Releasing Organization, a distribution company formed by David O. Selznick to wring whatever residual value remained in his older independent productions.

6. "Stix Still Nix British Pix," *Variety*, June 18, 1947, 1.

7. Bosley Crowther, "The Screen: For Adults," *NYT*, September 15, 1946.

8. *Time*, September 9, 1946.

9. Thomas M. Pryor, *NYT*, August 20, 1947.

10. *Time*, September 15, 1947.

11. Griffith, "Finance: Where Are the Dollars?," pt. 2, 40.

12. Richard Avol, "Innovations in Distribution: The Roadshowing of *Henry V*" (research paper, Department of Communication Arts, University of Wisconsin–Madison, 1978).

13. James Agee, *Time*, April 8, 1946.

14. Bosley Crowther, "The Public and 'Henry V,'" *NYT*, June 23, 1946.

15. Richard Griffith, "The Audience Over 35," *Films in Review* 1 (September 1950): 22.

16. Quoted in *Newsweek*, September 27, 1948, 87.

17. Meredith Lillich, "Shakespeare on the Screen," *Films in Review* 7 (June–July 1956): 255.

18. Bosley Crowther, *NYT*, September 30, 1948.

19. Bosley Crowther, "Olivier's 'Hamlet,'" *NYT*, October 3, 1948.

20. Sarah Street, *Transatlantic Crossings: British Feature Films in the USA* (New York: Continuum, 2002), 107.

21. Quoted in Street, *Transatlantic Crossings*, 107.
22. Ibid., 108.
23. *Life*, March 8, 1948, 110–11.
24. *VFR*, August 4, 1948.
25. Griffith, "Finance: Where Are the Dollars?," pt. 2, 40.
26. *Time*, October 17, 1949.
27. Arthur Knight, "A Visit to Ealing Studios," *Saturday Review*, October 13, 1951, 44.
28. *Time*, April. 14, 1952.
29. *Newsweek*, October 14, 1949, 91.
30. *Time*, January 23, 1950.
31. Bosley Crowther, *NYT*, January 15, 1950.
32. "Movie of the Week: *Kind Hearts and Coronets*," *Life*, June 19, 1950, 79.
33. Bosley Crowther, *NYT*, June 25, 1950.
34. Leda Bauer, "The Lavender Hill Mob," *Theatre Arts*, November 1951, 72.
35. *Time*, March 12, 1956.
36. "Arties Stress Films in English," *Variety*, September 5, 1951, 5.

Chapter 4. Market Dynamics

1. This figure is taken from Michael F. Mayer's *Foreign Films on American Screens* (New York: Arco, 1965). At the time Mayer was executive director and general counsel of the Independent Film Importers & Distributors of America, the trade association for the business. The theaters included in Mayer's appendix, listed by geographical area, regularly played foreign films, albeit not exclusively.

2. Arthur Mayer, "Hollywood Verdict: Gilt but Not Guilty," *Saturday Review*, October 31, 1953, 41–47.

3. "Art-House Boom," *Newsweek*, May 28, 1963, 102.

4. Ibid.

5. For an excellent study of art house exhibition practices, see Barbara Wilinsky, *Sure Seaters: The Emergence of Art House Cinema* (Minneapolis: University of Minnesota Press, 2001).

6. "Arties Stress Films in English," *Variety*, September 5, 1951, 5.

7. Max Laemmle, "The Art Theater," *Film Quarterly* 19 (Winter 1965–66): 24.

8. Alfred Starr, "The Lost Audience Is Still Lost," *Variety*, January 6, 1954, 61.

9 Geoffrey Wagner, "The Lost Audience," *Quarterly of Film, Radio, and Television* 6 (Summer 1952): 338–50; Kenneth P. Adler, "Art Films and Eggheads," *Studies in Public Communication* 2 (1959): 7–15. See also Dallas W. Smythe et al., "Portrait of an Art-Theater Audience," *Quarterly of Film, Radio, and Television* 8 (Fall 1953): 28–50.

10. Quoted in "Thar's Gold in Them 'Art' Houses," *NYT*, December 5, 1948; Wilinsky, *Sure Seaters*, 110.

11. "New Paris Theatre Ready to Open," *NYT*, September 5, 1948.

12. "Who's Who of New York Importers," *Variety*, April 26, 1961, 171.

13. "E.L. Kingsley, 47, a Film Importer," *NYT*, February 1, 1962.

14. Jerry Bauer, "Festival-go-round," *Theatre Arts*, June 1961, 24.

15. Vincent Canby, "Shock Therapy for N.Y. Execs," *Variety*, August 16, 1961, 3.

16. Arthur Knight, "A Domestic Film Festival," *Saturday Review*, September 11, 1954, 44.

17. Todd McCarthy, "Famous Fest Casts a Golden Showbiz Glow," *Variety*, March 24–30, 1997, 3.

18. Ibid.

19. Ibid.

20. Knight, "A Domestic Film Festival," 44.

21. A. H. Weiler, "Focus on Movie Fetes," *NYT*, July 30, 1961.

22. Herman G. Weinberg, "The Language Barrier," *Hollywood Quarterly* 2 (July 1947): 333–37.

23. Arthur Knight, "The Great Dubbing Controversy," *Saturday Review*, October 29, 1960, 28.

24. Quoted in Kerry Segrave, *Foreign Films in America: A History* (Jefferson, N.C.: McFarland, 2004), 111.

25. Eugene Archer, "To Cut or Not to Cut," *NYT*, January 22, 1961.

26. Bosley Crowther, "On Editing Imports," *NYT*, May 2, 1954.

27. Archer, "To Cut or Not to Cut."

28. Bosley Crowther, "Should Foreign Films Be Dubbed?" *NYT*, August 28, 1966.

29. "Future of the Dubbed Film," *Variety*, January 12, 1955, 7.

30. Bosley Crowther, "'Rififi' to Expand Run," *NYT*, September 26, 1956.

31. Bosley Crowther, "Changing Voices," *NYT*, September 7, 1958.

32. Quoted in "Crowther's 'Subtitles Must Go,'" *Variety*, August 17, 1960, 15.

33. "'La Dolce Vita' Blazes Subtitled Paths," *Variety*, November 1, 1961, 19. *La Dolce Vita* was re-released in a dubbed version by American International in 1966 and did very well at the box office.

34. Quoted in Hy Hollinger, "Foreign Pix Gain by Racy Take," *Variety*, June 30, 1954, 7.

35. "Art-House Boom," *Newsweek*, May 28, 1962, 102.

36. "High Cost of 'Artie' Come-On," *Variety*, February 15, 1961, 11.

37. Robert J. Landry, "Unsold in the Land of Sell," *Variety*, April 24, 1957, 3.

38. "High Cost of 'Artie' Come-On," *Variety*, February 15, 1961, 11.

39. Display ad, "New Yorker Theater, Starts Today: All Seats $1 at All Times," *NYT*, January 12, 1969.

40. Eugene Archer, "'Tom Jones' Is Due to Earn Record," *NYT*, April 4, 1964.

41. Bosley Crowther, "Oscar Is in Trouble," *NYT*, April 15, 1962.

42. Quoted in Eugene Archer, "Academy Awards Labeled 'Unfair,'" *NYT*, December 6, 1961.

43. Vincent Canby, "Oscar Rules Irk Film Importers," *NYT*, January 15, 1966.

44. Fred Hift, "Film Imports: 'Give 'Em Sex!'" *Variety*, January 8, 1958, 7.

45. Quoted in Archer, "'Tom Jones' Is Due to Earn Record."

46. Mayer, *Foreign Films on American Screens*, 64.

47. Richard S. Randall, "Censorship: From *The Miracle* to *Deep Throat*," in Tino Balio, ed., *The American Film Industry* (Madison: University of Wisconsin Press, 1987), 511.

48. Alan F. Westin, "'The Miracle' Case: The Supreme Court and the Movies," *Inter-University Case Program #64* (Indianapolis: Bobbs-Merrill, 1961), 5.

49. Laura Wittern-Keller and Raymond J. Haberski Jr., *The "Miracle" Case: Film Censorship and the Supreme Court* (Lawrence: University Press of Kansas, 2008), 73–74.

50. "N.Y. State Censor Data Show That Foreign Product 95% sans Seal," *Variety*, April 16, 1958, 7.

51. "Spellman Urges 'Miracle' Boycott," *NYT*, January 8, 1951; "Arties' Tabu on Pix with 'C' Rating," *Variety*, August 22, 1956, 5;"Foreigners Sing Censor Blues," *Variety*, September 8, 1954, 11.

52. Randall, "Censorship: From *The Miracle* to *Deep Throat*," 511–12.

53. Arthur Knight and Hollis Alpert, "The History of Sex in Cinema," *Playboy*, April 1968, 206.

54. Vincent Canby, "Foreign Films' U.S. Jackpot," *Variety*, April 20, 1960, 78.

55. Murray Horowitz, "TV Upgrading Foreign Pix," *Variety*, September 16, 1959, 23.

56. Thomas M. Pryor, "Film Society Movement Catches On," *NYT*, September 18, 1949.

57. Lisa Dombrowski, "The Rise and Fall of Cinema 16" (research paper, Department of Communication Arts, University of Wisconsin–Madison, 1996).

58. "Cinema 16: A Showcase for the Nonfiction Film," *Hollywood Quarterly* 4 (Summer 1950): 323–31.

59. Al Hine, "Cinema 16," *Holiday*, March 1954, 27.

60. R. J. Landry, "Who's Minding the Pantheon," *Variety*, January 26, 1966, 7.

61. Eugene Archer, "Janus to Curtail Its Film Imports," *NYT*, August 5, 1964.

62. Bosley Crowther, "Is There a System in Film Societies?" *NYT*, January 22, 1967.

Chapter 5. French Films of the 1950s

1. Arthur Knight, *Saturday Review*, May 24, 1952, 33.

2. "Film Center Planned," *NYT*, June 8, 1955.

3. Bosley Crowther, "Snows of Yesteryear," *NYT*, February 29, 1948.

4. Ibid.

5. Roy Armes, *French Cinema* (New York: Oxford University Press, 1985), 128.

6. Bosley Crowther, *NYT*, September 19, 1948.

7. John McCarten, *New Yorker*, December 18, 1948, 101.

8. *Time*, March 21, 1949.

9. "Legion 'Condemns' Film," *NYT*, May 30, 1949.

10. "Flaud's Theories, Not Facts, Denied," *Variety*, February 15, 1956.

11. "A Boost for French Films," *Business Week*, June 30, 1956, 104.

12. Bosley Crowther, *NYT*, December 9, 1952.

13. Bosley Crowther, *NYT*, December 14, 1952.

14. *Newsweek*, March 23, 1953.

15. *Time*, March 16, 1953.

16. Arthur Knight, *Saturday Review*, May 24, 1952, 33.

17. Bosley Crowther, *NYT*, January 14, 1953.

18. Arthur Knight and Hollis Alpert, "The History of Sex in Cinema," *Playboy*, December 1966, 244–45.

19. "Sex & the Censor," *Time*, October 22, 1951.

20. Luther A. Huston, "High Court Upsets Censors," *NYT*, January 19, 1954.

21. Bosley Crowther, *NYT*. March 17, 1954.

22. John McCarten, *New Yorker*, March 27, 1954, 61.

23. Bosley Crowther, "Films with Cachet," *NYT*, March 2, 1952.

24. *Time*, March 31, 1952.

25. Bosley Crowther, *NYT*, June 17, 1954.

26. Genêt, "Letter from Paris," *New Yorker*, September 12, 1953, 132.

27. Arthur Knight, *Saturday Review*, June 19, 1954, 30.

28. *Time*, July 5, 1954.

29. *VFR*, January 1, 1958.

30. *Newsweek*, November 10, 1958, 99.

31. *VFR*, December 12, 1956.

32. *VFR*, September 12, 1951.

33. "Of Local Origin," *NYT*, March 3, 1954.

34. Bosley Crowther, "On Editing Imports," *NYT*, May 2, 1954.

35. Bosley Crowther, *NYT*, April 6, 1954.

36. Quoted in Hollis Alpert, *Saturday Review*, March 27, 1954.

37. *VFR*, December 12, 1956.

38. Bosley Crowther, *NYT*, August 27, 1957.

39. *VFR*, April 29, 1953.

40. *Time*, February 21, 1955.

41. Knight and Alpert, "The History of Sex in Cinema," 244–45.

42. *Life*, May 19, 1956, 130.

43. *Time*, July 16, 1956.

44. *Time*, September 1, 1958.

45. "Of Local Origin," *NYT*, June 27, 1958.

46. "Of Local Origin," *NYT*, August 2, 1958.

47. Fred Hift, "Brigitte's Boxoffice Revel," *Variety*, April 16, 1958, 7.

48. "'BB' vs. 'C,'" *Variety*, July 16, 1958, 35.

49. Kevin Heffernan, "Censorship and the Art Film: The Production Code, Market Conditions, and Strategies for Distribution, 1951–1960" (research paper, Department of Communication Arts, University of Wisconsin–Madison, 1993).

50. Hift, "Brigitte's Boxoffice Revel."

51. Bosley Crowther, *NYT*, October 27, 1957.

52. "'BB' vs. 'C,'" *Variety*, July 16, 1958, 35.

53. Knight and Alpert, "The History of Sex in Cinema," 244.

54. Ibid.

55. *VFR*, May 7, 1958.

56. Seymour Peck, "It Must Be More Than Sex," *New York Times Magazine*, September 14, 1958.

57. Bosley Crowther, "French Fall-Out," *NYT*, June 14, 1959.

58. Cynthia Grenier, "Gallic Screen Scene," *NYT*, April 5, 1959.

59. "Films' Foreign Accent," *The Economist*, January 4, 1963, 453.

Chapter 6. Japanese Films of the 1950s

1. "A Religion of Film, *Time*, September 20, 1963.

2. Jane Cianfarra, "Japanese Film Wins Venice Festival Prize," *NYT*, September 25, 1951.

3. Greg M. Smith, "Critical Reception of *Rashomon* in the West" (research paper, Department of Communication Arts, University of Wisconsin–Madison, 1992).

4. Bosley Crowther, *NYT*, January 6, 1952.

5. Ray Falk, "Introducing Japan's Top Director," *NYT*, January 6, 1952.

6. Arthur Knight, *Saturday Review*, January 19, 1952, 33.

7. *Time*, January 7, 1952.

8. Robert Hatch, *New Republic*, January 14, 1952, 22; *Newsweek*, January 7, 1952, 59.

9. *Rashomon* Pressbook, Wisconsin Center for Film and Theater Research, Wisconsin Historical Society.

10. Teresa S. Becker, "Made in Japan: An Inquiry into the Critical Reception Afforded Japanese Films Aimed at the Art Cinema Market in the U.S., 1950–1963" (research paper, Department of Communication Arts, University of Wisconsin–Madison, n.d.)

11. Arthur Knight, *Saturday Review*, December 1, 1956, 54.

12. "Exquisite New Films from Japan," *Life*, November 15, 1954, 89.

13. Ibid.

14. Bosley Crowther, *NYT*, September 12, 1954.

15. *Time*, September 20, 1954.

16. "Exquisite New Films from Japan," 89.

17. Arthur Knight, *Saturday Review*, December 11, 1954, 26–27.

18. Bosley Crowther, *NYT*, December 14, 1954.

19. *Newsweek*, October 11, 1955, 116.

20. Arthur Knight, *Saturday Review*, December 11, 1954, 26.

21. Harold Strauss, "Glimpsed behind the Japanese Screen," *NYT*, January 2, 1955.

22. "Exquisite New Films from Japan," 89.

23. Bosley Crowther, "Little Things," *NYT*, February 5, 1956.

24. A. H. Weiler, "Of People and Pictures," *NYT*, March 31, 1957.

25. Bosley Crowther, *NYT*, June 5, 1959.

26. *Time*, June 15, 1959.

27. *Time*, December 12, 1955.

28. *LAT*, November 21, 1955.

29. Bosley Crowther, *NYT*, January 10, 1956.

30. John McCarten, *New Yorker*, January 28, 1956, 84.

31. *Time*, December 12, 1955.

32. "Columbia's Special Dept. to Handle Foreign Features," *Variety*, July 27, 1955, 3.

33. *VFR*, September 7, 1954.

34. Bosley Crowther, *NYT*, November 20, 1956.

35. Robert Hatch, *Nation*, December 8, 1956, 507.

36. Arthur Knight, "The Japanese Do It," *Saturday Review*, December 1, 1956, 54.

37. Michael Roemer, "Kurosawa's Way of Seeing," *Reporter*, March 17, 1960, 36.

38. A. Iwasaki," Japan's New Screen Art," *Nation*, May 12, 1956, 398.

39. Henry Hart, "New York's Japanese Film Festival," *Films in Review* 8 (March 1957):101.

40. Bosley Crowther, review of *The Japanese Movie: An Illustrated History* by Donald Ritchie, *NYT*, April 17, 1966.

41. Dave Jampel, "Japanese Arties Wow the Critics, but Horror Films Get Coin," *Variety*, April 15, 1959.

42. Arthur Knight, *Saturday Review*, February 13, 1960, 40.

43. Rick Lyman, "Akira Kurosawa, Director of Epics, Dies at 88," *NYT*, September 7, 1998.

44. Stanley Kauffmann, *New Republic*, March 7, 1960.

45. *Time*, February 15, 1960.

Chapter 7. Ingmar Bergman: The Brand

1. Pauline Kael, "'Brooding,' They Said," *New York Times Book Review*, February 21, 1965.

2. "Movie Director Ingmar Bergman," *Time*, March 14, 1960.

3. "Ingmar Bergman of Sweden," *Variety*, March 16, 1960, 15.

4. Bosley Crowther, *NYT*, October 27, 1954.

5. Robert Hatch, *Nation*, November 13, 1954, 430.

6. Arthur Knight and Hollis Alpert, "The History of Sex in Cinema," *Playboy*, December 1966, 248.

7. "'Monika' Stale Tale of Fjords," *LAT*, February 2, 1956.

8. "Film Dealer Gets Sentence," *LAT*, April 26, 1956.

9. *Time*, January 27, 1958.

10. "Slow-Going of Foreign Film Directors in U.S.—Per Kurosawa," *Variety*, December 13, 1961, 5.

11. *VFR*, May 29, 1957.

12. Bosley Crowther, *NYT*, October 14, 1958.

13. Robert Hatch, *Nation*, November 15, 1958, 367.

14. Jonas Mekas, *Village Voice*, November 19, 1958, 6.

15. Bosley Crowther, *NYT*, January 23, 1959.

16. Robert Hatch, *Nation*, July 4, 1959.

17. Stanley Kauffmann, *New Republic*, April 27, 1959.

18. Bosley Crowther, *NYT*, August 28, 1959.

19. Richard Nason, "Ingmar Bergman Lights 5 Screens," *NYT*, October 21, 1959.

20. Richard Corliss and Jonathan Hoops, "Hour of the Wolf," *Film Quarterly* 21 (Summer 1968): 34–35.

21. "Ingmar Bergman of Sweden," *Variety*, March 16, 1960, 15.

22. Kelly A. Wolff, "The Director Is the Message: Ingmar Bergman and His Films in the United States, 1949–1961" (research paper, Department of Communication Arts, University of Wisconsin–Madison, 1993).

23. *Time*, January 27, 1958.

24. James Baldwin, "The Precarious Vogue of Ingmar Bergrnan," *Esquire*, April 1960, 128.

25. Walter Ross, "Bergman's Landscape," *NYT*, November 26, 1961.

26. Oscar Hedlund, "Ingmar Bergman, The Listener," *Saturday Review*, February 29, 1964, 48.

27. Frederic Fleisher, "Sweden's All-Demanding Genius: Ingmar Bergman," *Variety*, April 26, 1961, 151.

28. Wolff, "The Director Is the Message."

29. Arthur Knight, "Speaking of Directors," *Saturday Review*, June 4, 1960, 26.

30. Werner Wiskari, "Another Bergman Gains Renown," *New York Times Magazine*, December 20, 1959.

31. "Movie Director Ingmar Bergman."

32. "Talk with the Director," *Newsweek*, November 23, 1959, 116.

33. Wiskari, "Another Bergman Gains Renown."

34. "Talk with the Director," 116.

35. "Movie Director Ingmar Bergman."

36. Fleisher, "Sweden's All-Demanding Genius," 151.

37. "Movie Director Ingmar Bergman."

38. Wolff, "The Director Is the Message."

39. Quoted in "Sweden's Ingmar Bergman," *Variety*, July 6, 1960, .26.

40. *Time*, June 12, 1960.

41. Eugene Archer, "Bergman Fetes in U.S. Next Year," *NYT*, September 24, 1960.

42. "Bergman Movie Stuns Audience," *NYT*, February 9, 1960.

43. Arthur Knight and Hollis Alpert, "The History of Sex in the Cinema," *Playboy*, July 1968, 130.

44. Bosley Crowther, *NYT*, November 15, 1960.

45. Stanley Kauffmann, *New Republic*, December 5, 1960.

46. Dwight MacDonald, *Esquire*, March 1960.

47. Bosley Crowther, *NYT*, November 15, 1960.

48. Eugene Archer, "'Tom Jones' Is Due to Earn Record," *NYT*, April 4, 1964.

49. Quoted in Werner Wiskari, "Stockholm Hails Film by Bergman," *NYT*, October 18, 1961.

50. Ibid.

51. Brendan Gill, *New Yorker*, March 17, 1962, 123.

52. Quoted in Werner Wiskari, "Ingmar Bergman's 'Silence,'" *NYT*, December 1, 1963.

53. *Variety*, March 20, 1963.

54. Bosley Crowther, *NYT*, May 14, 1963.

55. Dwight Macdonald, *Esquire*, August 1963.

56. Werner Wiskari, "Ingmar Bergman Tries New Theme," *NYT*, October 20, 1966.

57. Wiskari, "Ingmar Bergman's 'Silence.'"

58. Display ad, *NYT*, February 5, 1964.

59. "How Sweden's Film God Brings in the Kroner," *Business Week*, February 29, 1964, 130.

Chapter 8. The French New Wave

1. Jonas Mekas, "Cinema of the New Generation," *Film Culture* 21 (Summer 1960): 1.

2. "New Wave," *Time*, November 16, 1959.

3. Maryvonne Butcher, "France's Film Renascence," *Commonweal*, January 8, 1960, 415.

4. Genêt, "Letter from Paris," *New Yorker*, August 13, 1960, 88.

5. Genêt, "Letter from Paris," *New Yorker*, January 24, 1959, 94.

6. *Time*, January 25, 1960.

7. Ibid.

8. Robert Hatch, *Nation*, November 28, 1959, 407.

9. Hollis Alpert, *Saturday Review*, August 8, 1959, 24.

10. Arthur Knight and Hollis Alpert, "The History of Sex in Cinema," *Playboy*, December 1966, 244–45.

11. Genêt, "Letter from Paris," *New Yorker*, July 11, 1959, 81.

12. Bosley Crowther, *NYT*, November 17, 1959.

13. John McCarten, *New Yorker*, November 28, 1959, 228.

14. Ellen Lentz, "Berlin in Retrospect," *NYT*, July 12, 1959.

15. Bosley Crowther, *NYT*, December 3, 1959.

16. Robert Hatch, *Nation*, December 19, 1959, 475.

17. Richard Neupert, "'Dead Champagne': Variety's 'New Wave,'" *Film History* 10, no. 2 (1998): 227.

18. Genêt, "Letter from Paris," *New Yorker*, July 11, 1959, 78.

19. *Time*, November 16, 1959.

20. Hollis Alpert, *Saturday Review*, December 19, 1959, 12.

21. *Time*, November 16, 1959.

22. Vincent Canby, "British Humor Scores in the U.S.," *Variety*, April 26, 1961, 170.

23. Hollis Alpert, *Saturday Review*, December 19, 1959, 12–13.

24. Genêt, "Letter from Paris," *New Yorker*, July 11, 1959, 78–79.

25. Hollis Alpert, *Saturday Review*, May 21, 1960.

26. *Time*, May 16, 1960.

27. Dwight Macdonald, *Esquire*, September 1960.

28. Robert Hatch, *Nation*, May 28, 1960, 479.

29. *Time*, May 16, 1960.

30. Philip T. Hartung, *Commonweal*, June 10, 1960, 279.

31. Brendan Gill, *New Yorker*, December 3, 1960, 109–10.

32. *Time*, November 28, 1960.

33. Genêt, "Letter from Paris," *New Yorker*, August 13, 1960, 92–93.

34. Eugene Archer, "Nonconformist on the Crest of a 'New Wave,'" *NYT*, February 5, 1961.

35. *VFR*, January 1, 1960.

36. Roger Angell, *New Yorker*, February 11, 1961, 102–4.

37. *Time*, February 17, 1961.

38. Craig Fischer, "Films Lost in the Cosmos: Godard and New York Distribution and Exhibition (1961–1973)," *Spectator* 18, no. 2 (1998): 53.

39. Eugene Archer, "What Makes Us Hate—or Love—Godard?" *NYT*, January 28, 1968.

40. *VFR*, September 23, 1959.

41. Cynthia Grenier, "Gallic Censors Pounce," *NYT*, October 11, 1959.

42. "State Censors Let French Film Open," *NYT*, December 19, 1961.

43. Gene Moskowitz, "French Look beyond France," *Variety*, May 2, 1962, 65.

44. Bosley Crowther, *NYT*, December 19, 1961.

45. "A Religion of Film," *Time*, September 20, 1963.

46. *Time*, March 16, 1962.

47. Cynthia Grenier, "Notes on 'Marienbad' and the Paris Scene," *NYT*, November 12, 1961.

48. Robert Alden, "L'Affaire Marienbad," *NYT*, March 4, 1962.

49. Bosley Crowther, *NYT*, March 8, 1962.

50. Dwight Macdonald, *Esquire*, June 1962, 54.

51. *Time*, March 16, 1962.

52. Ibid.

53. Stanley Kauffmann, *New Republic*, March 26, 1962, 27.

54. Richard Neupert, *A History of the French New Wave Cinema* (Madison: University of Wisconsin Press, 2002), 192–93.

55. Brendan Gill, *New Yorker*, May 5, 1962, 184–85.

56. *Time*, May 4, 1962.

57. *Time*, July 5, 1968.

58. Bosley Crowther, *NYT*, July 24, 1962.

59. Cynthia Grenier, "Current Screen Activities along the Seine," *NYT*, July 1, 1962.

60. Bosley Crowther, "Waiving the 'Wave,'" *NYT*, November 9, 1962.

61. Stanley Kauffmann, *New Republic*, September 10, 1962.

62. *Time*, September 14, 1962.

63. Neupert, "Dead Champagne."

64. Bosley Crowther, *NYT*, November 13, 1962.

65. Hollis Alpert, *Saturday Review*, December 1, 1962, 75.

66. Cynthia Grenier, "Film Activities along the Seine," *NYT*, July 15, 1962.

67. *VFR*, June 20, 1962.

68. Brendan Gill, *New Yorker*, December 19, 1964, 151.

69. Bosley Crowther, *NYT*, December 17, 1964.

70. Hollis Alpert, *Saturday Review*, January 30, 1965, 40.

71. Eugene Archer, "France's Far-Out Filmmaker," *NYT*, September 27, 1964.

72. Bosley Crowther, *NYT*, September 24, 1963.

73. Stanley Kauffmann, *New Republic*, October 12, 1963.

74. *Time*, October 11, 1963.

75. New York Film Festival display ad, *NYT*, August 30, 1964.

76. Eugene Archer, *NYT*, September 19, 1964.

77. *Time*, November 6, 1964.

78. Stanley Kauffmann, *New Republic*, December 5, 1964.

79. Andrew Sarris, *Village Voice*, November 12, 1964.

80. Andrew Sarris, *Village Voice*, January 28, 1965.

81. Bosley Crowther, *NYT*, December 19, 1964.

82. Brendan Gill, *New Yorker*, December 25, 1964, 73.

83. *Time*, January 8, 1965.

Chapter 9. Angry Young Men: British New Cinema

1. Vincent Canby, "British-French in Sex Battle," *Variety*, February 8, 1961, 1.

2. Pauline Kael, "Commitment and the Strait-Jacket," *Film Quarterly* 15 (Fall 1961): 4.

3. Gene Moskowitz, "Angry Young Man vs. Britain," *Variety*, June 4, 1958, 3.

4. David Dempsey, "Most Angry Fella," *New York Times Magazine*, October 20, 1957.

5. V. S. Pritchett, "Pens Filled with Protest," *New York Times Book Review*, June 1, 1958.

6. Martin Esslin, "Where the Angry Young Men Led," *NYT*, May 8, 1966.

7. Kael, "Commitment and the Strait-Jacket," 4.

8. Clive Barnes, "Britain's New Actors—Rougher, Tougher, Angrier," *New York Times Magazine*, October 6, 1963.

9. Alexander Walker, *Hollywood UK: The British Film Industry in the Sixties* (New York: Stein & Day, 1974), 47, 51.

10. "Rogue's Progress," *New York Times Magazine*, March 15, 1959.

11. *Newsweek*, April 6, 1959, 113.

12. A. H. Weiler, *NYT*, March 31, 1959.

13. Stanley Kauffmann, *New Republic*, April 13, 1959.

14. Arthur Knight, *Saturday Review*, April 4, 1959, 28.

15. Stanley Kauffmann, *New Republic*, April 13, 1959.

16. Pauline Kael, "Commitment and the Straight-Jacket," 7.

17. "'Room at Top' to Get Major Yank First-Run-Dates," *Variety*, May 20, 1959, 3.

18. Heidi Kenaga, "The British 'New Cinema' in the United States, 1959–1963: Industrial Contexts and Critical Reception" (research paper, Department of Communication Arts, University of Wisconsin–Madison, 1993).

19. *VFR*, June 3, 1959.

20. Bosley Crowther, *NYT*, September 15, 1959; Bosley Crowther, *NYT*, October 13, 1959.

21. *Time*, September 28, 1959.

22. Bosley Crowther, "Angry Young Talent," *NYT*, September 20, 1959.

23. "The First Finney," *Time*, February 24, 1961.

24. Bosley Crowther, *NYT*, April 4, 1961.

25. Stanley Kauffmann, *New Republic*, April 17, 1961.

26. Moira Walsh, *America*, June 10, 1961, 430.

27. Edith Oliver, *New Yorker*, April 15, 1961, 154.

28. Walker, *Hollywood UK*, 81–82, 88.

29. A. H. Weiler, *NYT*, May 1, 1962.

30. *VFR*, September 20, 1961.

31. Hollis Alpert, *Saturday Review*, April 14, 1962, 57.

32. *Time*, May 18, 1962.

33. Bosley Crowther, *NYT*, May 20, 1962.

34. *VFR*, October 3, 1962.

35. Bosley Crowther, *NYT*, October 9, 1962.

36. *Time*, October 26, 1962.

37. Stanley Kauffmann, *New Republic*, October 1, 1962.

38. *VFR*, January 1, 1962.

39. Bosley Crowther, *NYT*, May 28, 1963.

40. *Time*, June 7, 1963.

41. Andrew Sarris, *Village Voice*, July 25, 1963.

42. *Time*, July 19, 1963.

43. *Time*, December 13, 1963.

44. Bosley Crowther, *NYT*, December 17, 1963.

45. John McCarten, *New Yorker*, December 21, 1963, 88.

Chapter 10. The Second Italian Renaissance

1. "Rebirth . . . in Italy: Three Great Movie Directors," *Newsweek*, July 10, 1961, 66.

2. Eugene Archer, "Artful Odyssey of an Aristocrat," *NYT*, August 18, 1963.

3. *VFR*, September 22, 1954.

4. In 1961 de Vecchi was employed by Astor Pictures as a vice president and oversaw the distribution of *La Dolce Vita*. In 1965 he distributed Visconti's *La Terra Trema*, and in 1974 he was working for Fellini as his personal representative and assistant.

5. Bosley Crowther, *NYT*, April 26, 1956.

6. A. H. Weiler, *NYT*, July 17, 1956.

7. Arthur Knight, "Italian Realism Refreshed," *Saturday Review*, June 30, 1956, 23.

8. Robert Hatch, *Nation*, July 1956, 106.

9. Thomas M. Pryor, "Fellini Honored by Film Directors," *NYT*, May 29, 1957.

10. A. H. Weiler, "Noted on the Local Film Scene," *NYT*, July 7, 1957.

11. Bosley Crowther, *NYT*, October 24, 1956.

12. *Time*, November 5, 1956.

13. Robert F. Hawkins, "Close-Up on Neo-Realism's Federico Fellini," *NYT*, November 25, 1956.

14. Ibid.

15. Arthur Knight, *Saturday Review*, November 9, 1957.

16. Philip K. Scheuer, *LAT*, January 18, 1958.

17. Cynthia Grenier, "Three Adventurous Italians," *Saturday Review*, December 24, 1960, 46.

18. Eugene Archer, "Roman Team on an Intellectual 'Adventure,'" *NYT*, April 2, 1961.

19. Bosley Crowther, *NYT*, April 5, 1961.

20. Edith Oliver, *New Yorker*, April 22, 1961, 144.

21. Hollis Alpert, *Saturday Review*, April 8, 1961, 41.

22. Andrew Sarris, *Village Voice*, March 23, 1961.

23. *VFR*, May 25, 1960.

24. Dwight Macdonald, *Esquire*, May 1962.

25. Bosley Crowther, "Italian Film Wins Cannes Top Prize," *NYT*, May 21, 1960.

26. "'La Dolce Vita,'" *New York Times Magazine*, April 9, 1961.

27. Mario de Vecchi, "'The Sweet Life's' Hard Knocks," *NYT*, April 16, 1961.

28. Vincent Canby, "Shock Therapy for N.Y. Execs," *Variety*, August 16, 1961, 3.

29. Howard Thompson, "'Dolce Vita' Due in Henry Miller's," *NYT*, March 8, 1961.

30. Robert Neville, "The Soft Life in Italy," *Harper's Magazine*, September 1960, 65–68.

31. Bosley Crowther, *NYT*, April 20, 1961.

32. Hollis Alpert, *Saturday Review*, April 22, 1961, 33.

33. Ibid.

34. Dwight Macdonald, *Esquire*, April 1961.

35. *Time*, April 21, 1961.

36. "'La Dolce Vita,' with 200 U.S. Prints," *Variety*, October 18, 1961, 3.

37. Grenier, "Three Adventurous Italians," 47.

38. Bosley Crowther, "Shocks from Abroad," *NYT*, July 2, 1961.

39. Stanley Kauffmann, *New Republic*, July 3, 1961.

40. Dwight Macdonald, *Esquire*, April 1961.

41. *Time*, July 21, 1961.

42. Archer, "Artful Odyssey of an Aristocrat."

43. Bosley Crowther, *NYT*, February 20, 1962.

44. Hollis Alpert, *Saturday Review*, March 3, 1962, 24.

45. *Time*, February 23, 1962.

46. Hollis Alpert, "A Talk with Antonioni," *Saturday Review*, October 27, 1962, 27.

47. "A Religion of Film," *Time*, September 20, 1963.

48. *Time*, February 19, 1965.

49. Stanley Kauffmann, *New Republic*, February 20, 1965.

50. Andrew Sarris, *Village Voice*, February 11, 1965.

51. *VFR*, April 17, 1963.

52. Bosley Crowther, *NYT*, August 13, 1963.

53. Andrew Sarris, *Village Voice*, August 22, 1963.

54. Stanley Kauffmann, *New Republic*, September 14, 1963.

55. *Newsweek*, August 26, 1963.

56. Hollis Alpert, "From ½ through 8½," *New York Times Magazine*, July 1, 1963.

57. Dwight Macdonald, *Esquire*, January 1964.

58. Bosley Crowther, *NYT*, June 30, 1963.

59. *Newsweek*, June 24, 1963, 112.

60. *Time*, March 1, 1963.

61. Bosley Crowther, *NYT*, June 27, 1963.

62. *Time*, June 18, 1963.

63. Andrew Sarris, *Village Voice*, November 11, 1965.

64. Andrew Sarris, *Village Voice*, November 18, 1965.

65. Stanley Kauffmann, *New Republic*, November 13, 1965.

66. Andrew Sarris, *Village Voice*, November 18, 1965.

67. "Europe's No. 1 Cover Girl: A Saga of Sophia," *Life*, August 22, 1955, 43.

68. Calvin Tomkins, "The Very Rich Hours of Joseph Levine," *New Yorker*, September 16, 1967, 58.

69. Ibid.

70. Bosley Crowther, *NYT*, May 9, 1961.

71. *VFR*, May 10, 1961.

72. Bosley Crowther, *NYT*, May 9, 1961.

73. "'Two Women' into 85 RKO Spots," *Variety*, September 20, 1961, 7.

74. *VFR*, December 27, 1961.

75. Bosley Crowther, *NYT*, September 18, 1962.

76. "Three Sophias for the Price of One," *Life*, April 10, 1964, 49.

77. Brendan Gill, *New Yorker*, January 2, 1965, 65.

78. *Time*, January 1, 1965.

79. Vincent Canby, "Noisy Debate Re 'Art' Film Future," *Variety*, August 12, 1964, 14.

Chapter 11. Auteurs from Outside the Epicenter

1. "A Religion of Film," *Time*, September 20, 1963.

2. Vincent Canby, "N.Y. Art Houses: Anglo-Yank," *Variety*, July 5, 1961, 11.

3. Bosley Crowther, *NYT*, March 25, 1952.

4. Arthur Knight, *Saturday Review*, September 15, 1951, 24.

5. Ibid.

6. Bosley Crowther, *NYT*, March 25, 1952.

7. *Time*, March 31, 1952.

8. Eugene Archer, "Movie by Buñuel to Be Seen Here," *NYT*, September 22, 1961.

9. *Time*, March 30, 1962.

10. Bosley Crowther, *NYT*, May 20, 1962.

11. Vincent Canby, *NYT*, September 21, 1970.

12. "A Religion of Film."

13. Bosley Crowther, *NYT*, September 28, 1958.

14. *Time*, October 20, 1958.

15. Arthur Knight, *Saturday Review*, September 20, 1958, 30.

16. *Time*, October 20, 1958.

17. Bosley Crowther, *NYT*, September 23, 1958.

18. Arthur Knight, *Saturday Review*, February 14, 1959, 37.

19. A. H. Weiler, "View from a Local Vantage Point," *NYT*, November 23, 1958.

20. *Time*, September 26, 1960.

21. Vincent Canby, "British Humor Scores in the U.S.," *Variety*, April 26, 1961, 170.

22. Gerard Alcan, "Satyajit Ray: India's One-Man Film Revolution," *LAT*, February 12, 1967.

23. "Devi—The Goddess," *NYT*, May 6, 1962.

24. "The Music Room," *NYT*, August 18, 1963.

25. Bosley Crowther, *NYT*, September 28, 1964.

26. Bosley Crowther, "With Luck, Full Speed Ahead . . . ," *NYT*, October 29, 1967.

27. Vincent Canby, *NYT*, October 9, 1972.

28. Arthur Knight, "Season in the Sun," *Saturday Review*, February 13, 1960, 40.

29. Jay Leyda, review of *The Films of Akira Kurosawa* by Donald Ritchie, *NYT*, January 2, 1966.

30. Stanley Kauffmann, *New Republic*, November 27, 1961.

31. *Time*, December 1, 1961.

32. Hollis Alpert, *Saturday Review*, September 15, 1962, 26.

33. Stanley Kaufmann, *New Republic*, September 17, 1962.

34. Bosley Crowther, *NYT*, November 23, 1961.

35. Bosley Crowther, *NYT*, January 23, 1963.

36. Stanley Kauffmann, *New Republic*, January 26, 1963.

37. *Time*, May 17, 1963.

38. Bosley Crowther, *NYT*, November 27, 1963.

39. Stanley Kauffmann, *New Republic*, November 23, 1963.

40. Bosley Crowther, "Speaking of Foreign Films," *NYT*, June 13, 1965.

41. "A Religion of Film."

42. Bosley Crowther, *NYT*, January 26, 1967.

43. Bosley Crowther, "Fans Flock to New York Film Festival," *NYT*, September 18, 1965.

44. *Time*, January 17, 1969.

45. Ibid.

46. *Time*, February 22, 1960.

47. Bosley Crowther, *NYT*, March 27, 1960.

48. *Time*, February 22, 1960.

49. Bosley Crowther, *NYT*, January 28, 1963.

50. Richard L. Coe, "'War, Peace' Story Told in Russ Film," *LAT*, May 25, 1968.

51. A. H. Weiler, "7-Hour *War and Peace* Booked Here," *NYT*, January 19, 1968.

52. Penelope Gilliatt, *New Yorker*, May 4, 1968, 163.

53. Renata Adler, "War and Peace—and Godard," *NYT*, May 5, 1968; Renata Adler, *NYT*, April 29, 1968.

54. *Time*, May 3, 1968.

55. Arthur Knight, *Saturday Review*, June 10, 1960, 37.

56. Cynthia Grenier, "Polish Phoenix from Ashes of War," *NYT*, October 21, 1962.

57. "A Religion of Film."

58. Bosley Crowther, *NYT*, May 30, 1961.

59. Stanley Kauffmann, *New Republic*, June 12, 1961.

60. "Pair from Poland," *Time*, May 19, 1961.

61. Bosley Crowther, *NYT*, May 10, 1961.

62. Stanley Kauffmann, *New Republic*, June 12, 1961.

63. Arthur Knight, *Saturday Review*, June 10, 1961, 37.

64. Bosley Crowther, "Promise from Poland," *NYT*, June 4, 1961.

Chapter 12. Enter Hollywood

1. Vincent Canby, "Hollywood Woos Foreign Talent," *NYT*, November 26, 1966.

2. Vincent Canby, "Overseas Films," *Variety*, May 2, 1962, 18.

3. *Time*, October 31, 1960.

4. Arthur Knight, *Saturday Review*, October 29, 1960, 28.

5. David Londoner, "The Changing Economics of Entertainment," in Tino Balio, ed., *The American Film Industry* (Madison: University of Wisconsin Press, 1985), 618.

6. Canby, "Hollywood Woos Foreign Talent."

7. Rafael Vela, "The American Critical Reception of Jean-Luc Godard: 1959–1968" (research paper, Department of Communication Arts, University of Wisconsin–Madison, 1993).

8. *NYT*, August 16, 1965.

9. Bosley Crowther, *NYT*, August 12, 1965.

10. Brendan Gill, *New Yorker*, August 21, 1965, 100.

11. *Time*, August 27, 1965.

12. Display ad, *NYT*, August 30, 1964.

13. Robert Hatch, *Nation*, April 4, 1966, 406.

14. Pauline Kael, *New Republic*, September 10, 1966, 27.

15. Display ad, *NYT*, September 11, 1966.

16. Bosley Crowther, *NYT*, September 19, 1966.

17. *Time*, October 7, 1966.

18. Brendan Gill, *New Yorker*, September 24, 1966, 112.

19. Arthur Knight and Hollis Alpert, "The History of Sex in the Cinema," *Playboy*, July 1968, 190.

20. Marilyn Bender, "Actress Is at Home in Haute Couture," *NYT*, October 4, 1962.

21. A. H. Weiler, *NYT*, October 19, 1962.

22. Bosley Crowther, *NYT*, December 26, 1962.

23. *VFR*, March 11, 1964.

24. Bosley Crowther, *NYT*, June 9, 1964.

25. *Time*, December 31, 1965.

26. Vincent Canby, "Brigitte Bardot Begins U.S. Tour," *NYT*, December 17, 1965.

27. *VFR*, December 8, 1965.

28. Robert Hatch, *Nation*, January 3, 1966, 27–28.

29. Alexander Walker, *Hollywood UK: The British Film Industry in the Sixties* (New York: Stein & Day, 1974), 69.

30. Quoted in Tino Balio, *United Artists: The Company That Changed the Film Industry* (Madison: University of Wisconsin Press, 1987), 239.

31. *Time*, October 18, 1963.

32. *Time*, July 9, 1965.

33. Ken Eakin, "Universal Failures: Jay Kanter and Universal's British Productions, 1966–69" (research paper, Department of Communication Arts, University of Wisconsin–Madison, 1995).

34. *Time*, November 18, 1966.

35. Hollis Alpert, "Alive and Well in Paris," *Saturday Review*, February 8, 1969, 18.

36. Bosley Crowther, *NYT*, November, 15, 1966.

37. Thomas Quinn Curtiss, "A Comeback for Love?" *NYT*, February 26, 1967.

38. *Time*, August 12, 1966.

39. Pauline Kael, *New Republic*, December 24, 1966, 34.

40. "All Majors Have Subsids," *Variety*, March 13, 1968, 7.

41. Peter Lev, *The Euro-American Cinema* (Austin: University of Texas Press, 1993), 30–31.

42. *Time*, December 25, 1964.

43. *VFR*, January 1, 1964.

44. Stanley Kauffmann, *New Republic*, January 16, 1965.

45. Bosley Crowther, *NYT*, December 18, 1964.

46. Piri Halasz, "You Can Walk Across It on the Grass," *Time*, April 15, 1966.

47. Walker, *Hollywood UK*, 331.

48. Yiota Mini, "Michelangelo Antonioni's Films" (research paper, Department of Communication Arts, University of Wisconsin–Madison, 1996).

49. Stephen Watts, *NYT*, July 31, 1966.

50. "Antonioni's Hypnotic Eye on a Frantic World," *Life*, January 27, 1967, 62.

51. Andrew Sarris, *Village Voice*, December 29, 1966.

52. *Time*, December 30, 1966.

53. Stanley Kauffmann, "A Year with Blow-Up," in *Figures of Light* (New York: Harper & Row, 1971), 6.

54. Bosley Crowther, "The Multinational Film," *NYT*, July 5, 1966.

55. Bosley Crowther, "The Tower of Babel Again," *NYT*, August 14, 1966.

56. Ibid.

57. Stuart Byron, "Don Rugoff: Ballyhoo with a Harvard Education," *Film Comment* 11 (May–June 1975): 21.

58. Bosley Crowther, "Too Few, Too Many," *NYT*, December 1, 1963.

59. Vincent Canby, "U.S. Majors Lead N.Y. Arties," *Variety*, September 9, 1964, 3.

60. Quoted in Vincent Canby, "N.Y. Foreign 'Art' Film Time Up," *Variety*, October 23, 1963, 21.

61. "U.S. Market for Foreigns," *Variety*, May 12, 1965, 3.

62. Ibid.

63. "Making a Loud Dollar," *Newsweek*, April 15, 1960, 80.

64. Ibid.

65. Bosley Crowther, "Critic Holler 'Help,'" *NYT*, April 23, 1967.

Chapter 13. The Aura of the New York Film Festival

1. Gordon Hitchens, "The First New York Film Festival," *Film Comment* 1 (Fall 1963): 2.

2. Vincent Canby, "The New York Film Festival: Why It Thrives," *NYT*, September 21, 1980. A jury system was instituted in 1966 consisting of "three knowledgeable

outsiders" to provide "more heads on which the praise and blame might fall in their unequal measures." The selection committee panel was later increased to eight. McCandlish Phillips, "Who Judges the Film Festival?" *NYT*, October 4, 1972.

3. The start of the festival was later moved to late September, which was better for attendance. The change placed the festival in conflict with the orchestra's season, which necessitated a change of venue within Lincoln Center, first to the 1,096-seat Alice Tully Hall and then to the 1,080 seat Vivian Beaumont Theater.

4. Amos Vogel, "Films: Fashion of the Fashionable," *NYT*, September 5, 1965.

5. "A Religion of Film," *Time*, September 20, 1963.

6. Eugene Archer, *NYT*, September 17, 1963.

7. Eugene Archer, *NYT*, September 20, 1963.

8. Eugene Archer, *NYT*, September 16, 1963.

9. Hollis Alpert, "Cinema: The Global Revolution," *Saturday Review*, October 5, 1963, 18–19.

10. Bosley Crowther, "A Repertory Cinema, Yes?" *NYT*, July 16, 1967.

11. Hollis Alpert, "One Man's Festival," *Saturday Review*, October 5, 1963, 67.

12. Vincent Canby, "Cannes: Focus On the Screen and Off," *NYT*, May 13, 1970.

13. Vincent Canby, "Festival Hits," *NYT*, May 29, 1970.

14. Alex Keneas, *Newsweek*, October 12, 1970, 112.

15. Vincent Canby, "Critic's Choice," *NYT*, December 31, 1972.

16. "Infuriating Magician," *Time*, February 16, 1968.

17. Display ad, *NYT*, September 5, 1965.

18. Phillip T. Hartung, *Commonweal*, November 12, 1965, 192.

19. Andrew Sarris, *Village Voice*, January 23, 1969.

20. Bosley Crowther, "One More Film Festival," *NYT*, October 8, 1967.

21. Robert Hatch, *Nation*, May 13, 1968.

22. Joseph Morgenstern, *Newsweek*, May 13, 1968.

23. Renata Adler, "The Ten Best Films of 1968," *NYT*, December 22, 1968.

24. Craig Fischer, "Films Lost in the Cosmos: Godard and New York Distribution and Exhibition (1961–1973)," *Spectator* 18, no. 2 (1998): 61–62.

25. Eugene Archer, "What Makes Us Hate—or Love—Godard?" *NYT*, January 28, 1968.

26. Raymond Sokolov, "The Truth 24 Times a Second," *Newsweek*, February 12, 1968, 90–91.

27. Display ad, *NYT*, September 1, 1968.

28. *Time*, November 1, 1968.

29. Andrew Sarris, *Village Voice*, December 5, 1968.

30. Roger Greenspun, *NYT*, April 27, 1970.

31. Display ad, *NYT*, September 1, 1968.

32. Quoted in Guy Flatley, "Godard Says Bye-Bye to Bardot and All That," *NYT*, May 17, 1970.

33. Vincent Canby, "He and She and Godard," *NYT*, February 25, 1973.

34. Bosley Crowther, *NYT*, October 31, 1963.

35. Brendan Gill, *New Yorker*, February 11, 1967, 134.

36. Andrew Sarris, *Village Voice*, February 2, 1967.

37. Bosley Crowther, "With Luck, Full Speed Ahead for 'Trains,'" *NYT*, October 29, 1967.

38. Vincent Canby, "The Personal Vision Endures," *NYT*, February 26, 1984.

39. Display ad, *NYT*, September 1, 1968.

40. Roger Greenspun, *NYT*, November 10, 1969.

41. Vincent Canby, "The Ten Best of 1969," *NYT*, December 28, 1969.

42. Vincent Canby, "Critic's Choice," *NYT*, December 26, 1971.

43. Vincent Canby, *NYT*, September 24, 1969.

44. Melton S. Davis, "Rohmer's Formula . . . ," *New York Times Magazine*, November 21, 1971.

45. Andrew Sarris, *Village Voice*, September 4, 1969.

46. Vincent Canby, *NYT*, September 24, 1969.

47. Davis, "Rohmer's Formula."

48. Vincent Canby, *NYT*, February 22, 1971.

49. Display ad, *NYT*, September 10, 1972.

50. Richard Schickel, *Life*, November 17, 1972.

51. Pauline Kael, *New Yorker*, October 7, 1972, 135.

52. Vincent Canby, *NYT*, September 11, 1970.

53. *VFR*, February 18, 1970.

54. Display ad, *NYT*, September 10, 1972.

55. Vincent Canby, *NYT*, October 12, 1972.

56. Display ad, *NYT*, September 9, 1973.

57. Charles Champlin, *LAT*, April 3, 1974.

58. Bosley Crowther, *NYT*, September 17, 1964.

59. *Time*, September 25, 1964.

60. Robert Hatch, *Nation*, September 28, 1964, 176.

61. Arthur Knight and Hollis Alpert, "The History of Sex in the Cinema," *Playboy*, July 1968, 197.

62. Robert Hawkins, "Italy's Rising Young Film Makers," *NYT*, January 12, 1958.

63. Stanley Kauffman, *New Republic*, August 17, 1963.

64. Bosley Crowther, "Too Few, Too Many," *NYT*, December 1, 1963.

65. Bosley Crowther, *NYT*, January 29, 1964.

66. Dwight Macdonald, *Esquire*, May 1964.

67. Eugene Archer, *NYT*, September 25, 1964.

68. Vincent Canby, "Sure, Hollywood Is Collapsing, But . . . ," *NYT*, May 2, 1971.

69. Leonard J. Berry, "Bertolucci Provides Bourgeois View of Fascist Psychosis," *LAT*, May 23, 1971.

70. Vincent Canby, *NYT*, September 19, 1970.

71. *Time*, April 5, 1971.

72. Melton S. Davis, "The 'Gospel' According to Pier Paolo Pasolini," *NYT*, April 10, 1966.

73. Bosley Crowther, *NYT*, February 18, 1966; Bosley Crowther, "The Greatest Story Simply Told," *NYT*, February 27, 1966.

74. Quoted in Howard Thompson, "Film about Jesus Sets Gross Mark," *NYT*, May 5, 1966.

75. Ibid.

76. Display ad, *NYT*, September 11, 1966.

77. Ibid.

78. "*Battle of Algiers* Wins Main Venice Film Prize," *NYT*, September 11, 1966.

79. *Time*, September 29, 1967.

80. Joseph Morgenstern, "The Terror," *Newsweek*, October 23, 1967, 102.

81. Bosley Crowther, *NYT*, September 13, 1965.

82. Display ad, *NYT*, September 17, 1967.

83. Howard Thompson, *NYT*, September 23, 1967.

84. *Time*, September 24, 1965.

85. *Newsweek*, February 7, 1966, 84.

86. Bosley Crowther, *NYT*, January 25, 1966.

87. Vincent Canby, "Film Importer Has Her Troubles," *NYT*, January 14, 1966.

88. "Czech Films Show 'New' Liberalization," *LAT*, August 20, 1968.

89. Display ad, *NYT*, August 28, 1966.

90. *Time*, September 23, 1966.

91. Bosley Crowther, *NYT*, October 27, 1966.

92. Penelope Gilliatt, *New Yorker*, July 1, 1967, 54.

93. Bosley Crowther, *NYT*, October 16, 1967.

94. Joseph Morgenstern, *Newsweek*, November 27, 1967, 97.

95. Display ad, *NYT*, September 1, 1968.

96. *Time*, December 6, 1968.

97. Andrew Sarris, *Village Voice*, November 7, 1968.

98. Crowther, "With Luck, Full Speed Ahead for 'Trains.'"

99. *Time*, May 23, 1969.

100. Display ad, *NYT*, September 1, 1968.

101. *Time*, September 27, 1968.

102. Display ad, *NYT*, September 11, 1966.

103. Vincent Canby, *NYT*, May 5, 1969.

104. Roger Greenspun, "Yugoslavs Reveal an Attractive Cinema," *NYT*, December 12, 1969.

105. Cyntia Grenier, "Yugoslav Entry Hailed at Cannes," *NYT*, May 24, 1971.

106. Display ad, *NYT*, September 12, 1971.

107. Justin Wyatt, "From Roadshowing to Saturation Releases: Majors, Independents, and Marketing/Distribution Innovations," in Jon Lewis, ed., *The New American Cinema* (Durham, N.C.: Duke University Press, 1998), 69–70.

108. Arthur Knight, *Saturday Review*, November 18, 1967, 57.

109. Bosley Crowther, *NYT*, September 30, 1967.

110. Stanley Kauffmann, *New Republic*, December 2, 1967.

Chapter 14. Collapse

1. Andrew Sarris, "Why the Foreign Film Has Lost Its Cachet," *NYT*, May 2, 1999.

2. Letter from James Bouras to Gerald Phillips, April 25, 1973. Quoted in Tino Balio, *United Artists: The Company That Changed the Film Industry* (Madison: University of Wisconsin Press, 1987), 290.

3. Arthur Knight and Hollis Alpert, "The History of Sex in Cinema," *Playboy*, April 1968, 206.

4. Quoted in "Anything Goes: Taboos in Twilight," *Newsweek*, November 13, 1967, 74.

5. "The Shock of Freedom in Films," *Time*, December 8, 1967.

6. Ibid.

7. Charles Champlin, "The 1960s: A Revolution in Movie Audiences," *LAT*, January 18, 1970.

8. Arthur Knight and Hollis Alpert, "Sex in Cinema: 1970," *Playboy*, November 1970, 164.

9. Christopher Sieving, "Revolution for the Sell of It: Mainstream and Alternative Responses to Hollywood's 'Revolution' Films" (research paper, Department of Communication Arts, University of Wisconsin–Madison, 1996).

10. Vincent Canby, *NYT*, May 26, 1969.

11. *VFR*, May 14, 1969.

12. Stephen Farber, "End of the Road?" *Film Quarterly* 23 (Winter 1969): 7–8.

13. Mel Gussow, "'Movies Leaving 'Hollywood' Behind," *NYT*, May 27, 1970.

14. Arthur Knight and Hollis Alpert, "Sex in Cinema: 1969," *Playboy*, November 1969, 168.

15. Ralph Blumenthal, "Porno Chic," *New York Times Magazine*, January 21, 1973.

16. Vincent Canby, "Foreign Pictures Enjoyed Big Earnings in 1966," *NYT*, January 18, 1967.

17. Bosley Crowther, "With Luck, Full Speed Ahead for 'Trains,'" *NYT*, October 29, 1967.

18. Werner Wiskari, "Ingmar Bergman Tries New Theme," *NYT*, October 20, 1966.

19. Display ad, *NYT*, May 9, 1967.

20. Vincent Canby, "Who's Going to Save the Mermaid?" *NYT*, April 26, 1970.

21. *VFR*, March 15, 1967.

22. Arthur Knight and Hollis Alpert, "The History of Sex in the Cinema," *Playboy*, April 1968, 204.

23. *Time*, March 31, 1967.

24. Vincent Canby, "*Ulysses* Plans Mass Premiere," *NYT*, August 31, 1966.

25. "Ulysses to Reopen for Unlimited Run," *NYT*, March 21, 1967.

26. Bosley Crowther, "The Ten Best Films of 1967," *NYT*, December 24, 1967.

27. *Time*, March 31, 1967.

28. Vincent Canby, *NYT*, June 20, 1967.

29. Pauline Kael, *New Yorker*, December 28, 1968, 56.

30. Renata Adler, "The Ten Best Films of 1968," *NYT*, December 22, 1968.

31. Pauline Kael, *New Yorker*, October 11, 1969, 157.

32. Arthur Knight, *Saturday Review*, April 6, 1968, 45.

33. Arthur Knight and Hollis Alpert, "The History of Sex in the Cinema," *Playboy*, July 1968, 189.

34. Robert Hatch, *Nation*, April 15, 1968, 517–18.

35. Pauline Kael, *New Yorker*, April 6, 1968, 162.

36. Stanley Kauffmann, *New Republic*, April 27, 1968.

37. Renata Adler, "How Movies Speak to Young Rebels," *NYT*, May 19, 1968.

38. Quoted in Ernest Betts, *The Film Business* (New York: Pittman, 1973), 305. In Britain "public" refers to private schools.

39. Andrew Sarris, *Village Voice*, August 22, 1968.

40. Vincent Canby, "The Ten Best of 1969," *NYT*, December 28, 1969.

41. Arthur Knight and Hollis Alpert, "The History of Sex in Cinema," *Playboy*, July 1968, 182.

42. Kevin Heffernan, "Prurient (Dis)Interest: The American Release and Reception of *I Am Curious (Yellow)*" (research paper, Department of Communication Arts, University of Wisconsin–Madison, 1994).

43. "Grovels Rosset: All Censors Wrong, Valenti Is Encouraging Vigilantes" *Variety*, September 17, 1969, 25.

44. "Swedish Movie Is Seized by U.S. Customs for Obscenity," *NYT*, January 19, 1968.

45. "U.S. Court Clears Swedish Sex Film," *NYT*, November 27, 1968.

46. *Time*, March 14, 1969.

47. Vincent Canby, *NYT*, March 11, 1969.

48. *VFR*, February 21–27, 2000, 16.

49. Joseph Morgenstern, *Newsweek*, December 15, 1969, 105.

50. Stanley Kauffmann, *New Republic*, December 13, 1969.

51. *Time*, December 5, 1969.

52. Stuart Byron, "Don Rugoff: Ballyhoo with a Harvard Education," *Film Comment* 12 (May–June 1975): 24.

53. Quoted in Neal Oxenhandler, "Satyricon," *Film Quarterly* 23 (Summer 1970): 39–40.

54. John Baxter, *Fellini* (New York: St. Martin's Press, 1993), 243.

55. Vincent Canby, *NYT*, March 12, 1970.

56. Andrew Sarris, *Village Voice*, March 19, 1970, 51.

57. Pauline Kael, *New Yorker*, March 14, 1970, 134.

58. Balio, *United Artists*, 287.

59. Vincent Canby, "Those Fanatical Fans of Foreign Films—Where Are They Now?" *NYT*, February 17, 1974.

60. Vincent Canby, *NYT*, December 21, 1970.

61. Quoted in McCandlish Phillips, "8 Foreign Films to Open in a 'Test,'" *NYT*, April 21, 1972.

62. Barbara Wilinsky, *Sure Seaters: The Emergence of Art House Cinema* (Minneapolis: University of Minnesota Press, 2001), 133.

63. Quoted in Guy Flatley, "The Victory of Vittorio De Sica," *NYT*, January 16, 1972.

64. *Time*, January 17, 1972.

65. Vincent Canby, "The Ten Best Films of 1972," *NYT*, December 31, 1972.

66. Canby, "Those Fanatical Fans of Foreign Films."

67. Pauline Kael, *New Yorker*, October 28, 1972, 130–39.

68. "Self-Portrait of an Angel and Monster," *Time*, January 22, 1973.

69. Judy Klemesrud, "Maria Says Her 'Tango' Is Not Blue," *NYT*, February 4, 1973.

70. Robert Hatch, *Nation*, February 12, 1973, 222.

71. Stanley Kauffmann, *New Republic*, March 3, 1973.

72. Canby, "Those Fanatical Fans of Foreign Films."

73. Quoted in McCandlish Phillips, "U.S. Filmmakers De-Emphasizing Sex," *NYT*, April 20, 1971.

74. Ibid.

75. Canby, "Those Fanatical Fans of Foreign Films."

Epilogue

1. Dan Cox and Jonathan Bing, "Overkill or Over-the-Hill?" *Variety*, October 2–8, 2000, 1.

2. Stuart Byron, "On Imported Films, U.S. Public Fickle," *Variety*, May 8, 1968, 40.

3. "The Walter Reade Organization Files Petition for Chapter XI Bankruptcy," *NYT*, June 6, 1977.

4. C. Gerald Fraser, "Rugoff Loses Theaters," *NYT*, February 15, 1979.

5. Leonard Klady, "When Oscar Talks, the B.O. Listens," *Variety*, April 4–10, 1994, 7.

6. Derek Elley, "Win Helps, but Won't Make Pic in Europe," *Variety*, January 4, 1993, 62.

7. Lawrence Cohn, "'Like Water' Crossover a Spanish-Lingo Record," *Variety*, June 21, 1993, 7.

8. Susan Karlin, "Sweet Shortcut for Hot 'Chocolate,'" *Variety*, August 30, 1993, 1.

9. Peter Bart, "Pushed to the Miramax?" *Variety*, December 20, 1999–January 2, 2000, 75.

10. Quoted in Winter Miller, "Sony Classics Plays by Its Own Rules," *Variety*, June 20, 2008.

11. Susan Sontag, "The Decay of Cinema," *NYT*, February 25, 1996.

12. Dan Yakir, "The Man behind Manhattan's Art Theater Boom," *NYT*, April 12, 1981.

Select Bibliography

Adler, Kenneth P. "Art Films and Eggheads." *Studies in Public Communication* 2 (1959): 7–15.

Agee, James. *Agee on Film*. New York: McDowell, Oblensky, 1958.

Armes, Roy. *French Cinema*. New York: Oxford University Press, 1985.

Balio, Tino. "The Art Film Market in the New Hollywood." In *Hollywood and Europe: Economics, Culture, National Identity, 1945–95*, ed. Geoffrey Nowell-Smith and Steven Ricci, 63–73. London: British Film Institute, 1998.

———. "Brigitte Bardot and Hollywood's Takeover of the U.S. Art Film Market in the 1960s." In *Trading Culture: Global Traffic and Local Cultures in Film and Television*, ed. Sylvia Harvey, 191–201. Eastleigh, U.K.: John Libbey Publishing, 2006.

———. *United Artists: The Company That Changed the Film Industry*. Madison: University of Wisconsin Press, 1987.

Beaver, Frank Eugene. *Bosley Crowther: Social Critic of the Film, 1940–1967*. New York, Arno Press, 1974.

Betz, Mark. "The Name Above the (Sub) Title: Internationalism, Coproduction, and Polyglot European Art Cinema." *Camera Obscura* 16, no. 1 (2001): 1–44.

Bordwell, David. *Making Meaning: Inference and Rhetoric in the Interpretation of Cinema*. Cambridge, Mass.: Harvard University Press, 1989.

———. *Narration in the Fiction Film*. Madison: University of Wisconsin Press, 1985.

Brandon, Thomas J. "Foreign Film Distribution in the U.S." *Film Culture* 2 (1956): 15–17.

Clarke, Shirley, et al. "The Expensive Art: A Discussion of Film Distribution and Exhibition in the U.S." *Film Quarterly* 13 (Summer 1960): 19–34.

Draper, Ellen. "'Controversy has probably destroyed forever the context': *The Miracle* and Movie Censorship in America in the Fifties." *Velvet Light Trap* 25 (Spring 1990): 69–79.

Fischer, Craig. "Films Lost in the Cosmos: Godard and New York Distribution, 1961–1973." *Spectator* 18 (1998): 47–66.

Gomery, Douglas. "The Coming of Television and the 'Lost' Motion Picture Audience." *Journal of Film and Video* 38 (Summer 1985): 5–11.

———. *Shared Pleasures: A History of Motion Picture Presentation in the United States*. Madison: University of Wisconsin Press, 1992.

Griffith, Richard. "Finance: Where Are the Dollars?" Pt. 1. *Sight & Sound* 18 (Autumn 1949): 39–40.

———. "Finance: Where Are the Dollars?" Pt. 2. *Sight & Sound* 18 (January 1950): 33–34.

Guback, Thomas. *The International Film Industry: Western Europe and America since 1945.* Bloomington: Indiana University Press, 1969.

Guzman, Tony. "The Little Theatre Movement: The Institutionalization of the European Art Film in America." *Film History* 17 (2005): 261–84.

Haberski, Raymond J., Jr. *It's Only a Movie: Films and Critics in American Culture.* Lexington: University Press of Kentucky, 2001.

Kael, Pauline. *I Lost It at the Movies.* Boston: Atlantic–Little, Brown, 1965.

Kauffmann, Stanley. *Figures of Light.* New York: Harper & Row, 1971.

———. *A World on Film.* New York: Harper & Row, 1966.

Knight, Arthur, and Hollis Alpert. "The History of Sex in the Cinema." *Playboy*, December 1966, 232–58.

———. "The History of Sex in the Cinema." *Playboy*, July 1968, 130, 181–98.

———. "Sex in Cinema: 1969." *Playboy*, November 1969, 168–80, 258–66.

———. "Sex in Cinema: 1970." *Playboy*, November 1970, 152–64, 217–26.

Lev, Peter. *The Euro-American Cinema.* Austin: University of Texas Press, 1993.

Lipkin, Steve. "The New Wave and the Post-War Film Economy." *Current Research in Film: Audiences, Economics, and Law* 2 (1986): 156–85.

Lopate, Phillip. *Totally, Tenderly, Tragically: Essays and Criticism from a Lifelong Affair with the Movies.* New York: Anchor Books, 1998.

Macdonald, Dwight. *Dwight Macdonald on Movies.* Englewood Cliffs, N.J.: Prentice-Hall, 1969.

Mayer, Arthur. *Merely Colossal.* New York: Simon & Schuster, 1953.

Mayer, Michael. *Foreign Films on American Screens.* New York: Arco, 1965.

Murray, Edward. *Nine American Film Critics: A Study of Theory and Practice.* New York: Ungar, 1975.

Neale, Steve. "Art Cinema as Institution." *Screen* 22 (1981): 11–39.

Neupert, Richard. "Dead Champagne: *Variety*'s New Wave." *Film History* 10 (1998): 219–30.

———. *A History of the French New Wave Cinema.* Madison: University of Wisconsin Press, 2002.

Ogan, Christine. "The Audience for Foreign Films in the United States." *Journal of Communication* 40 (Autumn 1990): 58–77.

Paletz, David, and Michael Noonan. "The Exhibitors." *Film Quarterly* 19 (Winter 1965–66): 14–41.

Randall, Richard. "Censorship: From *The Miracle* to *Deep Throat*." In *The American Film Industry*, ed. Tino Balio, 510–36. Madison: University of Wisconsin Press, 1987.

Sarris, Andrew. *Confessions of a Cultist.* New York: Simon & Schuster, 1970.

Schwartz, Vanessa R. *It's So French: Hollywood, Paris, and the Making of Cosmopolitan Film Culture*. Chicago: University of Chicago Press, 2007.

Segrave, Kerry. *Foreign Films in America*. Jefferson, N.C.: McFarland, 2001.

Smythe, Dallas W., et al. "Portrait of an Art-Theater Audience." *Quarterly of Film, Radio and Television* 8 (Fall 1953): 28–50.

Sova, Dawn B. *Forbidden Films: Censorship Histories of 125 Motion Pictures*. New York: Checkmark, 2001.

Staiger, Janet. *Interpreting Films: Studies in the Historical Reception of American Cinema*. Princeton, N.J.: Princeton University Press, 1992.

Street, Sarah. *Transatlantic Crossings: British Feature Films in the USA*. New York: Continuum, 2002.

Twomey, John E. "Some Considerations on the Rise of the Art-Film Theater." *Quarterly of Film, Radio and Television* 10 (Spring 1956): 239–47.

Wagner, Geoffrey. "The Lost Audience." *Quarterly of Film, Radio and Television* 6 (July 1952): 338–50.

Walker, Alexander. *Hollywood UK: The British Film Industry in the Sixties*. New York: Stein & Day, 1974.

Wasson, Haidee. *Museum Movies: The Museum of Modern Art and the Birth of Art Cinema*. Berkeley: University of California Press, 2005.

Weinberg, Herman G. "The Language Barrier." *Hollywood Quarterly* 2 (July 1947): 333–37.

Wilensky, Barbara. *Sure Seaters: The Emergence of Art House Cinema*. Minneapolis: University of Minnesota Press, 2001.

Wittern-Keller, Laura, and Raymond J. Haberski Jr. *The "Miracle" Case: Film Censorship and the Supreme Court*. Lawrence: University Press of Kansas, 2008.

Index

WISCONSIN FILM STUDIES

The Foreign Film Renaissance on American Screens, 1946–1973
Tino Balio

Marked Women: Prostitutes and Prostitution in the Cinema
Russell Campbell

Depth of Field: Stanley Kubrick, Film, and the Uses of History
Edited by Geoffrey Cocks, James Diedrick, and Glenn Perusek

Escape Artist: The Life and Films of John Sturges
Glenn Lovell

I Thought We Were Making Movies, Not History
Walter Mirisch

Giant: George Stevens, a Life on Film
Marilyn Ann Moss